The Prophetic Vision and the Real Jesus

The Prophetic Vision and the Real Jesus

*Growth of the Prophetic Vision and Its Impact on
the Mission of Jesus in Matthew's Gospel*

ADRIAN M. LESKE

WIPF & STOCK · Eugene, Oregon

THE PROPHETIC VISION AND THE REAL JESUS
Growth of the Prophetic Vision and Its Impact on the Mission of Jesus in Matthew's Gospel

Copyright © 2017 Adrian M. Leske. All rights reserved. Except for brief quotations in critical publications or reviews, no part of this book may be reproduced in any manner without prior written permission from the publisher. Write: Permissions, Wipf and Stock Publishers, 199 W. 8th Ave., Suite 3, Eugene, OR 97401.

Wipf & Stock
An Imprint of Wipf and Stock Publishers
199 W. 8th Ave., Suite 3
Eugene, OR 97401

www.wipfandstock.com

PAPERBACK ISBN: 978-1-5326-3415-4
HARDCOVER ISBN: 978-1-5326-3417-8
EBOOK ISBN: 978-1-5326-3416-1

Manufactured in the U.S.A.   SEPTEMBER 13, 2017

Scripture translations are by the author unless otherwise indicated

Contents

Acknowledgments | *vii*

Abbreviations | *viii*

Chapter I	Introduction	1
Chapter II	The Prophetic Vision before the Exile	7
Chapter III	The Beginning of the Exile, and the Priest Turned Prophet	24
Chapter IV	The Second Prophet of the Exile: A Prophet of Hope	39
Chapter V	After the Return from Exile	61
Chapter VI	Zadokites, Levites, and the Prophetic Vision	81
Chapter VII	The Prophetic Vision Under Pressure	98
Chapter VIII	The Prophetic Turns Apocalyptic	119
Chapter IX	Jesus and the Kingdom of God in Matthew's Gospel	149
Chapter X	The Prophetic Vision and the Mission of Jesus	184
Chapter XI	Conclusion	219

Bibliography | *225*

Modern Authors Index | *237*

Ancient Document Index | *241*

Acknowledgments

I wish to begin by acknowledging my indebtedness to Concordia Seminary, St. Louis, for the Study Scholarships I received to do my graduate studies, completing my doctorate there in 1971. Also my thanks go to Lutheran Life Insurance Company of Canada for the Alan Schendel Award for Theological Research in 1990. This allowed me to spend four months in Israel/Palestine doing research into the Jewish aspects of the Gospel of Matthew and its prophetic background. It was through this research that I became convinced of the priority of Matthew's Gospel. After this, at meetings of the Society of Biblical Literature, I attended and participated in sessions influenced by the late William R. Farmer and led by members of the Two-Gospel Hypothesis Group. I am particularly grateful to Bill Farmer for his encouragement and eventual invitation to contribute my commentary on "Matthew" for the *International Bible Commentary* he was editing.

My thanks also go to my colleagues at Concordia University of Edmonton for their encouragement, particularly Wayne Stuhlmiller. Wayne and I spent many hours in stimulating discussion, sharing ideas of our research while attending SBL meetings together. I am also thankful to many of my former students whose interest stimulated me to record much of what I had been researching and teaching, particularly Linda Maloney who read and commented on some of the earlier chapters.

However, this project would not have been completed without the patient understanding of my late wife, Tricia, and the continuing encouragement of our children, Kylie-Anne, Jane, and Andrew. But most of all, I want to express my thanks and gratitude to my wife and partner, Jenny Hawkins, for her careful reading of my manuscript, making corrections and suggestions for clarification, and for her loving encouragement.

Finally, a word of thanks to the editors of Wipf & Stock for accepting my work and for overseeing the manuscript to its final production.

Abbreviations

Ant.	Josephus, *Jewish Antiquities*
AB	Anchor Bible
ABD	*The Anchor Bible Dictionary.* 6 vols. Edited by David Noel Freedman. New York: Doubleday, 1992.
AnBib	Analecta biblica
BBR	*Bulletin for Biblical Research*
BETL	Bibliotheca ephemeridum theologicarum lovaniensium
Bib	*Biblica*
BibInt	*Biblical Interpretation*
BSac	*Bibliotheca sacra*
BTB	*Biblical Theology Bulletin*
CBET	Contributions to Biblical Exegesis and Theology
CBQ	*Catholic Biblical Quarterly*
Con BOT	Coniectanea biblica: Old Testament Series
CurTM	*Currents in Theology and Mission*
DSD	Dead Sea Discoveries
EBib	Etudes bibliques
ExpTim	*Expository Times*
HSM	Harvard Semitic Monographs
HTR	*Harvard Theological Review*
HTS	Harvard Theological Studies
HUCA	*Hebrew Union College Annual*
ICC	International Critical Commentary

Int	*Interpretation*
JAAR	*Journal of the American Academy of Religion*
JBL	*Journal of Biblical Literature*
JQR	*Jewish Quarterly Review*
JSJ	*Journal for the Study of Judaism in the Persian, Hellenistic, and Roman Periods*
JSJSup	Journal for the Study of Judaism Supplement Series
JSHJ	*Journal for the Study of the Historical Jesus*
JSNT	*Journal for the Study of the New Testament*
JSOT	*Journal for the Study of the Old Testament*
JSOTSup	Journal for the Old Testament: Supplement Series
KAT	Kommentar zum Alten Testament
NICOT	New International Commentary of the Old Testament
NovT	*Novum Testamentum*
NRSV	New Revised Standard Version
NTS	*New Testament Studies*
OTL	Old Testament Library
PRSt	*Perspectives in Religious Studies*
RB	*Revue biblique*
RevQ	*Revue de Qumran*
RSV	Revised Standard Version
SBL	Society of Biblical Literature
SBLDS	Society of Biblical Literature Dissertation Series
SBLEJL	Society of Biblical Literature Early Judaism and Its Literature
SBLMS	Society of Biblical Literature Monograph Series
SBLSCS	Society of Biblical Literature Septuagint and Cognate Studies
SBT	Studies in Biblical Theology
SJOT	*Scandinavian Journal of the Old Testament*
SJT	*Scottish Journal of Theology*
SNTSMS	Society for New Testament Studies Monograph Series
SVTP	Studia in Veteris Testamenti pseudepigraphica
VT	*Vetus Testamentum*
VTSup	Supplements to Vetus Testamentum

Abbreviations

WTJ	*Westminster Theological Journal*
ZAW	*Zeitschrift für die alttestamentliche Wissenschaft*
ZNW	*Zeitschrift für die neutestamentliche Wissenschaft und die Kunde der älteren Kirche*

Chapter I

Introduction

THIS BOOK IS A study of the development of the prophetic vision, beginning with the first writing prophets. It traces how the prophets learned from each other and responded to their changing environments as they were impacted by the events of history. It also touches on how the prophets influenced alternative visions, and particularly, how it found its fulfillment in the message and mission of Jesus as portrayed in the Gospel of Matthew.

Having taught both the prophetic literature and the Gospel of Matthew for many years, it had become quite apparent to me how closely they were related, and how the Gospel of Matthew and the teaching of Jesus therein were dependent on the prophetic literature. Of course, it had always been acknowledged that the writings of the New Testament had gained much from the Hebrew Bible for many of its concepts, ideas and terminology. However, the close connection of the Gospel of Matthew with the writings of the prophets, which exceeds that of any other New Testament writing, and in its portrayal of Jesus coming out of that prophetic milieu, has not always been acknowledged.

The prophetic vision was a gradual development over centuries. Once the message of the earlier prophets came to be written down and disseminated, it became natural for the later prophets to learn from those who had spoken out before and to build on their proclamations, expanding on their ideas for their own situation, often using their terminology and concepts. Out of this interconnectedness the prophetic vision developed to meet new circumstances as it grappled with social and political change, wars, oppression and disasters. So often in the past, study of individual prophets have been done in isolation and have not always taken into consideration the influence on the writings of the prophets who had spoken out earlier. The later prophets clearly built on or interacted with the ideas and messages of previous prophets, and one of the purposes of this study is to demonstrate this intertextuality. This becomes evident as the prophetic vision grows, moves through history and intensifies in time of persecution, injustice and oppression. Of course, the historical context plays an important part in the development of the prophetic vision, making it vital sometimes to reconstruct the historical context of a writing from the hints and allusions in the writing itself.

It is paramount, therefore, to trace the growth of the prophetic vision from the first writing prophets down through history to the time of Jesus. Using the approach of intertextuality, and seeing how the development of the prophetic vision interacts with and influences other movements, calls for a reevaluation of the significance of alternative movements such as the Levites, the Zadokite priesthood, and the origin of the Qumran community with its Teacher of Righteousness and their relation to the prophetic movement. Even more so, it calls for a reexamination of how Jesus, popularly proclaimed as a prophet in his own time, responded to the prophetic vision in his message and mission, its implications for Christology, and even the role of the author of the Gospel of Matthew.

So much of New Testament scholarship has been carried on with only superficial acknowledgment of the prophetic heritage from which the Gospels have emerged. The early church fathers had been mostly concerned with relating the gospel message to their own Gentile environment in the philosophical language of the time. They were thus inclined to interpret the prophets only as speaking of the coming of Christ, often with the use of allegory or typology. Even when interpretation was literal-historical, it was always christocentric and according to the rule of faith preserved in the churches and established in ecumenical councils. This set the general pattern in the West where Scripture was used more as proof texts for the growing doctrinal tradition of the church. During the Reformation period, particularly with Martin Luther's insistence on "sola scriptura," greater emphasis was put on exegesis. Luther contended that an understanding of the author and the time of each writing in its historical setting was important, although his interpretation of the prophets remained essentially christocentric.

However, with the development of Protestant orthodoxy during the seventeenth century, the emphasis returned to somewhat more rigid definitions of doctrine, often directed against Roman Catholic tradition. The period of Enlightenment in the eighteenth and nineteenth centuries was partly a reaction to the traditions and dogma of the church, both Protestant and Catholic. The effects of deism, religious skepticism, and rationalism that followed, eventually led to biblical criticism and a critical examination of how the Gospels were formed. This then led over time to the development of source, form and redaction criticism with virtually no consideration of the prophetic heritage as the precursor of the gospel. In this way, it so easily became open to the presuppositions prevalent at that time. The same must be said about the discussions that became prominent in this period regarding how the Synoptic Gospels related to one another.

Right from the beginning of the Christian movement the Gospel of Matthew had been universally held to be the first Gospel, originally written in Hebrew, and later translated into Greek for the growing number of Greek-speaking Gentiles and Diaspora Jews. Prior to that Greek translation, Papias (110–120 CE) tells us, Gentile Christians had to interpret the Hebrew as best as they were able (Eusebius, *Eccles Hist.* III.38.16). Yet despite their Gentile orientation, the early church fathers consistently show greater dependence on Matthew's Gospel than the other Gospels for their discussions of the life and teachings of Jesus. Clement of Alexandria (150–213 CE) reported that the Gospels with genealogies (Matthew and Luke) were written first, and that Mark wrote his Gospel based on Peter's preaching in Rome where he had served as Peter's assistant and interpreter (Eusebius, *Eccles Hist.* VI.14.5–7). Although it later became common to refer to the Synoptic Gospels in the order of Matthew-Mark-Luke, the order in which Irenaeus (120–203 CE) often cited them was Matthew-Luke-Mark (in *Against Heresies*, III, IV). The same order is found in Jerome's (347–420) *Concerning Illustrious Men* where he wrote about Matthew in ch. 3, Luke in ch. 7 and Mark in ch. 8. While Augustine used the order Matthew-Mark-Luke, he did so because he saw Mark as a summarizer of Matthew (*Harmony of the Gospels*, I.24) and, indeed, writing his Gospel in conjunction with both Matthew and Luke (*Harmony* IV.10–11).

It is no surprise, then, that when Henry Owen wrote his *Observations on the Four Gospels* in 1764, he followed this view that Mark had abridged both Matthew and Luke in writing his shorter Gospel. This was then taken up by J. J. Griesbach in Germany in 1776 and 1783 and followed by many scholars in biblical criticism. Other theories were developed, particularly with the idea that there must have been a primitive source from which the three Gospels evolved. Eventually what came to be established as the scholarly consensus in Germany, presented initially in 1863 by H. J. Holtzmann, was that the shortest Gospel, Mark, must have been the first, and that Matthew and Luke had then used Mark, separately of each other, as a framework filling in the narrative with sayings of Jesus supposedly collected into a hypothetical source referred to as Q. This is what eventually became known as the Two-Source Hypothesis. The more Jewish nature of Matthew's Gospel was attributed to the author's attempt to "rejudaize" Mark's Gospel.

Yet the popular view that Mark was the first Gospel was not just because of its brevity. This growing scholarly consensus was helped along by the politics of German unity under Kaiser Wilhelm II and his chancellor, Otto von Bismarck, during the *Kulturkampf*, which was the battle of Protestant Germany against Pope Pius IX's claim of papal infallibility in 1870 on the basis of Matt 16:18.[1] However, in all of this, the Jewish origins of Jesus, and the influence of the prophetic heritage on his life and teaching which would have given a different perspective on the whole question was lost in the shuffle. The form criticism of Martin Dibelius and Rudolf Bultmann, which saw Q as a collection of isolated sayings attributed to Jesus in the preaching of the early church further divorced the teaching of Jesus from its prophetic context. In the English-speaking world the two-source hypothesis was made popular in 1924 by B. H. Streeter although he actually argued for two extra sources, L and M, used by Luke and Matthew respectively for those sayings found exclusively in each. Since then, the two-source hypothesis has been followed by the majority of New Testament scholars and written into every textbook introducing the Synoptic Gospels.

It was on the basis of this hypothesis that the quests for the historical Jesus developed in an attempt to rediscover the real Jesus set free from the dogma of the church. Many of the "lives of Jesus" that emerged from these quests were governed by a fair amount of the current rationalism, skepticism or subjective imagination. With Mark, the shortest Gospel, as the basis for their lives of Jesus and with Q understood as a series of isolated sayings, it was easier to assert that many of these sayings and the stories about Jesus were the invention of the early church. Instead of finding Jesus in the Jewish culture and heritage in which he had lived, those involved in the quest tended to impose their own European culture on the Gospels and on the life of Jesus. Thus divorced from

1. See Farmer, "State *Interesse* and Markan Primacy," 15–49.

his Jewish roots, Jesus could become a teacher of ethics or wisdom with much of the rest regarded as myth, as David Friedrich Strauss expressed in his *Life of Jesus Critically Examined* of 1835–36.

This separation of the sayings of Jesus from their original historical context into a collection of isolated sayings open to subjective interpretations as general wisdom aphorisms caused one biblical scholar to fulminate: "The tendency (perhaps the agenda in some cases) of much of the recent analysis of Jesus' teachings rooted in form criticism has been to decontextualize, departicularize, de-israelitize or de-judaize Jesus. The most clearly Israelite elements in the Gospel tradition are determined to be secondary, created at later stages of the Jesus movement. . . . The method by which such judgments are made, however, is blatantly circular."[2] This approach to the life and teachings of Jesus has continued in its more provocative form by the "Jesus Seminar" which itself has recently come under some scathing attacks.[3]

However, every biblical scholar approaches the text with an arsenal of previous learnings and experiences, whether that be in the Greek classics, philosophy, Christian tradition, dogma, etc. Our tendency is to read into the text what we already know and understand and to impose our presuppositions on the biblical account. While all the disciplines studied before may help in gaining a wide understanding, they actually become peripheral to the unique background of the Gospels. This is particularly true in studying the Gospel of Matthew which bears a much more Jewish orientation than the other Gospels. Thus it is necessary to recreate as best as possible the cultural, religious, social and political milieu from which Jesus emerged. It means gaining an understanding of the whole cultural and prophetic heritage that lies behind the life of Jesus, consciously emptying ourselves of former presuppositions and letting Israelite prophetic history and culture become a part of our whole experience in order to understand the uniqueness of Jesus' message and mission in his own cultural context. Only in this way do we discover the *real* historical Jesus. With that understanding we are better able to apply his message to our own twenty-first-century situations and evaluate past traditions.

Given all this, it is important to acknowledge that the expansion of the early church around the Mediterranean was a story of a clash of cultures. The message of a Jewish Jesus was taken to the Diaspora Jews and to the Gentiles by the Apostle Paul. Gentiles, whether Greeks or Romans, would have received the message of Jesus with different understandings than their Jewish counterparts. This often led to different perceptions of Jesus and even conflict between Jewish and Gentile Christians. As the church became predominantly Gentile, there was a tendency to feel uncomfortable with those Jewish-Christian movements such as the Nazoreans and Ebionites, which often had a different understanding of the faith. So they soon became isolated from the mainstream of Christianity and became regularly included in the catalogues of heresies from the time of Irenaeus (ca. 130–200 CE) to that of Epiphanius (ca. 315–403 CE).

However, in the transition from one culture and language to another, there is always the danger that the essential meanings of some words and phrases are subtly changed. The author of the Gospel of Luke, writing his Gospel specifically for a Gentile audience,

---

2. Horsley, "Jesus and Galilee," 57–74, here 67. See further, Horsley, *Prophet Jesus*, 68–70.
3. Johnson, *Real Jesus*, and Jenkins, *Hidden Gospels*.

had to struggle with this. The Gospel of Matthew was initially written for a Jewish audience familiar with the prophetic vision (see chap. 9) and which sometimes caused concern for Gentiles (particularly Matt 10:5, 6; 15:24). In writing his Gospel, therefore, Luke had to transpose terminology and concepts loaded with prophetic meaning in a way that they could be meaningful to Gentiles. A good example of this is seen in the beatitudes. The beatitudes in Matthew (5:3–12) are loaded with religious meaning which draws on the prophetic vision, as we shall see, while in Luke (6:20–26) they are reduced to socioeconomic terms, losing some of their original meaning. The claim, then, that Luke holds the original form of the beatitudes shows a lack of understanding of the Jewish origins of the beatitudes. Another example of a change in meaning from one culture to another is the phrase "son of God." In Jewish history, Israel, as God's chosen people, was called "God's son" (Gen 4:22; Hos 11:1), and David and his descendants, chosen to represent God's rule, were given the same title (2 Sam 7:14; Ps 2:7). Jesus was called God's son in that context as one, who filled with the Holy Spirit, could represent God's word and authority. When this phrase entered the Graeco-Roman world, its meaning changed subtly, because in that culture the Roman Emperors were given this title with the implications of divinity and were worshiped as such. This led to many of the christological controversies of the first three centuries of the Christian era, leading up to the decrees of the Council of Nicea in 325 CE.

No quest for the historical Jesus can be successful without a thorough attempt to understand the kind of Jewish environment in which Jesus was immersed. This means taking the long journey through Israel's history and its developing religious hopes and beliefs. It means getting behind the person of Jesus and the writing of the Gospels instead of unconsciously imposing our own experiences onto those writings and the Jesus described in them. The incontrovertible fact is that Jesus was a Jew imbued with the prophetic vision. More recently a growing number of Christian scholars have been acknowledging the fact that Jesus came out of the Jewish context, gathered Jewish disciples and proclaimed his message to fellow Jews. Prompting this has been an increasing number of Jewish scholars writing on Jesus' Jewishness, promoting various Jewish points of view from which Jesus should be understood.[4] However, the implications of this fact need to be followed through.

Since the Gospel of Matthew was always understood to have been the first Gospel, originally written in Hebrew for Jewish readers, and since this Gospel more fully demonstrates the Jewish context with its numerous Semitic phrases and terminology, its many fulfillment quotations from and allusions to the prophetic writings, it stands to reason that we will find the more authentic Jesus in this Gospel. Once seen in relation to the prophetic vision, the teaching of Jesus takes on deeper meaning against its original background which is not always carried over in the other Gospels. Therefore, as this is recognized, the theory that Matthew used Mark's Gospel as his basic source and rejudaized it, adding material from a collection of isolated sayings (Q), makes little sense. The same must be said of the common idea, expressed so cogently by B. H. Streeter, that the Sermon on the Mount is an "agglomeration" of isolated sayings taken from Mark, Q and

---

4. See, e.g., Moore, "Jesus, an Emerging Jewish Mosaic," 58–81.

M (Matthew's so-called Jewish source) and then put together to make one big sermon.[5] Once again, a study of this sermon in the light of the prophetic vision will uncover the natural coherence and progression of the message.

While lip-service has increasingly been given to the Jewish background of the Gospel of Matthew, it is hoped that this study will make that indebtedness clearer. More and more the author of this Gospel is regarded as a Jewish follower of Jesus, but the implications of that have rarely been spelled out. Once that is fully understood, it raises a number of questions about the veracity of the two-source hypothesis, as well as the commonly held dating and authorship of the Gospel of Matthew. For over a century Old Testament scholars had dutifully followed the hypothesis of Bernhard Duhm that four Servant Songs had been imposed on the original work of Deutero-Isaiah before that theory was finally given up. Is it possible that the two-source hypothesis followed by the majority of New Testament scholars for well over a century now will eventually meet the same fate with a return to seeing Matthew as the first Gospel because of its Jewish orientation?

All the quests for the historical Jesus have been based on the two-source hypothesis, except perhaps that by Albert Schweitzer. That also includes the present-day quests, including those of the Jesus Seminar. That basis has hindered the seekers from finding him because of the presuppositions prescribed by that hypothesis, as well as the Gentile orientation taken to the quests. Johnson, in his criticism of present-day questers, argues that it is impossible to solve the quest. He says this because he himself works from the two-source hypothesis, and on the basis of that, he sees the problem as insoluble. For, he contends, "the majority of sources on which any historical reconstruction of early Christianity must be based are themselves impossible to locate historically because of the lack of firm geographical and chronological controls."[6]

However, my purpose in this study is not to deal with the various hypotheses of how the Gospels were formed, but I will argue for the priority of Matthew because it is the Gospel which portrays Jesus authentically against his Jewish background and particularly with the prophetic content which permeates the whole Gospel and the message of Jesus. For this reason, Jesus was popularly acclaimed to be a prophet. If we wish to find the Jesus of history, the "real Jesus," we will find him there in the fulfillment of the prophetic vision. For this reason, most of this study seeks to trace the development of that prophetic vision, and sometimes its opponents or alternatives, to see how the story of Jesus truly relates to its historical situation. Through this discovery of the real Jesus in his original historical context, we are better able to understand the significance of Jesus' life and teaching for us today. As Jesus told the Twelve when he sent them out to proclaim the good news of the kingdom: "Whoever receives a prophet because he is a prophet, will receive a prophet's reward" (Matt 10:41). May this be our reward too!

---

5. Streeter, *Four Gospels*, 249–53, 265.
6. Johnson, *Real Jesus*, 91.

Chapter II

The Prophetic Vision before the Exile

FROM THE BEGINNING

THE BASIC CONCEPT THAT ruled the lives of the early Israelites was the covenant, a bonding statement of relationship between God and people. In this corporate relationship, it was agreed that all would honor God and one another, and treat one's neighbors as sons and daughters of God, their heavenly Father and Creator. This double relationship defined and set down in the Sinai Decalogue, was not to be understood simply as a set of rules, but as the basis for faithful relationships with Yahweh their God and with one another. From time to time, prophets would arise to remind leaders and people to remain faithful to that covenant relationship.

When David was anointed as king by the people, he recognized the importance of that relationship and regarded himself as Yahweh's servant and son, called to represent God's justice and righteousness. As such, his kingdom flourished, and the people accepted the prophet Nathan's proclamation that David and his descendants would be on the throne forever (2 Sam 7:12–16). However, David's son, Solomon, had no desire to subordinate himself to the covenant and modeled his rule on that of the pharaohs of Egypt. The result of his autocratic rule led to the kingdom being split in two at the time of his death.

IN THE NORTHERN KINGDOM OF ISRAEL

As kings and officials of the northern kingdom sought to maintain their power and security, the covenant concept became increasingly ignored by them. After Solomon, the northern tribes no longer accepted the dynastic principle, and the people looked to a prophet to decide whether a contender to the throne was Yahweh's choice to represent his justice and righteousness. Those who sought kingship without prophetic designation left themselves open to assassination. To secure their position and power, some kings made alliances with other nations for protection and trade. This usually led to their acceptance and worship of their gods which nullified their covenant with Yahweh. Great prophets like Elijah, Elisha, and Micaiah ben Imlah were remembered and revered by the people for their fight to maintain the covenant tradition against King Ahab and his wife Jezebel, who sought to establish Baal worship in the kingdom (1 Kgs 17—2 Kgs 9). However, as powerful kings moved further from the covenant, it became necessary for the utterances of the prophets to be written down to reach a wider audience and be disseminated among the people. It is in these writings, carried down from one generation to another that we see how the prophetic vision developed. The first two writing prophets, Amos and Hosea, proclaimed their messages to the northern kingdom prior to its demise when the Assyrians deported most of the population in 722/1 BCE.

Amos was a mixed farmer (Amos 7:14) from Tekoa in the kingdom of Judah who had probably come north to trade in the northern markets around 760 BCE. He was shocked to find that, while the northern kingdom had become prosperous through trade alliances, his rural counterparts were being exploited, with many losing their ancestral land because of debt.[1] Meanwhile, their exploiters, merchants and court officials, were paying little to farmers for their produce but demanding high prices for poor quality goods while they celebrated their greed with lavish banquets in their extravagant residences (3:15; 4:1; 6:4–6). So Amos felt compelled to speak out and condemn the nation and its leaders for failing to live up to the covenant stipulations. Speaking as a prophet of God, he accused them of selling into slavery "the dispossessed for the sake of a pair of sandals," trampling "the head of the powerless into the dust," and being involved in cult prostitution (2:6–7; 5:11–12; 8:4–6). Their worship of foreign deities would soon lead to their exile (5:26–27), leaving only a remnant of the righteous (5:3, 15; 9:8).

The words Amos used to describe the faithful who were being exploited by the powerful became part of the covenant language of the prophets for the righteous. The designations, "dispossessed" (*ebyon*), one who was forced to forfeit his land, "afflicted" (*anaw, ani*), the righteous who suffered at the hands of the unrighteous, and "powerless" or "lowly" (*dal*), were terms used for those who were being treated unjustly according to the covenant. So all these terms are covenant descriptions of the afflicted and oppressed who become Yahweh's special concern because they have been deprived of their rights to the blessings guaranteed to them in the covenant. The terms "justice" (mishpat) and "righteousness" (sedaqah), used in parallel statement in 5:7, 24; 6:12, expressed for Amos the essence of the covenant relationship. For him, "justice" always had the meaning of carrying out God's judgment and purpose according to the covenant, and "righteousness" expressed faithfulness and commitment to this relationship both on the part of Yahweh and on the part of Israel.[2] Yet Israel had turned justice and righteousness into the bitterness of wormwood (5:6; 6:12). If only God's justice and righteousness would be permitted to roll down like an ever-flowing stream, then the people would be able to live and respond in righteousness to God and to one another (5:24)! Otherwise, the Day of Judgment would come upon them suddenly (5:18–20) and the leaders would go into exile while the covenant blessings would be restored to the faithful remnant as the planting of the Lord (9:15). After three months, Amos was forced to leave and return to Judah, leaving it to Hosea to proclaim the religious implications of their apostasy.

1. See Schottroff, "Prophet Amos," 36–39.
2. Leske, "Righteousness as Relationship," 125–37.

Hosea began his ministry a few years later as the "watchman for Ephraim" (9:8) and continued during the growing chaos until just prior to the siege of Samaria, a period of thirty years (ca. 754–724 BCE).[3] By the time of Jeroboam's death in 746 BCE, the economy was beginning to collapse and unrest and political turmoil were on the rise as the growing Assyrian Empire demanded heavy tribute from the smaller nations. During the political strife that followed, Hosea witnessed the assassination of four of the six kings that followed, the deportation of the tribes of Zebulon and Naphtali in 733, with the rest of the population finally being deported in 722/1 BCE. He saw that the covenant was consistently broken in every realm. Falsehood and violence were multiplying (12:2). Israel had become "a marauding band" of murderous thieves (6:9; 7:1), and the shrines at Bethel and Gilgal were corrupt and idolatrous. He consequently renamed Bethel (= "house of God") as Bethaven (= "house of evil," 4:15; 5:8; 10:5, 8). The priests were corrupt and evil (4:4; 5:1; 6:9–10), as were also the kings (5:1; 7:4–7; 10:7, 15) and officials (7:3, 5, 16; 9:15). Yahweh had a covenant lawsuit against them (4:1–4; 12:3–10).[4]

Nevertheless, Hosea's great contribution to the prophetic vision was by emphasizing the inherent nature of God's covenant love for his people in spite of their rejection of that relationship. This he illustrated in three striking metaphors—that of husband, father, and healer of Israel. Hosea had married Gomer, a former prostitute, who bore him three children to whom he gave symbolic names as messages for king and people. The first he called "Jezreel" to remind Jeroboam that bloodguilt still remained in the land (cf. 2 Kgs 9:1—10:11), the second "Lo-ruhammah," meaning "no mercy" if Israel did not repent, and the third "Lo-ammi," "not my people" because they showed no repentance. Yet in his love for his own children, Hosea saw the greater love of God for his people, a love which one day would once again graciously restore Israel to relationship as his covenant people. Then Israel would no longer be "Not my people" but would be known as "Sons of the Living God" (1:10).

Similar to his love for Gomer, Hosea reminded the people that it was Yahweh who had delivered them from Egypt, given them an identity and made them his own, and had continued to provide for them as a loving husband (2:14–17). If only they would return to Yahweh led by a faithful king like David (3:5), Yahweh would reaffirm his love with this vow: "I will betroth you to me forever; I will betroth you to me with *righteousness* and with *justice*, with *steadfast love* and with *compassion*. I will betroth you to me with *faithfulness*, and you shall *know* Yahweh" (2:19–20). Thus the ideal covenant relationship is expressed with all the intimacy of wedded love and faithfulness, expressed particularly with the verb, "to know." "Knowledge of God" for Hosea was never simply knowledge about God and his law, but referred to an intimate and faithful relationship with God. God's word to the priests who had rejected "knowledge" (4:4–6) was "I desire steadfast love and not sacrifice, the knowledge of God rather than a burnt offering" (6:6). So, like Amos before him (Amos 5:24), Hosea made a desperate plea to Israel to respond to God's love: "Sow for yourselves righteousness, harvest as a result steadfast love; break up your untilled ground for it is time to seek Yahweh that he may come and rain righteousness upon you" (10:12).

---

3. See Wolff, *Hosea*, xxi.
4. Cf. Huffmon, "Covenant Lawsuit in the Prophets," 285–95.

When Shalmaneser V became the Assyrian ruler in 727 BCE, Israel withdrew tribute and sought help from Egypt.[5] They were seeking to return to Egypt instead of returning to Yahweh! Hosea warned the leaders that as long as they refused to return to Yahweh, they would remain under the kings of Assyria and bear the yoke of servitude as they once had in Egypt (11:5–7). Building on Amos's image of Israel as God's family (Amos 3:1–2), Hosea spoke of God's parental love: "When Israel was a child I loved him, and out of Egypt I called my son. The more I called him, the more they went away from me. . . . Yet it was I who taught Ephraim to walk, I took them up in my arms, but they did not know that I was healing them" (11:1–3). However, Israel was an unwise son (11:13), and their king, Hoshea, was taken prisoner and their city of Samaria was besieged.

Yet Yahweh could not forever abandon his wayward son. Previously, Hosea had warned Israel that because of their waywardness, God "is not able to heal you or cure your wound." Yahweh would withdraw and leave them to suffer until they were ready to seek him in sincerity (5:13–15). Then he had pleaded with them: "Come, let us return to Yahweh; for he has torn, that he may heal us; he has stricken, and he will bind us up. After two days he will make us alive; on the third day he will raise us up, that we may live before him. Let us know, let us strive to know Yahweh!" (6:1–3a). However, their spiritual death would soon lead to their death as a nation. Yet Hosea could still hold firm to the hope of a future restoration of the people. His final call to them was: "Return, O Israel, to Yahweh, for you have stumbled because of your iniquity," and then they would hear the divine response: "I will heal their faithlessness, I will love them spontaneously, for my anger has turned from them" (14:2, 5).

This message of God's enduring love for his wayward people and his desire to heal their destructive ways became part of the prophetic vision, and would be further proclaimed in the generations to come.

IN THE KINGDOM OF JUDAH

The situation in the southern kingdom was not much better than in the north. Even though Judah had held to the dynastic principle, there had been assassinations and murders, foreign alliances, corruption, and practice of bribery. This led a young prophet in Jerusalem to express Yahweh's exasperation with his people: "Sons I have reared and brought up, but they have rebelled against me. The ox knows its owner, and the ass its master's feeding trough, but Israel does not know, my people do not understand" (Isa 1:2–3).

As a young contemporary of Amos and Hosea, **Isaiah** saw that much of the lawlessness described by them was going on in Jerusalem. He saw its leaders devouring the farmers' vineyards, their houses filled with the spoil of the afflicted; they were crushing God's people by grinding the face of the afflicted into the dust (Isa 3:13–15; cf. Amos 2:6–7; Hos 4:1–3). In a song, Isaiah depicted the house of Israel as the vineyard of Yahweh who had lovingly built and nurtured it only to find that it yielded rotten grapes which

---

5. Wolff, *Hosea*, 197.

he described with a play on words: "For the vineyard of Yahweh of hosts is the house of Israel, and the people of Judah are his pleasant planting. He expected justice (*mishpat*), but behold, bloodshed (*mispakh*), righteousness (*sedaqah*), but behold, a cry (*se'aqah*)!" (5:1–7). Calling for repentance Isaiah proclaimed a series of seven woes with covenant curses (5:8, 11, 18, 20, 21, 23; 10:1–2) decrying the lawlessness and the suffering inflicted on the righteous, but he saw no change. In a series of refrains, Isaiah reminded the perpetrators that God's "anger has not turned away and his hand is stretched out still" in judgment (5:25; 9:12, 17, 21; 10:4), and the rod of God's anger would be Assyria (10:5)!

Once, while in the temple, Isaiah had experienced a vision of Yahweh seated on his throne and surrounded by seraphim, God's heavenly attendants. Isaiah was taken aback that he, a person of unclean lips, had *seen* the King, Yahweh of hosts! Then a seraph cleansed his lips with a live coal from the incense altar and assured him that his sin had been erased, giving him the opportunity to become God's messenger (6:1–8). He was then given the strange commission to go to "this people" with this message: "Keep on hearing, but do not understand; keep on seeing, but do not comprehend. Make the heart of this people fat, and make their ears deaf, and their eyes glued shut! Lest they see with their eyes and hear with their ears and understand with their hearts and turn and be healed!" (6:9–10). Because of their obduracy God would hide his face from them. When Isaiah asked how long he would have to preach this, he was told until the cities lie uninhabited and the land is utterly desolate (6:11). The country would be devastated and the people exiled so that only a "stump" of the tree would remain, the holy seed of the faithful remnant (6:12–13). To proclaim this, like Hosea, Isaiah symbolically called his first son "Shear-yashub," meaning "only a remnant shall return."

Isaiah was soon to experience the deafness of Judah's King Ahaz who was confronted by Kings Pekah of Israel and Rezin of Damascus in 734 demanding that he join them in an alliance against Assyria or be forced off his throne. Isaiah warned Ahaz not to be afraid but put his trust in Yahweh, for soon these "smoldering stumps of firebrands" would be destroyed (7:3–9). But Ahaz would not listen nor ask God for a sign, so Isaiah responded: "Therefore Yahweh will give you a sign. Behold the young woman (*almah*) who is with child shall bear a son and shall call his name Immanuel" ("God is with us," 7:14). That is, by the time this young woman gave birth the threat of these two kings would have passed, and she would be able to name her son "Immanuel" out of thankfulness to God for deliverance. Shear-yashub accompanying Isaiah bore another name warning of consequences of not listening. However, Ahaz ignored the warning and sign, and instead sent a message and gifts to the Assyrian Tiglath-Pilesar III, saying: "I am your servant and your son. Come and rescue me" (2 Kgs 16:7). While this may have saved him from the threat of Pekah and Rezin, he had now put himself and Judah into servitude to the Assyrians. As a further sign, Isaiah named his second son "Maher-shalal-hash-baz," meaning "the spoil speeds, the prey hastens," as assurance that those kings would soon be destroyed.

However, the blindness and deafness of Ahaz and his advisers led Isaiah to declare that Yahweh, their rock of salvation (Isa 17:10; 26:4; 28:16; 30:29), would become for them "a stone to strike against, a rock of stumbling" and they would fall and be broken, snared and taken (8:14–15). Because of this Isaiah would close the book on them and wait for Yahweh (8:16–17). After hearing of the Assyrian ruler's decisive action against Pekah and Rezin and the deportation of the tribes of Zebulon and Naphtali, Isaiah pointed out that Judah would soon experience that same gloom and deep darkness. However, in the future those tribes who now sat in darkness would see the light of God's presence among them and see the rod of the oppressor broken, and in that light would return to Galilee of the nations (9:1–5). Then God would raise up a leader to sit on the throne of David, rule peacefully, and uphold justice and righteousness. As Yahweh's true representative he could be named with Yahweh's titles, "Wonderful Counselor [cf. Isa 28:29], Mighty God [cf. Isa 10:21], Everlasting Father [cf. Isa 1:2–4], Prince of Peace [cf. Isa 26:12]!"[6]

The alliance Ahaz made with the Assyrian ruler not only meant that the people had to carry the burden of paying tribute to their "protector," but also required them to acknowledge the Assyrian gods as superior to Yahweh with the altar to the Assyrian deity erected in the temple (2 Kgs 16:10–18). Because of this, Isaiah could see that "destruction is decreed, overflowing with righteousness" (10:22) from which only a remnant of the faithful would survive. Because of Yahweh's righteousness and faithfulness to the covenant, judgment was now inevitable, as it would also be on the oppressing nation. For with terrifying power Yahweh would cut down all the majestic trees and all will fall (10:33–34). However, after the pruning, Isaiah again prophesied, "there shall come forth a sprig from the stump of Jesse, and a shoot (*netser*) shall grow from its roots" (11:1). A new Davidic leader would emerge who would rule as an ideal representative of Yahweh's kingship, which would bring about a new society of the faithful in peace and security. This ruler would reflect God's wisdom and understanding, rule in the spirit of God's plan and power, carry out justice for the powerless and afflicted of the land, and the whole land would be full of the "knowledge of Yahweh" (11:2–9).

After the death of Ahaz in 715 BCE, his son Hezekiah acceded to the throne, made some attempts at reform, but he was still burdened with the Assyrian yoke and with the Solomonic tradition of having "wise men" as advisers. In 705 when Sennacherib became the new Assyrian leader, Hezekiah's advisers counseled him to make an alliance with Egypt against Sennacherib. Isaiah warned that this would be a "covenant with death" (28:15). These advisers were like the "drunkards of Ephraim" (28:1–4) whose counsel had led to the destruction of the northern kingdom in 721 BCE! Their response to Isaiah was ridicule: "To whom will he teach 'knowledge', and to whom will be explain the message? Those weaned from the milk, those taken from the breast?" followed by an imitation of the noisy babble of children learning the alphabet (28:9–10). Isaiah responded to this ridicule by warning them that they would soon be met with the babble of the alien tongue of their Assyrian conquerors (28:11–13)! By 701, Sennacherib's armies had destroyed Judah's fortified cities and laid siege to Jerusalem. Only surrender and paying a very heavy tribute saved the city (2 Kgs 18:14–16). Isaiah now counseled to put his trust in Yahweh, and God would cause Sennacherib to "hear a rumor, and return to his own land" where he would eventually die by the sword (Isa 37:1–7).

---

6. See Wildberger, *Isaiah 1–12*, 398–401; Williamson, "Messianic Texts in Isaiah 1–39," 254–58.

Basic Concepts in Isaiah's Vision

1. **Yahweh of Hosts, the Holy One of Israel.** Isaiah invests the common title for God, "Yahweh of Hosts," with deeper meaning. The seraphim which surrounded the throne of Yahweh in the vision are part of the heavenly host (cf. 1 Kgs 22:19–23) who act as covenant witnesses and agents, but the "hosts" also includes the armies ("hosts") of the nations which Yahweh uses as his unknowing agents in carrying out his will (cf. 13:4). The song of the Seraphim, "Holy, holy, holy is Yahweh of Hosts" (6:3) resulted in his more unique title, "The Holy One of Israel" which expressed for Isaiah the awesome majesty of the God of Israel as the great King over all peoples.

2. **Covenant.** While Isaiah never spoke explicitly of a covenant between Yahweh and Israel, his use of covenant concepts and terminology make it quite evident that the Sinai covenant was part of his thinking and the basis of his message. The Holy One of Israel can bring into force the covenant curses as well as the blessings, and comes in judgment as the same God who made himself known at Sinai (29:6; 30:27–28; cf. Exod 19:16–20). The Holy One demonstrates his holiness continually by his faithfulness to the covenant he had with his people at Sinai and reaffirmed through his covenant with David.

3. **Justice and Righteousness.** Isaiah gives these terms great emphasis. "Righteousness," both divine and human, is acting faithfully in the covenant relationship, as is also "justice" which is never used strictly in a juridical sense, but has the meaning of carrying out God's plan, purpose and judgment. Isaiah uses the same covenant terminology as Amos to describe the righteous as "afflicted," "powerless," and "dispossessed." When a king as God's agent fails to judge their case with equity according to the covenant (11:4), Yahweh will ultimately bring protection and peace to the afflicted in their vindication (14:30, 32; 29:19). It is the afflicted and dispossessed who will experience the covenant blessings and "will exalt in the Holy One of Israel."

4. **God's Plan and Human Wisdom.** Proverbial wisdom imported from Egypt and elsewhere by Solomon and perpetuated by scribal schools for the training of court officials had become the basis for decision-making rather than prophetic pronouncement in the Jerusalem court.[7] This had continued in Isaiah's time as is evident from the ridicule he received from Hezekiah's advisers (28:1–13). The book of Proverbs, chs. 25–29, are attributed to these advisers. Isaiah was familiar with this "wisdom" and condemned these "wise men," who give lip service to Yahweh but follow "the commandment of men learned by rote," and hide from God their "plan." They are like the clay that tries to tell the potter what to do. So, "the wisdom of the wise men shall perish, and the discernment of their discerning men shall be hid" (29:13–16). They are the rebellious children who carry out their own plan instead of Yahweh's and put their trust in foreign alliances instead of God. "When Yahweh stretches out his hand . . . they will all perish together" (30:1–5; 31:1–3).

---

7. See Whitelam, *Just King*, 165; Mettinger, *Solomonic State Officials*, 144–57.

So rather than covenantal obligations, Isaiah preferred to speak to them of divine "instruction" (*torah*) and God's "plan." For God also has a plan for all the nations, and "this is the plan which is planned concerning the whole earth, and this is the hand that is stretched out, and who will turn it back?" (14:26–27).

5. **House of David and Zion.** David's bringing the ark of the covenant into Jerusalem and establishing it on Mount Zion (2 Sam 6:1–15) was a symbolic act to emphasize that Yahweh now resided on this holy mountain and spoke and acted through the king as his "son." The royal psalms used in the worship continued to emphasize this intimate relationship between God and king and insured the continuing commitment in Judah to the dynastic principle. For Isaiah, then, Mount Zion would always be the "place of the name of Yahweh of hosts" (18:7). In the ideal future when Zion would be filled with justice and righteousness (33:5), the "mountain of the house of Yahweh shall be established as the highest of the mountains, and shall be raised above the hills." It would be a time when nations and peoples would recognize and come to Zion to worship the God of Israel as the only God, and to learn to walk in his ways. For the teaching which goes forth from Zion would lead nations to turn from war and destruction to peace and prosperity (2:2–4). Concomitant with that was God's establishing an ideal representative of his rule. This messianic hope which emerges explicitly for the first time in Isaiah comes out of a deep longing for a leader who would truly be a *mašiah Yahweh*, a true representative of God's justice and righteousness (11:1–9). Through him, Yahweh as *the* King (6:5) who breaks the rod of the oppressor and destroys the symbols of war, would restore his kingly rule.

6. **Isaiah and the Nations.** With the Assyrian domination, Judah's relationship to the surrounding nations was always an issue. Isaiah contended that God's almighty plan also encompassed these nations, often expressed in oracles against them. Those oracles, recorded in Isa 13–23 which have received considerable editing to make them relevant for later generations, reveal something of Isaiah's vision in regard to the nations.[8] As the creator and ruler of the universe, Yahweh sometimes uses foreign nations as his agents in chastising Judah (5:26–30; 7:17–20; 8:1–8; 10:5–6), but those who claim that power for themselves (10:7–19, 24–26, 33–34) or draw Judah into alliances (17:1–14; 14:28–32) will also be punished. However, as a consequence of Yahweh's universal sovereignty, redemption of these nations must inevitably come through the leadership of Yahweh's faithful remnant. This results in the hope expressed in Isa 2:2–4 that in the future all nations will seek Yahweh and walk in his paths.

Micah of Moresheth, as Isaiah's contemporary, expressed the anger and concern of the rural communities against the corrupt officials and judges in Jerusalem. As a country prophet living about thirty-two kilometers southwest of Jerusalem, he witnessed the growing hardships imposed on people of the land, caused by overtaxing as a consequence of Judah having to pay heavy tribute to Assyria. He had witnessed the destruction of Samaria in 722/1 BCE, and he could see that same disease of corruption and the

---

8. Cf. Davies, "Destiny of the Nations," 93–120, and Jenkins, "Development of the Isaiah Tradition," 237–51.

> **EXCURSUS**
>
> ## The Formation of the Book of Isaiah
>
> It has long been recognized that the sixty-six chapters of this book were not all written by Isaiah of Jerusalem who was active from 742–721 BCE. Much of chs. 1–39 are attributed to him during the Assyrian domination, which finally came to an end with the destruction of Nineveh in 612 and Haran in 610. Soon after, Judah came under the control of Babylonia, and through corrupt leadership and political intrigue suffered the loss of its leading people to deportation to Babylon in 597, and much of the population ten years later. Near the end of that long exile an anonymous prophet, whom we know as Deutero-Isaiah, proclaimed a message of hope around 545–540 BCE which was added to the book in chs. 34–35 and 40–55. By 539 Babylonia had fallen to the Persians under Cyrus, who permitted the exiles to return to Judah. In the first years of that return (ca. 538–518), disciples of Deutero-Isaiah, sometimes referred to as Trito-Isaiah, added chs. 56–66. Much later, probably during the time of Alexander the Great (ca. 330 BCE), chs. 24–27 were added which reflect the whole Isaiah tradition of God's universal judgment and final deliverance of Israel and the nations.

breakdown of covenant faithfulness, which had led to disaster in the north, spreading among his own people in Judah and Jerusalem. So the people had better prepare themselves for exile (1:9–16)!

Following Amos, Micah accused the officials of spending their nights devising ways to use their power to seize fields and houses, to "oppress a fellow and his house, a man and his inheritance" (2:1–2). Because of debt, they drove out women and children from the comfort of their homes into the streets, stripped of the dignity of possessing their rightful inheritance and forced into a life of servitude (2:8–9). With brutal clarity Micah described these leaders as cannibals intent on devouring the people and their land. They "tear the skin off my people and flesh off their bones, and eat the flesh of my people . . . , and their bones they break into pieces and spread them out as in a pot, as flesh in a cauldron!" (3:1–3). The time would come when those leaders would be prisoners, and their vast estates would be divided amongst their captors (2:4). For even judges, priests and cultic prophets in Jerusalem were all corrupt, and their claim that Yahweh was in their midst would not protect them, because Zion would be ploughed like a field and Jerusalem would become a heap of ruins (3:11–12).

In 701 when Sennacherib's armies overran the fortified cities and villages of Judah and put Jerusalem under siege, driving out people and taking as booty their animals and produce, the country was left in fear, and law and order was non-existent. Micah felt that the godly had disappeared from the land, and one could no longer trust one's neighbor or even the members of one's own household (7:2–6). All he could do was wait for Yahweh to demonstrate his righteous response and carry out his part of the covenant with chastisement of the whole nation (7:9).

However, Micah knew his role as a prophet was not only to warn of coming judgment and to plead the cause of the afflicted, but also to express the comfort and hope which the covenant relationship offered. Micah had reminded the people of Jerusalem that their ritual religion—offering multiple sacrifices even of one's first born child—would gain them nothing. What the covenant required was simply to do justice, to practice steadfast love, and to walk humbly with their God (6:6–8). True worship was not the cult with all its rituals and holy days, but living in faithfulness to the covenant relationship. For the temple was no guarantee of the presence of Yahweh among them and would be destroyed (3:12). But after the chastisement of his people, God would pardon them because of his steadfast love (7:18–20; 6:4) and would gather the lame and those driven away. They would become the remnant which will grow into a strong nation, "and Yahweh will reign over them in Mount Zion now and forevermore" (4:6–7; 2:12–13).

Micah did not question the traditions that God had chosen Zion for his dwelling place and David's descendants to be the earthly representatives of his kingship. The great prophecy of the restoration of Zion found in Isa 2:2–4 is repeated in Mic 4:1–4 with the addition of the rural idea that "they shall sit every man under his vine and under his fig tree, and none shall make them afraid." Yet he did not see the kings in Jerusalem as representatives of Yahweh's rule. God would choose a future ruler from a new line of David's descendants in rural Bethlehem rather than Jerusalem.[9] He would be a leader who could empathize with the common people in the covenant tradition and would gather those who had been led away captive, and "feed his flock in the strength of Yahweh" so that once again the people might know peace (5:2–6).

Understandably, while Micah had repeated the pious hope of Isa 2:2–4 that nations would come to Zion to turn their swords into ploughshares and their spears into pruning hooks, his eyes were still filled with the rapacity and devastation brought upon Judah by the nations. So he looked for judgment, particularly for Assyria, for the sufferings inflicted upon his people. The "many nations" who came to Zion to profane it were ignorant of God's plan: Yahweh would gather them to Zion as sheaves on the threshing floor where "daughter Zion" would crush them underfoot, and their wealth would be devoted to God (4:11:13). These hopes, expressed by both Isaiah and Micah, would live on into the future through the dark years ahead in spite of the suppression of the prophets during the long reign of Hezekiah's son, Manasseh.

The Prophetic Silence

After Hezekiah died in 687 BCE, his son Manasseh not only accepted the worship of alien gods but encouraged it. He took a strong pro-Assyrian stance and brutally suppressed any opposition from the prophets and others during his long forty-five-year reign (2 Kgs 21:10–16). Alien forms of worship were practiced in the Jerusalem temple, astral religion became popular in family worship with altars built on rooftops for "all the host of heaven." Worship of the sun god, Shamash, and Ishtar as the "queen of heaven" became common (cf. Jer 7:18; 44:19). Various forms of divination were practiced,

---

9. Cf. Hillers, *Micah*, 64–66.

sacrifices and libations offered to an array of deities, and firstborn sons were offered to the fire god Molech in the Valley of Ben-Hinnom (2 Kgs 21:4; Jer 19:5, 6). To supervise all this alien worship foreign priests (*kemarim*) were brought into Judah and Jerusalem (Zeph 1:4; 2 Kgs 23:5).[10]

These foreign practices had become firmly entrenched in Jerusalem and surrounding areas by the time of Manasseh's death in 642 BCE. His son Amon continued in his father's ways, but after a reign of two years he was assassinated by palace conspirators who, in turn, were executed by "the people of the land" who then put Amon's eight-year-old son, Josiah, on the throne. Under their guidance, Josiah gradually adopted an anti-Assyrian policy and eventually sought to bring Judah back to Yahwism. The first attempt at reform came in 626 BCE when the Babylonians under Nabopolassar, followed by the Medes, broke free from the Assyrian yoke. A more thorough reform followed in 621 when a scroll of the law was discovered in the temple during its renovation. It was during this period of Josiah's reign that the voice of the prophets began to be heard once again.

The prophet **Zephaniah,** whose ancestry is traced back to Hezekiah (1:1), spoke out prior to Josiah's attempt at reform. Prophesying at a time when syncretistic worship was still popular, and Josiah was still in his teens (ca. 635–626 BCE), Zephaniah denounced in the most graphic terms the false worship and corrupt ways which had been going on for so long. This had caused the reversal of creation leading to judgment (1:1–9; cf. Hos 4:1–3).[11] So at a harvest festival, he warned that instead of the sacrifices being offered by foreign (*kemarim*) and local priests (*kohanim*), they and all the idolaters, including "the king's sons" (1:8) who dressed in Assyrian attire and participated in foreign rituals, would soon become the actual sacrifice, a reversal with the coming of the Day of Yahweh. Taking a lesson from Amos (1:9—2:8), Zephaniah gave a series of oracles against nations beginning with Philistia and building up to Assyria, prophesying that the "exultant city," Nineveh, would become a desolation (2:14–15). Yet ultimate judgment would be for Judah and that "oppressing city," Jerusalem, with its faithless officials, judges, prophets and priests (3:1–4).

However, the greatest reversal of all would be those who inhabited Zion/Jerusalem in the future. Only "a people afflicted and lowly" who put their trust in Yahweh alone and acted faithfully would remain as the remnant, and God himself would be their King (3:11–20). Zephaniah no longer held out hope for a future Davidic messiah. The righteous remnant would be gathered together under the saving protection of their loving God to be his representatives.

Josiah's Reform

With Assyrian control weakening and Zephaniah's claim that Philistia and Moab would become the possession of the remnant of Judah (2:7, 9), Josiah began to extend his control over the territories that had once been part of the united kingdom. However, when

---

10. See further, Albertz, *History of Israelite Religion*, 1:188–94.
11. DeRoche, "Zephaniah I 2–3," 104–9; DeRoche, "Reversal of Creation in Hosea," 400–409.

the book of the law[12] was discovered in the temple and read to the king, he instructed Hilkiah the high priest and Shaphan the scribe to inquire of Yahweh concerning this book. They went to the prophetess Huldah who warned them of the consequences of not following this law. That, together with the backing of those faithful to Yahweh, led to Josiah initiating reform in 621. As it is described in 2 Kgs 23, the reform was thorough in seeking to get rid of all forms of foreign religious influences and syncretistic rites in Jerusalem and Judah, as well as in the former northern kingdom. While religious concerns were uppermost for some of Josiah's close advisers, political and national interests also fueled the reform. With the disintegration of the Assyrian Empire and with other nations against it, it seemed only a matter of time before "the exultant city" would be destroyed.

In this nationalistic fervor, the prophet **Nahum** warned Assyria that Yahweh is the God of universal justice and would take vengeance on those who had oppressed his people (1:3–6). For Yahweh is "a stronghold in the days of trouble; he knows those who take refuge in him" (1:7). Now was the time for Yahweh to break the yoke of the Assyrians and free his people to carry out their religious obligations. When in 612 BCE a coalition of Medes and Babylonians came against Nineveh, and after three months utterly destroyed it, Nahum was ecstatic! With Josiah once again celebrating the Passover with his people (2 Kgs 23:21–23), Nahum joyously proclaimed: "Behold, on the mountains the feet who brings good news, who proclaims peace! Keep your feast, O Judah, complete your vows!" (1:15). The rest of Nahum's prophecy is a passionate exaltation over the coming destruction of Nineveh, described in graphic and savage detail.

However, the exaltation was short lived. After Nineveh was destroyed, the Assyrian army retreated to Haran where they were again defeated. Josiah had moved north to establish claim to northern Israel, but Pharaoh Necho of Egypt had the same idea, and Josiah was killed at Megiddo in 609 BCE. With his death, Judah once again fell into chaos. The "people of the land" placed Josiah's younger son, Jehoahaz, on the throne, but he lasted there only three months before he was taken prisoner by Necho and replaced by his older pro-Egyptian brother who took the throne name, Jehoiakim. Under him the reform movement lapsed, and those who followed the syncretistic cult continued their practices (cf. Jer 44:15–19). Egypt required heavy tribute, which Jehoiakim collected from the people, particularly from the reform-minded "people of the land" who had bypassed him earlier for the kingship (2 Kgs 23:34–37). Egypt's claim to further territory led to their defeat at Carchemish by the Babylonians under Nebuchadnezzar in 605, and Jehoiakim now became an unwilling vassal to Nebuchadnezzar. When Nebuchadnezzar's further battle against Egypt in 601 left the outcome undecided and heavy loss of both sides, Jehoiakim rebelled and sought help from Egypt. Nebuchadnezzar quickly commanded his vassals in Syria, Moab and Ammon to send armies against Judah, which was already in enough trouble because of the corrupt and tyrannous leadership of Jehoiakim. It was in this situation that the prophet Habakkuk expressed dismay and sought answers from God.

Habakkuk, horrified at the corruption and ruthlessness of Jehoiakim, around 604 sought an answer from God why all this was allowed to happen. Why were the wicked

---

12. Generally understood to have been a substantial part of the book of Deuteronomy.

permitted to surround the righteous, so that justice is perverted (1:2–4)? In a series of woes (2:5–19), Habakkuk condemned Jehoiakim as arrogant and motivated by greed, heaping up what was not his, gathering evil gain for his house (2:5–9), similar to the description of Jehoiakim given later in Jer 22:13–19. After Jehoiakim's death these woes were expanded to refer to Nebuchadnezzar.[13]

God's answer to Habakkuk was to point out to him that he was still in control and would use the Babylonians, in spite of their cruelty, as agents to bring about judgment (1:5–11). Habakkuk's response to that was to acknowledge Yahweh's eternal justice, but he questioned why God would use such faithless and ruthless people to chastise Judah (1:12–17). The answer eventually came to Habakkuk in a vision (2:2–4) which he was told to write down in large letters, so that one running as a herald could read it, warning of impending judgment. The arrogant would ignore it, but the "righteous one by his faithfulness will live," and patiently enduring the strife, will survive the judgment on the arrogant. Then the "cup in Yahweh's right hand" of divine judgment would eventually be given to the Babylonians for their violence, corruption and false worship (2:15–19). By adding an ancient hymn to his prophecy, Habakkuk voiced his conviction that God is in control of his universe, a source of comfort, strength and joy for the faithful (3:2–19). He would wait out the coming events in that conviction.

The prophet *Jeremiah* received his call while still a youth in 627 BCE and continued as an irritant to priests and kings, calling all to repentance before disaster came, and Judah finished up in exile like the north. He lived through many crises and changing circumstances, constantly calling all to return to their covenant with Yahweh, until his death in Egypt sometime after 582. He came from Anathoth, a Levite town north of Jerusalem where his father served as a Levite priest. The Levites had served as priests at various shrines throughout the country for centuries, but with Josiah's reform of 621, all worship was now to be consolidated in the Jerusalem temple. Those shrines suspected of idolatrous worship were destroyed, and the Levite priests were invited to carry on their priestly duties in the temple. Most refused to do so, and the Zadokite priests in Jerusalem did not want this influx of rural priests. This caused upheaval and resentment for the Levites who continued to hold on to their priestly traditions.

Influenced by the prophets before him, Jeremiah, as a Levite prophet, came to Jerusalem to call the people to covenant faithfulness with the warning that there were other powers besides Assyria that could become God's agents and force them into servitude (Jer 1:13–16; 4:5–8; 5:10–17; 6:1–5). After the collapse of Josiah's reform under Jehoiakim, Jeremiah found that his message fell on deaf ears, and he was meeting with growing opposition. He saw Jehoiakim as a self-serving tyrant who used forced labor to build a new palace for himself, and who had "eyes and heart only for dishonest gain, for shedding blood, and for practicing oppression and violence." No one would mourn his death, and his body would be dragged out of the city and given the burial of an ass (22:13–19)!

Early in Jehoiakim's reign, when pilgrims were streaming into Jerusalem to celebrate the Feast of Booths,[14] Jeremiah stationed himself at the temple gate and preached his "Temple Sermon" in which he warned them not to think that the temple was

---

13. Cf. Roberts, *Nahum, Habakkuk and Zephaniah*, 84; Holladay, "Plausible Circumstances," 123–42.

14. Cf. Holladay, *Jeremiah I*, 2–3.

inviolable and always a place of refuge, repeating, "This is the temple of Yahweh" (7:4). They had turned this temple into a "den of robbers" by their failure to live by the covenant stipulations, their false confidence in ritual performance, and offerings to foreign deities (7:16–26; 26:1–19). Just as the ancient shrine of Shiloh had been destroyed, so this temple and Jerusalem would be destroyed also (7:12–15). This angered the priests and temple prophets and they wanted Jeremiah put to death for false prophecy, but some officials like Ahikam, the son of Shaphan, still trying to uphold the Josian reform, came to his aid by quoting a similar prophecy by Micah (Mic 3:12). Thus Jeremiah was saved but other such prophets were not so fortunate (Jer 26:20–24). However, Jeremiah was barred thereafter from entering the temple (36:5).

Yet Jeremiah was not deterred and only intensified his warning of coming judgment. Observing a potter working his clay on his wheel, he used this image to show that just as the potter reworks the clay when the vessel he is making is imperfect, so God would have to do the same with Judah (18:1–11). This only provoked some to plot against him (18:18). So he invited elders and senior priests to accompany him to the Valley of ben Hinnom, which he called the Valley of Slaughter. There, taking an earthen vessel representing the nation, he smashed it to pieces on the rocks! This, he told them, represented irrevocable judgment for their alien worship and their kings sacrificing sons to Molech in this valley (19:1–15). For this, he was put in stocks overnight to endure the jeering and mocking of the people (20:1–6). Because of his constant warning of judgment, even the men of Anathoth were threatening to kill him (11:18–23), and he was shunned even by members of his own family (12:6).

After Nebuchadnezzar's armies defeated the Egyptians at Carchemish in 605, they quickly advanced south. Because of the threat, a national fast was proclaimed throughout Judah, and people fled to the temple for refuge. Jeremiah had warned about this and quickly dictated all his oracles of coming judgment to his secretary, Baruch, and instructed him to read it in the temple (36:1–10). When the king's officials heard about this, they requested that it also be read to them. Knowing that they would have to report this to Jehoiakim, they advised Baruch and Jeremiah to go into hiding. As the scroll was read to him, Jehoiakim cut off sections and cast them into the fire, and ordered the arrest of Baruch and Jeremiah who were already in hiding (36:11–26). This did not deter Jeremiah; he simply dictated the oracles again with additions, including the curse that none of Jehoiakim's offspring would ever sit on the throne of David (36:27–31).

Judah now had to pay tribute to Babylon but when its armies suffered heavy casualties in fighting against Egypt in 601, Jehoiakim withdrew tribute in the hope that Egypt would come to his aid which they were in no position to do. By December 598, when Nebuchadnezzar arrived to lay siege to Jerusalem, Jehoiakim died and his eighteen-year-old son, Jehoiachin, became king, but within three months (March 597) the city had surrendered. Jehoiachin, his mother, many leading officials and citizens, as well as much booty, were taken to Babylon. Zedekiah was put in charge to collect tribute and serve Babylon. Jeremiah felt that those who had been left behind under Zedekiah were a basket of rotten figs, while the good figs, those officials who had supported him, were now in exile (24:1–10).

Zedekiah proved to be a weak ruler, easily influenced by pro-Egyptian advisers, which led to one crisis after another. Jeremiah, then wearing an ox-yoke around his neck, warned them and other conspiring nations to submit to the yoke of Babylon or they would be destroyed (27:1–22). He then sent a letter to the exiles appealing to them to reject the lies of the false prophets and diviners and settle in to a long stay—seventy years, the span of a lifetime (29:1–23). Nevertheless, in 589 with the promise of aid from Egypt, Zedekiah withdrew the tribute, and by January 588 Jerusalem was placed under siege and outlying cities were destroyed. Jeremiah warned Zedekiah to surrender in order to live, or he would die, but Zedekiah still held out hope for rescue. Jeremiah's constant calls for surrender only led to his imprisonment in a miry cracked cistern where he would have died had not an Ethiopian eunuch rescued him (38:1–13).

In July 587 the walls of Jerusalem were breached (52:5–7). Zedekiah and his officers were captured trying to escape as the city and temple were destroyed, leaders executed, and the majority of the people marched off into exile in Babylon (36:6–10; 52:12–17). Jeremiah was released into the protection of Gedaliah, a grandson of Shaphan who had been Josiah's secretary (39:11–14; 40:1–6). Gedaliah was appointed governor to administer the affairs of the poor of the land who were left behind to work the vacated vineyards and fields, but by 582 he was assassinated by an Ammonite group. Many of the people, fearing reprisals from Babylon, forced Jeremiah to flee with them to Egypt (42:1—43:7). There Jeremiah predicted that Nebuchadnezzar would again invade Egypt, and their escape would have been for naught (43:8–13). His last recorded sermon condemned their return to the worship of alien gods.

Jeremiah had seen his prophecies fulfilled, and in spite of the leaders' deafness and derision, he had felt compelled to speak out. For it was God's message, not his, that compelled him, as he confessed to God: "Your words were found and I ate them, and your words became to me a joy and the gladness of my heart, for I am called by your name, O Yahweh of hosts. I did not sit in the company of merrymakers, nor did I rejoice. I sat alone because your hand was upon me, for you had filled me with indignation" (15:16–17). It was this divine indignation and his proclamation of it that caused him so much suffering, like an incurable wound (15:18) from which he longed to be healed (17:14).

Following the prophets before him, Jeremiah had portrayed Yahweh as choosing Israel as his son and expected to be called "My Father," but Israel had acted as a faithless wife, playing the harlot (3:19–20; 4:13; cf. Hos 5:7; 6:7; 11:1). God had planted Israel in the desirable land as a choice vine, but it had become useless (2:20–21; cf. Isa 5:1–7). The people did not know Yahweh because "their kings, their officials, their priests, their prophets" had misled them (2:8, 26; 4:9). So the nation had become a "foolish and senseless people, who have eyes but do not see, who have ears that do not hear" (5:21; cf. Isa 6:9–10).

Jeremiah's call for repentance focused around the verb "to turn" (*šûb*) which could mean either "to turn away" from God or "(re)turn" to God. A sincere return to Yahweh alone in covenant faithfulness would mean the removal of all alien gods and injustices (4:1–4), but Judah seemed incapable of doing so. The consequences of turning away from the light of God's presence was to enter into darkness and to "stumble and fall" (6:15; 8:12; 18:15). Jeremiah described this stumbling as a "sickness" (6:7; 10:19), "wound" (15:18; 30:12), "pain" and "brokenness" (4:6, 20; 6:1, 14; 8:11, 21), often defined as "malignant" and "incurable." His plaintive cry: "Is there no balm in Gilead?" (8:21–22) would go unanswered. That healing would only come in the future after Judah had experienced the full brunt of the covenant curses. That promise finally came in Jer 30:12–17. By the grace of God the incurable would finally be cured.

Jeremiah's preaching was thoroughly covenantal, clear already from the influence of Hosea on his early proclamations, and reaffirmed by the discovery of the Deuteronomic scroll in the temple during renovations in 621. Its Levite orientation and emphasis on keeping the covenant made that discovery so important to him that he was understandably incensed by the arrogance and betrayal of the reform after Josiah's death, and he condemned the people for not having sincerely accepted the Deuteronomic covenant (11:1–17). In words reminiscent of Deuteronomy[15] Jeremiah reminded the people of the covenant curses, listed in Deut 27:15—28:15, which would come on all who did not heed the words of this covenant (11:3–4). These curses he summarized in constant threat of "sword, famine, pestilence, and captivity" (cf. 14:12; 15:2; etc). Jeremiah had one simple answer for the destruction of Jerusalem: "Because they forsook the covenant of Yahweh their God, and worshiped other gods and served them" (22:9). They would have to drink "the cup of God's wrath" (13:12–14; 25:15–27; cf. Hab 2:16).

Besides the kings, officials and Jerusalem priests condemned by Jeremiah, were the false prophets. These were often connected to the temple and were guilty of preaching "peace, peace" when there was no peace (6:13–15; 8:10–12). The fact that these prophets claimed to speak God's word by means of dreams and visions, led Jeremiah to reject them altogether. The word of Yahweh to him was: "When one of this people, or a prophet, or priest asks you, 'What is the *massa'* of Yahweh?' You shall say to them, 'you are the *massa*', and I will cast you off, says Yahweh" (23:33). The word, *massa'* from the verb *nasa'* "to lift up," can mean either "burden" or "oracular vision," deriving from the phrase "he *lifted up* his voice," often used of prophetic messages.[16] The temple prophets, claiming to have oracular visions, had become a burden (*massa'*) to Yahweh and he would *lift them up* and cast them away from his presence into everlasting shame (23:33–40).

The Vision of Hope

The covenant curses would have to run their course for a generation, and then Yahweh, the only living God and King (10:10; 8:19), would demonstrate his righteousness by restoring his people to covenant relationship with him (29:10–14). He would gather the people from all the countries into which he had driven them in his anger. He would bring them back to their land to dwell in security and covenant faithfulness (32:36–41) and give them shepherds who would care for them. Picking up on Isaiah's hope for "a shoot (*netser*) from the stump of Jesse" (Isa 11:1), Jeremiah used a more common term and predicted that Yahweh would "raise up for David a *righteous shoot* (*tsemah tsadiq*),"

---

15. See Jones, *Jeremiah*, 181–83; also Cazelles, "Jeremiah and Deuteronomy," 104–6.
16. Cf. Nah 1:1; Hab 1:1; Isa 13:1; 14:28; 15:1; Zech 9:1; 12:1; Mal 1:1; etc.

who would reign wisely and carry out justice and righteousness in the land. He would be called "Yahweh is our righteousness" (23:5–6) because he would be representing Yahweh's righteousness for all.

In his "book of consolation" (chs. 30–33), Jeremiah summarized these promises: "Behold, the days are coming, says Yahweh, when I will restore my people, Israel and Judah, from captivity, says Yahweh, and I will bring them back to the land which I gave to their fathers and they shall inherit it" (30:3). He would break the yoke from off their necks and burst their chains asunder and free them from servitude, and bring them healing (30:12–18). As a loving father he would gather them all from the farthest parts of the earth together with the blind and the lame, the woman with child and the woman in labor, and bring them back to Zion on the good path on which they would not stumble (31:7–9). There, he will keep them as a shepherd keeps his flock, ransomed and redeemed, and Rachel, refusing to be comforted because her children had all gone into exile, can then wipe her tears (31:15–22). The whole of creation would be renewed, and unlike the old covenant which was seen as a written document containing a set of laws to be obeyed or ignored, a new covenant would be written upon their hearts. Yahweh's teaching would be within them, leading them to live according to God's will, freely and willingly. Henceforth, there would be no need for one to teach the other to "know Yahweh," for all would be in an intimate, faithful relationship with God, experiencing his love and forgiveness (31:31–34).

Jeremiah's prophetic vision would have a profound influence on the prophets of the exile, and after them, on the prophets of the return and beyond. Because of the exile, that prophetic vision would be expanded and transformed.

Chapter III

The Beginning of the Exile, and the Priest Turned Prophet

THE CRISIS OF THE BABYLONIAN EXILE

By the time Jerusalem had fallen to the Babylonians in July 587, Jeremiah's constant warnings that they would die by "sword, famine, and pestilence" were already being fulfilled. Zedekiah was captured, saw his sons slain, then blinded, bound and taken captive to Babylon where he soon died. Many leading citizens, including leading Zadokite priests, were executed. The temple, the king's palace, buildings, and the walls of the city were destroyed by fire (2 Kgs 25:1–21; Jer 39:1–10; 52:4–27), and the rest of the people were marched off as captives to Babylon. Those who had been left behind were the poorest of the land or who had escaped captivity, but had lost everything. They had all become the downtrodden, the afflicted, and the dispossessed.

Those left behind, like the author of the book of Lamentations, inherited the city in ruins and the land plundered and devastated. There was no food, and women in their grief were even killing and eating their infants (4:9–10)! Their homes, and their possessions were gone, and now they even had to pay for their water and firewood (5:25). Law and order had given way to chaos, and neighboring nations were taking advantage of the situation and encroaching on Judah. At first, it was no better for those who had survived the long trek into exile, where they were put to work building and maintaining irrigation channels between the Tigris and Euphrates rivers near Nippur, mocked by the natives, as one psalmist mourned (Ps 137:1–3). While some blamed their leaders, others like the author of Ps 44 accused God of forsaking his people (vv. 11–14):

> You have made us like sheep for slaughter, and have scattered us among the nations.
> You have sold your people for a trifle, demanding no high price for them.
> You have made us the taunt of our neighbors, the derision and scorn of those around us.
> You have made us a byword among the nations, a laughing-stock among the peoples!

"Why?" the psalmist asks, professing innocence. "We have not forsaken you or been false to your covenant" (44:17; cf. Ps 74).

However, it soon became the major conviction that the exile happened because they *had* been false to the covenant, that Jeremiah had been right all the time. These disastrous events were the curses of the covenant which they would have to sit out and learn faithfulness before they could again experience the covenant blessings.

EZEKIEL AND THE ZADOKITE PRIESTHOOD

The book of Ezekiel is one of the major prophetical writings, yet it is never quoted and is rarely alluded to in any of the inter-testamental or New Testament literature, although it did have influence on part of the postexilic community, as we shall see. It becomes clear that the book does not, in itself, really contribute to the prophetic vision because of its priestly orientation, particularly with its emphasis on the temple and the future authority of the Zadokite priesthood outlined in chs. 40–48. Yet since it points in a priestly direction, which often led to differences and even opposition to the prophetic vision, we need to be familiar with its themes and characteristics.

Ezekiel was a Zadokite priest who was part of the first deportation to Babylon in 597 BCE. Trained as a priest with a good understanding of Israelite history and traditions, he was now no longer able to practice his priestly rituals and ordinances without altar or temple. Yet, since no other priest is mentioned, he had probably been forced to accompany these early exiles as their priest. Constant news of what was going on in Judah and Jerusalem affected him profoundly, and he was certainly influenced by reports of Jeremiah's speeches and activities. After five years in exile, since he felt he could not function as a priest, he assumed the role of prophet to pass on the messages of Jeremiah for the people in exile. He did this by carrying out some extreme symbolic acts as visual messages and as a graphic means of communicating with his fellow exiles.

The book of Ezekiel is carefully arranged into four major sections: oracles of judgment against Jerusalem and Judah, chs. 1–24; oracles against the nations, chs. 25–32; oracles mostly of deliverance, chs. 33–39; and plans for future restoration, chs. 40–48. The book is written in the first-person and is generally regarded as the work of Ezekiel himself,[1] although the plan of future restoration shows strong influences from the Zadokite priesthood generally. These latter chapters at least demonstrate that Ezekiel remained in his heart of hearts a Zadokite priest.

In order to fit into the role of prophet, Ezekiel, although he never mentioned or acknowledged Jeremiah, borrowed from his words and experiences to give credence to his claim to be a prophet. Jeremiah had claimed that Yahweh put forth his hand and touched his mouth (Jer 1:9) giving him the words to speak, words which he "ate" and which to him became a joy and the delight of his heart (Jer 15:6). So Ezekiel, in his call, was given the charge: "Open your mouth and eat what I have given you," and a hand was stretched out to him and he was given a scroll with writing on both sides, words of "lamentations, and mourning and woe" (Ezek 2:8–10). These were the words he was to

---

1. See Greenberg, *Ezekiel 1–20*.

speak to the "rebellious house" of Israel, yet when he "ate" the scroll, he said, "It was in my mouth as sweet as honey" (3:3).

Jeremiah had referred to prophets who, like himself, warned people of impending judgment, as "watchmen" (Jer 6:17), and because the people rejected the warnings of these watchmen, their rituals and sacrifices were unacceptable to God, and they would perish (Jer 6:16–21). Convinced of the rebellious nature of the people and the inevitable destruction of Jerusalem, Ezekiel saw his call thus to be a "watchman" to warn of the impending judgment (Ezek 3:16–21). Ignoring Jeremiah's rejection of the priestly rituals and sacrifices, he described his role as "watchman" in quasi-legal priestly language as warning the wicked and those who had strayed from their righteousness that they were under sentence of death. If he failed to warn the people, he would come under the same sentence.

Later, in ch. 33, Ezekiel returned to the "watchman" metaphor, again setting the function of prophet and the response of the people in the form of casuistic law (33:1–9). As requirements for repentance, he demanded not only living faithfully according to the covenant, but also maintaining the priestly laws. Part of those requirements are put in a negative, legal form, such as: "The righteousness of the righteous one shall not deliver him when he transgresses; and as for the wickedness of the wicked one, he shall not stumble by it when he turns from his wickedness; and the righteous one shall not be able to live by his righteousness when he sins" (33:12).[2] Much of this casuistry was brought over from Ezekiel's long discussion in ch. 18 of the common proverbial complaint: "The fathers have eaten sour grapes, and the children's teeth are set on edge" (18:2; cf. Jer 31:29–31). Ezekiel gave an extensive refutation of this proverb, giving greater weight to the stipulations of the Holiness Code than to the prophetic concerns for a true covenant relationship.[3]

Ezekiel's series of sign-acts (4:1—5:17) served as a prologue to his oracles of judgment. So Ezekiel was instructed to draw the city of Jerusalem on a clay brick, put siege works against it with a siege wall, ramp, enemy camps, and battering rams all around it. He was then to use an iron griddle as an iron wall between him and the city, and to press the siege against it (4:1–3). The symbol here was to illustrate God's judgment against Jerusalem. Ezekiel followed this sign-act with another in which he was to lie on his left side for 390 days and then on his right for forty days to symbolize the number of years of Israel's apostasy and subsequent divine punishment.[4] All this he was to do facing towards his model of Jerusalem under siege, prophesying against it (4:4–8). After illustrating with another sign-act that the besieged would be forced to eat that which is unclean in order to survive (4:9–17), Ezekiel was told to shave his head and beard with a sharp sword and to use the hair to depict the fate of the inhabitants of Jerusalem (5:1–17). While Ezekiel may have had in mind Jer 7:29 ("Cut off your hair and throw it away . . . for Yahweh has rejected and forsaken this generation"), the fact that it was forbidden for a priest to shave his head (Lev 21:5; Ezek 44:20) added to the drama. All this was to represent the covenant curses depicted in the Holiness Code (Lev 26:36–39)

2. See Graffy, *Prophet Confronts His People*, 76–77.
3. Cf. Greenberg, *Ezekiel 1–20*, 344.
4. So Block, *Book of Ezekiel: Chapters 1–24*, 180.

which would come upon even those who had escaped or been taken into exile (Ezek 5:1–4). To this he added Jeremiah's constant refrain of coming judgment—that the nation would be consumed by sword, famine, and pestilence (5:12, 17).

Jeremiah had spoken of two sisters, Israel and Judah, as both being wives unfaithful to Yahweh, with Judah being even more unfaithful than Israel (Jer 2:1—4:4). Ezekiel expanded on this concept in chs. 16 and 23 with some graphic embellishments. In ch. 16 Jerusalem is described as having been abandoned by her mother in the open field, still covered with blood, until the Lord Yahweh came by and commanded: "In your blood live, and flourish like a shoot of the field" (v. 7). So this female infant grew up in beauty and form, but was completely naked, until Yahweh passed by again, saw that she was "at the age of love" and adopted her as his wife in a marriage covenant (v. 8). Yahweh then washed off her blood, anointed, clothed, adorned, and fed her, so that her beauty became renowned among the nations (vv. 9–14). Then Jerusalem, trusting in her beauty, abandoned her husband, using the gifts she had been given in the practice of prostitution, giving herself to various nations, even paying her lovers rather than being paid by them (vv. 33–34)! Therefore, Yahweh would hand her over to her lovers to be stripped naked, stoned, cut in pieces with the sword, and all her houses burned. Only thus would Yahweh's anger and jealousy be requited (vv. 35–43). However, after the judgment, Jerusalem would be restored to bear her disgrace and feel shame, as an object of scorn and derision (vv. 53–58). For then God, who is always faithful, would say: "I will establish my covenant with you, and you shall know that I am Yahweh, that you may remember and be ashamed, when I make atonement for you, for all you have done" (vv. 62–63).

Apart from the explicit sexual language which Ezekiel has used for its shock value, priestly language and concerns permeate his description of Jerusalem as the unfaithful wife. His priestly sensitivity is evident particularly in regard to the defiling nature of blood and bloodguilt, also evident elsewhere in the rest of the book. So Jerusalem would finally finish up in "the blood of wrath and jealousy," death at the hands of her lovers (v. 38).[5] The curses of the covenant would be carried out, and God's justice would be satisfied. There is no hint of divine compassion, or of the people's repentance.

The same theme is carried further in ch. 23, where Ezekiel speaks of the two sisters, Samaria and Jerusalem. Samaria is called *Oholah*, meaning, "her own tent," and Jerusalem is named *Oholibah*, meaning, "My tent is in her," alluding to the Tent of Meeting, a priestly archaism for the temple.[6] Both sisters are seen as having been sexually promiscuous from the beginning in Egypt before the two were married to Yahweh, and both continued committing adultery after the marriage. Once again, Ezekiel describes their guilt in explicit sexual language. Oholibah is guilty of the ultimate defilement by having received lovers from afar into the innermost parts of the temple, seated on the "seat of glory" before the incense altar, the most sacred part of the temple! In seeking to make alliances with Egypt and neighboring provinces, Jerusalem had accepted the worship of their gods and given access to the temple for their idols and priests.[7] For this

---

5. Galambush, *Jerusalem in the Book of Ezekiel*, 94, 102–9.
6. See the discussion in Zimmerli, *Ezekiel 1*, 483–84.
7. Galambush, *Jerusalem*, 121–22.

priest-turned-prophet, the temple had been polluted beyond redemption. Both the city and the temple would have to be completely destroyed (vv. 46–49).

When finally Nebuchadnezzar laid siege to Jerusalem, Ezekiel was quick to remind the exiles with his allegory of the rusty pot (24:2–14) that any vestige of hope was inappropriate. Nor would it be right to mourn the city's destruction. Taking a cue from Jer 16:5–9, Ezekiel demonstrated this by showing no mourning for the death of his wife (24:15–18), and bade the exiles to follow his example (24:21).

Ezekiel, Priests, Prophets, and People

Considering Ezekiel's emphasis on the temple being irredeemably polluted, one would have expected that the Jerusalem priesthood would have become the focus of Ezekiel's castigation. However, he is strangely silent about their participation in the abominations he has described. Only twice does he mention his fellow-priests in a negative sense, and that is when he borrows lists of the failures of leaders from other prophets (e.g., Ezek 7:25–27 uses the words of Jer 8:18; Ezek 22:26 borrows from Zeph 3:4). Yet in his famous temple vision (chs. 8–11) where he is transported to Jerusalem and witnesses the abominations going on in the temple, he sees only elders and leading officials; there is no mention of any priest. It is difficult to see how the priests could be left out of the picture in their own temple!

Yet Ezekiel was quick to castigate the court prophets. While he picked up many of the phrases Jeremiah used to condemn both priests and prophets, he used them only against the prophets. This is particularly evident in Ezekiel's accusation that the prophets had misled the people saying, "Peace, peace, where there is no peace" (Ezek 13:10), a phrase clearly borrowed from Jer 6:14 where the perpetrators are described as "from prophet to priest, everyone deals falsely" (Jer 6:13). It had not been long after Jeremiah's letter to the exiles in 594 in which he denounced the prophets in Babylon who were 'prophesying a lie in [God's] name" (Jer 29:15–32), that Ezekiel took up the role of prophet himself and soon followed Jeremiah in condemning the lying prophets in both Babylon and Jerusalem. Using the imagery of an ill-built wall of defense desperately in need of repair, he described these false prophets as masons who simply covered over the defective structure with a mud plaster that washed away in the first storm, so that the wall crumbles (13:10–16; cf. 22:28). Condemned along with these false prophets were women among the exiles who, claiming to prophesy, used forms of divination and witchcraft taken from their Babylonian environment to delude the gullible by means of incantations and spells (13:17–23).

Because of the false prophets, the exilic community had become cynical, saying, "The days grow long, and every vision comes to naught" (12:22), doubting whether Ezekiel's prophecies of impending doom would happen in their lifetime (12:26–28). So when the elders came to him asking for a word from God, he was suspicious of their motives and warned them that deceit would earn them the same judgment as that for false prophets (14:1–11). When the news finally reached the exiles that Jerusalem had fallen, Ezekiel was now vindicated in their eyes. Many now came to him to hear the word of Yahweh. This new popularity made Ezekiel feel like "a sensuous love song" which people came to hear for its entertainment value. He questioned their genuineness, but felt vindicated that now they would know that a prophet had been among them (33:30–32)!

Ezekiel, the Elders, and the Deuteronomic Reform

Yet Ezekiel held his harshest words for the elders of the exile. These would have been many of those, including Shaphan and his family, who had assisted King Josiah in carrying out the Deuteronomic reform, and who had protected Jeremiah and had spoken in his defense during Jehoiakim's rule. These were some of the officials of Judah who, together with Ezekiel, had been taken into exile in 597 BCE. Jeremiah had regarded these early exiles as the basket of very good figs (Jer 24:1–10), and it was probably to these "remaining elders of the exiles" to whom Jeremiah had sent his letter "by the hand of Elasah the son of Shaphan and Gemariah the son of Hilkiah" (Jer 29:1–3) in 594.

Ezekiel's first mention of these elders came a little over a year after receiving his call to be a prophet (8:1). These "elders of Judah" who had come to his house and were sitting before him, precipitated a vision in which Ezekiel saw himself transported to the temple in Jerusalem where he witnessed abominations going on there. Besides seeing women weeping for the vegetation deity, Tammuz, and about twenty-five men worshiping the sun (8:14–18), he envisioned seventy elders of Israel offering incense before murals of unclean animals. One of these elders he pointedly identified as "Jaazaniah the son of Shaphan" (8:10–12). Obviously, Jaazaniah was specifically mentioned here because he was a member of the Shaphan family which had been so supportive of the Deuteronomic reform. This depiction of images of creeping things and loathsome animals (8:10) is not found elsewhere in contemporary criticisms of Judah's false worship.[8] The vision of these images and sun worshipers appear to be related to the prohibitions against this in Deut 4:16–19, part of the Deuteronomic law which the king and elders had imposed in the reform. Ezekiel had seen this as usurping the prerogative of the priesthood to teach the law.[9] For this they would be punished with death. Ezekiel envisions six executioners given orders to slay old and young, men and women, and even little children—all except those who, like himself, "sigh and groan" over the abominations (9:14; cf. 21:6–7; 24:17) and are marked on the forehead by "the man clothed in linen, with the writing case at his side," that is, a priestly scribe acting as judge (9:1–11; cf. Ezek 44:17–19, 24). The executioners would begin with the elders at the sanctuary and would fill the temple with the slain to emphasize its defilement beyond redemption (9:6–7). Consequently, God's Presence, the *kabod* of Yahweh, could no longer be there and heads east (11:22–24). This, it appears, was the message Ezekiel reported to the elders sitting before him (11:25).

When the elders appeared before Ezekiel a second time seeking an oracle from God (14:1–11), they were rebuffed. Ezekiel accused them of being insincere and of having "taken their idols into their hearts" (14:3). The third time that "certain of the elders of Israel" came to Ezekiel was on 14 August 591. They had come to inquire of Yahweh in accordance with Deut 4:29. Once again the elders were given the answer: "As I live, I

---

8. So Klein, *Ezekiel*, 55.
9. Cf. Block, *Ezekiel 1–24*, 290, 293.

will not be inquired of by you, says the Lord Yahweh" (20:3, 31). Yet the promise of Deut 4:29 was that those who inquired of Yahweh with all their heart and soul would find him and Yahweh would accept their returning with compassion (Deut 4:31; 7:6–13). Even though Ezekiel was familiar with this promise as is evident from his use of Deuteronomic terminology which he uses throughout ch. 20,[10] he still rejected it. He did not accept the message of Deuteronomy that sincere repentance could be followed by Yahweh's compassion and forgiveness. Israel would have to undergo punishment for her rebellion, for only then could the divine wrath be satisfied, and God would be ready to renew Israel (20:33, 34). In order to show that Israel's history had been one of constant rebellion which must inevitably lead to punishment, Ezekiel deliberately distorted the sacred traditions[11] to paint Israel in a consistent negative light (ch. 20). Each account of Israel's rebellion claimed by Ezekiel was followed with the indictment that God wanted to pour out his wrath and anger upon the nation, but refrained from doing so for the sake of his name lest it should be profaned in the sight of the nations (20:3–9, 13–17, 21–22).

The key to Ezekiel's antagonism towards the elders is revealed in his statement in 20:25–26: "Moreover, I gave them statutes [masculine form] that are not good, and judgment by which they will *not* live; and I defiled them through their gifts when they brought over every first issue of the womb, that I might desecrate them, that they might know that I am Yahweh." Since Ezekiel consistently used the feminine form for "statutes" for the priestly law throughout and particularly in this chapter, he has used the masculine form, in contrast, for the Deuteronomic law described as given on the plains of Moab prior to Israel's entry into the land (Deut 29:1). This he refers to as the "statutes of your fathers" (20:18) and the "not good" law (20:25).[12]

As a priest, Ezekiel regarded some of the Deuteronomic laws as subverting the priestly statutes of the Holiness Code (Lev 17–26), and thus inferior and threatening. Such laws as providing for profane slaughter (Deut 12:15–25), divorce (Deut 24:1–4), seven-year cycle of debt release (Deut 15:1–6), and the position of the Levite priesthood would have been "not good" in his eyes.[13] Ezekiel saw the Deuteronomic laws regarding the first issue of the womb of animals and the pouring out of blood on the ground mentioned in Deut 12:6, 15–28 and 15:19–23 as defiling and defective in contradiction to the priestly laws of Lev 17:1–9. Besides, the stated right of Levite priests to function equally in the centralized worship in Jerusalem (Deut 18:6–8) would not have sat well with Ezekiel as a Zadokite priest. The elders who had encouraged these "inferior" laws were therefore under judgment. Ezekiel accused their fathers of having been guilty of blasphemy and acting treacherously against Yahweh because they had permitted worship and the celebration of the sacrificial meals to happen upon any high hill and under any leafy tree, which was contrary to their own law (20:27–29; cf. Deut 12:1–7). It was likely a request on the part of the elders to institute such worship of Yahweh in Babylon that irked Ezekiel and led him to accuse them of wishing to defile themselves

---

10. See Pons, "Le Vocabulaire," 214–33.
11. Block, *Ezekiel 1–24*, 613.
12. See Hahn and Bergsma, "What Laws Were 'Not Good'?," 204–6.
13. Ibid., 208–10; also Kohn, "Prophet Like Moses?," 246.

after the manner of their fathers (20:30). Such practices of multiple sanctuaries, Ezekiel contended, had led to false worship and the practice of child sacrifice condemned in Deut 12:31 (20:31). That, Ezekiel accused them, is what they had in mind—to be like the nations worshiping wood and stone (20:32; cf. Deut 4:28; 12:30).[14]

As far as Ezekiel was concerned the elders and the people were all under judgment, all had been defiled by idolatrous practices in the past and now were guilty of using a defective law code. There would be no mercy or forgiveness. The word for "forgive" is never used, and only after the nations have witnessed the execution of God's judgment on Israel would God restore their fortunes and have mercy on the house of Israel (39:21–25).[15] It would be "with a mighty hand and an outstretched arm, and with wrath poured out" (cf. Jer 21:5) that God would be king over them, and would bring them into a no-man's land and enter into judgment with them before they could be brought back into the covenant relationship (20:33–38). Only then, after a thorough purge, could Yahweh lead them back to Mount Zion to serve him, and only then would God accept their gifts and offerings, and gather all the scattered. The people would then remember their past with loathing (20:38–44).

The Place of the Nations in Ezekiel's Thinking

Placed in between the oracles of judgment on Judah, which end with the siege of Jerusalem (ch. 24) and the transitional chapter announcing the fall of the city (ch. 33), are the oracles against the nations (chs. 25–32). Because judgment on Jerusalem and Judah was now imminent, it was necessary for Ezekiel's sense of divine justice to mention the pronouncements of judgment on the nations before speaking of Israel's future restoration. Seven nations are indicted (Edom, Moab, Ammon, Tyre and Sidon, Philistia and Egypt). Of these, Tyre (chs. 26–28) and Egypt (chs. 29–32) are given greatest prominence. Edom, besides an initial indictment in 25:12–14, receives further judgment in ch. 35 for betrayal and taking possession of Judah's land after Jerusalem's destruction. Babylon is nowhere included in these indictments, because Nebuchadnezzar had been God's agent in bringing judgment on Judah and Jerusalem, and would continue as divine agent in dealing with Tyre and Egypt. In the latest dated oracle of the book (29:17; April 26, 571 BCE), Ezekiel acknowledged that the destruction of Tyre by Nebuchadnezzar promised in a previous oracle (26:1–21) had been unsuccessful.

The indictments against the nations for the most part were that they had gloated over the destruction of Judah and the deportation of the people, or that they had acted in revenge, malice, and betrayal towards Judah at the time of its calamity. Tyre (26:2) and Edom (35:1–15; 36:5) had taken advantage of the exile to plunder or to take possession of Judah's land. Egypt had been guilty of drawing Zedekiah into an alliance against Babylon and away from Yahweh, only to prove to be a "reed staff" which caused harm to the house of Israel when it splintered under pressure (29:6–7). Even more than that,

---

14. Pons, "Le Vocabulaire," 226–28.
15. This is the only place (39:25) where the verb "to have mercy" is used in the book of Ezekiel.

both Tyre and Egypt were guilty of pride and arrogance, boasting of their beauty (27:3; 28:7, 12, 17; 31:8, 9) and regarding themselves as equal to God.

Since it had become common among the exiles to apply the story of Adam and Eve being cast out of the garden of Eden to their own situation of having been cast out of the land Yahweh had given them (Ezek 36:35; cf. Isa 51:3; Joel 2:3), Ezekiel used this metaphor also of Tyre and Egypt. Imagery taken from this story is used in two connected oracles of judgment on Tyre. In 28:1–10 Ezekiel accuses the leader of Tyre for claiming to be a "god" who sits on the throne of God in the heart of the seas, while in fact he is a human being (*Adam*) and no god. This leader regards his mind as *like the mind of God*, knowing good and evil (Gen 3:5). Such knowledge may have gained him much wealth, but he will soon be cast down to destruction. In the second oracle (28:11–19), the king of Tyre is described as having been in "Eden, the Garden of God," decorated with gemstones, having been adorned in this way from the day of his creation. He had been placed there "on the holy mountain of God" with "an anointed guardian cherub."[16] Like Adam he was blameless from the day of his creation until iniquity was found in him. So he was dismissed from the mountain of God and driven out of the garden by the guardian cherub

In the case of Egypt, the pharaoh and his multitude are likened to a cedar of Lebanon (like Assyria) in Eden, the Garden of God, which grew to a great height to tower over all the other trees, and because of its pride, was chopped down and destroyed. Egypt too, like this great cedar would be brought down with the trees of Eden to the netherworld, sharing the same fate as Assyria—cast out of the garden into the realm of the slain.

However, at the end of forty years the Egyptians would again be gathered into their land of origin to be a lowly kingdom, never again to exalt itself above others. Then they would know that Yahweh is God (29:13–16). This is the *only* expression of restoration for a nation other than Israel mentioned by Ezekiel, and may have been given because of the significant population of Jews in Egypt at that time.

Ezekiel's purpose in these oracles against the nations was twofold. First of all, it was to assure Israel that divine justice would be carried out for *all* nations. There would be a Day of Yahweh when judgment would be meted out to all those nations that had acted unjustly (cf. 30:1–3). Second, it was to show Israel that their calamity was a part of that universal justice. Like the nations they also had rebelled against God's universal plan and ignored his statutes. So they, too, had been cast out of the Garden of God, from his holy mountain.[17] Yet Yahweh would eventually gather Israel from the nations and restore the people to their own land where they would dwell securely, assured that universal justice would be done among the nations who had treated them with contempt (28:25–26).

---

16. See May, "King in the Garden of Eden," 169. Also, Stordalen, *Echoes of Eden*, 341–43.
17. Cf. Boadt, "Rhetorical Strategies," 196–99.

Ezekiel's Message of Deliverance and Restoration

After the many oracles of judgment on Israel and the nations, followed with the announcement of the fall of Jerusalem (33:21–22), Ezekiel abruptly changes to oracles of salvation. No reason is given for this change, no reference to Israel's repentance and reconciliation with God, no explicit reference to God's love and compassion for his people.[18] The underlying assumption seems to be that the covenant curses have been described and are taking their toll, and now it is time to talk of future covenant blessings.

In ch. 34 Ezekiel assured the exiles that God as the true shepherd of his people would soon gather them together and bring them back to their land. This chapter is essentially an expansion of Jer 23:1–8 in which the kings of the past are condemned as false shepherds who had been responsible for scattering the sheep which God will have to gather and bring back into his fold. Taking up this theme, Ezekiel has further condemned Judah's kings, but places a greater emphasis on Yahweh himself coming as the shepherd of his people, gathering them from the nations, feeding them upon the mountain pastures of Israel, binding up the crippled and strengthening the sick (34:11–16). The emphatic "I myself" in vv. 11 and 15 clearly expresses the direct action of God in caring for his people, making sure that the more powerful among the flock do not mistreat the weaker or act greedily in using the land only for themselves. God's justice will prevail for Israel not only among the nations but also among the people within Israel (34:17–22). It will be a covenant of peace and prosperity when Yahweh blesses his people and the land once again, and the people will know Yahweh, their God. They will remember that they are the sheep of *his* pasture (34:25–31). For the sake of his holy name, God would restore Israel to their land, so that the nations would know Yahweh and recognize his holiness (36:22–23).

Ezekiel believed that the people had proved themselves incapable of changing their nature, so Yahweh would have to intervene to bring about renewal. Since the people's polluted nature had been described like a woman's impurity, they would need to be sprinkled with the waters for impurity, as described in Num 19, to purify them of the guilt of past idolatrous practices. Then Yahweh would carry out a heart transplant by removing Israel's hardened, petrified heart and replacing it with a heart of flesh to restore the nation to life. After that, Yahweh would put *his* spirit within them to give the people the ability to live again in covenant relationship with God and with one another. Then the land would become fruitful again, the ruined cities rebuilt and repopulated to become like the garden of Eden (36:24–30, 35–36). "Then," the people are told, "you will remember your evil ways, and your deeds that were not good; and you will loathe yourselves for your iniquities and your abominable deeds. It is not for your sake that I will act, says the Lord Yahweh; let that be known to you. Be ashamed and confounded for your ways, O house of Israel!" (36:31–32).

In another graphic vision, given in response to those who felt that they were dead as a nation, Ezekiel described the restoration of the nation as a mass resurrection—dry bones which filled the whole valley would be restored to life as the nation of Israel when Yahweh breathed new life into them and filled them with his spirit. This vision was to

---

18. See especially Schwartz, "Ezekiel's Dim Vision," 43–67.

emphasize that only their God had the power to do the impossible: to bring back to life one nation from the scattered remnants of the northern kingdom as well as the exiles of Judah (37:1–14). All Israel would be gathered once again into one kingdom as in the days of King David (37:15–23). This would then complete Yahweh's saving act for all the people he had chosen for his own and the return to the covenant relationship would be a covenant of peace *forever*. For the exiles and their descendants would dwell and multiply in the land *forever*, with a descendant of David as their prince *forever*, and God would once again dwell among them in his temple *forever* (37:24–27). Then the nations would know that Yahweh had sanctified Israel when his sanctuary would be in their midst *forever* (37:28). The triple reference to the temple in these last three verses clearly indicated what was central to the theology of this priest-turned-prophet.

However, that "forever-ness" would be disturbed by a once-for-all great and horrendous event yet to come, the Day of Yahweh, which had been spoken of by the prophets from the time of the prophet Amos (38:17–22). All the nations under the leadership of Gog of Magog will come together against Israel to plunder and destroy. In the great battle that would ensue, it would not be the people of Israel but Yahweh himself who would defeat and totally destroy the hordes of Gog by means of pestilence and bloodshed, torrential rain and hailstorms, fire and brimstone (38:19–22). Their bodies would be left as prey for the vultures and wild beasts, and thus the Day of Yahweh would be accomplished (39:1–6, 8). So vast would have been the armies under Gog and so great their devastation that it would take seven years for the Israelites to use up all their weapons as firewood, and seven months to bury all the dead in order to cleanse the land (39:9–16).

Throughout these two chapters, the message is repeated and emphasized that all this would happen to fulfill God's ultimate purpose, to make God's name holy among the nations and before Israel. The nations and Israel would then understand why God had hidden his face from Israel and had handed them over to their adversaries for exile or sword. All must understand that God will not let his holy name be profaned any more (38:16, 23; 39:7, 21–29). Divine justice had to be carried out. Only then could God show mercy to Israel and pour out his spirit upon them

The Role of a Future Davidic King

Throughout his oracles, Ezekiel had put much of the blame for the exile on the failure of the kings of Judah, particularly Zedekiah.[19] The kings were supposed to be Yahweh's servants representing his divine rule and caring for his people, but they had appropriated his kingdom to themselves, and used the kingship for their own enrichment and gain. Ezekiel had condemned them as false shepherds who, instead of caring for the sheep, had devoured them and scattered them among the nations (34:1–10).

However, following Jer 23:5–6, Ezekiel could not entirely dismiss the concept of the Davidic covenant and its attendant messianic hope for an ideal king. So in the restoration Yahweh would still have his representative continuing the line of David: "I will set over them one shepherd, my servant David, and he shall feed them. . . . And I, Yahweh,

---

19. For a fuller discussion, see Joyce, "King and Messiah in Ezekiel," 323–37.

will be their God, and my servant David shall be leader in the midst of them" (34:23, 24). Later, when speaking of the two former kingdoms being one nation once again under one king (37:21–22), Ezekiel repeated the promise (37:24, 25). While Ezekiel has used the title "king" in this latter case to emphasize the one kingdom, he generally preferred to use the title "leader" (*nasi*) to emphasize the ruler's dependence and subordinate role to Yahweh's kingship. Using the traditional description of David as Yahweh's "servant" also highlighted that subordinate role. This messianic figure would be the means whereby Yahweh would carry out his shepherding. It is through him that people would know that Yahweh is their God (34:30–31). His reign would be one of peace, for he would come to the throne only after Yahweh had accomplished his judgments and initiated the new age with an everlasting covenant of peace and prosperity (34:25–31; 37:26). For Ezekiel this king would be a tender "shoot" from the lofty top of the cedar (17:22), a descendant of Jehoiachin,[20] which Yahweh would transplant in Zion to become a noble tree giving shelter to all and as a witness before the nations of the power of Israel's God.

The Ezekiel Plan of Restoration

As the time of the exile extended into years, Ezekiel and his fellow Zadokites sought to keep hope alive by developing a design for the restoration, which is set out in chs. 40–48. This series of visions was received some fourteen years after the destruction of Jerusalem and in the twenty-fifth year of Ezekiel's exile. The initial vision, which is dated on the day which normally would have been the beginning of preparation for the Passover (40:1; April 28, 573 BCE), is somewhat different in tone and message from the rest of the book. While this has led some to question the authenticity of these chapters,[21] there are good reasons for seeing this section as essentially from the hand of Ezekiel.[22] It carries on ideas expressed in the previous chapters and was probably written at this later time to set down some basic ground rules for the restored community from a priestly perspective.

Throughout this section, Ezekiel is seeking to establish a new set of laws to eradicate past problems. The return would be a new exodus which would require new laws for reentry into the promised land. So he would be the new law-giver, a new Moses—with a strong priestly bias! As Moses received his revelation on Mount Sinai (Exod 19:2–6; 24:12–18), so Ezekiel receives his vision "upon a very high mountain" (40:2). Ezekiel's detailed description of the temple, its furnishings and personnel has close parallels to the priestly version of the tabernacle and its specifications given by Moses in Exod 24–31. Many of Ezekiel's laws relating to temple worship are similar to earlier Mosaic laws, but others differ, particularly from some of the laws found in Num 28–29, 35–36. Even in his description of the consecration of the new altar of the future temple (43:13–27), Ezekiel assumes the role Moses had in Exod 29:35–46.[23] The fact that Ezekiel depicted himself

---

20. Klein, *Ezekiel*, 114–18.
21. E.g., Tuell, *Law of the Temple*, 14.
22. Greenberg, "Design and Themes," 1981; Klein, *Ezekiel*, 169–70.
23. Cf. Levinson, *Theology of the Program of Restoration*, 37–44; Greenberg, "Design and Themes," 183; McKeating, "Ezekiel the 'Prophet Like Moses'?," 97–109.

here as a new lawgiver is but the logical culmination of the legal approach he had been taking throughout his ministry in exile.

As a priest Ezekiel believed that the central focus of all law and life in the community would have to be the temple which he describes in great detail. It would contain an outer court which would be accessible to the Levites and the lay people, an inner court open only to the Zadokite priests, an entrance hall, main hall, and the holiest place as the dwelling place for Yahweh's *kabod*. Each area would be of increasing height and holiness. To maintain the separation of the sacred and the profane, the Zadokite priests were to change out of their priestly garments into their regular clothes before leaving the inner court and associating with the common people, lest the priestly garment be profaned and the people be sanctified by contact (42:14). This law of the temple was to maintain a clear distinction between the sacred and the profane at all times, and the temple protected from any form of defilement, even to the extent of the whole temple complex being surrounded by a boundary wall ten feet high and ten feet thick (40:5; 42:20).

Once all the details of the temple complex have been presented, Ezekiel returns to the outer east gate where he sees the *kabod* of Yahweh coming from the east, lighting up the earth with divine brilliance. Just as he had envisioned the *kabod* leave the polluted temple and head east in chs. 8–11, so now the *kabod* returns to this new sanctified, holy dwelling place. The *kabod* enters through the east gate and fills the innermost part of the temple. Then Yahweh announces to Ezekiel: "This is the place of my throne and the place of the soles of my feet, where I will dwell in the midst of the people of Israel forever" (43:7). This is the declaration of Yahweh's kingship to which no compromise is to be permitted. There will be no royal palace adjacent to this temple as it was in the time of Solomon (2 Kgs 11) whereby a king like Manasseh, who had fostered the worship of other gods, could be buried next to the temple (2 Kgs 21:18), and thus defile Yahweh's holy name (43:7–9). After a description is given of the altar of burnt offering (43:13–17), Ezekiel and the Zadokite priests are depicted making a series of burnt offerings over a period of seven days in order to "make atonement for the altar and purify it, and thus ordain it" (43:18–27). The central significance given to the altar makes it clear that for Ezekiel Yahweh's atonement could only come through the sacrificial system administered by the Zadokite priests. Ezekiel in his vision is then taken back to the outer east gate where he finds it closed. He is told that it will remain so permanently so that no one may enter where Yahweh has entered. This closure reinforces the idea of the continuing presence of Yahweh who will dwell in their midst forever. However, to indicate the lower and secular status of the future leader, he may eat his sacrificial meals at this gate (44:1–3). The Zadokite priests will eat theirs in a special room in the inner court (40:44–46; 42:13).

The sacredness of the temple is to be maintained also in another way: choice of personnel. So Ezekiel sets down "all the statutes of the house of Yahweh and all its laws" regarding three groups: foreigners, Levites, and the "levitical priests, that is, the sons of Zadok." Foreigners, who had served as temple guards and probably performed other general duties are to be excluded from the sanctuary entirely. The indictment against them is that they were uncircumcised in heart and flesh, that they had profaned the sanctuary by being present when sacrifices were offered, which had caused the covenant to be broken (44:6–9). The Levites are accused of leading the people of Israel astray with idolatry, thus becoming a stumbling block of evil to the house of Israel. They will take over from foreigners the function of being temple guards, they will serve in the outer court, slaughter sacrificial animals for the lay people, and supervise the people's activities. But they are not to enter the sanctuary or serve as priests (44:10–14). That function is to be the exclusive privilege of the sons of Zadok, the Jerusalem temple priesthood. These would be in charge of the inner court and the temple proper, to minister to Yahweh and offer him "the fat and the blood." This latter is described as giving Yahweh his food (44:7, 15)! The Zadokites are given this exclusive status, it is said, because they remained faithful and kept Yahweh's charge when the people of Israel, including the Levites, went astray after idols (44:15; 48:11; 40:45–46). As the holy priesthood they are to wear only linen garments and turbans while serving in the temple, and are to marry only virgins of Israel or widows of priests. Apart from their temple duties they are to educate the people in matters of the sacred and profane, clean and unclean, to act as judges, and to maintain the festivals and the holy days.

The surprising aspect of this description of temple personnel is that the Jerusalem priesthood, the Zadokites, who were responsible for the temple services prior to its destruction, are completely exonerated. Is it possible that they had been innocent of syncretistic practices when the temple was so polluted with idolatry as described in 2 Kgs 23:4–7 and Ezek 8–11? Previously, Ezekiel had avoided directing blame to the priesthood and directed it to the mountains of Israel, Jerusalem, the elders, those left behind in Judah, and now the Levites. The demarcation between the faithful and the unfaithful in this description is not on the basis of individual action as Ezekiel had argued earlier (e.g., ch. 18), but on the basis of class—*all* foreigners are to be excluded, *all* Levites are to be demoted for idolatry, *all* Zadokites are to be promoted to the highest office of priesthood because of their faithfulness. The Deuteronomic reform of Josiah had given the Levites, who had served at shrines outside of Jerusalem, equal opportunity to serve as priests in the Jerusalem temple (Deut 18:6–7). The resistance to this by the Zadokite priests is what is echoed here.

However, the Levites are not the only ones to be demoted; future kings are to be limited in their function as well. Ezekiel knew that such a secular leader would be necessary to deal with secular matters and to support the temple cult in the future, but because of previous abuses the ruler's function in the future would be reduced and power limited. The reason given for this limitation of power is clearly stated: "My princes shall no more oppress my people. . . . Thus says Lord Yahweh: Enough, O princes of Israel! Put away violence and oppression, and do justice and righteousness; cease your evictions of my people, says Lord Yahweh" (45:8–9). His ownership of land is to be limited and away from the temple (45:7–8). He is to be responsible for the regulation of just weights and measures (45:10–12), and for providing the cult with the sacrificial animals contributed by the people. His participation in the temple worship as leader of the lay community is to be strictly regulated (45:13—46:15). Limits are also set on what he can do with his land lest he be tempted to take away any of the inheritance of the people to give it to his sons (46:16–18). In this plan the prince's function as servant of Yahweh like David has lost some of its meaning since he has, in effect, been made subordinate to the Zadokite priesthood.

To indicate the renewal of the land, Ezekiel described in detail the vision of a life-giving stream which issues forth from the temple altar and spreads over the land even to the Dead Sea bringing new life and fruitfulness everywhere. The power for change and renewal is from God alone and is mediated through the sacrificial cult (47:1–12). After that, the final guidelines are given for dividing the land equally among the twelve tribes, the sojourners would live in their midst and receive an equal portion as their inheritance (47:22–23). Nothing is said here about the claims of those left behind in Jerusalem and Judah. These people had taken over the land and harvested the produce and now regarded it as their inheritance. Earlier, Ezekiel had strongly rejected their claims, saying they would all die by the sword, wild animals and pestilence (33:22–29; cf. 11:15). The land south of the temple area was to be for the new city which would be inhabited by representatives of all tribes (48:19) so that no tribe gained ascendancy over the others. This future city would be named "Yahweh is There" (48:35).

Conclusion

It has been evident throughout the book of Ezekiel that Ezekiel was a priest in prophet's clothing. Nowhere has this been so obvious as in his plan for the restoration. From the beginning he had modeled himself on Jeremiah. Although he mostly moved beyond Jeremiah's intentions and saw the crisis leading to exile through priestly eyes, using Jeremiah's language gave him a prophetic aura and gained for him a somewhat guarded acknowledgment as a prophet.

However, Ezekiel's concerns were centered on the temple cult. Together with the people, the temple had been polluted beyond redemption. So the temple had to be destroyed, and the people had to experience the full measure of God's wrath. Retribution and divine justice had to be carried out, and only then could there be renewal. Ezekiel's emphasis was always on the legal aspect of keeping covenant, rather than on the relational—the main aspect of the prophetic vision.

For Ezekiel, the Deuteronomic reform had been defective, so there would have to be a new priestly law code to guide them in the future, the law of the new temple, which Ezekiel felt called to proclaim, According to this new law, the Zadokite priesthood would maintain authority over all religious life—life centralized in the temple and its sacrificial cult. During the exile, the Zadokites had apparently been editing Israel's history and their priestly laws to emphasize this (the Priestly Work). While acknowledging that there would be a descendant of David in the future, his position would be limited and inferior to the priesthood.

Essentially, what Ezekiel had presented was the priestly vision of the future rather than the prophetic, and this would lead to growing tension in the community after the return. Ezekiel's vision, although modified after the exile, would, in effect, become the priestly opponent of the prophetic vision. The prophetic vision would need another prophet of the exile to express that vision in more positive terms for the changing circumstances of the future.

Chapter IV

The Second Prophet of the Exile: A Prophet of Hope

THE HISTORICAL SITUATION

As the years passed, the exiles settled down for a long stay. Jeremiah's advice to the early exiles to build houses and plant gardens, marry and have children (Jer 29:5–6), insofar as they were able as an indentured people, proved to be the only option. Those who remembered the plight of the northern tribes realized that there may never be an opportunity to return to their homeland. Was it because their God, Yahweh, had no power before the powerful Babylonian God, Marduk? Or had Yahweh simply rejected his people to experience the covenant curses forever? A new generation of exiles was growing up, and many may have been tempted to leave the God of their parents and, taken in by the brilliant pageantry and processions at the time of the New Year Festival, to turn and worship the God Marduk. Those who complained: "My way is hidden from Yahweh, and my judgment is disregarded by my God" (Isa 40:27), would have succumbed to the prevailing belief that the god of a suppressed nation was impotent and subject to the gods of the controlling power.

Even though their lot may have been made easier as the years rolled by, the exiles were still an oppressed people at the mercy of the Babylonians, "deeply despised, abhorred by the nations, the servant of rulers" (Isa 49:7). As such they were often humiliated at the hand of their tormentors (Isa 51:23) and felt they were a lost, rejected and forgotten people, "a people robbed and plundered, . . . trapped in holes and hidden in prisons, . . . a prey with none to rescue" (Isa 42:22).

Nebuchadnezzar maintained strong control of the empire until his death in 562 BCE. He was succeeded by his son Amel Marduk (Evil-Merodach), who freed King Jehoiachin from confinement and granted him special treatment within the royal court (2 Kgs 25:27–30; Jer 52:31–34). However, in the second year of his reign, he was assassinated by his brother-in-law, Neriglissar, who then ruled until his death in 556. While his short reign may have been peaceful, his son, Labashi-Marduk, who succeeded

Neriglissar was faced with rebellion and only reigned for nine months before being murdered, and a successor backed by the priestly party was enthroned in his place. This was Nabonidus who was king from 556 until the fall of Babylon in 539 BCE. Initially, he would have satisfied the Babylonian priesthood with the attention he gave to the great temple of Marduk, but his antiquarian interest in rebuilding other temples throughout the realm, such as to the sun god Shamash and to the moon god Sin led to trouble with the powerful priests of Marduk. His favoring of the worship of the god Sin, the god of his native city of Haran, soon resulted in growing conflict with the priesthood. For almost the last ten years of his reign he preferred to be absent from Babylon and lived in Tema, an oasis city and center for communication and trade in northern Arabia,[1] while his son, Belshazzar, served as co-regent in Babylon.

These were times of change which the exiles must have observed with some trepidation. Yet while there was growing unrest and turmoil within the Babylonian Empire, beyond it, Cyrus, who had becomes the Persian king in 559 after overthrowing the king of the Medes, had been expanding his empire both to the west and to the east. After his defeat of King Croesus of Lydia in 547, the only way for further expansion was south—Babylonia. Because of its internal strife Babylonia soon fell to Cyrus on October 13, 539 BCE, almost without a struggle. Nabonidus who had returned to Babylon earlier was captured, and Cyrus, presenting himself as a servant of Marduk, was welcomed as a liberator by the priests of Marduk.[2] The Babylonian Empire was now incorporated into the Persian Empire under Cyrus, an event which would mean great changes for the exiles in Babylon.

The Rise of a New Prophet

It was in the last decade of the Babylonian Empire (ca. 550–540 BCE) that a new prophet arose among the exiles. This anonymous prophet, regarded as responsible primarily for chs. 35, 40–55 in the book of Isaiah, has consequently been given the title, "Deutero-Isaiah." These chapters breathe a spirit of renewed hope; they are poetic, visionary, exuding an optimistic enthusiasm, drawing on the language of psalmic literature and the writings of the earlier prophets. The prophet transforms their messages with the positive conviction of God's steadfast love for his suffering people and the promise of deliverance near at hand.

From the message given in these chapters it becomes evident that they have been incorporated into the Isaiah corpus because the author has been influenced by and was responding to the oracles of Isaiah of Jerusalem. He had seen the fulfillment of the oracles of judgment in the disastrous events that had happened in Judah since Isaiah's time, events that had found their culmination in the exile.[3] However, Deutero-Isaiah's familiarity with the other prophets since the time of Isaiah of Jerusalem, particularly

---

1. Hermann, *History of Israel*, 294.
2. Ibid., 295.
3. Much has been written of this integration and unity of the book of Isaiah. See, e.g., Rendtorff, "Zur Komposition des Buches Jesaja," 295–320; Clements, "Unity of the Book of Isaiah," 117–29; Clements, "Beyond Tradition-History," 95–113; Vermeylen, "L'unite du livre d'Isaie," 12–27.

those of Jeremiah, Lamentations, the book of Deuteronomy, and the Psalms is evidence of the prophet's erudition and comprehensive understanding of Israel's past history.[4]

No prophetic writing has had greater influence on some of the postexilic prophets, the Qumran literature, and especially the New Testament than those of Deutero-Isaiah. Yet who is this influential prophet? While some had suggested that it was written by a group or by a prophetess,[5] it becomes clear that the author has striven so well for anonymity that further identity is impossible. The author had to fade into anonymity because the message is God's message, the plan is God's plan reaching back into the past and extending now into the future when Israel may finally recognize its God-given purpose. That divine word and testimony which Isaiah of Jerusalem had bound and sealed because of the blindness and deafness of the people of his time (Isa 8:16–17; 29:11–12; 30:8) was now to be revealed. This was to be the day when finally "the deaf shall hear the words of a scroll, and out of their gloom and darkness the eyes of the blind shall see. The afflicted shall obtain joy in Yahweh, and the dispossessed of humankind shall exalt in the Holy One of Israel" (Isa 29:18–19).

The New Commissioning: Isaiah 40:1–11

Isaiah 40:1–11 is the commissioning of this prophet patterned on that of Isaiah of Jerusalem in Isa 6:1–10. The opening scene in both is Yahweh speaking with his divine council. In both there is a "voice calling" (6:4; 40:3), in both a "voice saying" (6:8; 40:6), and in both the initial response is despair (6:5; 40:6). Both have references to the removal of "sin and iniquity" (6:7; 40:2) and emphasize the presence of the *kabod*, the brilliant presence of Yahweh (6:3; 40:5).[6] Yet while in Isa 6 that *kabod* is revealed to the prophet only, and it is only *his* sin which is blotted out when his "mouth" is purified for preaching, in Isa 40 the *kabod* of Yahweh is revealed to "all flesh, and it is God's people who are to be forgiven of their sin. For in this case, it is the "mouth of Yahweh" which has spoken, and it is this word which remains forever. But the greatest contrast of all is the message to be given. In the case of Isaiah of Jerusalem the message was the very bad news that the people were blind and deaf to the word of God and could not be healed, while in Isa 40:1–11 it is the very good news that God comes to comfort his people and bring healing and redemption.

The commissioning begins with Yahweh addressing members of his divine council, commanding them to comfort his people who have been mourning their loss and identity as a nation. The members of the divine council are to speak to the heart of Jerusalem, the devastated city which has had no one to comfort her (Lam 1:1–21) in response to the longing for comfort expressed in Isa 12:1 and Jer 31:13. This message of comfort for those who mourn becomes a constant theme throughout Isa 40–66, and the comforting word here is that the exile is soon to be over, and the covenant blessings will now be

---

4. See Sommer, "Allusions and Illusions," 156–86; Sommer, *Prophet Reads Scripture*; Willey, *Remember the Former Things*.

5. "Herald" is mentioned in both the feminine (Isa 40:9) and masculine forms (41:27) in the Hebrew. See McEvenue, "Who Was Second Isaiah?," 213–22.

6. See Seitz, "Divine Council," 239–40.

theirs. Jerusalem's time of service is ended, the debt of her iniquity has been paid out, and she has done "double for all her sins" (40:2) in fulfillment of Jer 16:18. The covenant curses have run their course, now is the time for the blessings!

In response, one of the divine council proclaims that the "way of Yahweh" is to be prepared by straightening out the hills and valleys to make a glorious highway through the wilderness. It will be a new exodus for God's faithful people where the *kabod* of Yahweh will be revealed to all flesh (40:3–5). As Deutero-Isaiah later expressed in a beautiful poem of God's act of redemption in Isa 35, it is the "Holy Way" on which only God's faithful people will travel as they return to Zion with singing, while "sorrow and sighing shall flee away." Then the voice of a divine council member is heard again: "Cry out, proclaim!" This is directed to our prophet, who as a true prophet, stands in the council of Yahweh (cf. Jer 23:18–22). But the prophet wonders whether it is helpful to proclaim anything to people who are not likely to listen, for "all flesh is grass, and all its steadfast love like the flower of the field. The grass withers, the flower fades when the breath [spirit] of Yahweh blows upon it. Surely the people are grass!" (40:6–7; cf. Isa 28:1–4). The heavenly voice then reminds the prophet that humanity may indeed be like grass and fading flower but "the word of our God stands forever" (v. 8), and it is this word which shall accomplish what God has planned (55:11; cf. 45:23). The people will be "the grass that shall become reeds and rushes" (Isa 35:7) among whom even "the bruised reed" will be cared for (Isa 42:3).

The prophet is now given the task of proclaiming the "good news," the traditional proclamation at the accession of a new king to the throne, to Zion, Jerusalem, and to the cities of Judah. The good news he is to shout from the mountain-top to the cities is: "Behold, your God!" For God comes like a victorious and triumphant King, offering reward and recompense, to lead his people back to their own land in fulfillment of the promise in Jer 31:16–17. He comes as the true Shepherd to gather the remnant of the flock and bring them back to their fold (cf. Jer 23:3), but without any promise of a descendant of David to rule over them. For God alone will be their King (Isa 41:21; 43:5; 44:6). This is the message which Deutero-Isaiah is to proclaim to the exiles, and with it will come the unfolding of God's plan for Israel and the nations.

Knowing the Lord Yahweh, the Only God and Creator

Deutero-Isaiah's first step now was to convince the exiles that Yahweh, the God of Israel, was ready and able to deliver them, that he had not abandoned them, that he no longer held them guilt-ridden because of the apostasy that had led to their exile. Those who had come to believe that the Babylonian gods had more power than their "regional" God had to be convinced that there is only one Creator of all things, one God, Yahweh, the Holy One of Israel, who had even created the Babylonians with their gods and which in his eyes were less than nothing, like stubble that is blown away in the wind (40:24).

Confronted by all the pageantry and opulence of the Babylonian cult of Marduk and other gods with their temples, festivals and processions, to many of the exiles Yahweh must have seemed non-existent with no image and no temple by which to identify him. So the prophet had to convince them that the God who comes to their rescue with tenderness and compassion is so great, so immense that no image could ever be made of him. For Yahweh holds the whole universe in the palm of his hand. To him the nations are like dust on the scales, they are less than nothing and emptiness in his sight (40:12–17). Such a God could not be compared to idols made out of wood and metals, nor to human officials and judges who appear to God like destructive grasshoppers here today and gone tomorrow, nor to the host of heavenly bodies which are his own creation, and doing his bidding (40:18–26). The exiles should know: "Yahweh is the Everlasting God, the Creator of the ends of the earth. He does not faint or grow weary" (40:28). Rather, he is the one who gives power and strength to those who *are* weary and exhausted, for "those who wait for Yahweh shall renew their strength; they shall mount up with wings like eagles, they shall run and not be weary, they shall walk and not faint" (40:31).

Deutero-Isaiah returned to this message repeatedly in the ensuing chapters emphasizing that there is only one God, and that is Yahweh. He is the God "who created the heavens and stretched them out, who spread forth the earth and what comes from it, who gives breath to the people upon it and spirit to those who walk in it" (42:5). He is Israel's creator who formed them from the womb and is solely responsible for everything that has been created, the only God, the First and the Last (41:4; 44:18, 24; cf. 43:15; 45:12, 18; 48:12, 13). A strict monotheism is constantly emphasized with the refrain, "Besides me there is no god" (43:11; 44:6, 8; 45:5–22; 46:9), also to counteract claims of Babylon as the only super-power, boasting, "I am, there is no one besides me" (47:8, 10). Eventually, the nations would have to acknowledge to Israel: "God is with you only, and there is no other, no god besides him" (45:14). The call would have to go out to "all the ends of the earth" to turn to Yahweh and be saved (45:22). Thus God's word which accomplishes his purpose and lasts forever is eventually to be fulfilled: "To me every knee shall bow, every tongue shall swear" (45:23; cf. 40:8; 55:10, 11).

Therefore, the Babylonian gods come under ridicule. The idols which their artisans make to worship are lifeless forms which cannot answer prayer or predict the future, and to worship them is the ultimate delusion (41:23–24; 44:9–20). The annual Akitu Festival with its processions through the streets of Babylon of the god Marduk (Bel) and his son and messenger god Nabu (Nebo) to the great shrine at Esagila came in for special derision (46:1–7). Even the dualistic features of Zoroastrianism, which had become so popular in the Persian Empire, are rejected: "I am, and there is no other, forming light and creating darkness, making peace and creating evil, I am Yahweh who does *all* these things" (45:6–7).[7] Yahweh in his uniqueness incorporates all the virtues and powers attributed to the nothing gods, and consequently cannot be defined by gender, so is described in both male and female terms, as in 42:13 and 14. The real proof of Yahweh's uniqueness and power, according to Deutero-Isaiah, is that he alone has stirred up Cyrus to come as his agent to take over the Babylonian Empire in the same way as he has already been victorious over other nations (41:1–7). The ends of the earth may tremble, but servant Israel can be assured that Cyrus is God's agent to deliver his people.

Deutero-Isaiah has taken over from Isaiah of Jerusalem the designation of God as "the Holy One of Israel" as part of the emphasis on the uniqueness and oneness of Yahweh as God. However, whereas that title was previously used to inspire fear and dread

---

7. Cf. Knight, *Servant Theology*, 89–90.

(Isa 8:13), Deutero-Isaiah uses it to give comfort and assurance in words of promise and salvation. God's royal power, often expressed as the "arm" of Yahweh, is always described as the power to save, except in the case of the Babylonians (48:14). The prophet's one reference to God as "the Rock" (44:8) demonstrates the influence of Deut 32 where that divine title is found six times (32:4, 15, 18, 30, 31, 37), and where also the term of endearment for Israel, "Jeshurun" is found three times (32:15; 33:5, 26), a term which is found elsewhere only in Isa 44:2.[8]

Comfort for Those Who Mourn

The good news that Yahweh has come as the King of the universe means that the people he has chosen to be his witness to the nations are about to be comforted. The opening statement of this prophetic work, "Comfort, comfort my people, says your God" (40:1), is a response to the promise in Jer 31:13b: "I will turn their mourning into joy, I will *comfort* them, and give them gladness for sorrow." So as the exiles warmed to the prophet's message of salvation and redemption they would soon join the heavens and the earth and sing for joy, "for Yahweh has comforted his people, and he will have compassion on his afflicted ones" (49:13). Even the ruins of Jerusalem would be called upon to break into singing because "Yahweh has comforted his people, he has redeemed Jerusalem" (52:9). Besides the terms "save, Savior" used of God twenty-five times in relation to Israel, the significant words, "redeem, Redeemer" are used eighteen times in parallel. The latter terms were originally used in the priestly law in regard to loss of property or honor through debt. In that law it was the responsibility of the next of kin to buy back or redeem the property sold because of debt. So also, when a person had become so impoverished that he sold himself into slavery, a near kinsman belonging to his own family might redeem him (Lev 25:48–49), and so restore him to honor and full membership in Israel. So Yahweh as Israel's kinsman is about to redeem Israel and restore the nation to honor.

The intimacy of Yahweh's kinship with oppressed Israel is expressed repeatedly using both male and female images. Yahweh is described as both father and mother to Israel whom he/she "formed in the womb" to be Yahweh's servant (43:21; 44:2, 21, 24; 49:5). He is both the father who begets and the mother who bears (45:10–11). Israel's redemption after the exile is described in terms of Yahweh giving birth: "For a long time I have held my peace, I have kept still and restrained myself, now I will cry out like a woman in travail, I will gasp and pant!" (42:14). When Zion says: "Yahweh has forsaken me," Yahweh responds: "Can a woman forget her sucking child that she should have no compassion on the son of her womb? Even these may forget, yet I will not forget you" (49:14–15). So like a faithful, nurturing mother, Yahweh says to Israel: "Listen to me, O house of Jacob and all the remnant of the house of Israel, who have been borne by me from your birth, carried from the womb, even to old age I am he, even to grey hair I will carry you. I have made you and I will lift you up, I will carry and will save" (46:3–4). It

---

8. Keiser, "Song of Moses," 488–90, also points out that both Deut 32:15 and Isa 44:8 use the term "Eloah" for God, the only time that term is used by Deutero-Isaiah.

is on the basis of this intimate kinship that Yahweh addresses Israel: "Fear not, for I have redeemed you, I have called you by name, you are mine.... For you are precious in my eyes, and honored, and I love you" (43:1, 4), and calls upon them to return from among the nations as "my sons and daughters" (43:6).

Even more, like the prophets before him since the time of Hosea, Deutero-Isaiah also used the metaphor of marriage to express Yahweh's relationship with Israel, and the reason for his redemptive work. Israel is described as a wife whom Yahweh has divorced because of her faithlessness but whom he will redeem (50:1–2), and Jerusalem is addressed as a barren widow who will once again be the mother of many children:

> For your husband is your Maker, Yahweh of hosts is his name;
> and your Redeemer is the Holy One of Israel, God of all the earth he is called.
> For like a wife forsaken and grieved in spirit Yahweh has called you,
> and like the wife of a young man when she is rejected, says your God.
> For a brief moment I forsook you, but with great compassion I will gather you.
> In overflowing wrath I hid my face for a moment from you,
> but with everlasting love I will have compassion on you,
> says your Redeemer, Yahweh. (54:4–8)

Using the popular language describing the covenant curses in terms of Yahweh "selling" his faithless people to the oppressor (cf. Judg 2:14; 3:8; 4:2; 10:7; 1 Sam 12:9), Deutero-Isaiah described the reason for the exile: "Because of your sins you were sold, and for your transgressions your mother was put away" (50:1). The exiles had complained: "You have made us like sheep for slaughter, and have scattered us among the nations. You have sold your people for a trifle, demanding no high price for them!" (Ps 44:13). To this Deutero-Isaiah responded: "Thus says Yahweh, 'You were sold for nothing, and you shall be redeemed without money!'" (52:3). While the psalmist had protested that they had always remained faithful to the covenant (Ps 44:18), the prophet made it clear that it was not on the basis of Israel's righteousness at all but on the basis of Yahweh's that redemption would take place. For Yahweh's message to servant Israel is clear: "I have swept away your transgressions like a cloud, and your sins like mist; return to me, for I have redeemed you" (44:22; cf. 40:2; 43:25). The exiles needed to understand that it was solely by the grace of God that they would be delivered. For it is only through forgiveness that renewal can come about.

However, deliverance needs human agency. Announced as Israel's only King, Yahweh still needed earthly representatives to carry out his plan. Israel is now continually described as the "servant" of Yahweh, a common designation for the vassal of a suzerain king who would act as the suzerain's representative in his region. But in order to accomplish that service, afflicted Israel would first have to be delivered from oppression. For that deliverance God would use a foreign ruler, Cyrus of Persia, as his agent. Earlier prophets had spoken of God using other nations or rulers as his servant to carry out his will (cf. Jer 43:10). What is new is that Cyrus is called Yahweh's "shepherd" (44:28) and "his anointed one" (45:1), terms which elsewhere were used only of kings of Israel. Jeremiah and Ezekiel had spoken of God's future shepherd being a descendant of David, but Deutero-Isaiah was asserting that God's shepherd now was this foreign ruler who had struck the coastlands and the nations with fear and dread. It would be Cyrus, designated by the only divine suzerain to bring about Israel's deliverance (45:4), rebuild Jerusalem and lay the foundation of the temple (44:28). Although Yahweh calls him by name and leads him by the hand (45:1, 3, 4), Cyrus does not "know" Yahweh (45:4, 5), that is, he is not in covenant relationship with God but simply acts as God's agent in carrying out the divine promise to Israel.

Calling this foreign agent "his anointed one" was calculated to shock some exiles who were used to it as a term denoting only Israel's kings. Yet implicit in the prophet's use of this term for Cyrus was the rejection of the need for any earthly king in Israel, for Yahweh alone would be their king. This "shocking" assertion may have been an initial response to those exiles who were bemoaning the loss of a Davidic king as "Yahweh's anointed" in Ps 89. Their negative reaction referred to in Isa 45:9–13 received the prophet's strong rebuke that Yahweh is the creator of all and carries out his purposes according to his will. Like his predecessor, Deutero-Isaiah reminded them that the clay has no right to question the potter (Isa 45:9; cf. Isa 29:15–16).[9] It seems that the prophet had to respond to their continuing criticism, again emphasizing that Yahweh is the *only* God who can use whatever means he chooses to carry out his plans. For he gives this divine response: "My purpose shall stand, and I will fulfill my intention, calling a bird of prey from the east, the man for my purpose from a far country. I have spoken, and I will bring it to pass, I have planned, and I will do it!" (46:8–11; cf. 44:24–28; 48:12–15).

The New Exodus

Given the situation of the exile under the yoke of Babylon, it was easy for the people to make comparisons with the plight of their ancestors at the beginning of their history in Egypt, and their subsequent exodus through the wilderness of Sinai to the promised land. Amos and Hosea had both referred to that exodus as indicating God's saving grace over against Israel's apostasy (Amos 2:10–11; 3:1; 9:7; Hos 2:15; 11:1; 12:9, 13; 13:4–6). Jeremiah, too, had spoken of a return after the destruction, a new exodus greater than the one from Egypt (Jer 16:14–15), and so had Ezekiel, but for Ezekiel it would be a time when God would enter into judgment with the people and would purge out the rebels from among them (Ezek 20:35–38).

Deutero-Isaiah also looked back on that first exodus and how God delivered his people then. He recalled the crossing of the Red Sea and the drowning of the Egyptian charioteers (42:3, 16–18; 51:10), God supplying water from a rock (48:21), and the guidance of God's *kabod* through the wilderness (52:12). But this new exodus would have no Moses, for God himself would both lead in front and be the protective rearguard as he leads them away from Babylon unhurriedly in triumphal procession (52:11–12). In stark contrast to Ezekiel's vision of the return, it would be a joyous exodus in which Lord Yahweh, their King, would lead them forth like a conquering ruler and caring shepherd (40:10–11) along a broad highway where the hills and valleys had been leveled (40:3–5; 42:15–16) for a pleasant return. Moreover, the barren wilderness would be furnished

---

9. For a somewhat different approach to this question, see Fried, "Cyrus the Messiah?," 373–93.

with springs of water, the whole barren landscape transformed with the springing up of trees of various kinds, supplying shade and nourishment (41:17–20; 43:19–21). They would neither hunger nor thirst, for Yahweh would feed them along the way and lead them by the springs of water (49:9–11). The exiles would come not only from Babylon but from all those places where God's people had been scattered (43:5–7; 49:12). It would be a joyous time when "the ransomed of Yahweh shall return, and come to Zion with singing, everlasting joy shall be upon their heads; they shall obtain joy and gladness, and sorrow and sighing shall flee away" (51:11; 35:10).

Even the whole creation would participate in this joyous return. For God's promise to the returnees as they leave Babylon is: "For you shall go out in joy, and be led back in peace; the mountains and hills before you shall burst into song, and all the trees of the field shall clap their hands!" (55:12). Along with the restoration of God's people would come the restoration of nature returning to that Eden-like garden before the fall when there were no thorns and briers (55:13). The way would lead to a renewed Zion, a garden of Eden, like the Garden of Yahweh (51:3). The highway back to Zion/Jerusalem would be the Holy Way of Yahweh for God's redeemed (35:8–9).

For those who feared the repercussions of the Babylonians or the power of Cyrus, Deutero-Isaiah had one answer: "The Lord Yahweh comes with might, and his arm rules for him; his reward is with him and his recompense before him" (40:10). Echoing the promise of the first exodus that "Yahweh will fight for you" (Exod 14:14), the prophet told the exiles: "Yahweh goes forth like a soldier, like a warrior he stirs up his fury; he cries out. He shouts aloud, he shows himself mighty against his foes" (42:13). This one and only universal God has merely to give his signal to the nations and raise his hand, and their kings and queens will humbly bring the scattered exiles back to their land (49:22–23; cf. 5:26; 11:10–12). "For even the captives of the mighty one shall be taken away, and the prey of the tyrant shall be rescued" (49:24–25).[10] Those who had been the oppressors of Israel would be brought low so that all flesh might know the power of Yahweh.

The destination of the new exodus is to be Zion/Jerusalem. Deutero-Isaiah carries on the Zion tradition of First Isaiah, but connects it to the new exodus rather than to the Davidic covenant tradition. For Yahweh alone will be King over Israel and will reign from Mount Zion (52:7). While Zion and Jerusalem are often mentioned together as the destination, the people return to Jerusalem, while Zion is the place where Yahweh anchors his salvation for Israel (46:13). For this reason the good news is announced first to Zion (41:27). Zion's barrenness will be transformed into the Garden of Yahweh (51:3), and although the prophet makes only passing mention of the temple foundations to be laid, he does speak of the returnees bringing back the sacred vessels of the temple (52:11). Most of all, Zion is to be a place of joy and gladness, thanksgiving and songs (51:3) rather than sacrificial offerings. Recalling the words of Nah 1:15, Deutero-Isaiah envisioned the good news being announced of the return of Yahweh to Zion: "How beautiful upon the

---

10. The MT in 49:24b reads, "or the captives of the *righteous one* be rescued." Baltzer (*Deutero-Isaiah*, 331) argues that this must be taken as the original version even though most interpreters follow 1QIsaa which has "tyrant," parallel to v. 25. If this is original, it would have to be understood ironically as "one who claimed the right" to that which had been taken. Cf. Matt 12:28–29.

mountains are the feet of the herald who announces peace, who brings good news, who announces salvation, who says to Zion, 'Your God reigns!' Listen! Your watchmen lift up their voices, together they sing for joy. For eye to eye they see the return of Yahweh to Zion" (52:7–8). Yahweh has not forgotten or forsaken Zion any more than a woman could forget her nursing child or have no compassion for the child in her womb (49:14).

Jerusalem has paid the penalty for her sin and is now to be redeemed. Now that cup of God's wrath from which Jerusalem had to drink (Jer 25:15–31) will soon be taken away and placed in the hand of her tormentors (51:17–23). Then the city will once again be able to put on her garments of pride and truly be called the "holy city." For the uncircumcised and the unclean will no longer be there (52:1), since God will have comforted his people and redeemed Jerusalem. Where Jeremiah (10:20) had complained of the threat of siege that Jerusalem's tent would be destroyed, the tent cords broken, and the children gone, in Deutero-Isaiah the barren one will become so populated with the returnees that God advises his city: "Enlarge the site of your tent, and let the curtains of your habitation be stretched out; do not hold back! Lengthen your cords and strengthen your stakes!" (54:2).

Those who feared returning to the desolation and isolation of Zion/Jerusalem are advised to look back to their ancestors, Abraham and Sarah, who were concerned over Sarah's barrenness, yet they became the ancestors of multitudes (51:1–2). Zion/Jerusalem is assured that her husband is the one God and Creator, her Redeemer, the Holy One of Israel, who will gather her to himself with great compassion and everlasting love. Like the Noachic covenant, Yahweh's covenant with his people is everlasting: "For the mountains may depart and the hills be removed, but my steadfast love shall not depart from you, and my covenant of peace shall not be removed, says the One who has compassion on you, Yahweh" (54:5–10). So the "afflicted one, storm-tossed, and not comforted" will surely be comforted and rebuilt with precious stones (54:11–12). Deutero-Isaiah's infectious and positive enthusiasm for the return and redemption of the exiles knows no bounds!

The Time for Healing

Long ago Hosea had called for his people to return to Yahweh so that they might be healed and their wounds bound up (Hos 6:1; 7:1; 11:3; 14:5). Jeremiah had echoed these same sentiments (Jer 3:22; 17:14; 30:17). Before him Isaiah of Jerusalem, confronted by the faithlessness of the nation, had received the revelation to speak words of judgment to this people whose ears were insensitive and whose eyes were glued shut "lest they turn and be healed" (Isa 6:9–10). Yet he, too, looked forward to the day when "Yahweh binds up the hurt of his people and heals the wounds inflicted by his blow" (30:26). However, he believed that would happen when a future righteous king reigned with loyal officials (32:1–4).

Even though Deutero-Isaiah used the word "heal" only once (53:5), he certainly believed that the time for the fulfillment of these promises was now to take place. Yet in spite of his positive enthusiasm, he was well aware that many of the exiles were slow to change from their old ways and were still tainted with the same spiritual blindness and deafness of Isaiah's day. Nevertheless, Yahweh had a plan and purpose for Israel and so confirmed the promises of old, assuring them that he would lead the blind by a way that they do not know and would turn the darkness before them into light (42:16). The spiritual darkness of being apart from God would be changed to light as they came into the brilliant presence of Yahweh (42:7; 49:9; 43:7; 48:11). So the exiles are called to listen and see because Yahweh has a purpose for Israel:

> Listen, you deaf ones, and look up and see, you blind!
> Who is blind except my servant, or deaf as my messenger whom I send?
> Who is blind as the one in a covenant of peace
> Or blind as the servant of Yahweh?
> He sees many things but does not observe them;
> Ears are open, but he does not hear! (42:18–20)

It is because of Yahweh's covenant faithfulness that he will bring sight and understanding to these people. In this way Yahweh will make his teaching great and glorious. Those still embittered by the exile are reminded that, yes, it *was* Yahweh who gave them over to the Babylonians, but it was because of *their* sin and rebellion (42:21–25). Now, the exiles are assured, Yahweh has redeemed them, called them by name, and will bring them back to their own land (43:1–7). So with the call: "Bring forth the people who are blind, yet have eyes, who are deaf, yet have ears" (43:8). Yahweh announces to them the purpose he has for them: they are to be his witnesses before the nations, to witness that Yahweh is the only God, the only one who has power to save (43:9–13).

Throughout Deutero-Isaiah's work there is the constant exhortation to "listen, hear," particularly in ch. 48 where the urging reaches an intensity with the word "hear" used twelve times, often in the imperative. The prophet does not mince words with the exiles, alternating between reminding them of God's gracious redeeming love and their stubbornness (48:4). The community is chided for professing allegiance to Yahweh "but not in faithfulness and not in righteousness" (48:1) because from of old they had not listened. But the people are now reminded that the former things, particularly the judgment of Isa 6:9–10, have passed, and new things are now being declared, "hidden things" that they have not previously known (48:6). This is the good news of God's reign with the redemption and deliverance of his people. It is these "new things," mentioned so often (41:22, 23; 42:9; 43:9, 18, 19; 46:8–9) that have called for a new song of praise to Yahweh (42:10–13). The "new things" declare that their sins are pardoned, their rebellions blotted out, swept away like a cloud, and their sins like the mist in the morning (40:2; 43:25; 44:22), not because they had repented, but because of whom God is, a loving and forgiving Father. Yahweh redeems his rebellious children "for his own sake" that Israel might be his witness before the nations (43:10, 25; 48:9).[11]

Eventually the positive proclamation of the prophet begins to have its effect on rebellious servant Israel, or at least on some of the exiles who come to understand that part of their purpose involved urging their fellow exiles to come into the light of God's presence and respond to the good news of God's reign. So now Yahweh's servant Israel,

---

11. See further Darr, "Isaiah's Vision," 847–82.

represented by those who have responded, can finally say: "My Lord Yahweh has given me the tongue of those who have been taught, to know how to aid the weary with a word" (50:4). Having heard this word and knowing that God is with him, the servant of Yahweh can now even put up with the ridicule and insults of the naysayers among the exiles (50:6–9).

The healing has begun, leading on to the triumphal summary statement of Deutero-Isaiah's message set down in ch. 35—a fanfare of what is coming and a response to some of the contentions of earlier prophets like First Isaiah and Jeremiah:

> Strengthen the weak hands and firm up the stumbling knees.
> Say to those who are fearful of heart: Be strong, fear not.
> Behold your God, he comes with vengeance.
> With the recompense of God he comes and saves you.
> Then the eyes of the blind shall be opened
> and the ears of the deaf opened up.
> Then the lame shall leap like a deer,
> and the tongue of the dumb shout for joy! (35:3–6a)

Israel as the Servant of Yahweh

When Deutero-Isaiah shocked his audience, particularly those who still hoped for a future Davidic leader, by announcing that Yahweh had named the Persian Cyrus as his "shepherd" and "anointed one" (44:28; 25:1) to rescue the exiles, he was indicating once more that Israel was to have no other king but Yahweh. In doing so he was opposing the views of not only the priestly group who followed Ezekiel's view of a dual messianism, but also of those who still held to the traditional hope for a Davidic messiah / anointed one. It is clear from some of the psalms, and particularly Ps 89, that this hope was still strong among many of the exiles. In Ps 89, which laments the loss of a Davidic king at the time and reminds Yahweh of his promise (2 Sam 7:12–16) of an *everlasting* covenant with David, David is frequently referred to as Yahweh's "anointed one" (89:39, 52), "servant" (89:4, 21, 40, 51) and "chosen one" (89:4, 20). While the prophet has used "anointed one" for Cyrus, he now uses the terms "my servant" and "my chosen one" as spoken by Yahweh, exclusively of the people of Israel, principally of the exiles.[12]

Already in 41:8–10, Deutero-Isaiah had Yahweh say: "But you, O Israel, *my servant*, Jacob, *whom I have chosen*, the offspring of Abraham, my friend; you whom I took from the ends of the earth, and called from the remotest area, saying to you, *You are my servant, I have chosen you* and not rejected you; fear not, for I am with you, do not be afraid, for I am your God; I will strengthen you, I will help you, I will uphold you with my right hand." Not only are the vassal terms, "servant" and "chosen one," transferred to the people, but other terms with royal overtones are used here in regard to Israel. References

---

12. I am in agreement with Mettinger (*Farewell to the Servant Songs*) that any attempt to isolate the so-called four Servant Songs (42:1–4; 49:1–6; 50:4–9; 52:13—53:12) from their context does a gross injustice to the whole proclamation of Deutero-Isaiah. Cf. also Clements, "Isaiah 53," 39–54.

to "taking by the hand" were used as a technical term in surrounding nations for a god installing a king.[13] So Yahweh is depicted here in these verses as installing Israel once again to be his witnesses (cf. 43:10, 12; 44:8; 55:4), as was the case prior to the monarchy. Calling Israel "the offspring of Abraham" tied Israel into the covenant promises and blessings made to Abraham—that his descendants would become a blessing to all the families of the earth (Gen 12:1–3; cf. Isa 51:1–3). Just as Abraham is addressed by God as "my friend, the one whom I love," so the same is said of Israel in 43:4.

Having assured the exiles that they truly have been reinstalled as God's servant, his chosen one, and under his guidance and protection, Deutero-Isaiah depicts Yahweh as now announcing to all the world what his servant is called to do (42:1–4):

> Behold my servant whom I uphold, my chosen in whom my soul delights.
> I have put my spirit upon him, he will bring forth justice to the nations.
> He will not cry out or lift his voice or make it heard in the street.
> A crushed reed he will not break, and a faint wick he will not extinguish.
> He will faithfully bring forth justice.
> . . . and the coastlands are waiting for his teaching.

The servant here is clearly Israel as the context demands, as well as the use of common wording.[14] The spirit of God is bestowed upon the servant, as it was on the judges prior to the monarchy (Judg 3:10; 6:34; 11:29; 13:25) and on kings (1 Sam 11:6; 16:13, 14; Isa 11:2), to equip the people for the awesome task of bringing forth justice to the nations. The term "justice" here is to be understood in its widest sense of conveying God's plan and purpose for his whole creation, the reason why he "gives breath to the people" on the earth "and spirit to those who walk in it" (42:5). It is the representative function of conveying God's justice and righteousness to all people to live in harmony and peace under him. It is for this reason that the "coastlands" are waiting for Yahweh's teaching (42:4; cf. 51:4–5) and will be able to sing his praises (42:10, 12). However, the servant will not carry out this task by fiat or edict, nor by violence, but by faithfulness to the spirit of God. Not breaking the crushed reed or extinguishing the faint wick refers to the way the servant would treat those of littleness of faith, whether among fellow exiles or among the nations (cf. Isa 35:7; 43:17), with patience and compassion. Nor will the servant become faint or be crushed himself because he has the assurance of God's spirit within him.

Having made this public proclamation, Yahweh now addresses Servant Israel once again (42:5–9), reminding the people that he has called them in faithfulness to his covenant with them. He has given them as a people-covenant and as a light to the nations. The term "people-covenant" (also in 49:8) is unusual but is evidently Deutero-Isaiah's response to the promise of Jeremiah that after the exile the covenant God would make with Israel would be to *put his teaching within them* and to *write it upon their hearts* (Jer 31:33). This is made clear when the people are addressed later: "Listen to me, you who know righteousness, you people who have my teaching in your heart" (51:7).[15] By living

---

13. See Baltzer, *Deutero-Isaiah*, 97.

14. See Mettinger, *Farewell*, 31; also Wilcox and Paton-Williams, "Servant Songs," 86–87.

15. Cf. Sommer, *Prophet Reads Scripture*, 48. Contra Hillers, "Berit 'am," 175–82; M. Smith, "Berit 'am / Berit 'olam, 241–43.

out their covenant relationship with God and fellow-beings they can become a light to the nations and bring freedom from the darkness of ignorance, injustice, and oppression, and be witnesses to the presence of the only God (*kabod*, 42:8) among the nations. This is the "new thing" Israel must learn to understand about their purpose. The former things of the Davidic dynasty have passed, and the image of an ideal king has given way to the image of an ideal people representing God.[16]

Yet the exilic community is not ideal. Many are still spiritually blind and deaf. But Yahweh will lead the blind by a road they do not know and turn the darkness into light. He will not forsake them. Yahweh's patience and encouragement of his blind and deaf servant to see and hear their calling is illustrated in the following chapters. They are constantly reminded of the intimacy of their covenant relationship with God, that Yahweh has created them, formed them in the womb, redeemed them and they are his (43:1; 44:1–2; cf. 44:21, 24). The blind and deaf servant is brought before the nations and reminded: "You are my witnesses . . . and my servant whom I have chosen, so that you may know and believe me and understand that I am he," the only God (43:10). They can be God's witnesses because he has now swept away their transgressions like a cloud and their sins like mist. They have the assurance that Yahweh always "confirms the word of his servant and fulfils the counsel of his messengers" (44:26). So, soon they will be able to "go out from Babylon, flee from Chaldea, declare this with a shout of joy, proclaim it, send it forth to the ends of the earth" (48:20).

Finally, the Servant responds (49:1–6). Deutero-Isaiah voices for his disciples and himself what faithful Servant Israel would say to the coastlands waiting for Yahweh's teaching (42:4; 51:4–5) and to nations generally. For Servant Israel has now come to understand that part of its role concerns the nations, and that had been planned from the beginning. By now recognizing that "Yahweh called me from the womb, from the womb of my mother he mentioned my name" (49:1), Servant Israel was acknowledging that Yahweh had chosen him to be his servant and witness to the nations before Israel was brought into being. In finally acknowledging this, the Servant describes that process of maturation and birth as his mouth being set like a sharp sword and his person made like a pointed arrow kept in God's sheath or quiver until the time when God would use him (49:2). While still in the womb, God had declared of his servant: "You are my Servant, Israel, in whom I will be glorified" (49:3). Having acknowledged that, Israel now confesses that in their preexilic past they had not understood this purpose, had labored in vain, and had expended all its strength "for nothing and vanity" (49:4a).

Now Servant Israel can affirm that the reason for its being is to be with Yahweh and carry out his plan (49:4b). Initially, during the exile that purpose had been expressed by Ezekiel as only gathering together all the tribes of Israel as one nation (Ezek 28:25–26). But Israel's purpose was to do more than that. Now Servant Israel is able to affirm to the nations that they have been called by Yahweh, not just to gather the survivors of Israel, but to be a light to the nations so that God's salvation "may reach to the end of the earth" (49:6; cf. 42:6).

That proclamation by the Servant to the nations is now followed by a response from Yahweh with a reality check and further encouragement and assurance for the

---

16. Sommer, *Prophet Reads Scripture*, 85, sees a number of parallels between Isa 11:1–10 and 42:1–9.

Servant (49:7–12). The Servant must keep in mind that after the restoration those kings and rulers who had despised and abhorred them will bow down to them with respect and honor. They will do this, bringing back the scattered exiles (49:7, 23) because they will confess: "God is with you only, there is no other" (45:14). Significantly, this honor in the future will be bestowed upon the people rather than on a king as proclaimed in Ps 72:8–11.[17] Once again (49:8), as in 42:6, they are reminded that they have been kept and given as a living people-covenant to reestablish their nation in Judah and to make sure that the returnees are given possession of their ancestral lands which had been left desolate. In carrying out this task Servant Israel was to call and gather the exiles scattered in all directions to be led back in the new exodus by Yahweh their God (49:9–12) in fulfillment of the promise given earlier (40:9–11).

In 50:4–9 the Servant speaks again and declares his dependence on the Lord Yahweh, listening to his every word day by day as those who are taught, so that he may be able to arouse the weary with God's promises (50:4; cf. 40:28–31). The Servant now emphasizes that he *listens* for now the Lord Yahweh has opened his ear. He knows that Yahweh now declares him righteous against those who declare him otherwise, claiming that he was misleading the people and misrepresenting Israel's purpose and mission (50:8–9). The Servant here is clearly those of the exiles who have now accepted the prophet's message and have become his disciples to proclaim the good news. As such they represent ideal Israel. That the prophet may be drawing on some of his own experiences does not negate the fact that the faithful are being portrayed here, since 50:10 refers specifically to those who "listen to the voice of his [Yahweh's] servant." Those who oppose and revile them, referred to in 50:11, are not Babylonian officials but fellow exiles who reject the message for various reasons.[18] Yahweh's response to the Servant's acknowledgment that he is now listening to Yahweh's teaching comes in 51:7–8:[19]

> Fear not the reproach of others, and be not dismayed at their reviling.
> For the moth will eat them up like a garment,
> and the moth-worm will eat them like wool;
> but my righteousness will be forever, and my salvation to all generations.

The prophet now turns his attention more to Zion/Jerusalem, the goal of the new exodus for the exiles. Zion is described in very much the same language as the Servant. Both have suffered oppression, affliction, shame and despair; both are promised vindication, deliverance and exaltation.[20] While Ezekiel had been angered by those left behind in the "waste places" in and around Jerusalem because of their claims that, like Abraham, they had now been given the land to possess (Ezek 33:23–29; cf. 11:14–21), Deutero-Isaiah has only a message of comfort. Yes, they are to look to Abraham, for Yahweh will comfort Zion and make her waste places like Eden (51:2–3). Zion, who had said, "Yahweh has forsaken me, my Lord has forgotten me" (49:14), is given the constant assurance that Yahweh has the compassion of a nursing mother and has not forgotten

---

17. Sommer, *Prophet Reads Scripture*, 115.
18. In agreement with McKenzie, *Second Isaiah*, 117.
19. So Mettinger, *Farewell*, 33.
20. See Willey, *Remember the Former Things*, 222.

(49:15–18) and that Zion/Jerusalem will soon be populated by the returning exiles. For this reason, Jerusalem is called upon to rouse herself (51:17–23); Zion/Jerusalem are commanded to awake, shake off the dust and rise up (52:1–2), for Yahweh is returning to Zion as their King with his exiled people. For he "has bared his holy arm before the eyes of all the nations, and all the ends of the earth shall see the salvation of our God" (52:10). With this announcement to Zion/Jerusalem the exiles are exhorted to depart. Having purified themselves, the people (not the priesthood) will carry the sacred vessels and return to their land with Yahweh leading them.

The Suffering Servant

It is in this context of the impending return that the Servant and his role of bringing light to the nations is now discussed once again (52:13—53:12). In the first strophe (52:13–15) Yahweh is depicted as announcing: "See, my Servant shall have insight, he shall rise up, be lifted up and be very high" (v. 13). The verb used in this announcement (hiphil of *sakal*) has the meaning of "having insight" gained through the "knowledge" of Yahweh, that is, through a faithful relationship with God.[21] The use of this verb affirms that the blindness and deafness of the Servant (42:18–19) has been healed, who through "knowledge" of Yahweh now has understanding of Israel's role. That the Servant "shall rise, be lifted up and be very high" affirms that intimate relationship of the Servant with Yahweh who was seen by First Isaiah in his vision "sitting on a throne, high and lifted up" (Isa 6:1).[22]

It is this Servant who had been so despised and abhorred by the nations (49:7), so disfigured that many were appalled (52:14), who will be the one to "sprinkle" many nations on Yahweh's behalf to bring about their purification and bring them into relationship with Yahweh (v. 15). The prophet has deliberately used this verb, "sprinkle" (*nazah*), employed in priestly law in regard to purification rites performed by the priesthood (Exod 29:21; Lev 4:6, 17; 8:11, 30; etc), to make the subtle point:[23] It is the people as a whole, as a living people-covenant, who will metaphorically "sprinkle" and purify the nations by causing many to be declared righteous (53:11). Kings and nations will now have a complete change of attitude toward Israel (v. 15; cf. 49:7) and will see and understand what they had not heard or experienced before. The reversal of Isa 6:9–10 would even involve the nations as well!

Deutero-Isaiah now expresses how he would hope the kings and nations might come to a new understanding of Servant Israel (53:1–6). Using language like that employed in hopes for a future Davidic king in Isa 11:1–10; Jer 23:5 and Ezek 17:6–22, he depicts the kings and nations describing the way they had observed Israel in the past— growing up before Yahweh as a young plant, like a root out of desert land, having no form or dignity, nothing pleasing in appearance, despised and rejected by others. They saw Israel as having pains and knowing sickness—the wounds and hurts that Jeremiah

---

21. Observe the use of this verb in relation to "knowledge of God" elsewhere. E.g., Isa 41:20; 44:18; Jer 3:15; 9:24; 10:21; 20:11.

22. See Gosse, "Isaïe," 538–39; Sommer, *Prophet Reads Scripture*, 95.

23. Cf. Ezek 36:25.

had regarded as incurable (Jer 6:7; 10:19; 30:15). These were such that others would turn away, despising and regarding Israel as of no value (vv. 2–3). But now they had come to realize that it was really *their* sickness, *their* pains which Yahweh's Servant had carried, whereas they had simply regarded him as stricken, struck down by God and afflicted (v. 4). So now the nations would come to confess: "But he was pierced because of *our* rebellions, crushed because of *our* iniquities, upon him was the chastisement by which *we* prospered, and now by his bruises *we* are healed" (v. 5). The nations would come to realize that they were the ones who had gone astray, yet Yahweh had caused their iniquity to come upon his Servant.[24]

The prophet now ponders the afflictions and humiliations of the exile (53:7–10) and expresses the suffering of the Servant in terms reminiscent of Jeremiah's lament (Jer 11:18–20) and Ezekiel's vision of the valley of dry bones (Ezek 37:1–14). In the affliction of the exile, the people had gone silently, like a lamb led to the slaughter (v. 7; cf. Jer 11:19), taken away because of oppression and judgment. There in exile, the Servant "was cut off from the land of the living, stricken on account of the rebellion of my people" (v. 8). More and more the faithful are being represented as the Servant, subjected to exile because of the transgression of the majority. While he borrows the phrase, "cut off from the land of the living" from Jer 11:19, the prophet uses a different verb for "cut off," one used in Ezek 37:11 of the exiles' complaint that they were completely *cut off*. The exiles had voiced the complaint that after all these years of exile they were dead as a nation. In response Ezekiel had given them God's answer: "I will open your graves and raise you from your graves, O my people" (Ezek 37:12, 13). So Deutero-Isaiah uses this same metaphoric language and says of the Servant: "They put his grave with the wicked and with a rich person in his death" (v. 9). The "rich person" may refer to Nebuchadnezzar who died in 562 BCE, and the "grave with the wicked" would be the idea of dying in an alien land among idol-worshipers.

Yet in his reflection of all of this, the prophet could see God's purpose at work and appears to half-address God in his musings: "Yet it was the purpose of Yahweh to crush him with sickness. Though you set his life as a guilt offering, he will see his offspring and prolong his days, and in his hand the purpose of Yahweh shall prosper" (v. 10). Israel had to experience the covenant curses with the chastisement of the exile, but now this would lead to their restoration as a nation to fulfill God's purpose for them and the nations. Ezekiel's plan of restoration had spoken of the necessity of the elaborate sacrificial worship as the means of atonement, but Deutero-Isaiah is saying here that Servant Israel has already accomplished that atonement in the exile, and through God's grace and purpose is being renewed in spirit (42:1). Earlier, the prophet had announced that God had blotted out their transgressions. So they did not need the priesthood, "the officials of the sanctuary" to carry out elaborate sacrificial rituals (43:22–28; cf. 40:2; 44:22).[25]

---

24. The context requires the "we" in this section to be the "many" of 52:14 and the "many nations and kings" of 52:15. Some have argued that the "many" and the "we" are identical but must refer to Israel or part of Israel. See, e.g., Steck, "Aspekte des Gottesknechts," 36–58. While the immediate context demands that the speakers in this strophe are the kings and nations, this does not rule out the possibility that Deutero-Isaiah may also have had in mind those of Israel who had escaped the exile. Cf. Clines, *I, He, We & They*, 29–33.

25. In agreement with Baltzer, *Deutero-Isaiah*, 421.

In the final section (53:11–12), Yahweh speaks once again, adding further remarks about those who have gone through the suffering of the exile and have come to see and find satisfaction in being in a faithful relationship with their God ("through knowledge," v. 11a). The emphasis on "seeing" and "knowing" affirms that the Servant is no longer blind and deaf (cf. 42:18–22; 43:8–10) but has come to an understanding of Yahweh's purpose for all to live in covenant relationship with Yahweh and be a light to the nations. Now, Yahweh proclaims, the Righteous One, my Servant, shall cause many to be righteous, and shall "bear their iniquities" (v. 11b). The phrases, "bearing their iniquities," "the one who bore the sin of many," and "make intercession for the rebels" all indicate that the Servant has taken over the role of priests who were previously responsible through sacrifice of bearing the sins of the people to Yahweh to receive pardon and forgiveness (cf. Lev 10:17; 16:22). The Servant is now to act as God's representative in forgiving iniquity.

Because of this renewed relationship, the promise of blessing is now given: "I will allot him a portion with the many, and he shall divide the spoil with the mighty, because he poured out his life to death and was numbered with the rebels" (v. 12a). It is because the faithful had endured the "death" of the exile together with the transgressors that they will now receive the blessings in a life renewed. In these verses Deutero-Isaiah appears to have had in mind the sentiment expressed in Isa 9:1–2 that those who have seen a great light would be as people who rejoice "when dividing the plunder."

The Servant as God's Representative

So now it is time for Zion/Jerusalem to burst into song because soon her children, the exiles, will be returning and will fill the area in and around the city to capacity (54:1–3). As if to negate as strongly as possible the statements of Ezekiel that the city and the people would remember their ways with shame and disgrace even after the restoration (Ezek 16:54, 61; 36:32; 43:10–11), Deutero-Isaiah piles up the words used to describe shame and disgrace and negates them all (54:4). For now, their God returns to Zion as her husband with everlasting love and compassion (54:5–8), and there will be an eternal covenant of peace like that at the time of Noah (vv. 9–10). Once more the bride of Yahweh will be adorned with jewels and precious stones and will be cared for by God with his teaching, righteousness and judgment. For "this is the inheritance of the *servants of Yahweh* and their righteousness from me, says Yahweh" (vv. 11–17). The plural, "servants," is used here for the first time, as some would argue, to refer to the offspring of the Servant mentioned in 53:10.[26] Certainly, those who followed this prophetic vision after the return continued to refer to themselves as "servants" rather than with the singular noun, as we shall see in Isa 56–66.

In his final chapter (55), the prophet draws together all he has said of the Servant's role and redemption to a glorious and climactic conclusion. It begins with an invitation to a banquet to celebrate Yahweh's blessings on his people, the fulfillment of promises to the afflicted and dispossessed that when they seek water and are parched with thirst,

---

26. See Sweeney, "Reconceptualization of the Davidic Covenant," 44–48.

Yahweh will answer them (41:17). The exiles can participate in this banquet "without money and without price" for it is God's gracious act. Moreover, this is the celebration of the inauguration of the new age in which Yahweh is their King (52:7), and the people will now be his witnesses to the nations. So Deutero-Isaiah now emphasizes the need for the people to "keep on listening" with their ears in the true sense (55:1–3a) in contrast to their previous deafness.

Given the emphasis on Zion in these last chapters (49–55), one would expect some reference to a Davidic king. Such an allusion only comes in this last chapter and only in the form of transferring the everlasting covenant made with David to the people. This transference to Servant Israel had already been hinted at in 42:1–4 and 49:22–23 where royal terminology had been used. That there were those who still put their hope in a future Davidic king has been seen from the lament in Ps 89. In this Psalm God is addressed with the words: "You said, 'I have made a covenant with my chosen one, I have sworn to my servant David: I will establish your descendant forever, and build your throne for all generations'" (89:4, 5). The permanence of that covenant is emphasized no less than seven times with the word "forever." Then after God is depicted as saying that the line of David would be "established forever, like the moon, an enduring witness in the skies" (v. 36), the psalm turns to lament and reproach: "You have removed the scepter from his hand, and hurled his throne to the ground!" (v. 45).

Deutero-Isaiah was certainly familiar with this psalm[27] and had already transferred the title, "my chosen one," "my servant" to the people. Now that everlasting covenant, Yahweh's "steadfast love for David" (emphasized so often in Ps 89) is transferred to the people as well (55:3). That the prophet saw this as an actual transference and not just a shared covenant[28] is made clear in the contrast between the role of David (v. 4) and that of the people (v. 5). The prophet acknowledges that David had been an enduring witness to the peoples as Ps 89:36 claimed, but now Servant Israel has been called to be witness to the nations that Yahweh is the only God (43:10, 12; 44:8). Borrowing a phrase from Ps 18:44 in which David had said that nations whom he had not known served him, the prophet says of the people that they will now call nations that they do not know, and nations that do not know them would run to them because of Yahweh, the Holy One of Israel. David's witness had been through military conquests, but Servant Israel's witness was to be peaceful in fulfillment of Isa 2:2–4. Contrary to the hopes expressed by earlier prophets for a Davidic messiah, it was clear that the Davidic dynasty was at an end. Yahweh would be the only King and the people would be his representatives. It would be a return to a pre-monarchic understanding of theocracy. For those who would question this development, the prophet reminded them that God's thoughts are higher than human thoughts and his purposes will be accomplished (55:8–11).

---

27. See Eissfeldt, "Promises of Grace," 196–207.
28. *Contra* Kaiser, "Unfailing Kindnesses," 91–98; Seitz, *Word Without End*, 161–63.

Covenant, Torah, and Righteousness

Deutero-Isaiah's theology is covenant theology. Elements of the Mosaic covenant may be in the background of the prophet's message, but no mention is ever made of that covenant.[29] We have already noted that the words of Jeremiah concerning a new covenant (31:31–34), which God would make with Judah and Israel in the future, was a strong influence on Deutero-Isaiah. Jeremiah had said that the new covenant would not be like the covenant God made with the people when he brought them out of the land of Egypt, but it would be Yahweh's teaching (*torah*) written in their hearts. The influence of this assertion is clear in Isa 51:7 where the people are addressed by God as those "who know righteousness (*tsedeq*)," "who have my teaching (*torah*) in your hearts." For this reason they had been addressed as a living "people-covenant" (*berit-am*, 42:6; 49:8).

In this whole section, 51:1–8, we have the use of a number of terms which illustrate the prophet's covenant theology clearly. It begins with the call: "Listen to me, you who pursue righteousness (*tsedeq*), you who seek Yahweh." The masculine noun for "righteousness" here is almost a synonym for "Yahweh." In fact, Deutero-Isaiah uses the masculine noun exclusively for Yahweh, never for human righteousness, because it is always Yahweh who takes the initiative for the deliverance of the exiles. The feminine form (*tsedaqah*) is used generally to indicate a response, either by the people or by Yahweh. This is clearly illustrated in Isa 45:8 where the prophet takes up a statement made by Hosea (10:12) and changes it to:

> Shower, O heavens, from above
> and let the skies rain down righteousness (*tsedeq*),
> let the earth open, that they may bring forth salvation
> and let it cause righteousness (*tsedaqah*) to sprout forth also.

Both these masculine and feminine forms of the noun refer to the initiative and response respectively, in acting faithfully to the covenant relationship.

However, the covenant implied in 51:1–8 is the covenant made with Abraham. While the initial reference is the promise of many offspring and that, likewise, Zion would again be populated by man (vv. 1–3), it continues on to speak of the blessings the offspring of Abraham were to bring to the nations (vv. 4–5; cf. Gen 12:1–3; 17:1–8; 22:15–18). The similarity of this proclamation to the task given to Servant Israel in 42:1–4 recognizes that Yahweh works through his covenant people as his witness and instrument to bring his teaching to the nations. Both here and in 42:1–4 the terms "teaching" (*torah*) and "justice" (*mishpat*) are used synonymously, and both are to be understood broadly as referring to passing on to the nations God's order, will and purpose.[30] Deutero-Isaiah never speaks of "torah" and "justice" as referring to individual laws, statutes, commandments as did Ezekiel. For it is the covenant relationship based on mutual faithfulness which is to be extended to all people, built on the trust that God's "salvation will be forever" and "his righteousness will never be ended" (51:6, 8).

---

29. Cf. Anderson, "Exodus and Covenant," 339–60.
30. Cf. Sweeney, "Book of Isaiah," 50–67.

Another indication of Deutero-Isaiah's constant emphasis on Yahweh's steadfast love and mercy rather than on Israel's obedience comes with his reference to the Noachic covenant in 54:9–10. There, as in 51:6, the assurance is given that the hills and mountains, heaven and earth, would be removed before God's steadfast love and compassion would ever be taken from them, just as God had promised about the waters of Noah.

Referring to such general covenants as those made with Abraham and Noah gives a more universal and permanent tone to the kind of covenant which is to be the motivating force in the lives of the people. This is evident also in the democratizing of the Davidic covenant discussed earlier. Apparently, the Mosaic covenant is not acknowledged by the prophet because it spoke only of Israel, was perceived as emphasizing rules rather than relationship, and did not fully appreciate that Yahweh was the only God of all the nations which needed to be drawn into covenant relationship with him.[31]

Israel's Mission to the Nations

Throughout, Deutero-Isaiah has emphasized that Yahweh is the only God and Creator to be worshiped by all nations. This emphasis has affirmed initially for the exiles that Yahweh alone has power to save, and so they have nothing to fear from the other nations (40:15–17). This had already been expressed in Isa 2:2–4 (Mic 4:1–4) and to some degree also in the earlier oracles against the nations. However, those oracles had generally concentrated on the divine justice to be carried out against nations for injustices and oppressions against Israel. This is still evident in the oracles against Babylon inserted in Isa 13 and 14, and is continued by Deutero-Isaiah in ch. 47 where Babylon and its people are indicted for arrogance, oppression and idolatry (cf. also 43:14; 48:14). Justice must be done so that all flesh knows that Yahweh is the only God and Savior (49:26). Cyrus the Persian, however, is spoken of in glowing terms as Yahweh's special envoy, addressed as God's agent in a way that rules out any Davidic messiah when he is addressed as God's "shepherd" and "anointed one" to carry out all of Yahweh's purpose to set the exiles free and rebuild Jerusalem (44:28; 45:L1–4, 13). Those coastlands that had feared and trembled at the coming of Cyrus (41:1–5) are called upon to turn to Yahweh, the only true God, and come to understand God's purpose for the nations. The nations would come to recognize that only in Yahweh would they find righteousness and strength (45:24) and blessing to live in peace. This is where Israel's purpose now comes into the picture.

For Yahweh's presence is to be revealed to all flesh, and Servant Israel has been chosen to be God's witness to the nations of Yahweh's saving presence. They will do so not only passively through God's deliverance of his afflicted and dispossessed people (52:10), but also through their active faithfulness to their relationship with God, their understanding of his will and purpose, and their willingness to share it (42:1–4). Through God's presence in their lives they are to become a light to the nations (42:6; 49:6–8), and thus a blessing to others. The covenants with Abraham (51:1–3), with Noah (54:7–10), and with David (55:3–5) which Israel is now to fulfill, all point to the universal task set

---

31. Cf. Lindblom, *Prophecy in Ancient Israel*, 380–82; Zimmerli, *Law and the Prophets*, 87–92; Stuhlmueller, "Deutero-Isaiah," 19–21.

before Israel to be a light to the nations and ultimately to universal salvation. Israel can no longer be concerned simply for its own survival and restoration, but to be a blessing to all the nations as well. The coastland and other nations are waiting and hoping for Yahweh's teaching and purpose which Israel is now to reveal to them (42:1–4; 51:4–5).

By demonstrating God's loving presence among them, the people of Israel not only bring about God's glory and praise among the nations but, as Yahweh's agents, they also become glorified for their witness to the strength and power of Yahweh to save, even in their suffering and weakness. In this way, as God's righteous ones, they will cause many to become righteous and drawn into the presence of the one and only God (53:1–12). Because of this witness, nations that they do not know shall run to them because of Yahweh their God who has thus glorified them (55:5).

Fittingly, Deutero-Isaiah concluded his proclamation of good news with a song of joyous return to Zion (55:12–13; cf. 35:8–10):

> For you shall go out in joy, and be led back in peace.
> The mountains and the hills before you shall burst into song,
> and all the trees of the field shall clap their hands.
> Instead of the thorn shall come up the cypress,
> instead of the brier shall come up the myrtle;
> and it shall be to Yahweh for a name,
> for an everlasting sign that shall not be cut off.

The prophetic vision is now directed to Yahweh as King over all the nations with Servant Israel to be his witness and representative to reflect his brilliance and light to all in confidence and faithfulness. Of all the prophets who have gone before or come after, none has transformed the prophetic vision into such a positive picture as has Deutero-Isaiah. During difficult times to come, this will be a vision that later prophets will cling to and recall.

Chapter V

After the Return from Exile

THE CITY OF BABYLON surrendered to Cyrus in 539 BCE, and its territories now became part of the Persian Empire. The following year Cyrus gave permission to the exiles to return to Judah, gave money for the rebuilding of the temple, and the temple vessels which had been taken from Jerusalem (Ezra 6:3–5). With Sheshbazzar as their governor, a small group of elders, priests, and others courageous enough to face an uncertain future returned (cf. Ezra 1:5–11). Some of the others were disciples of Deutero-Isaiah. This was far from the triumphal return envisaged by Deutero-Isaiah, but it was a beginning.

As the bearers of the prophetic vision of Deutero-Isaiah, these disciples would have had different ideas about what the restoration would entail than those priests who were eager to institute Ezekiel's program of restoration with the temple as central and Zadokite priests as the leaders of the restored community. The priesthood had worked diligently during the exile to maintain their cultic traditions. They had collected and codified their laws and recorded their history. For them the return to Jerusalem would be an opportunity to reestablish a cultic community centered round temple worship and governed by their statutes. For the followers of Deutero-Isaiah, the temple would have been almost unnecessary. During the years of exile they had developed forms of worship which did not include sacrifices and temple. For them, it would be a return to the original covenant relationship when Israel first possessed the land. In short, it would be the kingdom of Yahweh once again in which all the people would be a royal priesthood (Exod 19:6), exemplifying their covenant relationship in their dealings with one another, in bringing back the scattered of Israel and Judah, and being a witness before the nations to the power and glory of Yahweh to redeem and to save (Isa 42:6).

It was inevitable that there would be tension between these two ideologies, but there was another problem to be faced by both groups. Not all the people of Judah had been taken into exile. The Babylonians had left many "harmless" people behind in 587 BCE—men, women, and children from the poor of the land (Jer 40:7), and had given them fields and vineyards to cultivate, harvest and pay taxes. Those who remained after the murder of Gedaliah probably came under the jurisdiction of a neighboring provincial officer. People of Edom and Moab had encroached on Judah's territory, and taken over some of the land, and made life even more miserable for the survivors (cf. Lam

5:1–18). Social, political, and religious chaos and cynicism must have been rife with the main emphasis on survival. Yet some continued to offer sacrifices to Yahweh in the temple ruins (Ezra 4:2), sang their lamentations over Jerusalem (e.g., Lamentations, Ps 74), and fasted on the anniversaries of the destruction of Jerusalem, the temple, and the murder of Gedaliah (cf. Zech 7:4; 8:18–19), probably under the leadership of some of the Levites who had been left in the land.[1]

When the first exiles returned, the coming together of different ideologies and claims must have led to much confusion, distrust, and disillusionment. Very little was accomplished under Sheshbazzar. It was not until the priest Joshua and the new governor Zerubbabel, a Davidic descendant, arrived with a much larger group of exiles sometime around 525 BCE that the priestly leaders were able to gain some measure of control leading to the decision in 520 to rebuild the temple.

TRITO-ISAIAH

It is into this general context and time that Isa 56–66 must be placed. The setting of these chapters is clearly Judea after the return had occurred. Deutero-Isaiah's hope and message of restoration is still present, but also evident is disappointment, disillusionment, and conflict. It is obvious that these chapters have come from disciples of Deutero-Isaiah who sought to maintain his message of hope while at the same time relating it to their present situation without always fully comprehending all the implications of their master's vision. Consequently, these chapters are generally understood to be a collection of oracles coming from those who stood in the tradition of Deutero-Isaiah, written after the return during the period from around 538–520 BCE.[2] We can only know the author(s) as Trito-Isaiah.

Trito-Isaiah's Prophetic Community

The small prophetic community which had made the long journey to Judah knew that with the recognition of Yahweh as the only God of creation there had to be new ways of understanding God's purpose for them in relation to all the nations. They were no longer to remember the former things (43:18), but from now on they were to hear new things, hidden things that had not been known or understood before (48:6–7). They knew that they were to be the conveyors of this new and expanded teaching of God for a light to the peoples so that God's salvation would be forever and his righteousness never ending (51:4–8).

However, Trito-Isaiah's community was small, and the opposition to their ideals was strong. Their call to the larger community to practice justice and righteousness with the assurance that God's promised deliverance would soon eventuate and his righteousness be revealed (56:1; cf. 46:12, 13; 51:1–8) was largely ignored. The keeping of the Sabbath, which during the exile had become so important to them as a time for reflection

---

1. Cf. Achtemeier, *Community and Message*, 23.
2. See the discussion in Hanson, *Dawn of the Apocalyptic*, 32–46; Whybray, *Isaiah 40–66*, 39–40.

and worship,[3] and an expression of their covenant relationship with God, was treated like any business day (56:2; 58:13). Moreover, the Zadokite priesthood, following the directives of Ezek 44:9 and the priestly law of Lev 21:16–23, sought to exclude foreigners and eunuchs from participating in public worship at the temple site. Yet these traditions of exclusion were no longer to be remembered. The house of Yahweh was now to be a "house of prayer for all peoples" (56:7). The community of God's people could no longer be regarded as exclusive to Israel. Eunuchs faithful to the covenant would always be honored in the house of God (56:4–5), and foreigners who joined themselves to Yahweh to minister to him would be acknowledged as "servants" of Yahweh, a title by which the community of Trito-Isaiah preferred to be called (56:6–7; cf. 65:8, 13–15). So to the constant theme found in the book of Isaiah of gathering the outcasts of Israel (cf. 11:12; 40:11; 43:5; 45:20; 49:18; 54:7) is added the divine promise that other nations besides Israel would be gathered (56:8).

In the face of opposition motivated by greed, and complete indifference to their concerns, the prophetic minority soon came to the realization that they could no longer think of Israel, or even the returning exiles as "the Righteous One, my Servant, who will cause many to be righteous" (53:11). Stuck in the old tradition of exclusivity, Israel as a nation could not function as God's witness to peoples and nations. So the prophet laments that the Righteous One, as such, has perished, removed from evil and at rest—taken away once again from oppression and judgment because of the transgressions of the people (cf. 53:8, 9).[4] No longer could "Servant" be regarded as a collective term for "men of steadfast love" (57:1–2). From now on the faithful would be identified individually as "servants of Yahweh," as the offspring of the Servant (53:10), following the use of that phrase in 54:17.[5]

Thwarted by the priesthood in their desire to renew Zion, and resisted in their attempts to apportion the ancestral lands by those who had taken possession of them during the exile, the community of Trito-Isaiah felt they were fighting a losing battle and were just as crushed and humbled as the Servant of Isa 53:5, 10. But the divine assurance to them was still: "Whoever takes refuge in me shall inherit the land and take possession of my holy mountain" (57:13b). With the rousing call to "prepare the way, remove every stumbling-block from my people's way" (57:14), the announcement is given to the faithful to remember that they are God's people: "Thus says the high and lofty one, who inhabits eternity, whose name is Holy: I dwell in the high and holy place, and also with the crushed and humble in spirit to revive the spirit of the humble and to revive the heart of the crushed" (57:15). They are not to be discouraged, for God seeks to heal those who are faithless and lack understanding, to lead them, and comfort those who mourn. God desires healing for the far and near to bring about peace. But for those who persist in wickedness there will be no peace (57:16–21). So instead of losing hope the faithful are now told: "Shout out, do not hold back! Lift up your voice like a trumpet! Announce to my people their rebellion, to the house of Jacob their sins!" (58:1).

---

3. Westermann, *Isaiah 40–66*, 310.
4. In agreement with Hanson, *Dawn*, 197.
5. So Beuken, "Main Theme of Trito-Isaiah," 67–68.

This meant speaking out to those in Jerusalem who had not been exiled and had held fast days since the destruction of Jerusalem, mourning their losses (cf. Zech 7:3–5; 8:19). For this they expected judgments of righteousness from God, but were not ready to practice such themselves. Instead, they oppressed those who worked for them, and fought and quarreled with others. They carried out these ritual fastings for their own gain rather than for reflection on their own covenant failures. Their fasting had become a farce (58:2–5). So the prophet entreats the community to live as God's covenant people by setting free those they had enslaved, and removing the yoke of oppression (58:6). Instead of taking advantage of those less fortunate, the covenant called for them to care for the homeless and hungry, giving them every support. Only then could they expect healing and the fulfillment of all the blessings of God. For God's "hand is not too short to save, nor is his ear dull to hear" (59:1; cf. 50:2).

However, there was little change. The prophet saw the struggle for power and survival in the wider community descending into chaos and lawlessness. With its crookedness and greed, he perceived the present generation only producing a brood of vipers even worse than themselves, causing further desolation and destruction spiritually as well as physically (59:2–8). All this led the prophetic minority to raise a lament to God. They saw all the promises of Deutero-Isaiah for justice and righteousness, light and salvation disappearing before their eyes. It had become instead darkness and gloom as if they were blind "groping like those who have no eyes" (59:9–13). So they lamented: "Justice is turned back, and righteousness stands at a distance, for covenant faithfulness stumbles in the public square and uprightness cannot enter. Faithfulness is lacking and he who turns aside from evil is despoiled" (59:14–15).

God's answer to them is that his justice and righteousness will always be there to bring judgment on his adversaries, but "he will come to Zion as Redeemer, to those in Jacob who turn from transgression" (59:16–20). This is Yahweh's covenant with his people. Because of this, Trito-Isaiah's community is given the assurance that God's spirit is upon them and they and their descendants will continue forever to be the conveyors of God's word as the people who have God's teaching written in their hearts (59:21; cf. Isa 51:7).

The graphic description of Yahweh as the Divine Warrior, putting on "righteousness like a breastplate," a "helmet of salvation on his head," "garments of vengeance," and wrapped in a mantle of zeal (59:17) is taken up again in 63:1–6. There Yahweh is depicted as returning from Edom after having carried out the "day of vengeance" against his adversaries before carrying out the "year" of his redeeming work (63:4; cf. 34:8; 61:2). The brief section picks up the motif of judgment against Edom for its treachery from Isa 34, as an illustration to the faithful that Yahweh does bring judgment on his enemies. This is followed by a psalm of lament (63:7–14) which may have originated during the exile.[6] It confesses Israel's rebellion of the past but acknowledges God's deliverance of his people from Egypt through his agent Moses. This serves as a backdrop for an appeal by the disciples of Deutero-Isaiah to call on God to come down and bring about deliverance and restoration of all his people (63:15—64:11).[7]

---

6. Hanson, *Dawn*, 87–89.

7. Williamson ("Isaiah 63:7—64:11," 48–58) argues that all of 63:7—64:11 formed part of an exilic penitential liturgy taken over by Trito-Isaiah.

The call of the prophetic community to God: "Look down from heaven and see, from your holy and glorious habitation" (63:13) is a direct response to the assurance given in 57:15. The repeated cry: "For you are our father" (63:16; 64:7) had previously only been used in regard to Davidic kings (cf. 2 Sam 7:14; Ps 89:27), but since the everlasting covenant and steadfast love for David had been transferred to the faithful (55:3–5), the faithful servants of Yahweh could now address God in this way. While they acknowledged that they were the offspring of father Abraham (41:8; 51:2) and sons of Israel, they were even more so "sons" of the living God (63:8; cf. Hos 1:10) and could appeal to Yahweh as their father.[8] They needed help against their opponents. Yahweh was to return to Zion, but the prophetic community had to acknowledge that God's holy people had lost control of Zion to their adversaries in the Zadokite priesthood (63:18) who claimed sole rights to the temple site.[9] Yet it was the understanding of the prophetic group that just as the kingship had been democratized, so had the priesthood; it was to be a return to the original covenantal relationship in which they were to be "a kingdom of priests and a holy nation" (Exod 19:6; Isa 61:8; 62:12).

What the prophetic community was calling for was a dramatic theophany to cause Yahweh's adversaries to take notice and to turn to him (63:19—64:2). For, they acknowledge, as a nation they have failed, even their righteousnesses have fallen short, and God had hidden himself because of their transgressions. Nevertheless, in spite of their failures as a people, God is still their father, the one who has formed them like a potter who works the clay with his hands (64:7; cf. 29:16; 41:25; 45:9). But now God was silent; Zion and Jerusalem were still in ruins. When would the promise of redemption be fulfilled (64:9–11)?

The divine answer is given in 65:1–16: God has been waiting for the nation to ask and to seek him. But in spite of the warning to "seek Yahweh, while he may be found, call upon him while he is near" (55:6), the people as a whole had not responded but had gone their own way, following their own desires. For this there will be judgment. However, there are good and bad berries in a bunch of grapes, and so the ultimate judgment will be delayed so that the good can bring about the blessings God desires.[10] For the sake of the faithful, blessings will come and they will inherit the land in spite of the faithless among them. The nation as a whole will no longer suffer because of the wickedness of some. Instead, the servants of Yahweh will enjoy all the covenant blessings and be a blessing to others while the godless receive all the covenant curses (vv. 13–16). So the prophetic visionaries are reassured that God is still about to create a new heaven and a new earth. The former things are no longer to be remembered or come to mind (v. 17)—all will be renewed as had been promised, and the faithful will once again live in peace and harmony under the kingship of Yahweh (vv. 18–25; cf. Isa 11:6–9). Just as God

---

8. For a discussion of the wider use of the father-son terminology see Niskanen, "Yhwh," 397–407.

9. Beuken, "Main Theme of Trito-Isaiah," 75, 86, prefers to translate 63:18a as "since a while ago" rather than "for a little while" (NRSV). Hanson, *Dawn*, 95, argues on the basis of the latter translation that it was the Levitical priests who had remained in the land and had carried on worship at the temple site during the exile who are responsible for this lament and had, in opposition to the Zadokites, joined up with the prophetic minority. The fact that the Levites are mentioned in Isa 66:21 gives credence to this view. This view is also followed by Achtemeier, *Community and Message*, 116.

10. See Beuken, "Main Theme of Trito-Isaiah," 77.

had promised the Servant: "I will pour my spirit upon your offspring and my blessing on your descendants" (44:3), so now the offspring of the Servant are assured that "they shall be offspring blessed of Yahweh and their descendants with them" (65:23).

The opposition to the prophetic visionaries grew with the further influx of returnees from exile coming with the high priest, Joshua, and a new governor, Zerubbabel. With their arrival, the call to rebuild the temple was intensified and with it the idea of returning to the traditional sacrificial rituals of the past, as envisioned by Ezekiel. For the "servants of Yahweh," this was all part of the "former things" that were not to be remembered. The sacrificial cult had become tainted with syncretistic worship prior to the destruction of the temple and had not been practiced during the years of the exile. So for the prophetic minority, God's answer to this was (66:1–2):

> Heaven is my throne and the earth is my footstool.
> What is the house that you would build for me, and what is my resting place?
> All these things my hand has made, and so all these things are mine, says Yahweh
> But this is the one to whom I will look, to the one afflicted and crushed in spirit,
> who trembles at my word.

Those "who tremble at his word" (66:5) had argued that God is better glorified by acting in faithfulness to the new covenant relationship, but had been ridiculed and rejected. Yet it is they, who mourn over Jerusalem, who are given the promise that "as a mother comforts her child" Yahweh will bring comfort to them in Jerusalem (66:10–13). The new heaven and the new earth will still come about, and the name of his servants and their offspring will remain as part of it (66:22).

For the disciples of Deutero-Isaiah, the concern for Zion was as strong as their concern for apportioning and inheriting the land. Now that some had returned, it was important that Zion as the symbol of Yahweh's presence among them be upheld as the place where genuine worship could be carried on in covenant faithfulness. Only the faithful were to inherit God's holy mountain (57:13). Zion was to be a place where the afflicted of God's people would find refuge (Isa 14:32; cf. 66:2) and be joyful in his house of prayer (56:7). It was no longer to be a place for idolaters and meaningless ritual (65:3–5; 66:3). Yahweh's servants, his chosen ones, would inherit his mountains and settle there (65:9). Zion was to be a place where all flesh would see and come to know the brilliant presence of Yahweh among them (40:5; 66:18–20). Those who insisted on the necessity of the sacrificial rituals as a means of atonement (cf. Ezek 43:13–27) and as food for Yahweh (Ezek 44:6–8), as a priesthood which claimed greater holiness so as to exclude the faithful, would come under God's judgment (56:3; 65:5; 66:5, 6). Their sacrifices were no better than violence against humanity and the animal world, a mockery of God's creation (66:3).[11] So the prophetic group need not despair for Zion, for the barren one who had not been in labor (54:1), would suddenly and miraculously give birth to God's faithful people, and Jerusalem would be their wet-nurse to comfort them (66:7–13).[12]

---

11. Trito-Isaiah and his community do not entirely reject sacrifice (see 60:7), nor do they reject the temple as a house of prayer. But they do reject the false understanding of the purpose and use of the temple and sacrifice. See Wim Beuken, "Does Trito-Isaiah Reject the Temple?," 53–66.

12. Biddle, "Lady Zion's Alter Ego," 124–39, argues that because Zion has not changed, it will be

Trito-Isaiah's Opponents

The numerous expressions of conflict in Isa 56–66 make it clear that the background for these chapters is a constant struggle for power and influence going on in the Judean community. The first small group of returning exiles found that they were far outnumbered by those already living in Jerusalem and Judea and could not easily impose their leadership on the existing community. There were the powerful "people of the land" (Ezra 4:4; Hag 2:4; Zech 7:5; cf. Ezra 3:3; 9:1, 2, 11; 10:2, 11; Neh 9:30; 10:29, 31, 32) who had no intention of relinquishing the land they occupied for any redistribution program along the lines of Ezek 47:21–23 or the priestly ordinance regarding the Jubilee year, a law probably developed during the exile which required the return of property in the fiftieth year to its original owner (Lev 25:8–34; 27:17–24; Num 36:4; cf. Ezek 46:17 and Isa 61:2). These "people of the land" sent envoys with gifts to the Persian king when they heard of the impending return of the exiles in order to be guaranteed they would retain their land (57:9–13).[13] The issue of land inheritance continued to remain one of the contentious issues as more returnees arrived.

Levites who had remained in the land had continued worshipping and offering sacrifices at the temple site during the exile were loathe to move aside for the returning Zadokite priests who claimed authority from Cyrus to rebuild the temple, and took over the site. While the people of the land had continued to worship Yahweh and to keep fast days commemorating the siege and destruction of Jerusalem and the murder of Gedaliah (cf. Zech 7:3–5; 8:18–19), they often treated the returning exiles with contempt (58:6–7; 57:4).[14] The prophet pleaded with them to share their bread with the hungry, and bring the homeless into their houses, and so be a light in the darkness (58:7, 10) and witness the renewal of the land (58:11–12). But the pleas were often ignored, infighting, oppression and crooked ways continued, which led the prophet to describe them as a brood of vipers (59:3–8)!

The returning Zadokite priests had come with the intention of rebuilding the temple and beginning Ezekiel's restoration program. They began by excluding foreigners from participation in worship at the site on the basis of Ezek 44:6–9 and eunuchs on the basis of Lev 21:17–23. Trito-Isaiah, representing the prophetic minority, registered his strong protest against this narrow, conservative attitude, for it denied the Isaianic vision to accept all nations and people into the covenant community (56:1–8). Since Ezekiel described his role as "watchman" (Ezek 3:17; 33:2–7), the prophet called the priests "watchmen that are blind" and "without knowledge" of God, the "dumb dogs that cannot bark" (56:10). The Zadokites ousted the Levites from officiating at the temple site on the basis of Ezek 44:13 ("They shall not come near to me to serve me as priest, nor come near any of my holy things"), echoed in Isa 65:5 where the perpetrators of false

---

replaced. With the new heaven and new earth, there will a new Zion/Jerusalem.

13. Achtemeier, *Community and Message*, 42–43, argues that the envoys made their journey to "urge that their cultic life be restored." However, with the change in rule in Babylon they were probably more concerned about retaining the land Nebuchadnezzar had given them to work. Isaiah 57:13 would bear that out.

14. Cf. Blenkinsopp, *Isaiah 56–66*, 155–62; Schramm, *Opponents of Trito-Isaiah*, 128–33.

worship say, "Approach yourself, do not come near to me, for I am holier than you." In Isa 65:1–7, 11–12 the cultic abominations which Ezekiel had blamed on the Levites (44:10) are now attributed to the Zadokites.[15] They, together with the people of the land who have rejected Yahweh's call, are condemned in a series of curses (65:13–16) in contrast to the blessings given to the servants of Yahweh. Trito-Isaiah condemned in the strongest possible terms their cultic sacrifices as worse than pagan abominations (66:1–4). The Zadokite priesthood under the leadership of the high priest Joshua had firm control of the temple site, and this ridicule was addressed directly to them.[16] Nevertheless, the whole community was now permanently divided. The prophetic minority could now only wait for God's judgment on the priesthood (66:6) and look forward to a new heaven and a new earth in the future (66:22–23).

While the Levites generally sided with the prophetic minority in their opposition to the Zadokite priesthood and emphasis on covenant faithfulness, they disagreed with them on their democratization of both the priesthood and Davidic kingship. As followers of the Levite prophet Jeremiah, they held firmly to the promise of an ideal Davidic king and to the covenant with the Levites that they would serve at God's altar. To emphasize this, they apparently had added Jer 33:14–26, which is not found in the LXX version of Jeremiah, to the Hebrew text in the early postexilic period to counteract their rejection from serving at the altar by the Zadokites, and the claims of the disciples of Deutero-Isaiah that the everlasting covenant made with David had been transferred to the faithful.[17] In these verses the promise is repeated that God would cause a branch of righteousness to spring up for David (33:15; cf. 23:5), and the covenants made with David and the Levites would never be revoked any more than God would revoke his covenants with day and night and with the ordinances of heaven and earth (33:25, 26). Both covenants would be perpetuated and multiplied as the stars of heaven and the sands of the sea, along the lines of the promises to Abraham (33:22; cf. Gen 15:5; 17:5–7; 22:17). Trito-Isaiah responds to these claims with a restatement of the prophetic vision found in Isa 60–62.

The Renewed Prophetic Vision

In the midst of the tension and conflict, with the resulting disillusionment for many among the prophetic group, Trito-Isaiah comes out with a strongly positive reaffirmation of Deutero-Isaiah's program of restoration. The divine plan will be carried out in even more dramatic fashion in the future, but this time it will not be tied to a particular historical event. This renewed vision is set out in chs. 60–62 in the midst of the writings of Trito-Isaiah as the key to the whole. Speaking *as* faithful Israel, the Servant of Yahweh, who is filled with the Spirit of God (61:1; cf. 42:1), the prophet heralds the good news

---

15. See Hansen, *Dawn*, 147–50; also Achtemeier, *Community and Message*, 124. Cf. Tiemeyer, "Haughtiness of the Priesthood," 237–44.

16. Cf. Rofé, "Isaiah 66:1–4," 205–17.

17. The fact that Jer 33:14–26 is not found in the LXX has often been taken as evidence that this was a later insertion. See particularly Holladay, *Jeremiah II*, 227–35. See also Pomykala, *Davidic Dynasty Tradition*, 42–45; and Roberts, "Old Testament's Contribution," 47–49.

(61:1; cf. 40:9; 52:7) as one restored to the true covenant relationship with God in concert with Zion (61:10; cf. 50:1-2; 54:4-8).

The first major reaffirmation is that the faithful, as restored Israel, are to be the light to the nations (60:1-22). Zion is addressed as the focal point of the returned exiles, as the place where the faithful associate with, and are enlivened by, Yahweh as their King. So those who sit in darkness are assured that the light, which is the brilliant presence of God (*kabod*) has come upon them. This is the light they have been called to reflect to the nations (42:6, 7, 16; 49:6; 51:4). Whereas Ezekiel (43:2-5) had envisioned the *kabod* of Yahweh returning to Jerusalem to fill the temple, Trito-Isaiah speaks of the *kabod* as filling the people themselves as the true community of Zion (60:1-3):

> Arise, shine, for your light has come!
> For the *kabod* of Yahweh has risen upon you!
> For behold, darkness shall cover the earth,
> and thick darkness the peoples.
> But upon you Yahweh shall arise,
> and his *kabod* will be *seen* upon you.
> Then nations will come to your light,
> and kings to the brightness of your rising!

Yahweh himself will be their everlasting light (60:19, 20; cf. 66:18, 19). Through their relationship with God the faithful can reflect that light to the nations, so that those still living in exile will be permitted to return to Judah (60:4-16). That reflection of God's presence, as had been explained earlier (58:8, 10), happens when people respond to God's steadfast love with righteousness and compassion towards others.

As a result of their radiance, the nations and kings will shower their wealth on Zion, bringing gifts of gold and frankincense (60:6), acknowledging Yahweh as God and bringing their offerings (60:6-7; 61:9). Foreigners will help build their walls (60:10) because no longer will God's people be oppressed. Those nations that will not acknowledge Yahweh will perish or be brought to submission (60:12-14). So God's rule will be restored in Zion/Jerusalem with peace and righteousness (60:17). In this ideal situation Zion's people shall *all* be righteous and shall possess the land forever, for *they* are the "shoot" (*netser*) of Yahweh's planting, a term used previously in Isa 11:1 for an ideal descendant of David (cf. Jer 23:5-6 and 33:15-16). Restored to faithfulness they will glorify God in their righteousness (60:21-22; 61:3; 62:1-3).

Speaking as the Servant of Yahweh and herald of good news in ch. 61, Trito-Isaiah emphasizes not only the restoration which God will bring about, but also how God's faithful will play a part in that restoration and act as a corporate witness to the nations. Isa 61:1-3 draws in many allusions to Deutero-Isaiah, especially to chs. 42 and 49, to illustrate that he is speaking as the faithful in the role of the Servant. In 61:1 the Spirit of God has been bestowed as in 42:1; the good news of the reign of God is announced, as in 40:9; 41:27; 52:7, to the afflicted (49:13; cf. 41:17; 51:21; 54:11; 66:2); the Servant is to bind up the broken-hearted (cf. 42:3; Jer 23:9; Ezek 34:16), and to proclaim liberty to the captives as in 42:7; 49:9, 25. In 61:2, 3 Yahweh has anointed the prophet-Servant to proclaim the year of favor for Yahweh, as in 42:1 and 49:8 (cf. 58:5 and 60:10), and the day of vengeance as in 34:8; 35:4; 47:3 (cf. 57:19 and 63:4); to comfort all who mourn as in 40:1; etc (cf. 60:20; 66:13; Jer 31:13–15) so that they are clothed in joy and praise as in 35:10; 51:3, 11 (cf. 31:13) instead of a faint spirit (cf. 40:29–31; 42:3).[18]

As has been noted earlier, the transfer of the everlasting covenant made with David to the faithful is taken very seriously by Trito-Isaiah. Terms and descriptions of kings in the past are now used of the people. In 60:21, the righteous ones are called the "shoot" of God's planting (cf. 11:1). This "shoot" will grow into "oaks of righteousness, the planting of Yahweh" (61:3; cf. 11:4, 5). Speaking as representative of the righteous ones, the prophet announces that the Spirit of the Lord Yahweh is upon him, as upon the ideal king in 11:2 (cf. 42:1),[19] because Yahweh has anointed him, as was David (1 Sam 16:13; 2 Sam 23:1–5; Ps 89:21, 39, 52) to bring the good news to the afflicted (61:1). These "afflicted" become the recipients of the "oil of gladness" as was the king in Ps 45:8. That everlasting covenant is thus reaffirmed (61:8). As Zion's people, the faithful become the "crown of beauty" and a "royal diadem" in the hand of Yahweh who reigns (62:3).

As Isa 55:3–5 was a response to the cry of the royalists in Ps 89, so Isa 61:5—62:5 appears to have been a response to the disciples of Jeremiah who had emphatically claimed that God would not break his covenants with David and the Levites in Jer 33:14–26. Trito-Isaiah's response is that both of these covenants have been transferred to the people. In 61:6, the faithful are called the "priests of Yahweh" and "ministers of our God," the same terms used for the Levitical priests in Jer 33:18, 21, 22. This is a return to the ideal of Exod 19:6, which Paul Hanson has called "an astonishing democratization of the formerly exclusive sacerdotal office."[20] The faithful being clothed in the garments of salvation and the robe of righteousness, adorned as bridegroom and bride, rejoicing greatly (61:10) recalls the promise in Jeremiah of future renewal when there would be heard once again "the voice of joy, the voice of gladness, the voice of the bridegroom and the voice of the bride" (Jer 33:11; cf. 7:34; 16:9; 25:10, 11). Moreover, just as Jer 33:15 had reaffirmed the promise of Jer 23:5 with the words: "I will cause a shoot of righteousness to shoot forth for David," so Isa 61:11 says of the faithful "so the Lord Yahweh will cause righteousness and praise to shoot forth before the nations."

In response to the claim that because of the everlasting covenant with David and the Levites their offspring would be multiplied in Jer 33:22, 26, Isa 61:8–9 speaks of the everlasting covenant with the faithful leading to *their* offspring becoming known among the nations as the "offspring whom Yahweh has blessed." Finally, whereas Jer 33:16 mentioned that Jerusalem would be given a new name, "Yahweh is our Righteousness," Trito-Isaiah affirms that Zion/Jerusalem would be "called by a new name which the mouth of Yahweh will designate" (62:1–2). Instead of being called "Forsaken" and "Desolate," Zion/Jerusalem would be called "My Delight Is in Her" and the land "Married" (64:4; cf. Hos 2:20–23).[21] However, the faithful get a new name too: "They shall be called 'The

---

18. Cf. Hanson, *Dawn*, 65–67; Achtemeier, *Community and Message*, 88–90; Beuken, "Servant and Herald," 415–24.

19. See further Sommer, *Prophet Reads Scripture*, 86–87.

20. Hanson, *Dawn*, 67.

21. For different approaches see Anderson, "Renaming and Wedding Imagery," 75–80; Halpern, "New Names," 623–43; Williamson, "Isaiah 62:4," 734–39.

Holy People, the Redeemed of Yahweh'" (62:12). Holiness will not be something that can be claimed only by the Zadokite priesthood (cf. Ezek 44:19; 46:20).

When will all this happen? No specific time is given, but the faithful are to trust in their God that he will bring it to pass. In 60:22 they are told: "I am Yahweh; in its time I will accomplish it quickly." Yahweh will not keep silent or rest until righteousness and salvation have been accomplished for Zion/Jerusalem (62:1). In fact, the faithful are to be the watchmen on the walls of Jerusalem, never being silent day or night in reminding Yahweh to take no rest "until he establishes Jerusalem and makes it renowned throughout the earth" (62:6–7). In the meantime the people are to prepare for the return of all the dispersed of Israel and for the nations coming to Zion. For Yahweh has proclaimed to the end of the earth: "Say to daughter Zion, 'Behold, your salvation comes. Behold, his reward is with him and his recompense before him'" (62:10–11; cf. 11:11–16; 40:10). God's gracious desire to bring about righteousness is not in question, but the delay in the fulfillment has already been seen as the result of the people's general lack of response.

The dual democratization of the Davidic covenant and the role of the priesthood is again evident in the function of the prophet in 61:2–3 "to provide for those who mourn in Zion—to give them a *turban* instead of ashes, the oil of gladness instead of mourning." The "turban" was part of the required dress of a Zadokite priest (Ezek 44:18; cf. Exod 39:28) and, as noted above, the "oil of gladness" was the anointing for a king in Ps 45:8. The turban is mentioned again in 61:10 when the prophet, speaking collectively, describes himself as being clothed in the garments of salvation and the robe of righteousness "as a bridegroom priest-like decks himself with a turban."[22] The verb *kahan* ("act as priest") here clearly connects with 61:6 where the people are told, "you shall be called priests of Yahweh, ministers of our God." These expressions, combined with the allusions to Isa 11:1–16[23] and Jer 33:10–26 in these chapters (60–62) make for a strong emphasis of the democratization of both the royal and priestly functions. For *all* God's faithful people would be priests to instruct the nations in the ways of God and witnesses to his divine kingship. This would even include foreigners who "minister to Yahweh" (Isa 56:3, 6; cf. 66:21).

The prophet, as Servant, was sent to bring good news to the afflicted, to proclaim God's reign bringing justice for those who have been unjustly treated, to bind up the broken-hearted, to proclaim liberty to the captives and release to the prisoners (61:1). While for Deutero-Isaiah these meant freedom from exile, here, for Trito-Isaiah, they refer more to freedom from injustice and oppression causing economic slavery (cf. 58:3, 6, 9, 10). The faithful are promised that instead of shame and dishonor they will possess a double portion while those who rob others and present burnt offerings to God will be rejected (61:7, 8). This is a response to conflict within the community, referred to in Isa 58, where people practiced fasting while at the same time treating others unjustly,[24] and to the deceit used by some to claim inherited land by means of an oath at the altar with an offering (cf. Deut 29:13–21; 1 Kgs 8:31–32; Zech 5:1–4). There will be a day

22. Using the translation from Beuken, "Servant and Herald," 433.

23. Cf. Sweeney, "Reconceptualization of the Davidic Covenant," 57–60.

24. Beuken, "Servant and Herald," 430. The NRSV follows the LXX in translating, "I hate robbery and wrongdoing."

of vengeance, but it will be a year of Yahweh's favor towards the afflicted, the broken-hearted, the captives and prisoners, and those who mourn. These are the righteous ones who will eventually build up the ancient ruins, raise up the former devastations and repair the ruined city (61:1–4), as was promised by Deutero-Isaiah (44:26, 28; 45:13) and reaffirmed also in 58:12 and 60:10. But this time "they shall build houses and live in them; they shall plant vineyards and eat their fruit; they shall not plant and another eat" (65:21–22; 62:8–9). This expresses the reversal of what Jeremiah had predicted prior to the exile (Jer 5:17).

However, the recurring emphasis on possessing the land points to the ongoing struggle there must have been for the returning exiles to gain possession of land. Debt and enslavement seems to have been common. The phrase in 61:1, "to proclaim liberty to the captives" appears to be an allusion to the law of the Jubilee year in Lev 25:10 which proclaims that every person who lost his inheritance through debt and slavery was to be set free and was to be returned to his property (Lev 25:10, 13). The land was never to be sold in perpetuity because it belongs to God (Lev 25:23). The "year of Yahweh's favor" (61:2) in this context must refer to this jubilee year, expressing the hope for the redemption of the land by those who had returned from exile.[25]

Faithfulness to the covenant relationship is the basic criterion for the restoration of the reign of Yahweh. This is evident also in Trito-Isaiah's insistence that the foreigner and the eunuch who "hold fast my covenant" are to be part of God's community in the restored kingdom (56:4, 6). Such sincere faithfulness takes precedence over cultic purity, ritual, and racial origins as expressions of covenant relationship. On those who demonstrate such faithfulness Yahweh bestows his Spirit and puts his words in their mouths as his covenant response (59:21). Once again the marriage metaphor is used to emphasize the relational aspect of the covenant (61:10; 62:1–5; cf. 50:1–2; 54:4–8), as also is that of a father with his children (63:10; 64:8–9). The list of covenant blessings and curses appear in 65:13–16, a much shorter list than that given in Deut 27–28.

Trito-Isaiah's approach to the nations has sometimes been described as nationalistic and condescending.[26] However, he sees the nations as coming into the community of God's people on the basis of entering into the covenant relationship just as he does the people of Judah. That is evident already in 56:6–7 where the prophet maintains that "foreigners who join themselves to Yahweh, to minister to him, to love the name of Yahweh, and to be his servants, are to be accepted into God's house of prayer, which is for all peoples." It is the light of God's presence in Zion reflected through his faithful people that will draw the nations into that covenant relationship. So Zion is told: "Nations shall come to your light, and kings to the brightness of your dawn" (60:3). When they come they will be bringing back Zion's sons and daughters, gifts of gold and frankincense as to a king, and animals to be offered as sacrifices to God. In acknowledging Yahweh as the only God they will bring their wealth to build the walls of the city which they had previously broken down and to beautify Yahweh's sanctuary (60:4–13). However, any nation or kingdom that would refuse to serve Yahweh as their God would come under judgment (60:12). As the servants of Yahweh the faithful will becomes priests and min-

---

25. Cf. Whybray, *Isaiah 40–66*, 241; Gregory, "Postexilic Exile," 483–88.
26. See, for instance, Whybray, *Isaiah 40–66*, 231, 243.

isters to the nations who will reward them accordingly as a way of serving the true God (61:5–6). For the nations will acknowledge the descendants of the faithful as the people whom Yahweh has blessed (61:9).

With a final rebuke of those in Judah who persist in false worship (66:17), the prophet announces that God will gather all nations and tongues, and they will come and see his *kabod*. From these, some shall go to those peoples who have not heard of Yahweh's *kabod* among the nations. Thus, the promise in Isa 40:5 would be fulfilled. These nations will bring back all those of Israel who had been scattered among the nations as offerings to Yahweh. Some of those bringing these "offerings" will then serve Yahweh as priests, as Levites (66:18–21). All these new ways will be part of the new heavens and the new earth, the transformation which Yahweh will bring about in its time, and all flesh shall come to worship before him (66:22–23). In the writings of the unnamed authors of Isa 40–66, the prophetic vision has reached its height, to be fulfilled in God's time. The divine assurance given in Isa 55:11 that God's word shall not return to him empty but shall accomplish that which he purposes, still holds good.

DIFFERING CONTEMPORARY PROPHETIC VIEWS

Very little effort had been made during Sheshbazzar's governorship to rebuild the temple. It was not only the difficult struggle for the early returnees to adjust to the various challenges they faced, conflicts with those who claimed the land, but also poverty, taxes and conflicting ideologies. There were those also who felt that it was not yet the right time to build, that God's anger for seventy years had not yet been fulfilled (cf. Hag 1:2; Zech 1:12).[27] As well, the disciples of Deutero-Isaiah, while Zion was important to them, did not see the building of the temple as necessary with its implication of a return to the old sacrificial rituals (Isa 66:1–6).

Nevertheless, it was the Persian policy to encourage reconstruction and maintenance of regional temples, not only as religious centers for the local people, but also as centers for provincial administration within the empire. Part of the cost of maintaining the temple as such was to come out of the royal treasury (cf. Ezra 6:4–9; 7:15–22; 8:25–30). Such a policy encouraged loyalty to the empire and gave the people some degree of control over their own affairs. For that reason governors were usually chosen from the province's own leaders. Sheshbazzar himself had been one of the exiles and possibly was of Davidic descent (cf. 1 Chr 3:17–18: Shenazzar).[28]

Cyrus died in a military campaign in 530 BCE and was succeeded by his son, Cambyses. When Cambyses was in Egypt, having carried out a successful campaign to bring Egypt under Persian control in 525, he received word that his brother, Bardiya, had claimed the throne in his absence. Returning to deal with the revolt in 522, Cambyses died on the way, and one of his officers, Darius, took his place. By September 29, 522,

---

27. Cf. Bedford, "Haggai, Zechariah," 71–94; Kessler, "Building the Second Temple," 243–56; Hurowitz, "Restoring the Temple," 581–91.

28. Cf. Balentine, "Politics of Religion," 129–46; Trotter, "Was the Second Jerusalem Temple a Primarily Persian Project?," 276–94; Fried, *The Priest and the Great King*, 161–64.

Darius had slain Bardiya and taken over the Persian throne, but then had to deal with a series of revolts.[29]

Around this time, possibly appointed by Darius in 522 (or earlier by Cambyses) to strengthen Yehud's loyalty to the Persian Empire, came Zerubbabel, a grandson of Jehoiachin, as governor to replace Sheshbazzar. He was accompanied by the high priest Joshua, son of Jehozadak, together with a large contingent of returning exiles. Evidently, the task given to them was to get the temple rebuilt and develop an orderly system of administration and law in Yehud. Meanwhile, Darius found himself busy putting down a series of revolts within the empire which were to last until the end of November 521.[30] Against this background of continuing turmoil throughout the empire, the new returnees spent their time taking control of the province and settling in. But with the aspect of a new governor of Davidic descent and a Zadokite high priest with his priestly companions, there soon was a renewed cry to get on with rebuilding the temple and a growing hope for greater autonomy.

The Prophet Haggai

The first to call for action was the prophet Haggai who spoke out for a short period of three and a half months (from August 29 to December 18, 520) chiding the returnees for living in their paneled houses while the temple still lay in ruins, calling upon them to gather material for building the temple, and declaring that they were suffering drought because God had withheld his blessings from them because *his* house was still "lying in ruins" (Hag 1:1–11). Because of this they were still under the covenant curse uttered by Jeremiah (25:8–11), suffering from not having enough to eat or drink or clothing to keep them warm (1:6; Deut 28:48). Twice he urged them to ponder their self-centered ways (1:5, 7), and to turn to see God's ways and build his house. Then the curse would turn to blessing.

Three weeks after Haggai's initial call to rebuild the temple, Zerubbabel, Joshua and the returnees responded and began work on the temple site. But a month later, during the Feast of Booths, the harvest festival, which was also the anniversary of the dedication of Solomon's great temple, there was general disappointment over the slow progress being made and the poor harvests experienced. So Haggai had to encourage everyone to keep working on the project and God would fill it with splendor and would bring blessing. By December 18, the foundation was laid and Haggai could promise that from that day, they would be blessed.

Haggai probably came from a family which had never been deported.[31] In calling for the rebuilding of the temple he usually addressed the returnees explicitly as "Zerubbabel son of Shealtiel, governor of Judah, and Joshua son of Jehozadak, the high priest, and all the remnant of the people" (1:12, 14; 2:2). The prophet Zechariah (8:6, 11, 12) used

---

29. Darius later claimed that Cambyses had secretly killed his brother Bardiya prior to leaving on his Egyptian campaign in 525 BCE, and that it was a Magus named Gaumata who had claimed to be Bardiya and had usurped the Persian throne. See Olmstead, *History of the Persian Empire*, 107–9.

30. Ibid., 110–16.

31. In agreement with Wolff, *Haggai*, 17, 38.

the term "remnant" specifically of the returnees, as it was later used in Ezra 9:14; Neh 7:71; and 2 Chr 36:20. Yet at the harvest festival in October, where many of the country people would have been present, Haggai also called on "the people of the land" to take courage and soon the temple would be completed in splendor (2:4). The "people of the land," those who had remained in the country were generally regarded by the returnees as unclean, leading Haggai to question the priests about how they distinguished between clean and unclean. Holiness is not contagious, the priests affirmed, but uncleanness is (Ezek 44:25, 26). This gave Haggai the opportunity to make his point that it was the whole nation, not only the people of the land, but also the returnees including the priesthood, who were unclean by association, for all had neglected the building of the temple up to this time and had suffered lack (2:10-14). But now, with the foundation-laying, Judah's fortunes would turn from curse to blessing.

There are other indications that Haggai had become familiar with Ezekiel's plan of restoration (Ezek 40-48) with its central focus on the temple. According to him, the reason God gave to the people for building the temple (in 1:8) was "that I may accept [you] in it, and that I may be glorified." This picks up the description of the Presence of Yahweh entering the new temple (Ezek 43:2, 4, 5) with instructions for the final preparations upon which Yahweh would say, "I will accept you" (43:27). Yet Haggai's concern for the temple is not for the continuation of the sacrificial rites but that God would be present in it to bring blessing. This is clear from his use of the term *kabod* in 2:7-9 where it is understood in terms of the wealth the nations will bring to Judah in the great reversal that will happen when God will shake the nations with his presence (cf. Ezek 38:17-23). This is not the picture of the nations willingly bringing their gifts to Zion as in Isa 60:1-13.

However, it is in his final oracle (2:20-23) that Haggai shows his real colors. Whereas in his previous oracles he has always made sure to address both Zerubbabel and Joshua as leaders, this final message is for Zerubbabel alone. Conscious of the various rebellions within the Persian empire which have plagued Darius, Haggai saw this as possibly inaugurating the great and final battle in which Darius would be "Gog" of Ezek 38:18-23, and the Persian empire, would be overthrown. Then Judah would have the opportunity to become a kingdom once again with Zerubbabel as Davidic king at its helm. He thus addressed Zerubbabel as God's "servant" as was David in 2 Sam 7, and as "son of Shealtiel" to underline his Davidic descent as grandson of King Jehoiachin who had been taken into exile in 597 BCE. Jeremiah had spoken of Jehoiachin as God's signet ring which God had taken off his right hand and hurled into the land of exile (Jer 22:24-30). Now, Haggai believed, there would be a dramatic reversal of that prophecy, just as he had already promised such a reversal of Judah's fortunes. Now Zerubbabel would be God's signet ring, his representative, his chosen one (2:23). It would be a return to the Davidic dynasty as of old. But it was not to be.

The Prophet Zechariah

Zechariah was a prophet of priestly background. His grandfather Iddo (Zech 1:1) was one of the chief Zadokite priests who brought his family to Jerusalem from the exile in company with Zerubbabel and the high priest Joshua (Neh 12:17). As a Zadokite priest he favored the strong role that the high priest and priesthood were to play in the restoration as outlined in Ezek 40–48. However, he was also conscious of the criticisms made by some of his contemporaries against the Zadokite priesthood, as well as other differing points of view held by some regarding the rebuilding of the temple and the directions the community should take. Aware of the skepticism of the prophetic visionaries to his claim to be a prophet, he makes some concessions to their vision and frequently adds the refrain, "then you will know that Yahweh of hosts has sent me to you" (2:9, 11; 4:9; 6:15), after a prophetic pronouncement.

Zechariah's message is conveyed by means of a series of eight night visions (1:7—6:15) followed by a number of oracles (7:1—8:23). It is by means of these graphic images that the prophet conveys his message of how the restored community was to establish itself as the people of God under the leadership of the Zadokite priesthood. While his first proclamation, the call to repentance (1:1–6), was uttered around October 27, 520 BCE, before Haggai's final oracles at the time of the foundation-laying, his first vision comes a couple of months later, on February 15, 519. It is to announce that Haggai's hope for the overthrow of the Persian empire will not happen at this time, for "all the earth is quiet and at peace" (1:11), and Darius is now fully in control of his empire. Yet the comfort and compassion of God would still come about, for Yahweh has now returned to Jerusalem because the temple is being built: "Yahweh will still comfort Zion and will still choose Jerusalem" (1:13–17).

By means of the next two visions, using language reminiscent of Ezekiel, Zechariah assures his audience that God *will* judge the nations and diminish their power (1:18–21), and Jerusalem shall be expanded from its former boundaries with the return of those still living in exile. The only wall they will need for their security is the brilliant presence of God as a wall of fire (2:1–5). For these reasons he calls on those exiles still in Babylonia to flee from the coming judgment on the nations and come to Zion where Yahweh will protect them. Influencing this call is Ezekiel's picture of Gog who comes to plunder the cities without walls in Judah (Ezek 38–39) but who will be defeated by Yahweh (2:6–10). Yet, in expressing the hope that "many nations will join themselves to Yahweh on that day" (2:11), Zechariah goes beyond Ezekiel and makes some concession to the Isaianic hope and the appeal that aliens and foreigners who "join themselves" to Yahweh would be accepted in the community of God's people (Isa 2:2–4; 14:1; 56:3–6; 66:18–21).

Nevertheless, Zechariah is committed to Ezekiel's plan for the Zadokite priesthood and affirms this in his fourth vision (3:1–10). In response to Trito-Isaiah's claim that the priesthood has been democratized, that all are priests and ministers of God (Isa 61:6), and Haggai's assertion that *all* are unclean (Hag 2:14), Zechariah depicts Joshua the high priest and his associates in a heavenly tribunal being declared clean and given increased power and authority by God. Joshua stands as defendant in the heavenly court before God as judge with the accuser, Satan, at his right hand (cf. Ps 109:6). But Satan's accusation of past corruption is rendered out-of-date, for God has again chosen Jerusalem and is no longer angry (3:2; cf. 2:12). The high priest was to be seen as "a brand plucked from the fire," of God's wrath (Isa 66:15, 16; Ezek 22:21–22, 26–31).

Zechariah thus sees the high priesthood exonerated as a symbol of divine favor rather than of divine judgment. As a consequence, Joshua is divested of garments filthy with excrement (3:4; cf. Ezek 4:12–15), symbolizing the former guilt and uncleanness of the priesthood, and is clothed in fine garments, the holy linen garments to be worn by the priests in the holy place of the temple (Ezek 42:14; 44:19). All this was to symbolize that the priesthood was now cleared of all past guilt and was ready to receive the new powers promised in the restoration plan of Ezek 40–48. Impulsively, Zechariah himself then interjects in the vision with the statement: "Let them put a clean turban on his head." One would have expected him to use the word employed for a priestly turban found in Ezek 44:18; Exod 39:28 (cf. Isa 61, 3, 10), but he preferred to use the term employed in Isa 62:3 to describe faithful Zion as a "royal turban" in the palm of God. The turban was a symbol of bearing the authority of God which Zechariah was claiming exclusively for Joshua the high priest in accordance with Ezek 44:15–24. Joshua is then charged to walk in the ways of God and to render judgment in God's house and have charge of his courts. The function of judging, formerly a royal responsibility, is passed onto the high priest as upholder of God's covenant law (3:7) as was specified in Ezekiel's restoration program (Ezek 44:24).[32] But now even the privilege of access to the divine assembly, up to this time recorded only of prophets (e.g., 1 Kgs 22:19–22; Isa 6:1–8; 40:1–9; Zechariah himself in this vision), is given to Joshua and his Zadokite priesthood. Thus *all* theocratic rule is to be channeled through the priesthood.

The Zadokite priesthood is referred to as "men of portent" (3:8), men who will serve as "signs" or "symbols" of God's action and plan, just as Isaiah and his children (Isa 8:18; 20:3) and Ezekiel (Ezek 12:6, 11; 24:24, 27) were said to be. The Zadokite priesthood now established in its central position is to be seen as the God-given sign that the priestly plan will be brought to completion with the building of the temple under the auspices of "my servant the Shoot" (v. 8), that is, Zerubbabel. Haggai (2:23) had specifically referred to him as "my [God's] servant," and being of Davidic descent he was seen as the one who would fulfill the hope expressed in Jer 23:5 and 33:15 as the "righteous shoot" from David's line. From Zechariah's point of view, it was Zerubbabel as such a future king who would be responsible for the completion of the temple (6:12, 13). Thus the plan outlined in Ezek 45:7–25 would be carried out with the future messianic king in a diminished role. This was a subtle correction of Haggai's giving the central focus to Zerubbabel as the potential king (2:20–23).

After this brief reference to Zerubbabel, the focus is returned to Joshua in his high-priestly clothing, specifically, to the stone affixed to his ephod. According to Exod 28:9–12 two onyx stones engraved with the names of the twelve tribes of Israel were to be affixed to the ephod of Aaron to indicate that he represented them all before Yahweh. Here only "a single stone with seven facets" is mentioned, inscribed, presumably, with the "nation of Judah," to indicate that it is through Joshua that the guilt of the whole land is now removed and the prosperity mentioned by Haggai will soon be evident (vv. 9–10).[33]

With all that authority invested in the priesthood, the question of the relationship of the high priest to the Davidide Zerubbabel needed to be dealt with. This is the point of the fifth vision (4:1–14) in which Zechariah sees a golden menorah on the top of which

---

32. Cf. Segal, "Responsibilities and Rewards of Joshua," 720–26.
33. See Vanderkam, "Joshua the High Priest," 533–70.

is a bowl containing oil which in turn feeds seven lamps, each of which contains seven wicks. Patterned somewhat on the menorah described in Exod 25:31–35 and 37:17–20, the seven lamps, each with its output intensified by the seven wicks, give a picture of brilliant light beaming out in every direction, thus symbolizing the brilliant comforting and guiding presence of God (cf. Ps 18:29; 119:105). On either side of the menorah is an olive tree presumably feeding its essential oil into the bowl at the top of the menorah (4:2–3). These two olive trees represent the two leaders in the restored community as Ezekiel had outlined (44:15—46:18). Both priest and prince have their specific roles as channels in the people's worship of Yahweh. According to Ezekiel, the priesthood was to carry out the sacrificial rituals using the offerings brought to them by the prince who, in turn, had gathered them from the people.

Zechariah's question as to the meaning of this vision is brushed aside momentarily, and the vision is interrupted by statements made to Zerubbabel (4:6–10a). While these verses are often seen as a later insertion,[34] they nevertheless prepare the audience for the answer to be given in vv. 10b–14. In these statements the position and function of Zerubbabel is addressed in the light of the previous vision which emphasized the authority of the high priest, Joshua. First Zerubbabel is addressed: "Not by might, not by power, but by my spirit, says Yahweh of hosts" (v. 6). Zerubbabel is not there in order to establish independent leadership or to oppress the people (with Ezek 45:9 in mind). Those who see in Zerubbabel hope for the reestablishment of the traditional Davidic kingship are mistaken. He is to carry out his role only as Yahweh's spirit leads him. For the present, that role is to complete the building of the temple. The great mountain of stones at the site are to be used in the building until that mountain becomes a level plain under Zerubbabel's leadership and the job is completed. So then the people can shout enthusiastic approval as Zerubbabel lays the final headstone in place (v. 7).[35] This message, directed to Zerubbabel, is now confirmed by Zechariah (v. 9) with the assurance that those who scorned the day of the foundation laying will rejoice when they witness Zerubbabel actively completing the temple (v. 10a).

Now that the role of Zerubbabel has been clarified, Zechariah can continue with the explanation of the vision. The seven lamps are "the eyes of Yahweh" who keeps watch over everything that happens (v. 10b). The two stalks of the olive trees pouring their liquid gold through golden pipes into the bowl are interpreted as "two sons of oil" standing by the Lord of the whole earth (v. 14). The word for "oil" here is the word used for the olive oil used in the lamps. The point here is that both Joshua and Zerubbabel were to be channels for the people's offerings to God and thus were to function as a dual leadership. There is no indication here that either was "anointed" (NRSV). A different word was used for anointing with oil (cf. 1 Sam 16:13; Ps 45:8; Isa 61:3).

Two more visions follow which in their own way reiterate and affirm the message of Ezek 33:10–16 (and Ezek 18) that each individual will suffer for his own covenant transgressions (5:1–4), and that now the corporate guilt of the land can be removed to allow a renewal of the covenant relationship (5:5–11). The final vision (6:1–8) emphasizes that

---

34. Cf. Petersen, *Haggai and Zechariah 1–8*, 244; Meyers and Meyers, *Haggai, Zechariah 1–8*, 242.

35. Cf. Meyers and Meyers, *Haggai, Zechariah 1–8*, 246–49; Bruehler, "Seeing through the *eynim* of Zechariah," 436.

God has constant surveillance and control over the Persian Empire, and so the people can continue to rebuild the temple and reestablish their covenant community with the assurance of security.

To close off the section of prophetic visions, Zechariah is called upon to carry out an action that summarizes and extends the previous visions. Taking gold and silver from recently arrived exiles, Zechariah is commanded to make crowns (plural), but then only one person is mentioned as being crowned, Joshua the high priest (6:11). Yet in the next verses (12, 13) it states that he is called "the Shoot" who is to "shoot up" and build the temple of Yahweh. This is both the title and function of Zerubbabel (3:8; 4:9–10; but cf. Jer 33:15 and Isa 61:11). It appears that the words "and on the head of Zerubbabel the son of Shealtiel" have been deleted from the end of v. 11, possibly by an editor after Zerubbabel was withdrawn as governor by the Persians at a later date. Verse 13 clearly points to a royal contender and priest sitting on thrones side by side in peaceful coexistence. The dual leadership referred to in 4:14 is reaffirmed now with messianic overtones.[36] However, the crowns are to be kept in safekeeping in the temple of Yahweh until the time is right (v. 14). With this symbolic action, Zechariah was sending a message to all exiles that in these two leaders they already had Ezekiel's restoration plan of a dual leadership fulfilled in embryo. So all should not only support the building of the temple with contributions, but should return to Judah to bring that plan to fruition (v. 15).

The last two chapters of Zech 1–8 are dated to 7 December 518 BCE, almost two years after the day celebrating the laying of the temple's foundation (18 December 520, Hag 2:18). The occasion for these oracles is a delegation sent from Bethel, about 20 kms north of Jerusalem, with a question for the priests. By this time the building of the walls of the temple would have been well advanced. The delegation wished to know whether they should still weep and fast during the fifth month (the month during which Jerusalem was burned and the temple destroyed) which they had been doing for many years (7:3). Zechariah takes this opportunity to speak on behalf of the priests to "all the people of the land" to question their sincerity of motive (7:4–7; cf. Isa 58:3–5), call them to repentance, and remind them of what had happened to their fathers who had not heeded the warning of the former prophets (7:8–14).

However, Zechariah assures the people of the land that things can change. Zion will once again be inhabited with a large population and become a thriving center as it once was, because God is very jealous for Jerusalem and will return to Zion with blessing. Many more exiles will return and soon fill the area of the city (8:1–8; cf. 1:14, 15). Part of the reason behind the question of the people of Bethel was evidently the concern whether the land was still under the seventy-year curse, because the prosperity that had been promised at the time of the foundation-laying for the temple (Hag 2:18, 19) had not come about. Zechariah's word to them was to be patient and remain strong and live in covenant faithfulness (8:9–17). Then all those fasts commemorating the disasters surrounding the destruction of Jerusalem will be turned into joyous festivals (8:18–19).

The people of Bethel had also come to Jerusalem with a view to entreating the favor of Yahweh (literally, "to soften the face of Yahweh," 7:2). Zechariah now concludes his response to them with what he has voiced before—that many nations shall join themselves

---

36. Cf. Petersen, *Haggai and Zechariah 1–8*, 274–79; Meyers, "Messianism," 129–31.

to Yahweh in the future. The inhabitants of many cities will come to entreat the favor of Yahweh. Indeed, many peoples and strong nations of every language will come seeking God's favor, showing their readiness to belong to the covenant community by holding onto tassels of a Jewish man's prayer shawl (8:20–23; cf. Num 15:38–40; Deut 22:12). While Zechariah thus finally accepts the overtures made by the people of Bethel he, nevertheless, reflects a certain priestly condescension towards the people of the land (cf. Ezek 11:14–21; 33:23–29) which eventually led to rejection under Ezra (cf. Ezra 9:2, 11; 10:2, 11). In spite of Zechariah's expressed hope for all nations joining themselves to God, there is apparent a growing tendency among the recent returnees to see themselves exclusively as the true people of God.

Conclusion

It has become very evident that with the recent influx into the Judean community of a substantial number of Zadokite priests with Joshua that the community is being formed and brought under the authority of the priesthood with the temple and its sacrificial rituals being placed at the center of community life. The restoration plan of Ezekiel with its priestly and royal authorities is to be implemented. The prophetic visionaries are gradually being sidelined, and are being told that when they see the temple completed they will know that it was the right thing. The main concession Zechariah had made to the prophetic vision is that eventually nations will come to Zion and accept Yahweh as the one and only true God (2:15; 8:20–23). However, that will be on the basis of acceptance of the priestly tradition.

Chapter VI

Zadokites, Levites, and the Prophetic Vision

THE TEMPLE WAS COMPLETED in 515 BCE (Ezra 6:15), and with it the Zadokite priesthood became the controlling force in the religious life of Judah. Darius I who had supported the temple services, died in 486 BCE. Those who succeeded him (Xerxes [486–465] and Artaxerxes I [465–423 BCE]) withdrew support from temples, and increased taxation in the provinces to finance military campaigns against Greece. The ability of the Persian Empire to maintain its power was diminishing along with its economy. This exploitation of the provinces led to increasing unrest and social upheaval. In Judah the temple and priesthood suffered from the loss of imperial funding, so the priesthood sought to enforce tithing on the people of Judah who were already stretched to the limit by the increased taxation. All of this, together with poor harvests and drought, forced many into debt, eventual loss of property, and enslavement of family members to creditors. The breakdown of the social fabric of the temple community led to growing resentment and despair.[1] It was in this situation that around 460 BCE a prophet arose in Judah calling for change in the attitudes of both priests and people.[2]

THE PROPHET MALACHI

We know this prophet as "Malachi," a title probably drawn from Mal 3:1: "Behold, I send my messenger . . ." (*mala'ki*), but not necessarily his name. He was a person of deep faith and concern about the worship and life of the people of Judah and saw the opportunism and corruption in his society as directly attributable to the indifference and depravity of the Zadokite priesthood. His references to the covenant with Levi would identify him as belonging to that group of Levites who had contended some years earlier that God's covenant with the Levites was as permanent as God's covenant with day and night (Jer 33:15–26). It was that same covenant that, according to Deut 33:8–11, was made with the Levites to teach Israel God's law and to serve at God's altar. Furthermore, Malachi's

---

1. See Berquist, *Judaism in Persia's Shadow*, 87–106; Grabbe, *Yehud*, 207–8.
2. It is evident that the temple had been completed and in use for some time, but the initial enthusiasm for worship and hope for blessing had degenerated into indifference and corruption. The prophet raises issues which are later addressed by the comings of Ezra (458 BCE) and Nehemiah (445 BCE).

strong concerns about matters of temple worship and priestly service, as well as for proper tithing (a part of which was income for the Levites), and his conviction that God would eventually reject the Zadokite priests and purify the Levites to take their place, all point to the author being a Levite himself. There is evidence also that he had been influenced by prophetic concerns for covenant faithfulness and the coming Day of Yahweh.

Following the pronouncement of Ezekiel (44:10–14), the Zadokite priests had not permitted Levites to function as priests at the altar, although they could do the chores around the temple such as slaughtering animals for sacrifice and overseeing the temple gates. However, because of their education and scribal skills, the Levites were indispensable, not only for the temple administration, keeping records, copying sacred texts, and doing preparation for sacrifice according to established practice, but also for provincial administration, and collection of taxes and tithes.[3] As such, the Levites had firsthand knowledge of what was happening in both the secular and religious realms. Malachi's primary concern here was with the failure of the Zadokite priesthood to render faithful leadership.

Malachi's Concerns

Fundamental to Malachi's message was his understanding of the covenant God had made with his people, a covenant of love and faithfulness on God's part, but mostly not reciprocated by the people. The promises of coming prosperity made at the time of the building of the temple by Haggai (2:18–19) and Zechariah (8:11–15) had not come about and had led to disillusionment and distrust within the community. Drawing on Deuteronomic language Malachi pointed out that in spite of it all, there was clear evidence that God still loved Israel.[4] For while the people of Edom had lost their land, Yahweh had restored the people of Judah to theirs (1:2–5). Yet did they show honor and respect to God to deserve his blessings? Certainly not in the way they offered animals for sacrifice to God which were blind, lame, or sick. "Try presenting that to your governor," Malachi pointed out, "and see whether he will show favor!" (1:8).

However, the prophet quickly moved to a strong indictment of those who were privileged to pronounce the divine blessing—the Zadokite priesthood. They had carried out their priestly tasks with such indifference as to turn the Aaronic blessing (Num 6:23–27) into a curse! Their temple services had become a charade, and their sacrificial offerings were abominations (1:6–10). Consequently, the prophet contended, those scattered among the nations—those of the Jewish diaspora and their proselytes who could only call upon God in prayer—were making the pure offerings which the Jerusalem priesthood had claimed only they themselves could do through sacrificial rituals (1:11–13).[5] The Zadokite priests had forgotten that God is the great suzerain King

---

3. See Grabbe, *Yehud*, 152–53, 230.

4. Moran, "Love of God in Deuteronomy," 77–87.

5. Glazier-McDonald, *Malachi*, 60–61, claims v. 11 must be understood as expressing the hope of what will happen in the future. However, while such hope, as expressed in Isa 42:4–6; 49:6; 51:4, may be the background, the context calls for the present. In agreement with Rudolph, *Haggai—Sacharja 1–8—Sacharja 9–14—Maleachi*, 262–63.

over all the nations, who sees all and who both blesses and curses (1:14). Because their priestly blessing had become a curse, they should be declared unclean and removed as dung (2:1–3)! Such a hard-hitting condemnation should lead to the priestly office being handed over to the Levites (2:4).[6] The Levites had always been faithful in instructing the people as the true messengers of God in spite of Ezekiel's condemnation of them (2:5–7; cf. Ezek 44:10–13). While the Levites had turned many from iniquity, Malachi claimed, the present priesthood had caused many to stumble by their false instruction. Therefore, they should be despised by the people (2:8–9).

In the next verses (2:10–16), Malachi seems to be addressing the whole community, accusing the people of Judah and Jerusalem of acting deceitfully to one another and profaning the covenant of the fathers and the sanctuary of Yahweh by men casting off their first wives to marry foreign women. However, by the use of certain terminology, the prophet was also subtly pointing specifically at the priesthood. Using phrases like "abomination done in Israel" (v. 11), "profaning the covenant" (v. 10), "profaning the sanctuary of Yahweh" (v. 11), and using the unusual phrase "daughter of a foreign god" (v. 11), Malachi was alluding to Ezek 44:6, 7, 13. In those verses, Ezekiel had condemned the practice of using foreigners to do the menial tasks around the temple and had then decreed that the Levites could take over those tasks, although they were not to come near any of the sacred offerings because of their "abominations" (Ezek 44:13). By alluding to this Malachi was making the point that the Zadokite priests had participated in breaking the very rules on which the rebuilding of the temple and their exclusive priesthood had been based. Besides, in this whole section, Malachi used the verb *bagad* five times (vv. 10, 11, 14, 15, 16) from which the noun "garment," derives. So the verb originally had the meaning "to cover over with a garment," hence "to act deceitfully." This appears to be a deliberate play on words because the noun *beged* was often used for the holy linen garments of the priests (e.g., Ezek 42:14; 44:17–19; Zech 3:4–5). The prophet was implying that the actions of the priests indicate that they wear this holy garment to cover their deceit and treachery!

However, it appears that many priests and people had married foreign women, who retained their own religious beliefs and practices, either for economic reasons or for participating in fertility rites of the foreign religion in the hope of better harvests. The sexual language of v. 12 ("May Yahweh cut off from the tents of Jacob anyone who does this—both the one aroused and the one who submits") would suggest the latter.[7] Such syncretistic practice, the cause of the first temple's destruction, could not be tolerated. By doing so they had profaned the covenant of their fathers which forbade marriage with foreign women who would only lead them into idolatry (Exod 34:15–16; Deut 7:1–6), and had acted treacherously towards God and their own people in divorcing the wives of their youth with whom, under God, they had a covenant, and only from whom they could expect godly offspring.[8]

---

6. Mason, *Books of Haggai, Zechariah and Malachi*, 147, correctly translates this verse as "Then you will know that I issued this decree to you, that my covenant should be with Levi."

7. Cf. Glazier-McDonald, "Malachi 2:12," 295–98.

8. Glazier-McDonald, "Intermarriage, Divorce," 603–11.

The sacredness and meaning of the marriage covenant is given its strongest affirmation here, and the prevailing practice of divorce is condemned. According to the lists of those who married foreign women recorded in Ezra 10:18–44, while there was a large number of non-priestly citizens involved, there was also a considerable number of Zadokite priestly families and a handful of Levites who were called upon to put away their foreign wives.

Another concern of the prophet was the failure of the people to tithe. Many of the farmers were finding it difficult enough paying taxes and tribute when they were suffering from locust plagues and droughts, while their leaders seemed to be doing well and their injustices condoned. The complaints of the people that "all who do evil are good in the sight of Yahweh" and their question: "Where is the God of justice?" (2:17) would indicate that the people saw these injustices as encouraged by the priesthood. This had led them to conclude: "It is vain to serve God" (3:14). But by not tithing they were leaving the Levites without any livelihood at all, forcing them to find work in the fields as day-laborers (cf. Neh 13:10). Malachi's warning to the people was that they were only bringing a curse upon themselves by withdrawing the tithe. If they would only bring the whole tithe, they would receive an overflowing blessing of prosperity (3:8–15). The corruption of the priesthood was having its negative effect in different ways within the community.

Consequently, the Day of Yahweh was approaching, Malachi warned, about which the prophets of the past had spoken so often. The announcement of the coming of this day is described in terms used of a king sending out a messenger to prepare the people for his coming to their towns and cities: "Behold, I am sending my messenger to prepare the way before me" (3:1a). It is similar to Isa 40:3 where a voice cries: "In the wilderness prepare the way of Yahweh, make straight in the desert a highway for our God," the call for a messenger to announce that Yahweh will be leading the exiles back to the promised land. However, the real issue here is that God himself is coming to judge the people, and the blessing will be only for the righteous. The messenger and the deity sending the message become absorbed into one.

The people had raised the question: "Where is the God of justice?" (2:17), and the prophet gave the answer: "The Lord whom you are seeking will suddenly come to his temple, the messenger of the covenant in whom you delight, indeed, he is coming!" (3:1b). This answer carried the threat of coming judgment, and in this case drew on the language of the theophany in Isa 29:5b–6 ("And in an instant, suddenly, you will be visited by Yahweh of hosts, with thunder and earthquake and great noise with whirlwind and tempest and the flame of a devouring fire"). This motif had been further expanded by Trito-Isaiah in Isa 66:15 ("For Yahweh will come in fire and his chariots like the whirlwind to pay back his anger in fury, and his rebuke in flames of fire"). It is little wonder that the author (or an editor) identified the messenger of 3:1a with Elijah the prophet (4:3) who was taken up in a whirlwind into heaven by a chariot of fire (2 Kgs 2:11). He would come to bring warning and to call the people to return to covenant faithfulness and thus avoid utter destruction (4:6).

So the Day of Yahweh "is coming, burning like an oven, when all the arrogant and all evildoers will be stubble; the day that comes shall consume them, says Yahweh of hosts, so that it will leave them neither root nor branch" (4:1). The evildoers are described in general terms as sorcerers and adulterers (cf. Isa 57:3), those who swear falsely (cf. Zech 5:4), those who oppress their workers (cf. Isa 58:3), widows, orphans and aliens (cf. Deut 24:17–21; Zech 7:9–11). Yet the Day of Yahweh would be a time when the Levites will be refined like gold and silver (cf. Isa 48:10) to become the bringers of offerings to Yahweh in righteousness (3:3). The faithful will pass through the fires of judgment unharmed to tread down the ashes of the wicked (3:16—4:3; cf. Isa 43:2) as the "sun of righteousness," that brilliant presence of Yahweh (cf. Isa 60:1), encompasses them and brings healing from their hardships.

While Malachi's primary concern has been with temple and priesthood and the reinstatement of the Levites, his oracles nevertheless indicate the influence of the prophetic vision on his thinking, particularly as it had developed in Trito-Isaiah. Many of the social concerns of Malachi are reminiscent of Trito-Isaiah's complaints about the lack of uprightness, honesty, and righteousness in the community (Mal 3:14–15; cf. Isa 59:14–15). His criticisms of the Zadokite priesthood are similar to Isa 66:3–5. Malachi refers to God as "Father" (1:6; 2:10) in a way familiar from Isa 63:16 and 64:8, and his question (2:10), "Has not one God created us?" echoes the frequent reminder in Isa 40–55 that the one and only God (Isa 43:10–13; 44:6–8; 45:14, 18, 20–23; 46:9; 48:10) has created Israel (43:1) and formed his chosen one from the womb (44:2, 24; 49:1) to be his faithful servant. His triple emphasis on the greatness of God's name among the nations (1:11, 14), while perhaps limited in its extent, bears the mark of Deutero-Isaiah's emphasis on Israel's purpose to be a light to the nations (Isa 42:6; 49:6). Malachi can speak of the covenant with Levi in concert with Jer 33:14–26 but he makes no mention of the corresponding covenant with David. Indeed, for him God is the only King (1:14; cf. Isa 40:9–11; 52:7), and like Deutero-Isaiah, Malachi sees the ideal situation as that prior to the monarchy where God is King and the people are God's "treasured possession" (3:17; cf. Exod 19:5; Deut 7:6; 14:2; 26:8), and God can say to the faithful, "You are mine" (3:17; cf. Isa 43:1).

The Response: Ezra and Nehemiah

Evidently, the message of Malachi got back to the Jewish community in Babylon where the priests had already set down in writing their priestly laws and traditions. They must have been concerned about the reported breakdown of those laws and about the threat of worship in the new temple becoming syncretistic. It appears that the Jewish community there acted as a strong lobby group under the leadership of Ezra, a scribe and priest who traced his ancestry through Zadok back to Aaron (cf. Ezra 7:1–6). By convincing Artaxerxes I that the province of Yehud was in real danger of slipping into chaos and even rebellion, and that its stability and loyalty was important for the security of the Persian empire, Ezra was able to gain permission to go to Jerusalem and take with him a large group of exiles. There was not only the continuous threat of Greeks seeking control of the coastlands, but the satrapy of Egypt had revolted, forcing the Persian empire to strengthen its presence in the western provinces.⁹ To maintain the services of the temple Ezra was given funds from the king's treasury as well as receiving contributions from the Babylonian Jews. The priesthood and those involved in temple administration were to be freed from paying taxes and tribute themselves in order to retain their loyalty in collecting and handling of the taxation revenues of the province. Ezra was instructed to teach the law of his God and the law of the king and to appoint judges and magistrates to carry them out (Ezra 7:7—8:20).¹⁰

Ezra and his group of returning exiles left Babylon in the first month of 458 BCE and arrived in Jerusalem in the fifth month of that year (Ezra 7:7-9). For the next two months Ezra spent time reorganizing the temple service and personnel after which he led public readings of the priestly law to a large assembly in Jerusalem with others assisting in its interpretation (Neh 8:1-12). Since this was the seventh month and they had heard in the law that they were to celebrate the Feast of Booths in that month, they did so for the next seven days (Neh 8:13-18; cf. Lev 23:39-43). Once the law had been read and interpreted and had been studied by the leaders of the people, the matter of intermarriage with "the peoples of the lands" could be dealt with. By recalling the names of those peoples who had originally inhabited the land of Canaan when the Israelites first entered it, Ezra was able to appeal to the edicts against intermarrying with the peoples in Judah lest they be led astray into worshipping false gods and practicing their abominations (Exod 34:11-16; Lev 18:24-30). However, the main emphasis was placed on the returned exiles maintaining their ethnic purity by separating themselves from the peoples of the land and thus keeping the "holy seed" (Ezra 9:2) undefiled. Those who were involved in marrying foreign women were mostly the leaders and officials of the temple community, who were seen as defiling God's holy place (9:8, 11). This, for Ezra, was the real issue, since according to priestly law (Lev 15:1-30) anyone who married outside the community of the returned exiles was in danger of being defiled by a partner who was not familiar with the purity laws and so would be unclean and thus would also render the land unclean (Ezra 9:11).¹¹ So anyone who would insist on staying married to a foreign woman was under threat that they could not be part of God's holy people, risked the forfeiture of property and being banned from the assembly of the exiles (Ezra 10:8). For the priest Ezra this was the only way for the "holy seed" to maintain its ethnic purity and escape the judgment of God.

This endeavor to maintain purity of worship and good law and order led to a process of isolation of the returning exiles from the rest of the population of the province. No longer could the seed of Abraham be understood as a blessing to the nations. A sharp distinction was drawn between the "peoples of the land(s)" (Ezra 9:1, 2, 11, 14; 10:2, 11; Neh 9:30; 10:31) with their "foreign women" (Ezra 10:2, 10, 11, 14) and those who were referred to as "the children of the exile" (Ezra 6:16, 19; 8:35; 10:7, 16; cf. 6:21; 9:4; 10:6), or "the assembly of the exiles" (10:8) who were "from the captivity" (8:35). Except for

---

9. E. Meyers, "Persian Period," 516.

10. Whether the Letter of Artaxerxes (Ezra 7:12-26) was genuine or not, the mission of Ezra to bring relief to the temple and establish law and order to maintain the loyalty of the province is clear. Cf. Janzen, "Mission of Ezra," 619-43.

11. See Janzen, "Scholars, Witches, Ideologies," 60-66.

the few who had joined the returnees and separated themselves from the "pollutions" of the nations to worship Yahweh (6:21), Ezra's reforms had concentrated on those who had returned from exile. Those Judeans who had not been exiled appear to have been covered by the term "peoples of the land" together with Greek and Tyrian traders and those who had gained land in the province through foreclosure or other means.[12]

The situation does not seem to have been much different during the governorship of Nehemiah. Because of reports of the precarious situation in Judah reported by Nehemiah's brother Hanani, Nehemiah was granted a leave of absence from his service as cupbearer to Artaxerxes I to serve as governor of Yehud for twelve years (445–433 BCE). His mission was to strengthen Jerusalem and to maintain the province's loyalty to the Persian Empire. So Nehemiah was accompanied by officers of the Persian army and cavalry whose function was not only to guarantee protection on the way but also to enforce Nehemiah's authority as governor and thus to strengthen Persia's presence in the province. They would reside in the temple fortress which was to be repaired (Neh 2:8, 9).[13] In spite of Ezra's attempt to make Judah a temple community, there were still disturbances and corruption, while leaders in the satrapy, Beyond-the-River, and the surrounding area sought greater autonomy and consequent wealth for themselves. The officials in Judah, including the priesthood, were not above participation in this pursuit.

Nehemiah's first concern was to rebuild the walls of the city in spite of the opposition of those who saw the fortification of Jerusalem as a regressive step in their plans to gain autonomy and control in the area. Even the Jerusalem priesthood and officials had to be kept in the dark regarding Nehemiah's plans until he was ready to start the work, lest his endeavors be undermined (Neh 2:16). Nehemiah's major adversaries were Sanballat, governor of Samaria (2:10, 19; 4:1–23; 6:1–14; 13:28), Tobiah of a powerful Jewish family who governed Ammon (2:10, 19; 3:35; 4:1; 6:1, 12–19; 13:4–8), and Geshem the Arab, king of the Qedarite kingdom to the south of Judah (2:19; 6:1–6). It is clear that Nehemiah saw the high priestly family and many of the Jerusalem officials as working in collusion with these adversaries (6:10–19; 13:4–9).[14] Nehemiah's derogatory way of referring to Tobiah as "the Ammonite servant" (2:10, 19) and his later angry removal of Tobiah from the room in the temple provided by the high priest Eliashib (13:7) indicates that he viewed Tobiah not only as compromising the province's loyalty to him and the Persian authority, but also as seeking control of business operations in Jerusalem. The local Jerusalem administrators, however, obviously saw Tobiah's activities as of benefit to them (6:17–19). Yet in spite of opposition, Nehemiah was able to get the whole wall completed in fifty-two days (6:15).

Tied in with all of this was Nehemiah's concern to stem the tide of the exploitation of the people of Judah by the Jerusalem nobles, officials and local bureaucrats. People had been mortgaging their fields and vineyards and borrowing from creditors to pay their taxes and tribute. Because of high interest rates, people were not only losing their property through foreclosure, but family members were being sold into slavery because

---

12. See Grabbe, *Yehud*, I, 287, who comes to the conclusion "that many, if not all, these 'peoples of the land' were Jewish descendants who were not deported."

13. Fried, *The Priest and the Great King*, 194–200.

14. Ibid., 202–3.

of debt. The nobles and officials were even selling off debtors to foreign traders, so that fellow Jews often finished up as slaves in other nations. The priesthood, as overseers of the collection of taxes and tithes, were participants in this (5:1–13). Nehemiah was able to stem the tide of some of this corruption during his twelve-year term as governor. However, after a period of absence, when he returned for a second term, he found that the leaders were back to their old tricks, temple services had broken down because Levites and temple singers were not being paid, the Sabbath was not being kept, and traders were insisting on doing business in Jerusalem during that day. As well, there was further intermarriage with foreigners, and the priesthood had fallen back into corruption. Once again, Nehemiah sought to bring law and order to the province and separation of the people from all things foreign (13:1–31). Yet the priesthood continued to wield power through their double function of temple service and supervision of the collection of taxes and tithes, as well as through intermarriage with powerful families such as Tobiah and Sanballat (13:4–5, 28). Nehemiah found himself more in sympathy with the Levites (13:10), a sentiment he shared with the prophet Malachi. Nevertheless, those who held to the prophetic vision found themselves powerless and a minority, and with the weakening of the Persian Empire, the Province of Yehud was only falling further into corruption in a constant struggle to survive.

Already during the reign of Artaxerxes I (465–423 BCE) increased taxes had put Judah under severe stress, and many farmers were losing their property to creditors. Even though trade with the Greeks had increased with the sale of olive oil and grain, increasingly people who had become indebted in Judah were being sold into slavery to the Greek and Phoenician traders.[15] These circumstances seem to have continued under his successor, Darius II (423–404 BCE). During the reign of Artaxerxes II (404–359 BCE) revolts by some of the Greek states were put down, leading to what was known as the King's Peace (386), accomplished mostly by Persia playing the Greek states off against each other.[16] However, Egypt also had revolted earlier and the Persian armies had suffered a number of defeats there, unable to gain a footing in the Nile Valley.[17] It was only during the reign of Artaxerxes III (359–338 BCE) that the Persian armies after initial defeats in 361–351 were able to amass enormous forces, cross the Nile and bring Egypt under their control in 343–342.[18] During this whole period of wars with Egypt, one can assume that large numbers of foot soldiers and cavalry marching through Palestine would have required enormous supplies of food on their way to Egypt. Travelling armies were sometimes like a plague of locusts consuming everything before them. This must have had a debilitating effect on the people of Judah and others in the coastlands.

---

15. Berquist, *Judaism in Persia's Shadow*, 109.
16. Briant, *From Cyrus to Alexander*, 637–49.
17. Ibid., 652–55.
18. Ibid., 682–87.

CONCERNS OF THE CHRONICLER

With the attempts of the Zadokite priesthood to form Judah into a hierocracy, the Levites, and probably only those who had been part of the exile, could serve in temple activities as outlined in Ezek 44. Meanwhile, the Zadokite priests still in Babylon had been redacting and expanding the historical traditions of Israel in order to incorporate and maintain their own traditions and claims to priestly authority. From now on the chief priests would be anointed as had the kings prior to the exile (Lev 4:3, 5, 16; 6:20, 22).

The Priestly Work and the Chronicler

This Priestly Work, embodied in the exodus traditions in the books of Exodus, Leviticus, and Numbers, sought to establish in writing all the priestly laws and cultic practices that had developed over the centuries, and also aimed at refining and incorporating into the early history of the exodus the distinction between priests and Levites addressed in Ezek 44. For this reason, in its reformulation, the Zadokite priesthood could no longer be referred to as "sons of Zadok" but would henceforth be known as "sons of Aaron" to fit into that early history with Zadok as a later descendant of Aaron. Consequently, the Priestly Work gives a detailed description of the functions of the various Levites descending from Gershon, Kohath, and Merari, the sons of Levi, in Num 3 and 4 affirming that only Aaron and his sons could serve within the sanctuary. The rest of the Levites were under their command (Num 4:27–28), with the threat of death if they touched the holy things or even looked upon them (Num 4:15, 20).

The explanation given for the subordinate position of the Levites is embedded in the story of rebellion against Moses and Aaron by the Levite Korah and the Reubenites Dathan and Abiram in Num 16–18. These had questioned Moses' and Aaron's claim to superiority because, as they said, "all the congregation are holy, all of them, and Yahweh is in the midst of them" (Num 16:3). It would appear that the priestly redactors saw the Levites, particularly those who regarded themselves as followers of Jeremiah, as being in the same camp as the prophetic visionaries (see Isa 62:12 and 65:5!). Those who followed them would be swallowed up by the earth just as Korah, Dathan, and Abiram and their followers were for questioning the authority of Moses and Aaron (Num 16:23–35)! As a result of this rebellion, Aaron and his sons were reaffirmed and would retain the privileged position of carrying out the sacrifices on the altar and serve in the holy place, while the Levites would be given to them as a gift to do all the subordinate tasks (Num 18:1–7). All this is depicted as a divine decree given through Moses as a permanent arrangement, as a "covenant of salt forever before Yahweh" (Num 18:19; cf. Ezek 43:24; Lev 2:13).[19]

---

19. The influence of Ezek 44 on these three chapters (Num 16–18) is evident from the use of terminology common to Ezekiel but rare in Numbers. E.g., *meri* (rebellion) is found in Ezek 44:6 plus 14 times and only in Num 17:25 (Eng. 17:10); *khalal* (to profane) in Ezek 44:7 plus 21 times and only in Num 18:32; *nasu avonam* (bear their guilt) in Ezek 44:10, 12 plus 8 times and only in Num 18:23. Note also the double use of *rab-lakem* (enough!) in Ezek 44:6 and 45:9 and in Num 16:3, 7. These examples would indicate that the Priestly work has used Ezek 44 rather than the other way around. *Contra* Cook, "Innerbiblical Interpretation," 193–208.

It had been Ezra's mission to respond to Malachi's criticism and to bring the priestly law to the Province of Yehud. He had apparently participated in the writing of the Priestly Work since he is described as "a scribe skilled in the law of Moses" (Ezra 7:1–6) with his goal "to teach statute and judgment in Israel" (Ezra 7:10). He did this by reading the book of the Priestly Law to the people assembled in Jerusalem, with the Levites he had brought from Babylonia giving the required interpretation (Neh 8:1–8; cf. Ezra 8:15–20). The result was that "all the people wept when they heard the words of the law" (Neh 8:9). Many would not have welcomed the exclusiveness of the priestly law, nor the claims to authority of the Zadokite priesthood, nor the oath they were required to make in submission to that law (Neh 9:38—10:31). But the threat of having to forfeit all their property and be banished had its decisive effect.

The work of the Chronicler is a Levite response to the Priestly Work and the increasing authority and power wielded by the priesthood in the latter part of the Persian Empire.[20] Because of the special emphasis given to the prophet Jeremiah at the end of his writing (2 Chr 35:25; 36:12, 21, 22) and the constant emphasis on the permanence of the covenants with the Levites and with David, it is likely that the Chronicler belonged to that group who honored the memory of Jeremiah and the claims that the covenants made with David and the Levites were permanent (Jer 33:14–26). The author was evidently a gifted leader among the Levites with experience in the workings of the temple, its ritual, administration, and personnel, as well as a thorough familiarity with the history, literature and archival records up to that time.

The purpose of the Chronicler then was to do his own reformulation of history in order to demonstrate the real position of Levites from the beginning and to do so in an erudite and diplomatic manner. Whereas the Priestly Work had gone back to Moses as the founder of their rites for the tabernacle in the wilderness, the Chronicler goes back to David as the one who set down the form and function of worship to be carried out in Jerusalem. Because David established Jerusalem as his city, brought the Ark of the Covenant to Mount Zion, planned the temple and established the form and the cultic personnel of the worship, he is the true founder of the cult.[21] The Chronicler's goal is not to take away the priesthood from the Zadokites but to demonstrate that the Levites with their different functions should have an equal partnership in the worship in the Jerusalem temple. In his presentation, he also speaks to other issues raised by Ezra and the priesthood, as well as claims made by the prophetic visionaries.

Purpose of the Genealogies

The Chronicler begins his work with nine chapters of genealogies of the twelve tribes which make up Israel as the people of Yahweh. These are placed into the context of the nations of his world, beginning with Adam down to the Chronicler's time. He wants to

---

20. The actual date of writing is uncertain, but I would concur with those who put the date of completion of the work somewhere between 400 to 350 BCE. See Klein, *1 Chronicles*, 13–16. Also, Pomykala, *Davidic Dynasty Tradition*, 88, who argues for a date between 435 and 348 BCE. The "work of the Chronicler" refers only to 1 and 2 Chronicles.

21. Cf. Riley, *King and Cultus*, 60–62.

bring his contemporaries, conscious of their own genealogies, to see the wider, more leveling perspective of their history and legacy, with the understanding that of all the nations of the world, Israel is but one nation; of Israel, Judah is but one tribe; of the Levites, the Zadokite priesthood is but one part—and all are interconnected as the people of Israel.[22]

By the use of these archival and oral genealogies, the Chronicler thus lays the foundation for three major fundamental issues he elaborates throughout his large work: (1) the unity of all Israel over against the exclusive claims of those who have returned from exile; (2) the primary position of David as the founder of the cult in Jerusalem; and (3) the position of all of the Levites, whatever their functions may be, as equal in importance to the claims of the Zadokite priesthood.

In contrast to the exclusive way the Passover was celebrated since Ezra's reform (Ezra 6:19–21), the Chronicler observed that Hezekiah had sent written invitations to the Passover celebration "to all Israel, from Beersheba to Dan" (2 Chr 30:5), and even though some from the northern tribes had not cleansed themselves according to the law, they were still able to eat the Passover and benefit from it (2 Chr 30:17–20) in spite of Lev 7:19–21. Similarly, the enormous Passover celebration prepared by Josiah was kept not only by the priests and Levites, but by "all Judah and Israel who were present" (2 Chr 35:1–19).

However, the understanding of the term "all Israel" was another issue the Chronicler aimed to clarify. According to Ezra/Nehemiah the exiles accommodated to themselves the title "all Israel" since they saw only themselves as the true representatives of the chosen people of God (cf. Ezra 2:70; 6:16, 17; 7:28; 8:25; 10:5; Neh 7:72; 11:3; 12:47). So the Chronicler affirmed, in response, through the genealogies that "all Israel" is made up of all twelve tribes. Israel, as the people of God, is more than Judah or any exclusive group within it.

In regard to the concern of the returned exiles for ethnic purity, the Chronicler quietly observed that Judah itself was never ethnically pure since even their ancestor had married a Canaanite woman. He then went on to list without censure some six cases of such intermarriage in Judah's genealogy (1 Chr 2:3—4:23) to Canaanites, Egyptians, Moabites and others—some of the very peoples rejected by Ezra (Ezra 9:7) because they would contaminate the "holy seed" (Ezra 9:2).[23] However, since Judah had become the focal point of the postexilic community, the Chronicler gave Judah's genealogy first (1 Chr 2:3–55 and 4:1–23), its two parts wrapped around the genealogy of David (3:1–24). Even though David's genealogy is centered in Judah, throughout his work the Chronicler emphasizes that David was anointed as king over "all Israel" (1 Chr 14:3) and that "all Israel," participated in the dedication of the temple in Jerusalem (2 Chr 7:4–6) and in Israel's subsequent history.[24]

The genealogy of Levi is placed in the very center of all the tribal genealogies to indicate its importance and significance for all the tribes. This is also borne out by the

---

22. Levin, "Who Was the Chronicler's Audience?," 242–43.

23. See esp. Knoppers, "Intermarriage," 15–30; Knoppers, *1 Chronicles 1–9*, 358–59; Klein, *1 Chronicles*, 108; Japhet, *Ideology*, 349–50.

24. See Japhet, *Ideology*, 272–99.

length of the record (6:1–80), second only to that of Judah. While the function of the "sons of Aaron," is described as making offerings on the altars of burnt offering and incense, doing all the work of the most holy place, and to make atonement for Israel (6:49), the Chronicler states: "their brethren the Levites were given for *all* the service of the tabernacle of the house of God" (6:48).

The implications of the Chronicler regarding the priests and Levites are clear: First of all, they are all Levites, sharing a common genealogy but with different functions. While the sons of Aaron function as priests in the most holy place, the Levites carry out all the other services related to the worship. All are thus ministering to Yahweh contrary to Ezek 40:46; 44:15–16. Second, while the priests carry out their function according to all that Moses commanded, the Levites carry out theirs as David had ordered. Third, there is no hint here of subordination or inferiority on the part of the Levites to the priesthood—all are related and equal with different roles to play. Finally, the description of the towns given to the Levites (6:54–81) shows that they were spread equally throughout the territory of the twelve tribes to minister to *all* Israel.

The concluding chapter of the genealogies (ch. 9) begins with the statement: "And Judah was taken into exile because of their unfaithfulness" (9:1) as a reminder that the returned exiles can hardly claim to be the "holy seed" (Ezra 9:2). This is made much more explicit at the end of the Chronicler's work (2 Chr 36:14) where it states emphatically that the reason for the exile was because "all the leading priests and the people were exceedingly unfaithful, following all the abominations of the nations, and they polluted the house of Yahweh that he had consecrated in Jerusalem." This would be the Chronicler's final rejection of the claims of the Zadokites against the Levites as expressed in Ezek 44:9–16.

Importance of the Davidic Dynasty for the Chronicler

The Chronicler's portrayal of David is both positive and ideal. There is no Bathsheba incident, no family strife in his account. The only somewhat negative story is David's call for a census, but even that has a positive ending with the establishment of an altar to Yahweh on the threshing floor of Ornan the Jebusite (1 Chr 21).

David's accession to the throne comes about democratically with all Israel gathering together at Hebron, and all the elders anointing him king over Israel. Every one of the leaders is consulted by David regarding bringing the ark of the covenant to Jerusalem and join him in the venture (1 Chr 13:1–6). All this had happened, the Chronicler declares, according to the word of Yahweh by Samuel, the Levite priest-prophet (1 Chr 11:2–8; cf. 6:33). So David's kingship is thus established by divine authority, and becomes "greater and greater because Yahweh of hosts was with him" (1 Chr 11:9) as he reigns on Yahweh's behalf. For David and his descendants "sit upon the throne of the kingdom of Yahweh over Israel" (1 Chr 28:5; cf. 29:23; 2 Chr 9:8; 13:8).[25] The emphasis on the permanence of the Davidic covenant in 1 Chr 17:1–15 is recalled often (2 Chr 6:4, 10, 15, 16; 21:7), and is repeated even more strongly in 2 Chr 13:5 as a "covenant of salt,"

---

25. See the discussion in Japhet, *Ideology*, 395–411.

an expression taken over from priestly language (Lev 2:13; Ezek 43:24; Num 18:19), to remind the Zadokite priesthood that the Davidic covenant is as permanent as any claim that they may have to divine authority, as well as contrary to the claim of Isa 55:3–5 that that covenant has been handed over to the faithful. While the Chronicler does not press the issue, he is conscious of the presence of David's descendants in the community (1 Chr 3:19–24).

Since the Ark of the Covenant (referred to as "the ark of the God Yahweh, who is enthroned on the cherubim which is called by his name," 1 Chr 13:6) represents God's rule, David is concerned to bring it into Jerusalem. Only the Levites are to carry the ark, for they have been chosen by God "to minister to him forever" (1 Chr 15:2). David himself leads the procession clothed in a linen ephod, functioning as high priest (1 Chr 15:27; cf. Exod 28:33; 39:2–22; Lev 8:7), offers up sacrifices, and pronounces Yahweh's blessing on the people (1 Chr 16:1–3). He then appoints some of the Levites to serve regularly before the ark, offering prayer, praise, and thanksgiving accompanied by their harps, lyres and cymbals—and with two priests appointed to blow trumpets. Meanwhile, Zadok and his priests, accompanied by some of the Levites, are left serving before the tabernacle in Gibeon, about 10 kilometers away.

Bringing the ark into Jerusalem also emphasized David's commitment to the covenant tradition. The Chronicler now calls it the "ark of the covenant of Yahweh" (1 Chr 15:25–29). Later, when the ark was brought into the new temple, the point was made: "There was nothing in the ark except the two tablets that Moses put there at Horeb, where Yahweh made a covenant with Israel" (2 Chr 5:10), implying that there was no "rod of Aaron" (Num 17:10), and thus no superior controlling authority of the priesthood. David was thus binding himself to the covenant relationship. While David cannot build the temple himself because he has shed much blood and waged wars (1 Chr 22:8), he nevertheless supplies all the plans, the details, the materials, the money, and even all the skilled craftsmen (1 Chr 22:2–7, 14–19; 28:1–5). All the preparations are made by David before he dies, particularly the appointment and the complete organization of the temple personnel—priests, musicians, gatekeepers, treasurers, Levite officers, and judges. Even the military and civil administration is organized in detail (1 Chr 22–28). Twice the reason given for these detailed preparations and the plea to the leaders of Israel to help Solomon is that Solomon is still "young and inexperienced" (1 Chr 22:5; 29:1). For the Chronicler, the important focus of all this detailed preparation is God's plan and direction. First Chr 28:19 makes that clear: "All this, in writing from the hand of Yahweh upon me. He caused me to have insight of all the tasks of the plan." This being so, the implication is that this should also be the basis for the second temple administration and organization.

The whole story given by the Chronicler is how David, with divine authority, planned the whole worship enterprise and set down the order of the work of both priests and Levites for the service of the house of God. The story continues with how the "good" kings, those who "walked in the ways" of their ancestor David, like Hezekiah and Josiah, sought to restore the temple and its cultus in accordance with "the written directions of King David of Israel, and the written directions of his son Solomon" (2 Chr 35:4). The story ends, then, with the promise given by King Cyrus of Persia to rebuild the house of Yahweh, the God of heaven, in Jerusalem. The implication lingers that the divine plan established through David is to continue with the new temple in the time of the Chronicler.

The Place of the Levites in Chronicles

For the Chronicler, the status of the Levites is integrally related to the Davidic authority. It is David who has set down the functions and permanent forms of service for the Jerusalem temple. While the Chronicler never mentions the second temple built under Zerubbabel, it is quite obvious that he has given a foundation for the Levites to validate their claims for equal participation in the worship activities of this temple in his time.[26]

Next to the Davidic authority over the temple worship and administration, the primary focus of the Chronicler is on the Levites and their role. Much more space is given to the Levites than to the priesthood. That is evident particularly in the genealogy of Levi (1 Chr 6:1–81) and in David's succession narrative (1 Chr 23–27). The duties of the sons of Aaron, the priests, is set out briefly as: to make offerings on the altar of burnt offering and on the altar of incense, for all the work of the most holy place, and to make atonement for Israel (1 Chr 6:49), and to minister to Yahweh and pronounce blessings in his name forever (1 Chr 23:13). Considering the role that the priesthood had taken on in the postexilic period as representatives of the Persian rulers, this was a reminder of what the limitations of their role should be.

However, the Levites, who alone were to carry the ark of God (1 Chr 15:2), were to be singers, musicians, gatekeepers, in charge of the chambers and treasuries of the house of God, take care of the ordinary and holy utensils, the furniture, flour, wine, oil, incense and spices for the temple, make flat cakes and prepare the rows of bread for each sabbath, as well as serve as officers and judges (1 Chr 9:17–33; 23:4). Whereas the Priestly Work had claimed that the Levites were "given" to Aaron and his sons to "minister to him [Aaron]" (Num 3:6–9; cf. 4:15, 27, 33), the Chronicler makes the point that the Levites were rather "given for all the service of the tabernacle of the house of God" (1 Chr 6:48), and "to minister to him [Yahweh] forever" (1 Chr 15:2).

The Chronicler emphasizes in his history how priests and Levites have worked together as equals in the past (cf. 2 Chr 23:1–21 and 2 Kgs 11:4–20). The same prominence to the Levites and priests working together as equals is also evident in the account of Hezekiah's reform, with the roles complementing each other in the cleansing of the temple (2 Chr 29:1–30). In the ensuing thanksgiving for the restoration of the temple (29:31–36), the Levites are given greater prominence because they had been more conscientious in sanctifying themselves than the priests and so were called upon to help the priests in their duties. The same is true of Hezekiah's Passover celebration which had to be delayed for a month "because the priests had not sanctified themselves in sufficient number" (2 Chr 30:3). Consequently, the Levites were required to slaughter most of the lambs for the people and were commended for showing "good skill in the service of Yahweh" (2 Chr 30:22). Both priests and Levites share in giving the blessing for the people

---

26. De Vries, "Moses and David," 638–39; Knoppers, *1 Chronicles 10–29*, 797.

(v. 27), a function usually exclusively that of the priests (Lev 9:22–23; Num 6:22–27; 1 Chr 23:13). Again, in Josiah's Passover celebration, the Levites take the prominent part as "those who instructed all Israel and who were holy to Yahweh" (2 Chr 35:3). Following the written instructions of David and Solomon they were to serve Yahweh and his people Israel, take their position in the holy place, slaughter the Passover lambs, sanctify themselves, skin the animals and carry the blood to the priests who pour it out at the foot of the altar (35:3–6, 11). The Levites also prepare the Passover lambs for the priests who are busy with the burnt offerings (35:14). Once again, the Chronicler mentions that these are their required functions since they no longer carry the ark (35:3; cf. 1 Chr 6:31; 15:2; 23:26). Contrary to the Priestly Work where the Levites are clearly subordinated to the sons of Aaron, the Chronicler has described them as sharing equally in the work of service for the house of Yahweh. The Levites are to work "at the side of the sons of Aaron" (1 Chr 23:28).[27]

In the summarizing verse of the role of the Levites (1 Chr 23:32), the Chronicler uses a rather ambiguous phrase, often used in the Priestly writings: "keep watch over." Num 18:5 follows Ezek 40:45 in asserting that only the sons of Aaron are to "keep watch over the sanctuary and watch over the altar." The Chronicler makes use of this ambiguous language to say that the Levites are to keep watch over the tent of meeting, over the sanctuary, and to keep watch over the sons of Aaron. Not only is this implying a greater role for the Levites than the Priestly Work would allow them,[28] but some kind of "censorial oversight over the priests."[29] In Ezekiel's plan for the temple, it was to be the priests who would wear the linen garments (44:17–19; cf. Exod 39:27–29; Lev 16:4, 23, 32), teach the people (44:23; cf. Lev 10:10–11; 2 Chr 15:3), and act as judges (44:24). But in Chronicles it is the Levites who are mentioned wearing linen garments (1 Chr 15:27; 2 Chr 5:12), Jehoshaphat is recorded as sending out five officials, eight Levites, and only two priests to travel around all the cities of Judah to teach the people from the book of the law of Yahweh (2 Chr 17:7–8). According to 1 Chr 23:4 and 26:9, to act as judges is a Levite responsibility.

So the evidence is there that this learned Levite scribe was making a claim for enhanced worship in the temple of Yehud with the Levites playing an equal and important part in the services. After all, these were the written directions set down by David as the founder of the temple cult. The Chronicler does not openly condemn the Zadokite priests for corruption or argue that the Levites should take over from the Zadokites as the author of Malachi had threatened. However, he does imply that the Levites need to be there to censure and curb priestly corruption. For history had shown that the priesthood was not always up to the standard expected of them. Certainly, the author of Chronicles wanted to clear up once and for all the false image of the Levites portrayed by Ezekiel and the Priestly Work. The priestly claims to faithful service (Ezek 44:15–16) and subordination of the Levites because of idolatry did not stand up to scrutiny. For, the

---

27. Knoppers rightly argues that the phrase refers to the roles of Levites and Aaronides as being complementary to each other. See his "Hierodules, Priests or Janitors?," 59; Knoppers, *1 Chronicles 10–29*, 822.

28. Knoppers, "Hierodules, Priests, or Janitors?," 63.

29. De Vries, "Moses and David," 639.

Chronicler reminded his readers, it was "all the leading priests and the people also who were exceedingly unfaithful, following the abomination of the nations; and *they* polluted the house of Yahweh that he had sanctified in Jerusalem" (2 Chr 36:14).

Levites and the Prophetic Visionaries

There is no questioning the importance of the prophetic movement in the eyes of the Chronicler.[30] It was the word of Yahweh by the prophet Samuel that David was made king (1 Chr 11:3). Prophets appear throughout Chronicles at momentous occasions as the "messengers of God" (2 Chr 36:15–16). As such they carry an authority even greater than kings. For when kings listen to the prophets they are delivered by God (e.g., 2 Chr 12:2–12; 15:1–16). However when they refuse to listen to a prophet, it would result in judgment or death (e.g., 2 Chr 16:7–13; 25:14–24).[31] Thus the prophets are the upholders of theocracy—it is God who decides on victory or defeat.

The Chronicler used various terms for these messengers of God—prophet (*nabi*), visionary (*kozeh*), seer (*ro'eh*), and twice "man of God" (2 Chr 11:2; 25:7–9), a title also used of Moses (1 Chr 23:14; 2 Chr 30:16) and David (2 Chr 8:14). He mentions those prophets found in his source, as well as introducing the reader to others.[32] He goes beyond his source by attributing the historical records of kings, particularly the ones he favors, to the writing prophets.[33] Of all the prophets of the past, Samuel is given the most prominence. He and his sons were regarded as Levites (1 Chr 6:28) and Heman, one of the leaders of the singers, was claimed to be his grandson (1 Chr 6:33).

So with Samuel installed as a Levite, the next step was to claim prophetic authority also among the Levites in general, thus giving them greater prestige. Among the leading singers organized by David to bring the ark into Jerusalem was one Chenaniah who is described as a leader of the Levites in oracular visions (1 Chr 15:22, 27). Also the three leading singers, Asaph, Heman, and Jeduthun, and their families are described as prophesying, implying that there was a close connection between the singing of psalms with music and prophesying (1 Chr 25:1–8). Each of these leaders is referred to as the "king's visionary" (Heman: 1 Chr 25:5; Asaph: 2 Chr 29:30; Jeduthun: 2 Chr 35:15) and are directly responsible to the king (1 Chr 25:6). One of the descendants of Asaph, Jahaziel, was filled with the spirit of Yahweh to encourage Jehoshaphat not to fear the great army coming against Judah because "the battle is not yours but God's" (2 Chr 20:14–15). This prophetic action had the right response from Jehoshaphat who then exhorted the people: "Believe in Yahweh your God and you will be established; believe his prophets" (20:20).

Only in the last couple of chapters of his work does the Chronicler refer to the Levite-prophet who had been his mentor, Jeremiah. Jeremiah's influence on his thinking and theology has been evident throughout, as, for instance, when he puts the language

---

30. Cf. Petersen, *Late Israelite Prophecy*, 55–56.
31. See further, Japhet, *Ideology*, 179–80.
32. See the lists in Jonker, "Chronicler," 276–78.
33. Cf. Klein, *1 Chronicles*, 41–42.

of Jer 29:18 into the mouth of Hezekiah in 2 Chr 29:8. Jeremiah is first mentioned by name at the time of the death of King Josiah as one who uttered laments for him, a custom which was being continued by the Levitical singers "to this day" (2 Chr 35:25). Then he is mentioned as the prophet who spoke "from the mouth of Yahweh" (2 Chr 36:12). Jeremiah's favorite phrase, "I have *persistently sent* my servants the prophets" (Jer 7:25; 25:4; 26:5; 29:19; 35:15; 44:4) becomes "Yahweh *sent persistently* to them by his messengers" in 2 Chr 36:15. The long period of the Babylonian exile is seen as the fulfillment of "the word of Yahweh in the mouth of Jeremiah, until the land has made up for its sabbaths. All the days that it lay desolate it kept sabbath, to fulfill seventy years" (2 Chr 36:21; cf. Jer 25:12; 29:10). Even the coming of Cyrus of Persia as liberator is attributed to the fulfillment of the word of Yahweh spoken by Jeremiah (2 Chr 36:22). The Chronicler probably had in mind here Jer 29:10–14, although it was Isa 44:28 and 45:1 that first mentioned Cyrus. The reason why the Chronicler has completed his work with references and allusions to Jeremiah rather than any other prophet is clear: as a Levite he has been influenced by and honors the work of Jeremiah as the great Levite-prophet of the past whose word is fulfilled.[34]

There is much that the Chronicler has in common with the prophetic visionaries. His universal appeal to all Israel and inclusion of foreigners and sojourners in the people of Israel would be well received by the prophetic call to be a light to the nations. The greater role for the people in the covenant relationship, and the theocratic understanding that it is essentially the kingdom of Yahweh in the hands of David and his descendants (1 Chr 17:14; 28:5; 29:11; 2 Chr 13:8) would meet some of the prophetic concerns. However, the visionaries would not have been able to go along with the emphasis on cultic ritual, nor the Chronicler's insistence on the permanence of the Davidic dynasty, claiming that Yahweh had given the kingship to David and his sons "by a covenant of salt" (2 Chr 13:5). That the Chronicler was disputing the prophetic claim that the everlasting covenant made with David had been transferred to the faithful in Isa 55:3–5 is clear from the way he changed the wording in the quotation of Ps 132:8–10 from "for the sake of your servant David" to "remember *your steadfast love for David* your servant" in 2 Chr 6:42. His use of the phrase "steadfast love for David" was taken from Isa 55:3.[35] While differing from the visionaries in regard to the reestablishment of the Davidic monarchy, the Chronicler has shown how the prophetic vision had influenced the Levites on some issues, agreeing particularly with the opposition to the growing power and claims of the Zadokite priesthood.

---

34. Jonker suggests that it was because of "the Chronicler's strong tendency to merge different traditions in his version of the past" ("Chronicler," 291–92). Leuchter, "Prophets," 31–47, would argue that all the prophets of Jeremiah's time were Levites which then explains why the Chronicler changed "the priests and prophets" in his source (2 Kgs 23:2) to "the priests and the Levites" in 2 Chr 34:30.

35. See Leske, "Context and Meaning," 667–69. For a different view see Riley, *King and Cultus*, 196–200.

Chapter VII

The Prophetic Vision Under Pressure

MEANWHILE, THE PERSIANS UNDER Artaxerxes III (359–338 BCE) were occupied trying to maintain control of the empire. Attempts to regain Egypt had led to a humiliating defeat for Artaxerxes in 351 BCE. Kings of Phoenicia and Cyprus took the opportunity to revolt, but the Persian armies were sent against them, and this finally led to their surrender and the destruction of Sidon in 346 BCE.[1] In the meantime, Artaxerxes had been gathering together an enormous army of 300,000 infantry, 30,000 cavalry, as well as 300 triremes and 50 other transport vehicles to bring Egypt under Persian control. Moving with these enormous forces from Phoenicia in 343, the army was able to cross the Nile, put the Egyptian army to flight and to return with much booty. Egypt once again came under Persian control.[2]

The need for the Persians to raise and maintain such enormous armies required revenue. This meant that the administrators of the Province of Yehud, which included the Jerusalem priesthood, found themselves once again under pressure to supply increased tribute. This, in turn, required collecting more taxes from the people of the land who were already burdened and facing loss because of growing debt. One can understand that this only led to further distrust and conflict between the people of Judah as a whole and the administration in Jerusalem.[3]

These were unsettling times, and with the growing turmoil throughout the Persian Empire, anxiety and fear among the people of Yehud led them to look for God's answer to this troubling period. Those who sided with the Chronicler looked with renewed hope for a Davidic messiah to arise and bring about independence. The Zadokite priesthood turned to Ezekiel's claims that Yahweh would gather all the armies of hostile nations to the hills of Judah under Gog of Magog to finally destroy them there (Ezek 38–39). These hopes for release from economic oppression, for freedom and independence, as well as the extension of their territory to the boundaries known in the time of David, were only

---

1. Briant, *From Cyrus to Alexander*, 682–85.
2. Ibid., 686–87.
3. See, e.g., Redditt, "Nehemiah's First Mission," 672–73. However, beside the tithe for local taxes, Ezra-Nehemiah speaks of tribute, poll tax, and property tax, Ezra 4:13, 20; 6:28; 7:24; Neh 5:4. Moreover, Zech 9–14 gives evidence of a later date when the situation was clearly worse.

heightened during the annual eight-day Feast of Booths when they celebrated the gifts of harvest and the promises of God (cf. Deut 16:13–15; Exod 34:22–24; Lev 23:33–43).

THE MESSAGE OF ZECHARIAH 9–14

Against all this background around 350–345 BCE, an unknown prophet, who authored Zech 9–14, spoke out, imbued with the Isaianic vision. Like Haggai, this prophet whom we refer to as Deutero-Zechariah, took advantage of the assembly of the people in Jerusalem at an annual Feast of Booths to respond to the situation in Jehud. His first response was in the form of an oracular vision (*massa'*) during the Feast (chs. 9–11). This was followed by a more insistent response at a later harvest festival (chs. 12–14) when the threat of approaching armies seems to have been more imminent.[4] Much of what is found in these oracles is in reaction to the two groups—mildly corrective of the Davidic claims of the Chronicler, and strongly against the actions of the priestly group and their reassertion of the claims of Ezekiel.

These oracles appear to have been affixed to the earlier writings of the priest-prophet Zechariah (chs. 1–8) because of common hopes for the universal spread of the worship of Yahweh evident in Zech 8:20–23 and in Zech 9:1–8 and 14:9–21. Apart from that the two sections (1–8, 9–14) have little in common.

The First Oracular Vision (9–11)

The prophet begins his first oracular vision with an affirmation (9:1–8) of an old promise repeated at the three major festivals: "I will cast out nations before you and enlarge your borders" (Exod 24:34), alluding particularly to how that promise is expressed in Ezek 47:13–23 (cf. Num 34:1–12) and with the contemporary political situation in mind: "The word of Yahweh *is* in the land of Hadrach, and Damascus is its resting place. For to Yahweh is the eye of humankind and all the tribes of Israel, and also Hamath which borders on it" (9:1–2a). In this brief summary the prophet has emphasized that *all* the tribes of Israel (cf. Ezek 47:21–23) look to Yahweh, and combines this with the promise of Isa 17:7 that "in that day humankind will look to their Maker, and their eyes will see the Holy One of Israel." This promise was echoed in Isa 52:10 which, after the joyous announcement to Zion that "Your God reigns!" (52:7), affirms, "Yahweh has bared his holy arm before the *eyes of all the nations*, and all the ends of the earth shall see the salvation of our God."

The prophet can see the action of God in the armies sent from Damascus[5] against the Phoenician cities of Tyre and Sidon (9:2b–4). The Philistine cities will be next to come under judgment and will eventually be included within the extended borders of Israel, and incorporated into Judah as a clan, just as the Jebusites were at the time of

---

4. Leske, "Context and Meaning," 669–71.

5. Damascus was an important center between Babylonia and Egypt (cf. Briant, *From Cyrus to Alexander*, 487) and was included in the ideal Davidic kingdom (cf. Num 34:1–12; Deut 1:7; Josh 1:3–4; 2 Kgs 14:24–27; Ezek 47:16–20) and probably included some Israelites among its inhabitants.

David (9:5–7). This appears to be a reminder to those who still held to the exclusive views of Ezra that even Ezek 47:22 speaks of "aliens" becoming citizens of Israel. Once God has established that, he will stand guard over his people so that no longer will any tyrant march over them (9:8).

After this proclamation, the means by which Yahweh will accomplish this is announced: "Rejoice greatly, O daughter Zion! Shout aloud, O daughter Jerusalem! Lo, your king is coming to you . . . " (9:9). This draws on a number of prophetic declarations of the past where Yahweh is announced as "King of Israel," as in Zeph 3:14–15; Isa 40:9–11; 52:1–9; and 62:11. It is the kingship of Yahweh that is being announced. But the description of the king is in terms never used of Yahweh, or of a Davidic king. God's representative is here depicted as "righteous and saved" (*tsadiq wenosha'*) and "afflicted" (*'ani*). These were terms frequently used of Servant Israel. The prophet evidently had in mind that the announcement of the good news of God's reign in Isa 52:7–10 was the prelude to the announcement of the Servant in 52:13—53:12 as the one *afflicted* (Isa 53:4, 7) and *saved* (53:10; cf. 45:7) who is "the righteous one" who will "make many righteous" (53:11). This, then, was followed with the announcement in Isa 55:3–5 that the everlasting covenant made with David was transferred to the faithful who are now to be God's witnesses to the nations.[6]

Moreover, to make it even clearer that it is the people of Judah as the Servant who will represent Yahweh's kingship, the prophet further describes the "king" in terms of Gen 49:10–12, an allusion to Judah as leader prior to the monarchy coming to Shiloh for the Feast of Booths, mounted on a young male donkey, offspring of a she-donkey to emphasize his peaceful and democratic leadership. Symbolically, his mount is neither a horse (an animal of war), nor a mule (the traditional mount of David and Solomon) but a purebred donkey, an animal of service. So no Davidic king, or hierocracy will act as the instruments of God's reign. It will be the people of Judah, joined by all the tribes of Israel (9:9, 10, 13; 10:6–12), who will "command peace to the nations" (9:10; cf. Isa 42:1, 6; 52:7) without chariot, warhorse, or battle bow (cf, Isa 2:4; 43:15–17). Picking up on Isa 49:2, Judah and Ephraim are described again as bow and arrow and sword in the hand of God (9:13) to bring about God's rule.

Speaking out at the Festival and using language and metaphor alluding to Isa 40–66 which the faithful would discern, the prophet reminds them that they have been given as a people-covenant to be a light to the nations, and that Yahweh has set their prisoners free from the exile to be that light (9:11–12—Isa 42:6–7; 49:6–8; 61:1), assuring them again that they will be restored to a double portion of joy (9:12b—Isa 61:7). For Yahweh will use their mouth like a sharp sword (9:13b—Isa 49:2) against "the sons of Greece." The Greeks were renowned as traders throughout the Persian Empire as well as for serving as mercenaries in both Persian and Egyptian armies. Greek traders had been prominent throughout Phoenicia and Palestine centuries before the coming of Alexander.[7] Already during the exile Greece (Javan) was known for trading in slaves and bronze vessels (Ezek 27:13), and that was still going on near the end of the Persian era (cf. Joel

---

6. Leske, "Context and Meaning," 671–72. In agreement with Mason, "Use of Earlier Biblical Material," 42–44; Petersen, *Zechariah 9–14*, 58–59.

7. See Smith, "Hellenization," 108–9.

3:6). So the faithful are to participate in Yahweh's theophany as he executes judgment (9:13–14; cf. Isa 66:15–16). But Yahweh will protect them so that they are able to trample on the slingstones (9:15; cf. Isa 54:17) and continue to eat and drink and noisily celebrate their harvest festival.[8] For they are the sheep of Yahweh's flock (Isa 40:11), the jewels of his crown (9:16; cf. Isa 54:11; 62:3). Their young men and women will soon once again be able to enjoy the *fullness* of the harvest without most of it taken by foreigners (9:17; cf. Isa 62:8–9; Jer 31:10–14).

Speaking more directly, the prophet decries the false leaders of Yehud and their faithless ways, for they have left Yahweh's people like sheep afflicted (as in 9:9) and without a true shepherd (10:1–2). The false leaders under divine condemnation are referred to as "shepherds" and "he-goats" (10:3), terms that cover both the priestly and secular leaders of Yehud. The flock, those who are to represent Yahweh's kingship (9:9), are identified further as "the house of Judah" which is to be Yahweh's agent in bringing about deliverance from oppressive forces and fulfillment of divine promises. They are to be the "cornerstone" of Isa 28:16, the "tent peg" of Isa 33:20 and 54:2, the "battle bow" of Isa 49:2 and Zech 9:13, and the righteous "taskmaster" of Isa 60:17 (10:4). As such, they will be Yahweh's fighting force (10:5) which he will strengthen through union with northern Israel (10:6–7). Even all those scattered among the nations, in Egypt and Assyria (cf. Isa 52:3–6), would be gathered to fill up the land, extending its borders to Lebanon and Gilead (10:8–10). This was a hope that had often been expressed by the prophets (Isa 11:11–16; 54:1–3; Jer 31:1–22; Ezek 37:15–22) and it would soon happen to make the faithful strong in Yahweh as they walk in his name (10:12).

The mention of extending the borders to Lebanon (cf. Deut 1:7–8; 11:24; Josh 1:3–4; 13:5–6) led to a further triumphal denunciation of Phoenicia's pride and arrogance (cf. 9:2–4), depicted here in terms of fire destroying the cedars of Lebanon and the oaks of Bashan (11:1–2; cf. Isa 2:12–13; 10:34). Already the consequences of Sidon's revolt may have become evident. This would affect the leaders in Jerusalem, for their cover would be destroyed (11:3; cf. Jer 25:34–38). What that cover is, is now to be revealed (11:4–17).[9]

Using again somewhat cryptic language, the prophet now gives a very pessimistic view of the situation of his time which virtually puts on hold everything he had expressed before. Speaking in allegorical terms of being commissioned to be a shepherd of the "sheep for slaughter," a term borrowed from Jer 12:3, Deutero-Zechariah brings a bitter indictment against the leaders of Yehud, for the people of Judah are being sold into slavery to foreigners! "Those who buy them slaughter them and are not held guilty, and those who sell them are saying, 'Blessed be Yahweh, for I have become rich,' and their shepherds show no compassion for them" (11:5). The situation has become far worse than during Nehemiah's time when debts "to pay for the king's tax" led many to lose their property to creditors and, together with family members, to be sold into slavery

---

8. Translations of 9:15 which speak of the faithful drinking the blood of the slingers (e.g., RSV, NRSV) are misled by the addition of "blood" in the LXX which seems to have been influenced by Ezek 39:17–18. See also Petersen, *Zechariah 9–14*, 65. The literal translation of the Hebrew is: "Yahweh of hosts will give protection over them, and they shall eat and trample the clingstones, and they shall drink, and be noisy as from wine, and be full like a bowl, like the corners of the altar."

9. Cf. Petersen, *Zechariah 9–14*, 85.

to other nations by the nobles, officials, and priests in Jerusalem (Neh 5:1–13). With higher taxes now heavier, the "buyers" who sacrificed the debtors to the slave markets of Tyre and elsewhere are the Greek traders mentioned in 9:13, the sellers and the shepherds who have no compassion for the sheep are the priests and officials of 10:3. For the priesthood and administrators of Yehud were responsible for paying the "king's tax"[10] as officials of the Persian government, since temples in the empire often functioned as gathering centers for tribute and as treasuries.[11] Because of this moral corruption and lack of compassion, the prophet declares that Yahweh will show no compassion on the inhabitants of the land, and the people will be left in the hands of their neighbors (probably neighboring provinces) and the Persian king, who will devastate the land (11:6).

So the prophet takes up the role of the shepherd of the sheep for slaughter, that is, "the afflicted of the flock" mentioned in 10:2.[12] As a sign of his desire to bring about God's favor for all peoples and the unity of Judah and Israel, the focus of 10:6–12, the prophet took two staffs which he labeled "Favor" and "Unity." But it was of no avail, for while he was able to eliminate three corrupt leaders in one month, he realized that he did not have the people behind him (11:7–8). So he resigned his position realizing that Yahweh's declaration of judgment (11:6) was inevitable (11:9). As a sign that God's grace and favor had been withdrawn, he broke the staff, "Favor," which the afflicted of the flock knew was the word of Yahweh (11:10–11). Thus the covenant that God had made with all the peoples was annulled. For it was the people God had given as a people-covenant to be a light to the nations that had failed in their mission (cf. Isa 42:6; 49:6, 8). So for his trouble the prophet was paid off with thirty shekels of silver, ironically the price of a slave (Exod 21:32), which he was bidden by God to throw to the smelter in the temple (11:12–13).[13]

As a sign that the leaders were also rejecting the unity between Israel and Judah, the prophet now broke his second staff, "Unity." For the priestly claim that they were following Ezekiel's plan to unify all Israel, was hypocritical when they continued to exclude all those they regarded as ritually impure. Their actions had completely negated the very message of Ezekiel (37:15–22) that they professed to follow. As a consequence, they had also lost the grace and favor of God.[14] But it was more than that. While this passage (11:4–17) hits hard at the priestly and civic leaders of the province, it is really to show that the people of Yahweh as a whole had failed to achieve their God-given purpose. That purpose was twofold: "to raise up the tribes of Jacob" and to be "a light to the nations," so that salvation might reach "to the ends of the earth" (Isa 49:5–6). As a consequence, they would continue to experience what the prophet is then called upon to act out: a worthless shepherd who abuses and exploits those under him to the full extent for his

---

10. In agreement with Hanson, *Dawn*, 342–43.

11. See Schaper, "Jerusalem Temple," 528–39; Schaper, "Temple Treasury Committee," 200–206.

12. I follow the MT here in 11:7, 11, which has *laken aniyye hatson*. Most interpreters have emended this to *lakenaani*: "to the Canaanites (traders) of the sheep," in accordance with 14:21 as in RSV, NRSV, etc. Cf. on this point Larkin, *Eschatology of Second Zechariah*, 110–11.

13. See Schaper, "Jerusalem Temple," 536–39.

14. In agreement with Hanson, *Dawn*, 342–46.

own selfish gain (11:15–17). So the priesthood as the worthless shepherds will be the very epitome of the false shepherds Ezekiel had condemned (Ezek 34:1–6).

Second Oracular Vision, Zechariah 12–14

The oracles in this section were probably delivered at the gathering of the people in Jerusalem for a later Feast of Booths. There had been a growing threat of armies on the march, causing further anxiety about the future. The response by those who had followed the leadership of the priesthood appears to have been to turn to the triumphal message of Ezek 38–39, while royalists and Levites increased their hope for a Davidic leader to be their deliverer. These oracles respond to both groups but give a different view of what will happen "on that day" (a phrase used 14 times in this oracular vision) from a clearly prophetic understanding.

The prophet begins this section (12:1) with an abbreviated quotation from Isa 42:5, a passage which emphasizes that all power and all life is God's creation, and which leads on to announce that God has given Israel as a people-covenant and a light to the nations (42:6). But foremost in the prophet's mind is the similar description of God in Isa 51:12–16 in which Deutero-Isaiah reminded the exiles that they were fearful because they had forgotten Yahweh their Creator who is the one "who stretched out the heavens and laid the foundation of the earth" (Isa 51:13). He had promised release from the exile and it had happened. What followed in Isa 51:17–23, is now taken up in Zech 12:2, where the prophet points out that the promise that Yahweh would take the cup of reeling from his people and give it to their oppressors is now to be fulfilled. For Jerusalem will become that cup of reeling for her attackers because in Jerusalem, in Zion, Yahweh has laid a foundation stone, a precious cornerstone (Isa 28:16), described as the faithful of Judah in 10:4, which nations, by trying to remove it, will only bring harm to themselves (12:3). For the covenant curse of Deut 28:28 will come upon those nations which come against that foundation stone, and both horse and rider will be thrown into panic and confusion. However, Yahweh will be watching over the leaders of Judah, and they will recognize, in spite of some tension, that their strength lies with the inhabitants of Jerusalem "in Yahweh of hosts, their God" (12:4, 5). For that cornerstone which cannot be moved is the basis for renewal of the community with justice and righteousness (Isa 28:17).[15]

For it is the clans of Judah which Yahweh will use to maintain Jerusalem in its place: "On that day I will set the clans of Judah like a pot of fire on a pile of wood and like a flaming torch among the sheaves, and they will devour to the right and to the left all the peoples round about, and Jerusalem will continue to dwell in its place, in Jerusalem" (12:6). One naturally thinks of Samson sending flaming torches tied to the tails of foxes through the sheaves of the Philistines (Judg 15:1–5),[16] but the prophet is drawing primarily on Gen 15:17–21, in which God made a covenant with Abram to give the land from the Nile to the Euphrates to his descendants, a passage familiar to celebrants of the

---

15. Cf. Mason, "Use of Earlier Biblical Material," 146.
16. As does Mason (ibid., 150).

Feast of Booths. In that passage the "smoking pot" and the "flaming torch" were the signs and seal of that covenant. Thus the emphasis in Zech 12:6 is on the clans of Judah being God's agents in carrying out God's covenant promise to his people.

In that final imaginary battle, Yahweh will give deliverance to "the tents of Judah" first, so that "the pride of the house of David and the pride of the inhabitant of Jerusalem may not be greater than Judah's" (12:7). All are put on an equal level. While "the inhabitants of Jerusalem" must refer to the Zadokite priests and their associates in administration (12:5; 13:1), when the prophet uses the singular as he does in 12:7, 8, 10, he may be focusing more directly on the high priest as head of that group. The equalizing of the power and pride of the three groups in 12:7 is carried further in v. 8. For the authority of the high priest will be curtailed, and the "feeblest among them" (cf. Isa 35:3; 40:30; 59:10), that is, the "tents of Judah,"[17] will be like David, following the democratizing of kingship in Isa 55:3–5. But the statement that "the house of David shall be like God, like an angel of Yahweh before them" is unusual and deliberately ambiguous. The hopes for restoration after the exile were often depicted in terms of the garden of Eden restored (Isa 51:3; 58:11; Ezek 36:33–35; Joel 2:3). The only other reference to being "like God" in Scripture is in Gen 3:5 where the serpent promises Adam and Eve that they shall be "like God, knowing good and evil," which eventually led to them being cast out of the garden. The addition of "like an angel of Yahweh" only continues this theme, for the phrase is an allusion to 2 Sam 14:17, where the woman of Tekoa flatters David by telling him that he is "like an angel of God to discern good and evil" (see also 2 Sam 19:28). Compare Ezekiel's condemnation of Tyre for claiming to have a mind "like the mind of God" (Ezek 28:2, 6) for which he is cast out of the garden of Eden (Ezek 28:7–13). These descriptions of the house of David thus do not elevate its position but bring it down to a very human level. So, "on that day," when God destroys the nations that come against Jerusalem (12:9), all authority will be thoroughly democratized under the rule of God.

While Deutero-Zechariah has been emphasizing the role of the faithful (clans of Judah) over against the royalists and the priesthood, he has also had in mind the Chronicler's claims, and that becomes clear in the following verses (12:10—13:1). Yahweh will pour out a spirit of favor and supplication "on the house of David and on the inhabitant of Jerusalem." The word "favor" always has the meaning of looking with favor on someone, and "supplications" are always addressed to God, seeking help, forgiveness, and cleansing. This is the spirit which will be given to the house of David and the "inhabitant" of Jerusalem in the future, leading them to be filled with sorrow and regret when they realize what they have done. They will look on the "one whom they have pierced" and yet has been God's instrument of their deliverance. For the one whom they have pierced are the people of Judah who have already been referred to earlier as the "afflicted" (9:9; 10:2; 11:7, 11), the "sheep for slaughter" (11:4, 7). So their mourning will be like that at the death of King Josiah in the plain of Megiddo, which the Chronicler had mentioned as continuing "to this day" (2 Chr 35:20–25).

To emphasize the extent and thoroughness of the mourning needed to show repentance, the prophet gives a list of mourners imitating the genealogical lists of the

---

17. See Leske, "Context and Meaning," 676.

Chronicler[18] with four specific names mentioned—David, Nathan, Levi, and Shimei. It is unlikely that the "Nathan" mentioned here is one of the sons of David (cf. 1 Chr 3:5; 14:4)[19] since he plays no significant role in history. "Nathan" must refer to the prophet Nathan[20] who was given such a prominent role in the Chronicler's work—as the one who had announced the everlasting Davidic dynastic rule (1 Chr 17:1–16) and was partly responsible for the histories of David and Solomon (1 Chr 29:29; 2 Chr 9:29). The family of the "house of Levi" is a label, the Chronicler had argued, which referred to all priests and Levites, while the "family of Shimei" was one of the prominent Levite families mentioned a number of times by the Chronicler (1 Chr 6:16, 17, 42; 23:7, 9, 10; 25:17). By mentioning each family by itself and their wives by themselves, the emphasis is placed on the need for each and every individual as equal persons to make the commitment to change (12:12–14). Only then, "on that day," will the house of David and all the inhabitants of Jerusalem be cleansed from sin and impurity by Yahweh, the fountain and source of living waters (13:1; cf. Jer 2:13; 17:13; Pss 36:10; 68:27). That is what the flow of living waters mentioned in Ezek 47:1–12 is to accomplish. It will need more than the ritual sprinkling with clean water of Ezek 36:25.

Significantly, the house of Judah is not mentioned in this mourning and cleansing since they are the righteous and the saved (9:9), the group the prophet represents. He uses the word for impurity (*niddah*), which has the general meaning of menstrual impurity (cf. Lev 12:2, 5; 15:19–23) because it is the term used in Ezek 36:17–18 for Israel's idolatrous practices (cf. Ezek 16, 23). Already, idolatry and false prophecy had been linked in Zech 10:2. Thus the prophet implies that the claims of the house of David and the official cult with its practice in Jerusalem have been idolatrous, bolstered up by false prophets and the "spirit of uncleanness." This "spirit of uncleanness," while recalling Ezek 36:17, 25, 29, may also refer to the way the priestly laws of uncleanness (cf. Lev 15:3–31) have been used to isolate the priesthood and their adherents from the rest of the population (Ezra 6:21; 9:11). However, when this great cleansing happens, those who have misled the people will be ashamed (Ezek 36:32) of their false visions, and with Ezekiel's reference to Eden in mind (Ezek 36:35) will claim to be simply "a tiller of the soil which Adam caused them to possess" (13:4–5, alluding to Gen 2:15). But they will bear the marks of the past: The wounds they received in the house of their lovers (13:6) alludes to Ezekiel's description of Israel's past idolatrous relationship with other nations which Yahweh promised he would gather against them on every side (Ezek 16:36, 37; 23:22).

After talking about the ideal future, the prophet turns somewhat abruptly to the contemporary scene with all its inequities and injustices being done to the people, described in 11:4–17. Justice will come before there can be renewal. Again, using some of Ezekiel's imagery (Ezek 5:1–12; 21:21:9–17) he describes the sword of God (11:17; cf. Isa 34:5–6; 51:9) striking the shepherd, who claims to be Yahweh's representative, and scattering the sheep with the result that two thirds perish. The one third left will be tested

---

18. Cf. Mason, "Use of Earlier Biblical Material," 166.

19. As understood by many interpreters. E.g., Mason, ibid., 167; Petersen, *Zechariah 9–14*, 122; Meyers and Meyers, *Zechariah 9–14*, 346–47.

20. Hanson, *Dawn*, 366.

and refined like silver and gold in the furnace of affliction (Isa 48:10) and will acknowledge Yahweh as their only God (13:7–9). These verses are a poetic cry of impatience and a desire to see the final vindication of the faithful and the sincere renewal of the covenant relationship once again.[21]

In the final oracle (Zech 14:1–21), the prophet focuses particularly on Jerusalem and its inhabitants. He does this partly to correct the priesthood's triumphal view of the future based on their understanding of Ezek 38–48 which, presumably, they had been feeding to the people during these anxious times. News of the Persians gathering together an enormous army to overthrow Egypt would have caused a lot of anxiety in Yehud. Yet Deutero-Zechariah particularly wants to present the prophetic vision in which the nations will come to acknowledge Yahweh as their only King.

So, whereas Ezekiel's vision of Gog of Magog gathering all the nations to come against Israel in a final great battle, only to be struck down by God with sword, famine and pestilence before they can plunder or harm Israel (Ezek 38–39), Deutero-Zechariah depicts Yahweh as gathering the nations to take Jerusalem, to plunder and rape, and divide the spoil in their midst, sending half the population into exile. But there would be a remnant which would not be cut off from Jerusalem because it was to be the seat of Yahweh's earthly rule (14:1–2). Thus, the covenant curse (Deut 28:25–30) could be carried out to cleanse Jerusalem of the faithless *before* Yahweh would carry out judgment on their aggressors (14:3). Only then would Yahweh appear in a great theophany in which the land would shake, mountains be thrown down, cliffs fall, and walls tumble (Ezek 38:19–21). Yahweh would appear on the Mount of Olives, the Mount from which he departed and on which he would return, according to Ezek 11:23 and 43:2. But the splitting of the mountain alludes to the revealing of those who have entered "the caverns of the rocks and the clefts of the crags from the terror of Yahweh and from the glory of his majesty, when he rises to terrify the earth" (Isa 2:10, 19, 21; cf. Isa 40:3–5).[22] These "idolaters" (Zech 13:2; Isa 2:20), thus revealed, will flee when Yahweh takes over Jerusalem with all his holy ones (v. 5). These are the faithful who have not been cut off from Jerusalem, who will carry out God's judgment (Isa 13:3) and are the redeemed (Isa 4:3; 62:10–12). The prophet's reference to "Yahweh *my* God" (v. 5) indicates his rejection of those inhabitants of Jerusalem and their worship who will be revealed as unfaithful on that day, and clearly aligns himself with the "holy ones."[23]

"On that day," which only Yahweh knows, all the prophetic promises will come to fulfillment. The promise that on the day when Yahweh heals his people, "the light of the moon will be like the light of the sun, and the light of the sun will be sevenfold" (Isa 30:26), and the promise that when nations come to the light reflected by the faithful (Isa 60:1, 3), "the sun shall no longer be your light by day, nor for brightness shall the

---

21. Some have argued that 13:7–9 is misplaced and should be attached to 11:17 (e.g., Mason, "Use of Earlier Biblical Material," 118–30; Mitchell, *Critical and Exegetical Commentary*, 314–18). However, these verses really set the pattern for the final chapter (14); in agreement with Petersen, *Zechariah 9–14*, 129.

22. For a more complete study of the use of biblical allusions in Zech 14, see Schaefer, "Zechariah 14," 66–91.

23. In agreement with Mason, "Use of Earlier Biblical Material," 183–84.

moon give light to you, but Yahweh will be your everlasting light" (60:19–20) will be fulfilled. So this is what Deutero-Zechariah sets down as the first aspect of the ideal future: night and day are no longer relevant for the light of God's presence will always be there (14:6–7). Then, partly in response to Ezekiel's vision of water flowing from below the threshold of the temple to the east giving life to all it touches (47:1–12), he speaks rather of the living waters flowing from Jerusalem (avoiding any mention of the temple) to both east and west (14:8), largely in line with Isa 59:19. Thus, Yahweh will become King over all the earth in fulfillment of the Isaian vision (Isa 2:2–4; 40:9–11; 52:7).

As the one and only King, Yahweh will need no intermediary (14:9). Jerusalem will be the earthly seat of Yahweh's reign, and those who survive of the nations will be able to come every year to Jerusalem to acknowledge Yahweh as their King and to celebrate the Feast of Booths in thanksgiving in fulfillment of the hopes expressed in Isa 60. Thus, the priestly codes for distinguishing between "holy and common, clean and unclean" (Ezek 42:13–14, 20; 44:5–6, 19, 23; 46:20) will become null and void. According to the priesthood, the phrase, "Holy to Yahweh," engraved on a gold plate was to be worn only by the high priest on his turban (Exod 28:36–38; cf. Zech 3:5) to indicate his power and authority. Yet it had been the priesthood that had condoned the selling of the indebted into slavery to foreign merchants like the Greeks (11:4–17), and as such, they were nothing more than "traders (Canaanites) in the house of Yahweh" (Zech 14:21). This priestly claim to exclusiveness and power had been rejected by the prophetic group before (Isa 65:1–5). But here, with biting sarcasm, the prophet proclaims that even the bells of the horses bringing these foreigners, who had been rejected as unclean by the priesthood (Ezek 44:5–7; Isa 56:3–8), would be inscribed with "Holy to Yahweh" (14:20). Nor will distinctions of holiness be made between pots and bowls, nor for that matter, by implication, between people and priesthood. For all are to be holy before God. With so many people coming to Jerusalem to worship their King, there would be no place for the exclusivity of the Zadokite priesthood to declare what is holy and what is not. All God's faithful people will be called "priests of Yahweh," "ministers of our God" (Isa 61:6; cf. 66:21), God's "holy ones."

THE PROPHET JOEL'S RESPONSE TO THESE UNCERTAIN TIMES

Little is known about the prophet Joel or about his time of writing, but it appears likely that his strong warning of the proximity of the Day of Yahweh would place him near the end of the Persian Empire. His prophetic proclamations demonstrate that he was well educated, and thoroughly familiar with the prophetic literature of the past, which he was able to quote or allude to freely. His writing also shows that he was intimately acquainted with the rituals, liturgies and laments of the temple worship in Jerusalem.

His message is a call for repentance from the people of Judah and Jerusalem in the face of imminent destruction. Using the imagery of a locust plague and drought (1:4; 2:25) he sees God's army coming to bring destruction on that great and terrible Day of Yahweh (2:2, 11—alluding to Mal 3:2, 23) first on Judah and Jerusalem and then on all the nations that have humiliated and harassed Yahweh's people (2:20; 3:1–15, 19). With this imminent threat of judgment, the prophet gives an urgent call to the people of

Judah and Jerusalem to return to Yahweh their God with sincerity, for God is gracious and merciful (2:12–14). No particular transgressions are mentioned, but the priests in particular are addressed to lead in the act of repentance and return (1:9, 13; 2:17). Only those who faithfully call on the name of Yahweh will be saved and escape the judgment.

After this "cleansing" of the people of God, all the nations will be gathered together in the valley of decision for their own destruction, as Yahweh wreaks vengeance on them for their persecution of his people and their looting of his possessions (3:1–15). It would be like the great battle during the reign of Jehoshaphat, described in 2 Chr 20, when the surrounding nations in great multitudes were coming against Judah and Jerusalem. At that time, the Levite prophet Jahaziel called upon Jehoshaphat and the people to not be afraid "for the battle is not yours but God's" (2 Chr 20:15). So approaching the enemy with Levite choirs loudly singing the praises of Yahweh (2 Chr 20:18–22), God caused the nations to turn against each other until they were utterly destroyed. So the Day of Yahweh would be like the valley of Jehoshaphat, a total destruction of the nations. The message of hope for the nations in Isa 2:2–4 and Mic 4:2–3 would be reversed (Joel 3:9–10).

Then Israel would know that their God dwells in Zion, and Jerusalem will be holy with no aliens ever again contaminating it by their presence (3:17). Then Judah and Jerusalem will experience peace and prosperity and inhabit their land forever (2:18–27; 3:18, 20; cf. Amos 9:13), and the spirit of God would be poured out on everyone (2:28–29).

For his graphic image of that Day of Yahweh when God carries out his judgment on Israel and the nations, Joel draws on all the references to that Day in the writings of previous prophets. He uses the distinctive language of Mal 3:2; 4:5, a warning to the Zadokite priesthood, and finds fertile ground for his description particularly in Isa 13, an oracle against Babylon, and also in Obadiah's oracle against Edom. But he also uses the language of Amos 5:18 and Zeph 1:7–8, 14–16, which are warnings for Israel, Judah, and the nations of the coming judgment. His reference to the Day in 1:15: "Alas for the Day! For the Day of Yahweh is near, and as destruction (*shad*) it comes from the Destroyer (*shaddai*)," is a quotation from Isa 13:6 where the same play on the ancient name of God (El Shaddai) is used. His second reference in 2:1–2 draws heavily on Zeph 1:14–15. Joel has combined all the previous references to the Day of Yahweh whether they were directed against the nations or against Israel/Judah and used them in the first instance against Judah and Jerusalem (1:15; 2:1–2, 30–31), and then against the surrounding nations (3:13–15).

Joel and Zechariah 9–14

There is much that Joel has in common with Zech 9–14. They both denounce Tyre and Sidon and Philistia for their amassing of silver and gold (Joel 3:4–5—Zech 9:1–7). Both condemn the practice of the people of Judah being sold into slavery to the Greeks and Phoenicians (Joel 3:3–6—Zech 9:13; 11:4–14). Both demonstrate a strong criticism of the ruling priesthood (Joel 1:9, 13–15; 2:12–17—Zech 10:1–3; 11:4–14). Both allude to the great final battle with the nations (Joel 3:1–2, 9–16—Zech 12, 14). In that event both speak of the Day of Yahweh in which the judgment will first be visited on Jerusalem with only the remnant of the faithful as survivors (Joel 2:32—Zech 14:2).[24] However, while Zech 14:16 sees the survival of those of the nations who accept Yahweh as King, there is only total destruction of the nations in Joel's account.

Like Zech 9–14, Joel demonstrates a considerable knowledge of the prophetic and other writings. Yet, while Deutero-Zechariah shows a strong dependence on the Isaianic vision and the idea of the faithful witnessing to the nations, Joel prefers other prophetic writings, particularly those speaking of the Day of Yahweh, and has a greater interest in true temple worship. The unusual phrase, "sons of Zion," is used by both Joel (2:23) and Zech 9:13, and is found elsewhere only in Ps 149:2 and Lam 4:2. But Joel refers frequently to Zion as the place where Yahweh dwells, commands, and gathers the faithful (3:16, 17, 21; 2:32) while Deutero-Zechariah prefers to speak more generally that Yahweh "encamps" at his house (9:8). Both say that no oppressor (Zech 9:8) or alien (Joel 3:17) will ever again pass through Jerusalem. Again, reference to the eastern and western seas are found only in Zech 14:8 and Joel 2:20. However, whereas in Zech 14:8 it is God's life-giving waters flowing from Jerusalem in both directions in the future, in Joel it is the army from the north that will finish up in both seas destroyed by Yahweh. There are also references in both to early and late rains as divine response to the faithful (Zech 10:1–2; Joel 2:23),[25] and to grain and wine overflowing as blessing (Zech 9:17; Joel 2:24).

All these close connections would indicate that both prophets are contemporaneous with one another, and that one is familiar with the work of the other. However, there are differences in outlook between the two. In Joel's work there is a greater intensity, a greater feeling of political uncertainty and a sense that the final struggle is imminent. This may indicate that Joel's is the later work.

Joel and the Priesthood

The book of Joel demonstrates a real familiarity with the various forms of liturgical worship to the extent that some have seen the temple as the center of his religion, serving Yahweh with proper cultic worship in accordance with covenant righteousness.[26] Yet in spite of this, Joel is highly critical of the priesthood and certainly does not see compliance to their priestly law as fundamental to living according to the will of God.[27]

The first explicit mention of the priests (1:9) announces simply that the grain offering and the drink offering have been cut off from the house of Yahweh, and so the priests, the ministers of Yahweh mourn. Later (1:13), it speaks of those offerings as being withheld "from the house of your God." According to Lev 2:1–10, the priestly law was that only a handful of the grain offering was to be burned on the altar for God, and the rest was to be eaten by the priests as the most holy part. According to Ezek 44:28–30, this is how all the offerings were to be used, and eaten only by the Zadokite priests in the holy chamber (Ezek 42:13). The implication is that the priests mourn and wail because

---

24. Cf. Wolff, *Joel and Amos*, 34
25. Cf. Ahlstrom, *Joel and the Temple Cult*, 108–9; Crenshaw, *Joel*, 155.
26. So Ahlstrom, *Joel and the Temple Cult*, 26.
27. Cf. Wolff, *Joel and Amos*, 12.

they have been cut off from their food supply. In the light of this, and *with* references to drink offerings in 1:9, 13, it is likely that Joel is alluding to the priests also when he calls upon "drunkards" and "all you wine-drinkers" to weep and wail because the wine is cut off from their mouths in 1:5.[28]

Joel is also clearly making a point with his emphasis on the priesthood as the "ministers of Yahweh" (1:9; 2:17), "ministers of the altar" and "ministers of *my* God" (1:13). Like the use of the term "my God" in Zech 14:5 (cf. 11:4), its use here by Joel is meant to set him apart from the priesthood, particularly since he contrasts that with the "house of *your* God" in the same verse.[29] The focus on the term "ministers" alludes to those claims in Ezek 40:46 that only the sons of Zadok may approach Yahweh to *minister to* him. Only the Zadokites could serve as *ministers* of Yahweh "between the vestibule and the altar" (Joel 2:17; cf. Ezek 8:16). So with the threat of impending judgment Joel taunted the priests to put on sackcloth and sanctify a fast and gather all the people of Judah to come to Jerusalem to the house of Yahweh for prayer and lamentations. Having claimed to rule on Yahweh's behalf, they themselves had come under the threat of Yahweh's judgment.[30] The call to repent with all sincerity and to rend their hearts and not their garments (2:12–13) is clearly directed to the priesthood.

While Joel demonstrates familiarity with the book of Ezekiel, he is by no means influenced by it. His reference to the land being like the garden of Eden before and like a desolate wilderness after the coming of "a great and powerful army" (Joel 2:2–3) is a reversal of Ezek 36:35 (cf. Isa 51:3). His reference to Yahweh pouring out his spirit on Israel (2:28; cf. Ezek 39:29) will not lead to the kind of cultic hierocracy of Ezek 40–48, nor even to mere repentance of Zech 12:10, but to all the people becoming prophets and visionaries (2:28–29). Instead of Joel's fountain flowing forth from the house of Yahweh (3:18) to the Dead Sea to both the eastern and western seas, it flows out to irrigate the wadi of the acacias. Considering that according to the Priestly Work (in Exod 25–38) all the furniture of the temple was to be made of acacia wood, this may allude to a total reform of the cultic worship within the house of Yahweh.

It is noteworthy that Joel also makes use of the Levite prophet Malachi who earlier criticized the cultic worship of the Zadokite priests and has elements in common with the book of Jeremiah, particularly Jer 33:10–26, and the Chronicler (2 Chr 20:15–20). All this would seem to indicate that Joel himself was a Levite prophet who adhered to the Chronicler's contention that the Levites had the spirit of prophecy (cf. 2 Chr 15:1; 20:14).[31]

So part of the reason for Joel's criticism of the ruling Zadokite priests came out of that continuing tension between the Zadokites and the Levites. Yet it was not the "right

---

28. Cf. ibid., 31.

29. Cf. Mason, "Use of Earlier Biblical Material," 174.

30. Cf. Wolff, *Joel and Amos*, 36.

31. It is interesting to note that prior to the time of the Chronicler and Ezra-Nehemiah only one "Joel" is mentioned, the first son of Samuel (1 Sam 8:2). However, the name appears a number of times in the Chronicler's work and some of the leading Levites are so named (e.g., 1 Chr 15:7, 11; 23:8; 26:22; 29:12).

cult" that Joel regarded as the "only foundation for the future of the people,"[32] but the right relationship with their God. In the light of the harsh criticism of the priesthood by Deutero-Zechariah, and Joel's indictment of the nations for selling the people of Judah and Jerusalem into slavery (3:2–8), it is likely that the priesthood's involvement as officials within the Persian satrapy led to Joel's condemnation of the priests as well as the nations.

Joel and the Locusts

Joel's graphic description of a locust plague which he describes as a nation invading the land, powerful and without number, and with teeth of a lion and fangs of a lioness (1:6), coming as a great and powerful army like blackness spread over the mountains (2:2), has such intensity about it as if such a thing had never happened before. Yet locust plagues were not uncommon in the ancient near east. It is difficult to see how one such plague would cause the earth to quake and the heavens to tremble (2:10), and be heralded as the harbinger of the terrible Day of Yahweh. The destruction is described as fire that had devoured the pastures of the wilderness and flames that have burned all the trees of the field (1:19), fire and flames that go before them and follow after them (2:3). The account of the plague as having the appearance of war horses, rumbling chariots, and of a powerful army drawn up for battle (2:4, 5) gets bolder as it moves along until it is identified as an army from the north (2:20).[33] The intensity of the threat continues through to 2:17 when it suddenly changes to promises of deliverance and great harvests and a prophetic future for the faithful without any mention of an actual return to Yahweh (2:18–32). It is as if the threat had suddenly passed on or dissipated. After that the focus of the Day of Yahweh is directed with much bitterness to the nations that had harassed and humiliated Judah for so long (3:1–15, 19).

References to locusts in the Hebrew Bible as a whole are used in two basic ways: either (1) as the curse against Egypt (Exod 10:4–19; Pss 78:46; 105:34) or as a covenant curse (Deut 28:38; cf. Amos 4:9; 1 Kgs 8:37 / 2 Chr 6:28); or (2) as armies of various nations coming like locusts, too numerous to count (Judg 6:5; 7:12; Jer 46:23; 51:14, 27; Isa 33:4; Nah 3:15–17). It seems that Joel makes use of both these concepts. On the one hand, he speaks of "God's army" (2:11) as locusts coming to invoke the covenant curse, and on the other, as a cipher for a great army coming from the north, eating up the produce of the land as they head south.[34] He may be using this cipher as a way of preventing any possible retribution for criticism of the Persian government. It is clear that this great army does not attack Jerusalem but passes on leaving nothing but devastation behind (2:3).

---

32. So Ahlstrom, *Joel and the Temple Cult*, 61.

33. The mention of a northern army, also found in Jer 1:14–15; 4:6; 6:1, 22 and Ezek 38:6, 15; 39:2, cannot simply be brushed aside as a mythical idea (so Wolff, *Joel and Amos*, 62, and Crenshaw, *Joel*, 150). Judah's major enemies always came from the north, whether they were Assyrians, Babylonians, or Persians.

34. See the cogent arguments by Andinach, "Locusts in the Message of Joel," 433–41.

The detail and intensity of the description of this army argues for it being a present reality rather than an imaginary horde like Ezekiel's Gog of Magog, and this may give us a clue as to the date of Joel's writing. For Artaxerxes III gathered together an enormous army of Persian soldiers and cavalry, as well as many mercenaries, and led them south from Phoenicia to defeat the armies of Egypt and sending them into retreat in 343 BCE. Such an enormous army would have been like a plague of locusts pillaging and destroying harvests as they moved south. Joel saw the approaching army initially as a divine threat to the leaders of Jerusalem, and then, when the imminent danger had passed, he was filled with indignation and resentment for all the humiliations the surrounding nations had inflicted on Judah. For this the nations would be destroyed.

Thus the book of Joel finished up with the same outlook as Ezek 38–39 with the total destruction of the nations, as well as Egypt and Edom. The only difference is that, like Zech 14, Jerusalem and Judah would experience the Day of Yahweh first. But, unlike Zechariah, there is no glimmer of hope for the nations that some might "go up to the mountain of Yahweh" (Isa 2:3; cf. Zech 14:16), or that the people of Yahweh might be a "light to the nations" (Isa 42:6; 49:6). This was another form of exclusivism, and it would not go unanswered.

THE RESPONSE TO JOEL: THE BOOK OF JONAH

In the postexilic period we have observed a growing division between those who believed that the foreign nations must be destroyed on that great and terrible Day of Yahweh so that Israel could lead a pure and holy life under God, and those who believed that God had called them to be his witness to the nations, to bring them, by example, into a faithful relationship with the one and only God, Creator of heaven and earth.

The book of Jonah is a satirical response by a proponent of the latter to the former group represented by Joel. The unknown author has taken the name of a minor prophet of the past, Jonah the son of Amittai, who lived in northern Israel during the reign of Jeroboam II and whose only claim to fame was that he had prophesied that Jeroboam would restore "the borders of Israel from Lebo-Hamath as far as the Sea of Arabah" (2 Kgs 14:25). Jonah is made the main character representing nationalistic exclusivists like Joel. "Jonah" means "dove," and may have been chosen because of its irony, since the character is portrayed more like a "hawk."

The satire begins by God calling up Jonah to go to the great city of Nineveh to warn of judgment on its wickedness. But Jonah flees, taking a ship in the opposite direction to Tarshish, trying to escape from the presence of God (1:1–3). But like Ps 107:24–28, God, who Jonah later acknowledges is "Yahweh, the God of heaven, who made the sea and the dry land" (1:9), causes a great storm on the sea, putting fear into the hearts of the mariners who cry out to their gods and throw their cargo overboard. Meanwhile, Jonah is unperturbed and asleep in the hold of the ship. When it is recognized that Jonah is the cause of the storm because of his flight from Yahweh, Jonah, without showing any contrition, acknowledges that the only way the ship and the sailors can be saved is for them to throw him overboard. This done, and the sea calm, these foreign sailors recognize the sovereign power of Yahweh and offer a sacrifice to him and make vows. Throughout this whole ordeal, these representatives of foreign nations have shown greater compassion and fear of Yahweh than Jonah himself, who was the one who had claimed allegiance to Yahweh (1:7–16).

Jonah goes down to the realm of death or Sheol, depicted as Yahweh causing him to be swallowed by a great fish (1:17; 2:2). Drawing on the idea expressed in Hos 5:14—6:6 where the prophet had said that Israel had to undergo a death experience until "in their distress they seek" Yahweh and are then raised up on the third day to live before him, the prophet speaks of Jonah being in the fish for three days and three nights. This death and resurrection experience had also been mirrored in Isa 53 where the exile was depicted as dying to the old ways and being raised up with the new purpose of being a light to the nations. So using a collage of psalm verses, Jonah in his distress seeks Yahweh's favor. The psalm verses making up this collage seem to have been chosen for their cries to Yahweh in distress, ultimate thanksgiving for rescue, and references to the deep and Sheol, waves and billows (e.g., Ps 18:5–7; 42:7).[35] In brief, the psalm verses illustrate Jonah's plight, his confidence that Yahweh will deliver him, and his vow to offer thanksgiving in the temple to Yahweh (2:10). Of course, the foreign sailors had already done this. The implication is that Jonah would expect God's mercy for himself, but didn't accept that that mercy could extend to those outside of Israel. As a Levite, Joel would have been used to chanting these psalms.

So Yahweh delivers Jonah and sends him again to Nineveh. This time Jonah obeys but gives only a harsh message to the Ninevites: "Forty days more, and Nineveh shall be overthrown!" (3:4). There is no call for repentance, just this announcement of coming destruction, which is probably what Jonah wished for. But the people of Nineveh do just what Joel had called on the priests in Jerusalem to do (Joel 1:13–14): they proclaim a fast and put on sackcloth (3:5). To carry the satire further, the author has the king of Nineveh decree that every human being and *every animal* shall go on a fast, and put on sackcloth and repent (3:6–8). This clearly alludes to Joel 1:18, 20 where the same words ("flock"; "cattle"; "animal") are used and where it states that the animals had no feed and water and cry out to Yahweh (Joel 1:20). To carry his point even further, the author has the king of Nineveh repeat the very same assurance of divine mercy in response to their repentance as Joel had given to Judah and Jerusalem: "Who knows? God may turn and relent, he may turn from his burning anger, so that we do not perish" (3:9; cf. Joel 2:14a). The prophet is making the point that the same repentance and response of divine mercy is open to all God's creatures—it is not just limited to Israel.

So when the people of Nineveh turn from their evil ways, God relents from the evil he had intended (3:10). But Jonah is angry and now reveals why he had fled in the beginning: because he knew that God would be merciful according to the formula of Exod 34:6–7. Now the author deliberately has Jonah quote that formula exactly as it is found in Joel 2:13, including Joel's addition, "and relents from evil," which was not part of the formula.[36] The message of this prophet to Joel and all who claimed God's grace and

---

35. For a complete list of psalm verses used, see Wolff, *Obadiah and Jonah*, 133–39; Dell, "Reinventing the Wheel," 85–101.

36. See the discussion in Dozeman, "Inner-Biblical Interpretation," 207–23; Kim, "Jonah Read Intertextually," 512–16.

mercy only for themselves was that God cannot be limited by their nationalistic mind-set. Justice is never a mathematical equation, but a recognition and acceptance with great rejoicing when *anyone* turns to God in faith and lives under Yahweh's kingship (cf. Jer 18:7–10). Selfishly, Jonah could rejoice greatly only over the *qiqayon* plant that gave him shade (4:6). He had received God's unmerited grace and forgiveness after he had fled from Yahweh and had been rescued from death, yet he could feel only anger when the Ninevites were shown the same mercy and forgiveness (4:3–4).

Joel's unbridled anger at the surrounding nations is answered in God's twice-repeated question to Jonah: "Is it doing good for you to be angry?" (4:4, 9) which may be an allusion to Ps 37:1–8, where it emphasizes that one should refrain from showing anger toward the evildoer, for anger can only lead to evil. It is better to do good and to trust in Yahweh, to commit one's way to him and *he* will act. That point is made again in the final discussion between God and Jonah (4:10–11). There Yahweh points out to Jonah that he can show compassion for a plant for which he did nothing and which lasts but a day, yet he resents God having compassion on Nineveh which represents a sizable part of his creation. Joel had called on the priests to pray for Yahweh to have compassion on his people (2:17). The author of Jonah has emphasized that all nations are God's people as well, and he will exercise his love and compassion on all.[37]

The message of Hosea's death and resurrection motif (5:14—6:6) had been that the people needed to die to their old ways and be raised to a new life of faithfulness to God, to which was added the newly revealed purpose to be a light to the nations to the glory of God in Isa 53. The observation which the author of Jonah is making is that Israel in the exile had gone through that death and resurrection experience, but that many, like Jonah, still seemed to be stuck in their old mind-set of not seeing further than their own nation. God's steadfast love is fundamental to his being and his compassion thus reaches out to all his created world.[38]

CHANGES FOR THE BETTER

After the defeat of Egypt in 343 BCE, palace intrigues eventually led to the murder of Artaxerxes in 338. His successor, Arses (338–336 BCE), fared no better. He was succeeded by Darius III (336–331 BCE). Around the same time, Philip of Macedonia had become the acknowledged leader of the Greek states and planned an all-out war on Persia (337). However, in the summer of 336 Philip also was murdered, and the leadership fell to his twenty-year-old son, Alexander. By 334 BCE Alexander was ready to launch the war against Persia. So he moved his army of 5,000 cavalry and 30,000 foot soldiers to Troy and was met there by the Persian army at the River Granicus. The Persians were defeated, and many prisoners (mostly Greek mercenaries) were sold into slavery. The Greek and Persian armies met again in battle at Issus a year later (333) in which Alexander again defeated the Persians. Darius III escaped, leaving his family to be captured by Alexander.

---

37. Wolff, *Obadiah and Jonah*, 174.
38. Cf. Fretheim, *Message of Jonah*, 129–30.

From there Alexander triumphantly continued south with little resistance, except from Tyre against which Alexander laid siege for seven months before taking the city and destroying it, with those not killed being sold into slavery. From there, moving further south, Judah and Jerusalem readily submitted to Alexander, seeing him more as a liberator than a conqueror. Gaza resisted but was defeated. By 332 BCE Alexander was in Egypt where he was crowned as Pharaoh, founded the city of Alexandria, and was declared to be the son of the Egyptian god Amon. The following spring of 331, Alexander headed northeast with his army and engaged Darius III once again in a decisive battle at Gaugamela, in which the Persian army was routed. Although Darius again fled the battle, he was later killed by his satraps. Alexander was now in control of the Persian Empire, marched to the Persian capital of Persepolis where he burned the great palace of Xerxes and was acknowledged as emperor in 330 BCE.

ISAIAH 24–27—THE SO-CALLED ISAIAH APOCALYPSE

It has been almost universally recognized that the four chapters of Isa 24–27 were not written by any of the "Isaiahs" previously discussed. However, it has previously been difficult to identify the situation which called for these prophecies or the time when these chapters were written. Nothing is known about the author, the city mentioned in these chapters is not named. There are no specific references to historical events or political or religious figures. Consequently, there has been a great variety of proposals as to the time and circumstances which led to these chapters.[39] These chapters were inserted into the book of Isaiah following the oracles against the nations (chs 13–23), and because the author frequently uses the language and phrases from those chapters, particularly from the oracles against Babylon, many have assumed that these chapters (24–27) must have been written during the time of the Babylonian Empire.[40]

However, we have noticed that the prophets during the time of the Persian Empire have been very careful never to make any reference to the Persian government, obviously out of fear of reprisals. So they have often used the language of the oracles against Babylon, even to the extent of quotations, as in Joel (e.g., 1:15 = Isa 13:6; cf. also 2:10 which draws on Isa 13:10, 13), for their indictment against the Persians and their allies. So it is conceivable that these chapters also were written around the end of the Persian Empire with the coming of Alexander's armies. These chapters, imbued with Isaianic traditions, give a message of triumphant judgment on the oppressors, a cautious but joyous expectation of liberation, and a vision of future universal peace and prosperity, a new age.

The prophet begins with a triumphant proclamation that "Yahweh is laying waste the earth and devastating it, ruining its face and scattering its inhabitants." No matter who the inhabitants are or what status they have, all will be leveled by this. For the earth is being utterly laid waste, utterly plundered. "For Yahweh has spoken this word!" (24:1–3). "This word" appears to be the oath of Yahweh to "sweep with the broom of

---

39. See the discussion in Wildberger, *Isaiah 13–27*, 460–67; Millar, *Isaiah 24–27*, 1–22.
40. E.g., Otzen, "Traditions and Structures," 205–6; Seitz, *Isaiah 1–39*, 198; Childs, *Isaiah*, 176–98.

destruction," and carry out his plan set out in 14:23–27: "This is the plan that is planned concerning the whole earth . . . and this is the hand that is stretched out over all the nations" (cf. Isa 40:10–17). Originally, this was spoken against Assyria (14:25; 37:26), but it is now directed against Persia and the city of Tyre. That is made clear in Isa 23:13. For Yahweh has now stretched out his hand over the sea (23:11). Later, our prophet praises Yahweh for having carried out wonderful things, "*plans* formed of old, faithful and sure" (25:1). This same point is echoed in the oracle concerning Tyre with the rhetorical question, "Who has *planned* this against Tyre?" and with the answer, "Yahweh of hosts has *planned* it" (23:8, 9).

In the light of this it becomes clear that the prophet of Isa 24–27 is living during the time when Alexander has besieged Tyre and brought about its destruction. The oracle concerning Tyre (Isa 23:1–14) in all likelihood also comes from his hand. With Alexander's triumphs over the Persian armies at the River Granicus and again at Issus, together with the destruction of the proud city of Tyre, the prophet can see that God's plan is being fulfilled and that the world as he has known it has finally come under judgment so that a new age can soon begin.

Borrowing some of the language used by Joel (1:5–12) to describe the devastation of Judah, the prophet now directs it against the nations of his world who have not lived according to the everlasting covenant made with Noah after the flood (24:4–9; cf. Gen 9:8–17). But the real focus of the devastation is the city of Tyre which has now become the "nothing city" (cf. Isa 40:17), now completely desolate, its gates smashed to ruins (24:10–12; cf. 13:9). The judgments forecast in Zech 9:2–4 and Joel 3:4–8 have now happened. Tyre has become an example of what will happen to the nations as God carries out his plan. Again, borrowing language used in Isa 17:6, which spoke of only a small remnant of Israel escaping judgment, the prophet now transfers that to the nations to indicate that only a remnant of the nations would survive (24:13).[41]

With Alexander's victories over Israel's oppressors, and his peaceful approach to Judah and Jerusalem, the people of Israel can now raise their voices and sing a new song (cf. Isa 42:10–13) and praise the beauty of Yahweh, the Righteous One, for he has acted according to his righteousness (24:14–16a; cf. 45:8, 21; 59:19). However, the judgment is not all over yet. For then the prophet, with allusions to Isa 21:2 and 33:1, utters the rather enigmatic cry: "I have a secret! I have a secret! Woe is me! For the treacherous deal treacherously, the treacherous deal very treacherously!" (24:16b). The implication here is that not only will the treachery of the Persians be dealt with treacherously but that also Alexander will eventually come under the same judgment that comes to the whole earth. No one can escape (24:17–18; cf. Jer 48:43–44), for it is like the time of the flood when "the windows of heaven were opened" (24:18; Gen 7:11). The whole heaven and earth come under judgment before the new heavens and new earth mentioned in Isa 66:22–23 can come into being with Yahweh of hosts as King on Mount Zion in fulfillment of Isa 52:7–10 (24:19–23; cf. Zech 14:9). Even the sun, moon, and stars will come under judgment because the nations have worshiped them. But Yahweh's brilliant presence will shine forth from Zion and give light to all (Isa 60:1–3, 19–20; Zech 14:7, 9).[42]

41. Cf, Sweeney, "Textual Citations," 42–43.
42. Cf. Wildberger, *Isaiah 13–27*, 509.

With that, the prophet offers a thanksgiving psalm rejoicing that the fortified city of Tyre has become a heap of ruins, that the palace of aliens is no more and will never be rebuilt (25:1–2; cf. 23:13; 37:26). Now a strong people will experience God's presence, but violent nations will fear. For Yahweh has always been a fortress for the lowly and a refuge for the dispossessed in his distress (25:3–5; cf. 4:5–6; 14:30, 32; 32:1–2; Zeph 3:12–13). The "lowly," the "dispossessed," and the "afflicted" (26:6) had long been terms for the faithful in conflict. Now the establishment of Yahweh as King over all the nations calls for a celebration. The hope expressed in Isa 2:2–4 of nations coming to Mount Zion to worship Yahweh and to learn his teaching was expanded into a meal celebrating Yahweh's kingship in Isa 55:1–5, expressed later as nations bringing their wealth to Jerusalem in Isa 60. Zech 14:16 had described it as the survivors of the nations coming to Jerusalem to celebrate the Feast of Booths. Now, in Isa 25:6–8, it becomes a great banquet for all peoples, when the shame covering the nations will be withdrawn, and the disgrace and suffering of Israel will be removed. For death, that which separates one from the life-giving force, from God, will be done away with, as all peoples and nations turn to Yahweh as their King and Savior and live together in peace under him.

This utopian vision of the future is unfortunately spoiled by one nation, Moab, which has persisted in its pride (25:10b–12). The threat of their rejection parallels the threat that was held over Israel in the past in Isa 2:6–21.[43] The prophet thus has to return to his present reality. Yet the obstinate pride of Moab reminds him that Yahweh has brought down to the dust that lofty city, Tyre, for its pride. That reassurance of God's plan being fulfilled calls for a song of faith and continuing trust (26:1–6). Once again, recalling the vision of nations streaming to the mountain of Yahweh to learn his ways in Isa 2:2–4, he acknowledges that Yahweh makes smooth the path of the righteous so that they can learn righteousness. The song echoes the promises of Isa 60:10–11 that the gates will always be open to the coming of faithful nations to Zion. But he laments that the wicked do not take that path and do not see the blessings that come to the faithful. They are like the dead that do not rise (26:7–14).

Nevertheless, while Alexander may have permitted Judah to expand her borders, stability has not yet returned to the region. Alexander is still carrying out his conquests. The past has changed, but the future is not yet. The faithful are once again caught in between.[44] Only Yahweh can bring about change for the better. Using the metaphor of the agony of childbirth, the prophet confesses on behalf of the faithful that even though their chastisement was like the pain of giving birth (cf. 13:8), they were not able to bring about salvation to the earth or cause the fall of the world's inhabitants (26:16–18). They would have to wait until Yahweh would once again give birth to another delivery—like the restoration of Judah from exile (cf. Isa 42:14). Recalling that that restoration was depicted in Isa 53 as a rebirth from the dead, the prophet assures his audience: "Your dead shall live. As a corpse they shall rise! Awake and sing for joy, you who dwell in the dust. For your dew is fruitful dew" (26:19; cf. Hos 6:1–2 and 14:4–6).[45]

---

43. Sweeney, "Textual Citations," 46–47.
44. Cf. Childs, *Isaiah*, 190–92.
45. Cf. Schmitz, "Grammar of Resurrection," 145–49.

On that Day, Yahweh's Day, Yahweh will finally destroy the forces of chaos (Leviathan), and then the Song of the Vineyard (Isa 5:1–7) will be reversed. Yahweh will water and guard his vineyard, Israel; and so it will take root and fill the whole world with its fruit (27:1–6). As he contemplates this new relation of peace, the prophet looks back reflectively on Israel's past. Yes, Yahweh had struck them with the rod of his wrath, but not as severely as he had dealt with those who had struck them. Yes, he had sent them into exile and by this their guilt had been atoned for. But the real fruit of their relationship with Yahweh now would be complete faithfulness and understanding in contrast to Isa 6:9–11. That fortified city, Tyre, was now desolate and forsaken, for their people had been without understanding, and so their Creator could show them no compassion (27:7–11). So on that Day, Yahweh will gather all the people of Israel together from the four corners of their world, and the words of Isa 11:11–16 and 60:8–9 will finally by fulfilled (27:12–13). But in the meantime, the faithful would be waiting with renewed hope.

Chapter VIII

The Prophetic Turns Apocalyptic

DURING THE SHORT REIGN of Alexander there was tolerance toward the conquered nations, seeking to blend the various cultures under Greek influence, and at the same time maintaining respect for the religious beliefs of the peoples. All that came to an end when Alexander died in 323 BCE.[1] Perdiccas, one of Alexander's generals, was appointed regent and sought to continue Alexander's policies. Other generals, who had been given satrapies to govern, but wanted more power to amass wealth for themselves, were opposed to these policies and assassinated Perdiccas in 321 BCE. Then, for the next twenty years, these generals, known as the *Diadochoi* ("Successors"), fought one another to extend their control over various parts of the empire. As a consequence, the lives of people living in Syria-Palestine were constantly disrupted and chaotic.

In 320, Ptolemy I Soter, satrap of Egypt, invaded Syria-Palestine and annexed it to Egypt. Five years later, another general, Antigonus, invaded Palestine and set up his garrisons in various cities. By 312, Ptolemy had taken it back, but the victory was short-lived, because a few months later the land was back in Antigonus' possession. Many of the Jewish leaders, including the high priest Hezekiah, who had favored Ptolemy over Antigonus, fled to Egypt.[2] However, Antigonus' expansion policies and his claim to rule over the empire eventually led to other generals forming a league in 302 to fight against him. Ptolemy took the opportunity once again to overrun Palestine, and when the other generals defeated Antigonus at Ipsus in 301 and divided the empire among themselves. Ptolemy, who had not participated in the battle, insisted Syria-Palestine was to remain under his rule.

These twenty years of fighting over the control of Syria-Palestine had wreaked havoc on the people of the land. The multiple conflicts between Antigonus and Ptolemy over the land often left confusion, chaos and humiliation in their wake. Meanwhile, the Jewish leaders, including the Jerusalem priesthood, sought to retain some kind of power for themselves under the tyrant of the day. Taking sides in the conflict was dangerous, yet offering gifts and services was often the only way to maintain some semblance of power and authority. One of these services was to become agents for the collection of

---

1. Tcherikover, *Hellenistic Civilization*, 7–8.
2. Ibid., 57.

tribute and taxes. Of course, to the common people this was seen as collaboration with the enemy, particularly by those who could not meet the heavy demand for taxes, lost their ancestral land, or were forced into slavery. These generals were only interested in the revenues they could harvest from the territories they had conquered, and it was the common people who were exploited, not only by these foreign rulers but also often by the leaders of their own people.

One way to escape this exploitation was to leave the urbanized areas and find refuge in the more isolated reaches of Upper Galilee and Gaulanitus where collection of tribute and taxes was often difficult and dangerous.[3] Archaeological evidence has shown that this area long resisted any Hellenistic influence and continued to honor Jewish traditions. Many of those who took refuge in Upper Galilee were deeply religious,[4] were in tune with the prophetic vision, and had a strong distrust of the priesthood in Jerusalem. Here they formed communities supportive of each other.

All hopes for judgment on the oppressors and for vindication of the righteous, with the new heavens and the new earth mentioned in Isa 65:17 and 66:22 and described in Isa 24–27, now remained unfulfilled. The cry of the faithful for the coming Day of Judgment on the oppressors and their agents became more pronounced. Those who held to the prophetic vision sought to communicate with and encourage one another by expressing themselves in apocalyptic language. By the use of visions and dreams purported to be experienced by the patriarchs of old, they sought to reveal the "hidden things" (cf. Isa 48:6) to those who had ears to hear and eyes to see. In this way the faithful would understand the message of comfort and the exhortation to remain faithful in the face of evil, while their detractors would see it all as harmless fantasy. The authors of this apocalyptic literature by necessity carried on scribal activity as a means of sharing the prophetic vision with the wider community of those who followed the prophetic tradition as well as those of Levite background who shared with them opposition to the Zadokite priesthood in Jerusalem.

1 ENOCH

The Enoch literature, originally written in Aramaic, but extant now only in Ethiopic, appears to have originated in Upper Galilee. First Enoch is made up of a number of books written at different times. The Astronomical Book (chs. 72–82) is generally regarded as the oldest, the Book of Watchers (1–36) was written as early as the period of the Diadochoi,[5] the Epistle of Enoch (chs. 91–105, which includes the Apocalypse of Weeks in 93 and 91:12–17) around the beginning of the second century BCE, with the account of the Birth of Noah (chs. 106–107) and the closing chapter (108) added later. The Dream Visions (chs. 83–90) were formulated during the Maccabean era, and the Parables of Enoch (37–71) saw the light of day soon after the death of Herod the Great, about 4 BCE.

---

3. Cf. Meyers and Strange, *Archeology*, 40–42, 45–46; Frankel, "Prehellenistic Galilee," 894.
4. Meyers and Strange, *Archeology*, 47.
5. See Nickelsburg, *1 Enoch 1*, 170.

The Book of the Watchers: 1 Enoch 1–36

Having observed and often experienced the atrocities visited on the people by the Macedonian overlords, the author(s) of these chapters recalled the message of Isa 24:17–23 which referred to the coming Day of Judgment being similar to the time of the flood when both the hosts of heaven and the kings of the earth would be punished, and Yahweh of hosts would reign on Mount Zion.

Wishing to encourage their companions to remain faithful during these difficult times without alerting the overlords to what could be construed as inciting resistance, the authors used those ancient stories leading up to the flood in Gen 5–7. The enigmatic account of the sons of God coming down to earth and procreating with human women and fathering giants (Gen 6:1–4) is interpreted in relation to Isa 24:21, and became the basis for understanding the violence and corruption the faithful had experienced and which would lead to the final judgment. The ancient patriarch, Enoch, who "walked with God; then he was no more because God took him" (Gen 5:21–24) became the vehicle for their revelation to the faithful, with the story of Noah and his family becoming the model of their final vindication.

Throughout 1 Enoch, the faithful are addressed in Isaianic terms as "the chosen and righteous ones," "the plants of righteousness and faith" (Isa 60:21; 61:3), and Enoch is "the blessed and righteous man of the Lord," the "scribe of righteousness" who reveals to the chosen ones what he learned from the Holy One in the heavenly realms. Much of the story of the Watchers is an elaboration of the message of Isa 24–27 with frequent allusions to concepts from Isa 60–66 combined with the stories in Gen 6.[6]

The ancient idea that the "sons of God" were originally Yahweh's divine representatives to or "watchers" over the various nations (cf. Deut 32:8–9) but were eventually condemned for not maintaining justice in light of the evils done by nations against Israel, led to the conviction that the offending sons of God would die like human beings (Ps 82; Isa 24:21). These "sons of God" are interpreted as 200 of the watchers lusting after the beauty of human women, who make a pact on the peak of Mount Hermon to come down to earth, have intercourse with them and beget children. Thus, they defile themselves and humanity with sorcery, divination, godlessness, and violence. Through this union, their wives give birth to giants who devour the produce of the land and then turn on the people themselves, killing and devouring them. Even the animals, birds, and fish do not escape their insatiable appetite and violence. They then turn on each other to devour and destroy (7:1–6). Thus, the actions of the *Diadochoi*, who claimed to be descended from the gods,[7] are explained.

Eventually, the growing wickedness on earth leads to Noah being advised to hide himself because the end is coming (cf. Isa 26:19–20), for after the flood he is to renew the "planting of the Lord," the righteous (10:1–3; cf. Isa 60:21). The rebel watchers are to be bound and cast into outer darkness, imprisoned until the Day of eternal Judgment after witnessing their bastard sons perishing in wars of destruction. Thus all evil will be banished from the face of the earth and the "plants of righteousness and faith" (cf. Isa

---

6. Ibid., 148.

7. Tcherikover, *Hellenistic Civilization*, 11.

61:3) will appear and be a blessing to all, and they will be planted forever. Thus the earth is to be purified and be filled with righteousness.

Much of the story, as it is elaborated, revolves around Upper Galilee. When the irrevocable judgment on the rebel watchers has been ordered, they plead with Enoch to present their petition for forgiveness for themselves and their children to God. This Enoch does by going to the sacred waters of Dan, just south-west of Mount Hermon, and recites the petition of the rebel watchers to God (13:4–7). God's negative response comes in a vision which Enoch then conveys to the watchers who are waiting nearby at Abel-Main (13:8–10). For they have broken the natural order of the separation between heaven and earth, the spiritual and the physical, the immortal and the mortal. Therefore they cannot return to heaven but will be bound until "the day of the consummation of the great judgment." However, their sons, the giants, will die of the flesh but their evil spirits will remain as demonic forces causing corruption, violence and illness among human beings until the day of consummation (14:24—16:4).

The purpose of this elaboration of the story of the fallen angels is to explain that while the wars of the Diadochoi may be over, the exploitative situation has not changed for the better. Their evil spirits have remained like demonic forces influencing those in power, having penetrated all parts of society with godless ways until the final Day of Judgment. Behind the elaboration of the indictment of the rebel watchers that they have usurped their role as priests of the heavenly sanctuary, there appears to be an indictment against their earthly counterparts, the Zadokite priests in Jerusalem, for their failures to carry out their function as priests and intercessors for the people, thus nullifying their ability to teach God's word.[8]

One other point that is significant in this section is the setting of these chapters. The specific references to Mount Hermon, the waters of Dan in the land of Dan (13:7), and the reference to Abel-Main, accurately located between Lebanon and Mount Hermon (13:9), would indicate that the author is quite familiar with this area, regards the waters of Dan as sacred, and probably resides in Upper Galilee among those who have moved there to escape the exploitation of the land and who regard themselves as "the planting of the Lord."[9] The area below Mount Hermon, a sacred place since the tribe of Dan moved there in the early days of settlement (Judg 18), appears to have been adopted as their sacred place by the prophetic visionaries who regarded the Jerusalem temple and Mount Zion as polluted by the Zadokite priesthood.

In his visions, Enoch travels to "a chaotic and terrible place" burning with fire where the rebel watchers are imprisoned forever (21:1–10). Later, he sees seven beautiful mountains, the highest of which is the throne of God, which God will use when he descends to earth to bring blessing. It is surrounded by fragrant trees, and one of these never withers, and bears beautiful fruit which no human being may touch until after the great judgment. This is the tree of life which will be transplanted from God's paradise to a renewed Jerusalem,[10] where the righteous, pious, and chosen will be able

---

8. Evidence for this point has been given in detail by Suter, "Fallen Angel, Fallen Priest," 115–35, and Nickelsburg, "Enoch, Levi, and Pete," 575–600.

9. Nickelsburg, "Enoch, Levi, and Pete," 582–87.

10. Nickelsburg, *1 Enoch 1*, 313–15. However, this transplanting of the tree of life to the new

to enjoy its fruit and live long, free of torments, plagues, and suffering. There they will be worshipping and praising God, for the fragrance of the tree "will be in their bones" (24:2—25:7) as the "oaks of righteousness (Isa 61:3).

This vision leads Enoch to journey to the center of the earth, to look upon the new Jerusalem and Mount Zion, with sprouting trees all around which are watered by a stream flowing from beneath the holy mountain. All is blessed except the valley on the west, the Valley of Hinnom, long cursed because idolatry had been practiced there (cf. Jer 19). There, all those who have blasphemed God will be gathered for a curse on the Day of Judgment in the presence of the righteous (26:1—27:5; cf. Isa 65:14-15; 66:24).

For those who have been experiencing constant humiliation and injustices because of the Ptolemaic exploitative policies, and who have been despairing of ever seeing the fulfillment of the prophetic promises, these chapters give the assurance that God is still in control of his universe, and his plans will be carried out in due time. The sinners will get their just deserts, and the righteous will experience the new heavens and new earth in a new Jerusalem. Those who have died in the meantime will not miss out but will be raised to enjoy the new garden of God together with all the righteous and chosen, and be able to eat of the tree of life. The promises of Isa 25:6–10a and 26:19 will be carried out according to God's almighty plan.

The Astronomical Book: 1 Enoch 72–82: This earliest document (before 3rd century BCE) emphasizes the use of the solar calendar of 364 days, as part of the natural order of creation. This calendar continued to be used by the prophetic community and the Levites, who rejected the lunar calendar adopted by the priesthood in Jerusalem.

THE CHANGING POLITICAL SITUATION

In 199 BCE the Seleucid Antiochus III decisively defeated the Ptolemaic general, Scopus, in battle at Panion in Upper Galilee, and so the whole of Syria-Palestine soon came firmly under the control of the Seleucids.[11] The rule under Antiochus III appears to have been somewhat more benign than that under the Ptolemies and the inhabitants of Jerusalem benefited, allowing the priesthood and wealthy families to gain more wealth and power as the agents for the collection of taxes and tribute, with the high priest responsible for the sum payment to the king. The temple served as a bank for the wealthy and so had become a financial and political institution as much as a religious one, with the high priest as head administrator. During the reign of Seleucus IV (187–175 BCE), who succeeded Antiochus, the vast accumulation of wealth in the temple became a point of contention. Seleucus who desperately needed money at that time to pay Rome for the peace treaty between them demanded it, but the attempt of the king's agent to confiscate the temple treasury failed (2 Macc 3:1—4:6).

Jerusalem of the future may indicate that the author is thinking of the future transfer of the worship of the faithful from Mount Hermon to Mount Zion. The description of Mount Zion in the new Jerusalem with its life-giving stream flowing from under the mountain in 1 En 26:2 really mirrors Mount Hermon with its spring beneath it flowing out as the source of the Jordan.

11. Tcherikover, *Hellenistic Civilization*, 73–75.

When Seleucus' brother, Antiochus IV Epiphanes, succeeded him in 175 BCE, Joshua, the brother of the high priest Onius III, took the Greek name Jason, and offered Antiochus IV higher tribute for the office of high priest. That money would be collected from the common people as part of their taxes, tribute, and tithes to a greater degree than before. At the same time, he offered even more money for the privilege of making Jerusalem a Greek *polis* with the name of Antioch, and set about transforming Judaism in conformity with the Greek way of life. Jewish law and traditions were regarded as primitive and were replaced by Greek law and customs, as well as Greek language and dress. The endeavor was the secularization and Hellenization of the Jewish state to gain status and power for the wealthy leaders of Jerusalem that would equal that of their Greek contemporaries (2 Macc 4:7–22).

However, in 172 BCE the desire for control of Jerusalem's wealth led one of Jason's officials, Menelaus, to offer a much higher amount of tribute to Antiochus IV for the high priestly office, and when this was granted, Jason had to flee, and Menelaus was left to maintain his position as high priest by means of force, bribes, and even murder (2 Macc 4:23–50). The striving for more wealth and power by the Jerusalem aristocracy on the backs of the rest of the population during this period led Ben Sira, to remark: "Wild asses in the wilderness are the prey of lions, likewise the poor are the feeding grounds of the rich" (Sir. 13:19).[12]

The Epistle of Enoch: 1 Enoch 92–105

This was composed during this period with its woes against the rich for the exploitation of the people by the Jerusalem priesthood and aristocracy.[13] The Epistle is addressed to the community of the righteous to encourage them to remain faithful in these difficult times and to assure them of God's ultimate plan for their vindication. In this Epistle, the author presents what is known as the *Apocalypse of Weeks* (93:1–10; 91:11–17). This is addressed to "the chosen of eternity," "the plant of truth" (93:2) and describes periods of world history, past, present and future, in terms of weeks. The *first* week is the period ending with the time of Enoch. In the *second* week, deceit and violence become evident, leading up to the time of Noah and the flood, the first universal act of divine judgment. By the conclusion of this period iniquity is seen as already increasing again (93:4). The *third* week covers the period leading up to the time of Abraham who is portrayed as the father of the faithful who are "the plant of righteousness forever and ever" (93:5). The *fourth* period is highlighted by the theophany at Sinai in which the covenant is given through Moses (93:6). Following this, the *fifth* period is the age ending with the building of the temple by Solomon, described as "the house of glory and kingdom built forever" (93:7). But then in the *sixth* week, the period ending with the Babylonian exile, speaks of the temple of the kingdom being burned with fire because the people had become blind (93:8). The *seventh* week is the era in which the author and his community live. It is the time of the "perverse generation" who are the perpetrators of the same kind of deceit

---

12. See further, Horsley, *Scribes, Visionaries*, 36–66.
13. VanderKam, *Enoch and the Growth*, 149; Nickelsburg, *1 Enoch 1*, 440–41.

and violence exhibited during the period leading up to the flood. At the end of this age the chosen will be "witnesses of righteousness" as part of "the eternal plant of righteousness." To them will be given wisdom and knowledge sevenfold, which will include these revelations of Enoch. Then they will uproot the foundations of violence and deceit. No mention is made of the second temple since it is the seat of much of the evil that has been inflicted on the people (93:9, 10; 91:11).[14]

The *eighth* week will then be a period of righteousness in which "a sword will be given to the righteous to execute judgment on all the wicked" as God's agents. The consequence of the judgment will be that the righteous will acquire possession in a just way, unlike the rich who had acquired houses and property unjustly (cf. 94:7; 97:8).[15] Thus the righteous will inherit the land. In this future era of righteousness a new temple of the kingdom of God will be built in splendor for generations to come, and will be ready for all the nations to come to Zion to worship the one true God. The *ninth* week (91:14) will see the whole law of God revealed to people of the whole world, evil will disappear and humankind will walk in the way of righteousness. The witness of the righteous as a living covenant and light to the nations will have accomplished its purpose, and the new earth established. In the *tenth* week (91:15-16) the rebel watchers and the false stars will experience eternal judgment, and the words of Isa 24:21-23 will be fulfilled. The new heaven will appear and the luminaries will shine sevenfold brighter in fulfillment of Isa 30:26. After this there will be weeks without end in which sin is no more, and righteousness and piety prevail.

The Six Discourses (chs. 94-105) that follow are a series of woes against the rich as the perpetrators of deceit and violence, constantly accused of oppressing and persecuting the righteous, treading on the lowly with their might (95:7; 96:5, 8), dehumanizing people by forcing them into slavery with no redress (98:4; 103:11-12). The rich are guilty of murder (99:15), of burning the righteous with fire (100:7) and favoring the murderers of the righteous and covering up their evil (103:15). They build themselves palatial homes by confiscating land and materials and using forced labor (94:7; 99:13; cf. Jer 22:13). On the Day of Judgment they will finish up for all eternity in the flaming fire (103:58), the fiery furnace (98:3; 102:1).

The background of these woes is the lawlessness brought on by Jason and Menelaus fighting each other for the high priesthood by paying more and more tribute to Antiochus IV and placing the burden on the people of the land who became indebted, losing their land to the tax agents and Jerusalem aristocracy, and sold into slavery or put to work at a subsistence level as tenant farmers on what had formerly been their land. They had rejected the covenant and sought to impose Greek culture on the population. Their greed soon led to war between their parties in which many people were killed. This then led to a revolt of the people against the Hellenizers. When Antiochus heard of the revolt, he took Jerusalem by storm, and ordered his soldiers to slay any they found in the city. Thousands were slaughtered and many were sold into slavery, leaving the Hellenizers in control of Jerusalem. Antiochus then decreed the prohibition of the use of the Torah, the practice of circumcision, and the observance of the Sabbath. At the end of the year 167

---

14. Cf. Nickelsburg, *1 Enoch 1*, 447-48.
15. Ibid., 449.

The Prophetic Vision and the Real Jesus

he had the "desolating sacrilege" erected on the altar and ordered the worship of Zeus Olympius to be practiced in the temple in Jerusalem (1 Macc 1:41–63).

The enforcement of these decrees in the towns and villages finally led an old priest, Mattathias, to kill the king's officer and the villager who sought to comply and to head into the Judean hills with his five sons and other followers. They were soon joined by many of the Hasidim ("the pious") who were ready to fight for their faith. These formed a kind of guerilla army, rejecting the king's decrees and punishing those Hellenizers who had gone along with them. Under the leadership of Mattathias's third son, Judas (known as "Maccabeus"), the prohibition against self-defence on the Sabbath was abolished, and the armies Antiochus sent against them were no match for the strategic acumen of Judas. By December 164 BCE Judas had become master of Judea, gained control of Jerusalem, cleansed the temple and restored the traditional worship. Antiochus IV died soon after in Parthia.

For the Enochic community in Upper Galilee and surrounding area, the events that took place mostly in Judea were part of the divine judgment forecast in the Epistle, but the final Day of Judgment was yet to come. A member of that community wished to emphasize that and to elaborate further on how he saw the plan of God unfolding. This was presented as two dream visions which Enoch is said to have had at the beginning of his revelations when he was still a youth. These dreams were incorporated into 1 Enoch as chs. 83–90. They were probably written sometime just prior to Judas Maccabeus's death in 160 BCE.[16]

The **First Dream Vision (chs. 83–84)** sees the Day of Judgment being imminent when all heaven and earth would sink into a great pit, as described in Isa 24:17–23, with a plea to God to leave a remnant as a "seed-bearing plant forever" (83:7; 84:5–6).

The **Second Dream Vision**, known as *The Animal Apocalypse (chaps 85–90)*[17] divides human history into three ages—the distant past, the more recent past to the present, and the ideal future. The history is allegorized by depicting human beings as animals or birds, the rebel watchers as fallen stars, and the archangels have "the appearance of white men" who bind the stars hand and foot and cast them into the abyss. The present age ends with the Great Judgment (90:20–27) with God sitting on his judgment throne. The archangels will bring the false Watchers, and their followers who are then bound, condemned, and cast into an abyss full of fire. Likewise, the blind sheep are to be judged and cast into the fiery abyss in the Valley of Hinnom to the south-west of Jerusalem, the final fulfillment of Isa 66:24. In the final age, Yahweh makes a new covenant with the *house* of Israel in which divine teaching will be written in the people's hearts and they will all *know* the Lord from the least of them to the greatest (cf. Isa 61:7–9). The people themselves thus will be a living covenant and a light to the nations (Isa 42:6; 49:6, 8). All the nations will serve them (90:30) as the faithful act as priests and ministers to them (Isa 61:5–7). All those who had previously been destroyed and scattered will now be gathered into "that house" (90:33), an affirmation of the resurrection. All will have their eyes open, and there will no longer be any sin, for they will all be righteous (cf. Isa 60:21).

---

16. Cf. VanderKam, *Enoch and the Growth*, 163; Nickelsburg, *1 Enoch 1*, 361.

17. For a full discussion of this Dream Vision, see Tiller, *Commentary on the Animal Apocalypse* and Nickelsburg, *1 Enoch 1*, 354–408.

The two historical apocalypses, the Apocalypse of Weeks and the Animal Apocalypse, are essentially attempts to set down the divine plan for humanity—that plan that had been spoken of in Isa 14:24–27 and 46:10–11, and which the author of Isa 25:1 had seen as coming to fulfillment with the arrival of Alexander the Great. Alexander's early death and the period of the Diadochoi had suspended that hope, and as suppression and violence continued, the faithful needed assurance that God really had a plan in which they would be vindicated. The Apocalypses seek to assure the faithful that God's plan is real and that it will, in its time, lead to the purification of all humanity. All history moves towards the Day of Judgment, after which the righteous will have authority and will complete the renewal of all humanity in the new age. The influence of the Isaianic traditions on the Enochic literature has been evidenced throughout, even more so in the Parables of Enoch (chaps 37–71) which we shall discuss later.[18] Moreover, Isa 24–27 appears to be the base from which the early Enochic literature emerged. While Enoch is described as having dreams and visions like the prophets of old as the source for his revelations, he is never described as a prophet, only as "a righteous man and scribe of faith" (15:1; 92:1). This is obviously because he is depicted as initially recording his visions rather than proclaiming them orally. The authors of the Enochic literature disseminated these revelations in writing as a more covert method of communication to their communities. Thus, they and Enoch can be described as prophetic scribes, bent on encouraging their communities, among which they lived, to remain faithful in spite of persecution.

THE BOOK OF DANIEL

The book of Daniel in its final form was written during the time of Antiochus IV Epiphanes, and so is roughly contemporaneous with the Dream Visions of Enoch. It is written partly in Aramaic and partly in Hebrew, the first six chapters are tales of how Daniel and his companions acted faithfully while living in exile under Babylonian and Persian kings, and the last six chapters are apocalypses in which Daniel receives dream-like visions of the future. The first half of the book contains tales *about* Daniel, while in the second half Daniel himself is speaking. The tales are set in a time long ago, no longer familiar to the author as is evident from historical inaccuracies.[19] The apocalypses have obviously been written during the difficult years of Antiochus IV. Yet in spite of these differences there is a certain unity about the book and a continuity of themes.[20]

The stories of Dan 1–6 appear to be tales which were told to illustrate how people who recognize their calling to be the Servant of Yahweh will live out their faith in an alien environment. For the Servant "*will have insight*, he will be exalted and lifted up and be very high" (Isa 52:13) so that kings and nations will open their eyes and recognize Israel's divine purpose for them (Isa 52:15). The term "have insight" is used in that verse to describe those who have come to understand God's plan for them and thus act as

---

18. Cf. Knibb, "Isaianic Traditions in the Book of Enoch," 217–29.

19. E.g., references to Belshazzar as king in Dan 5:1; 7:1; 8:1 and to "Darius the Mede" in Dan 5, 6, 9, 11.

20. Established long ago by Rowley, "Unity of the Book of Daniel," 247–80.

God's witnesses before the nations. The unity of the book of Daniel is evident from the use of the term, "*those who have insight*" (*maskilim*) in both parts of the book. It is used in Dan 1:4, 17 as a description of Daniel and his three companions. The verb is used again in the prayer for insight in Dan 9:13, 22, 25, and the term is used significantly in 11:33–35; 12:3, 10 to describe the faithful leaders of the people in terms of the Servant of Isa 52:13—53:12. The use of this term at the beginning of the book and at the end form a kind of *inclusio* to indicate that all in between deals with what it means to be "those who have insight," and to act as Yahweh's Servant in difficult situations.[21] The calling of Israel to be the Servant of Yahweh meant to be *witnesses* to the power of the one and only true God, Yahweh, before peoples and nations (Isa 43:8–12; 44:8). In this way, the Servant would "cause many nations to be purified; kings will shut their mouths because of him; for that which had not been told them they shall see, and that which they had not heard they shall seek to understand" (Isa 52:15).

Daniel 1–6

While the stories in Dan 1–6 may exemplify the advice given to the first exiles to "seek the welfare of the city" where they have been sent, because in its welfare they will find their welfare (Jer 29:7),[22] the author of these tales had more in mind. By describing Daniel and his companions as "those who have insight," he wanted to encourage his followers that, like them, they can live out their role as the Servant while living under alien rulers and thus, by being faithful to their God, can bring about change. It is because of their standing firm in their faith that Daniel is acknowledged as "servant of the living God" (6:21; cf. Matt 16:16) and his companions are referred to as "servants of the Most High God (3:26, 28). As God had given his spirit to his Servant in Isa 42:1, so Daniel is endowed with the spirit of the holy God (4:8, 9, 18; 5:11).[23]

In Isa 44 where Israel is called to be God's witnesses (v. 8), the promise was given to them: "I am Yahweh . . . who frustrates the omens of liars, and makes fools of diviners; who turns back the wise, and turns their knowledge into foolishness, but who confirms the word of his servant, and fulfils the prediction of his messengers" (vv. 25–26). This is demonstrated in Dan 2 where the king's wise men, enchanters, magicians and diviners cannot tell the king his dream or its interpretation, whereas Daniel is able to do so after seeking God's help. This witness caused the king to acknowledge God as "God of gods and Lord of kings, and a revealer of mysteries" (Dan 2:47), and Daniel is "exalted, lifted up and made very high" (Isa 52:13) as ruler over the province of Babylon (Dan 2:48). The same kind of message is repeated in the stories in Dan 4 and 5 with similar results.

Much of Isa 44 and 46 spoke of the folly of prostrating oneself before images of wood, gold and silver which cannot move or answer or save, so it is important to witness to the power of the true and living God. The same motif is carried over into Dan 3, 5

---

21. Cf. Davies, *Daniel*, 111.
22. So Collins, *Daniel*, 51.
23. Many of the illustrations of the Isaian influence given below have already been pointed out by Gammie, "On the Intention and Sources of Daniel I-VI," 282–92.

and 6. It is significant that the word used in Isa 44:15, 17, 19 and 46:6 for prostrating oneself before an idol (*sagad*) is found elsewhere only in Dan 3 where it is used some eleven times of worshiping the golden statue set up by the king. In this story, Daniel's companions are cast into the fiery furnace because they would not serve the gods of the king nor worship his golden statue. These three young men showed their readiness to face death like the Servant in Isa 53:12 rather than deny their God. Because of their covenant faithfulness they are saved, their faith vindicated, and God acknowledged as the only God who can save (3:28, 29), while their detractors perish in accordance with the promises to the Servant in Isa 50:10–11. As a consequence, Daniel's companions are "exalted and lifted up" as well (Dan 3:30).

A similar lesson is taught in Dan 6 where Daniel who is thrown into the lion's den because he continued to pray to God in spite of the edict against it. Again, Daniel demonstrated his readiness to confront death rather than not witness to his faith, God saved him, God is acknowledged as "the living God who endures forever" (6:26–28), and Daniel is exalted by the kings (6:29). Because of his witness, and that of his companions, and being a light to the nations, the words of Isa 45:14–17, 23 are being fulfilled.

Besides these major Isaianic themes in Dan 1–6, there are a number of other allusions to phrases and terminology found in Isa 40–66 and in some of the Psalms which further illustrate the dependence of the author of Daniel on the prophetic vision expressed by Deutero-Isaiah. The essential message to the faithful, then, living under Gentile kings, is to live up to their calling as the Servant of Yahweh, remaining firm in their faith while they serve those who rule over them. In this way, they can witness to the power of Yahweh as the only true God, and so bring about acceptance of their faith and ultimate transformation of the nations. Under the Ptolemies and Seleucids up to and including Antiochus III such a message was still viable. For in spite of heavy taxes imposed on them, they were still free to practice their religion. However, with the coming of Antiochus IV Epiphanes with his strategy of Hellenization and his insistence on the Jews worshiping his god under the name of Zeus Olympius, the situation began to change. This called for a different approach and focus.

Daniel 7–12

With the growing impact of the reign of Antiochus IV on the religious practices and beliefs of the Jews, as well as the expanding influence of the Hellenizers supporting him, it was now necessary to communicate to the faithful more covertly and with some urgency. So the author turns from speaking of Daniel as an interpreter of dreams to Daniel himself experiencing dream visions which needed to be interpreted. In these latter chapters Daniel himself becomes the spokesman, describing his visions with an angel as interpreter, similar to the role played by Enoch.

These chapters have much in common with the Enochic literature, and it is likely that the author of Dan 7–12 was familiar with it and sympathetic to its message on the whole, even to elaborating on some of its themes. In the Animal Apocalypse, Enoch saw that "a throne was constructed in the *pleasant land*, and the Lord of the sheep sat upon it, and he took all the sealed books and opened these books" (1 En 90:20) for judgment on the seventy shepherds. Similarly, Daniel sees that "thrones were set in place, and an Ancient of Days took his throne. . . . The court sat in judgment and the books were opened" (Dan 7:9–10). This throne scene is further described in terms taken from 1 En 14:28–22. The designation of Palestine as "the pleasant land" in 1 En 89:40; 90:20 has its equivalent in Dan 8:9; 11:16, 41. The archangels Michael and Gabriel are featured in both (1 En 10:9, 11; 20:5, 7 and Dan 8:16; 9:21; 10:13, 21; 12:1), and Daniel seems to assume the function of these two as described in Enoch. Both the Enochic literature and the book of Daniel have been influenced by the Isaianic vision, although Daniel has emphasized more of the role of the Servant. Both are indebted to Isa 24–27 specifically, and both have resurrection scenes (1 En 92:3; 103:4; Dan 12:1–2; cf. Isa 26:19) and names of the faithful written in the book of life (1 En 103:3; Dan 12:1). Moreover, in both, the faithful will shine like the luminaries (1 En 104:2; 108:11–12; Dan 12:3). That the imminent end-time will happen at God's appointed time is emphasized in 1 En 92:2, and even more so in Dan 8:17, 19; 9:27; 11:27, 29, 35, 40. The concern for faithfulness to the everlasting covenant and "the commandments of the Most High" is essentially the same in both (1 En 99:2, 10; Dan 9) although Daniel's prayer of confession and supplication is more explicit (Dan 9:11; but see 1 En 89:36).[24]

However, there are two major differences. Although both are influenced by the Isaianic vision, they differ in their attitude to the Maccabean revolt. In the Apocalypse of Weeks (91:12) as well as the Animal Apocalypse (90:19) a sword is given to the righteous to execute judgment upon the wicked, although after that has been accomplished, the sword is to be sealed up in the presence of the Lord (90:34).[25] Yet for Daniel, it is only by word, attitude and action that the Servant would cause many to become righteous, for the rest is to be left to God. This is evident already in the tales of Dan 1–6, particularly in Dan 2 where the stone that destroyed the great statue of the nations was "cut out, not by human hands" (2:33, 45; cf. Zech 12:3). So Antiochus IV will be broken, "and not by human hands" (8:25). The Maccabean revolt as a consequence is dismissed as only "a little help" (Dan 11:34).

The second major difference is in regard to the temple and its services. While in 1 Enoch the priesthood is condemned and the second temple regarded as polluted (1 En 89:73), Daniel has no polemic against the priesthood and is distressed over the abolishing of the regular burnt offerings and the setting up of the "abomination that desolates" and violation of the covenant (Dan 8:11–14; 9:27; 11:31). His prayer of supplication is "on behalf of the holy mountain of my God" (9:20). The leaders who violate the covenant are seen as seduced by Antiochus who is always the primary target. Considering that the heroes in Dan 1–6 were actually officials in the alien administration, it may be that the author of Daniel was close to the action in Jerusalem and sought to encourage particularly those in administrative positions to remain faithful to their tradition, including those priests and officials who sought to continue in spite of the Hellenizers. It is likely

---

24. See below. Daniel's prayer can mention Moses as servant of God (9:11, 13), but because Enoch is purportedly speaking about the future Moses, he can only speak of him as "the sheep that became a man" and built the "house," the covenant relationship (1 En 89:36).

25. Cf. Zech 12:6–7; 14:1–5.

that the author of Daniel was himself one of the *Maskilim* ("those who have insight"), seeking to keep the role of the Servant (Isa 52:13—53:12) as a model before the faithful.

Daniel 7

Daniel 7-12 is made up of four visions given at different times in the escalating violence of Antiochus Epiphanes' reign. The first vision (ch. 7) was given somewhere between 169-167 BCE, before the desecration of the temple in December 167.[26] Antiochus's explicit attacks on Jerusalem and the faithful made it impossible for the *Maskilim* to think in terms of bringing about a transformation of Seleucid rule by their words and behavior. This was now the time for the announcement of the final judgment on the evildoer and vindication for the righteous.

The kingdoms of the Babylonians, Medes, Persians, and Greeks (2:44-45) are now portrayed as great predatory beasts being drawn out of the sea of chaos by the four winds of heaven. The fourth one, Greece, is described as more terrifying, dreadful, and exceedingly more destructive than the others. It features ten horns as symbols of powerful kings, among which an eleventh, a small horn, appears with its mouth speaking arrogantly—clearly a reference to Antiochus Epiphanes (7:1-8). The court of judgment is set up, following the descriptions in 1 En 14:8-23 and 90:2, except in this case "thrones" are placed. That is, another throne is set up next to the throne of the Ancient of Days (7:9-10). The books are opened and the little horn with the arrogant words is condemned to death and his body burned with fire. Dominion and power is also taken away from the other kings and kingdoms (7:11-12).

Then in stark contrast to the kings as beasts coming forth from the waters of chaos, there comes "one like a son of man"[27] with the clouds of heaven to whom is given dominion and glory and kingship, the everlasting kingdom of Dan 2:44-45. The Aramaic term, *bar enash* ("son of man") is the equivalent of the Hebrew *ben adam*, which is used of Daniel, one of the *Maskilim*, in Dan 8:17. He is given glory, dominion, and kingship "that all peoples and nations, and languages should serve him" (7:13-14). This alludes to the joyous proclamation of Isa 60-62, particularly 60:4-16 and 61:1-7, where it speaks of nations coming to the faithful bringing gold and frankincense and proclaiming the praise of Yahweh. This proclamation in Isaiah finishes with the words: "they shall be called, 'The Holy People, the Redeemed of Yahweh'" (Isa 62:12; cf. 63:18). The scene here is really an enthronement celebration in which Yahweh hands over his everlasting kingdom to this "one like a son of man" to reign as his representative, similar to the liturgies of Pss 2 and 45. In fact, the words of Ps 45:8-9 are echoed in Isa 61:1-3 where the Servant of Yahweh is anointed as God's righteous people who shall possess the land forever as the shoot of God's planting (Isa 60:21; cf. Isa 11:1, 4). All this is based on the transfer of the everlasting covenant made with David to the faithful, God's holy people, in Isa 55:3-5. In this context and in view of the central theme of the book of Daniel,

---

26. Hartman and Di Lella, *Book of Daniel*, 214-15.

27. The contrast between the predatory beasts and the righteous appearing in the form of a "man" is the same as in the Animal Apocalypse where the oppressors are seen as predatory beasts, while Moses, as the righteous one, is a sheep who becomes a "man."

the "one like a son of man" can only be the Servant of Yahweh, that corporate figure standing for the righteous ones referred to repeatedly in Isa 40–55, and specifically in Isa 52:13—53:12. The extra throne mentioned in Dan 7:9 is for that Servant to sit at God's right hand (Ps 110:1; cf. Ps 80:18) as his earthly representative.

The interpretation given that it is the "holy ones of the Most High" who receive the kingdom and possess it forever (7:18) is a natural rendition of the corporate figure of the Servant. They are God's holy people. Daniel sees "the horn that had eyes and a mouth that spoke arrogantly" (7:20) making war with the holy ones and prevailing over them until the Ancient of Days came and gave judgment for the holy ones so that they gain possession of the kingdom (7:19-22). This is Antiochus Epiphanes, the one who speaks words against the Most High, wears out the holy ones, and attempts to change the sacred seasons and the law, so that the holy ones are "given into his power" for a limited time ("for a time, two times, and a half a time"). Soon, however, he will come under judgment and his power totally destroyed, and kingship and dominion will then "be given to the people, the holy ones of the Most High" (7:23–27). Behind this can be seen the tyrannous acts of Antiochus as described in 1 Macc 1:41–51. Those who continued to keep the sabbaths and festivals suffered at his hands.

That those faithful to God should be called "the holy ones of the Most High" simply picks up on the refrain in Leviticus: "Be holy, for I am holy" (11:44, 45; 20:7, 26; 21:6; cf. Num 5:40; 16:3), just as the faithful are called "the holy ones" in Pss 16:3; 34:10. The Aramaic phrase in 7:27 should be translated as an appositional construct: "the people, the holy ones of the Most High,"[28] and is equivalent to "the holy people," in Isa 62:12; 63:18. In Zech 14:5, it is these holy ones who accompany their God to fight and establish his kingdom, while others flee.[29] That the holy ones will "gain possession of the kingdom" (7:22, 27) is the culmination of the fervent hope of the faithful that they would eventually possess the land (Isa 54:3; 57:13; etc).

The contention that the "one like a son of man" is the archangel Michael and the "holy ones" are angels is to disregard the continuity and direction of the prophetic vision. The kingdom has never been promised to angels in any of the prophetic literature.[30] While it is true that in 1 Enoch the "holy ones" usually refers to the heavenly watchers, the faithful are also described as "the righteous and holy ones" in 1 En 93:6; 100:5.[31] The whole focus of Dan 7 is to give assurance to the faithful that the vindication that they have been longing for since the time of the exile is finally to come about.

---

28. Hartman and Di Lella, *Book of Daniel*, 95.

29. That this passage was interpreted this way at the time of the writing of Daniel is evident from 1 En 90:18–19 where the earth is split, the predatory beasts and birds flee, and a sword is given to the good sheep.

30. In agreement with Davies, *Daniel*, 104.

31. *Pace* Collins, "Son of Man," 50–66; Collins, *Apocalyptic Imagination*, 78–85; Collins, *Daniel*, 294–324; also Koch, "Der 'Menschensohn,'" 369–87.

Daniel 8

After Daniel's first vision and the interpretations given, the hopes of the people for a speedy end to the persecution under Antiochus IV would have become evident, but the situation only became worse. After banning burnt offerings and sacrifices in the temple and forbidding the practice of circumcision, reading the Torah, or keeping sabbaths and festivals on pain of death, Antiochus had an altar to Zeus Olympius erected on the altar of burnt offering in December 167 BCE (1 Macc 1:54–63). In forbidding the worship of the God of Israel and claiming divinity for himself, Antiochus also rejected the gods of his ancestors (Dan 11:36–39). This is delineated in this second vision where the "little horn" grows exceedingly great, as high as the host of heaven, and throws down some of the host and some of the stars, and tramples on them (8:9–10). The gods of his fathers are seen as part of the host, often depicted as stars (cf. Isa 24:21–22; 1 En 18:14–16). However, Antiochus also acts arrogantly to the one true God, the "prince of the host," by forbidding sacrifice and worship in the temple (8:11). Yet he continues to succeed in his evil.

In this vision, Daniel then hears one of the faithful ("a holy one") speaking to another and asking the question that would have been on the minds of all the faithful: How long is this ban on sacrificial worship and the desecration of the temple ("the transgression that makes desolate") going to go on? The answer that it would last for 3,300 evenings and mornings (8:14), is roughly equivalent to the three and a half years given in the first vision (7:25). First Macc 4:52–53 reports that it was actually December 164 BCE before the burnt offerings could be resumed.

Since Daniel is portrayed as receiving this vision centuries before these events take place, he needs an interpretation of his vision. This is supplied by the angel Gabriel who is described as having "the appearance of a *geber*" ("male, warrior," v. 15), a play on the name Gabriel (= "warrior of God"). Gabriel assures Daniel that the vision is for the end of the period of wrath (8:19; cf. 11:36). The later time of that period is described in terms of Antiochus destroying both the mighty and the people, the holy ones (8:24), deceiving many, and without warning destroying many of them (8:25). The author apparently has in mind the slaughter and enslavement of the Jerusalem population described in 1 Macc 1:29–32. However, Antiochus's arrogant attack on Yahweh (the Prince of princes) finally leads to himself being destroyed by God. It is evident that that period of wrath is also extended to those Hellenizers who were ready to reject their God for the sake of economic and social gain. That idea is now expanded upon in the next vision.

Daniel 9

As the period of wrath dragged on, and the struggle with Antiochus and his forces led to the loss of more innocent lives, the question came up again: How long will this persecution go on before the godless come under judgment? The author has Daniel, therefore, turn to Jeremiah's prediction given after the first deportation by Nebuchadnezzar. Jeremiah had predicted that the period of wrath against Judah would be seventy years before Yahweh would restore them and then judge Nebuchadnezzar (Jer 25:11–12;

29:10). Deutero-Isaiah had long ago announced that that period was over and they had paid double for all their sins (Isa 40:1–2), and that had been reaffirmed in Zech 9:11–12. Yet since the return from exile the people had been continually under the domination of foreign powers which had now become intolerable (Dan 9:12).

So Daniel now turns to God with a prayer of confession and supplication offered on behalf of "the people of Judah, the inhabitants of Jerusalem, and all Israel" including those Jews living in other countries (9:7). Daniel appears to be confessing all the sins of the nation from the time of the monarchy to the present (9:8). Acknowledging that God has acted in covenant righteousness in bringing this present evil upon them, Daniel confesses that they, the nation, have been rebellious in not heeding God's laws set before them by God's servants the prophets (9:4–10). Significantly, that rebellion is described in more specific terms: "We did not entreat the favor of Yahweh our God to turn from our iniquities and *to have insight* into your faithfulness" (9:13).

While Daniel is still praying, "the man Gabriel" appears in response to his prayer and to answer his question about Jeremiah's seventy years. In response to the prayer Gabriel announces that he has come *to give* Daniel *insight* and understanding (9:22). The answer to the question about the seventy years, however, bears resemblance to the seventh week of the Enochic Apocalypse of Weeks. The archangel's answer that "seventy weeks [of years] are decreed for your people and your city to finish the transgression, to put an end to sin, and to atone for iniquity, to bring in everlasting righteousness, to seal both vision and prophet, and to anoint a most holy place" (9:24). In the Apocalypse of Weeks, this period in which the Hellenizers have led many astray, is described as the rise of "a perverse generation" whose many deeds will be perverse, but at the end of this "week" the chosen from the "everlasting plant of righteousness" are to act as witnesses of righteousness, and they will be given sevenfold wisdom and knowledge (1 En 93:9–10). Then, at the conclusion of the eighth week, "the temple of the kingdom of the Great One will be built in the greatness of its glory for all the generations of eternity" (91:13). Thus the anointing of a most holy place (Dan 9:24) will take place after the judgment announced in 7:11.

Daniel, too, is given knowledge and insight (v. 25) about the seventy weeks which are divided up into three periods. The first period of seven weeks stretches from the return from exile until the time of an anointed leader, understood to be the high priest Joshua at the time of the rebuilding of the temple (Hag 1:12–15; 2:1–9). The second period of sixty-two weeks is from the establishment of that temple in 515 BCE until another anointed one is cut off, a reference to the murder of the high priest Onias III in 171 BCE.[32] The final week (seven years) describes Antiochus Epiphanes coming and destroying Jerusalem and its temple and slaughtering many people (1 Macc 1:20–35). "Desolations are decreed," an ominous echo of Isa 10:22 (cf. Isa 28:22), implies righteous judgment because of those who have followed the Hellenizers with whom Antiochus had made a "strong covenant." His banning of sacrifices and setting up of the altar of Zeus Olympius, the "abomination that desolates" (1 Macc 1:54–59) is described as taking place for "half a week," the three and a half years mentioned in Dan 7:25. The end of that time will mark the end of Antiochus (9:27). While the answer given by Gabriel again

---

32. Porteous, *Daniel*, 142; Hartman and Di Lella, *Book of Daniel*, 251–52; Collins, *Daniel*, 356.

focuses on the climactic evil of Antiochus, the essential message is that the consequences of the sin of the Hellenizers must run their course before judgment will finally be brought upon Antiochus.

Daniel 10–12

In these chapters one gets a heightened sense of the developing drama from the time of the Persian Empire to the increasingly vicious retaliations of Antiochus Epiphanes and the horrific suffering of the people who refuse to relinquish their faith in their God Yahweh.

Chapter 10 serves as a prologue to the thinly veiled but increasingly accurate and specific details of the Greek overlords in ch. 11, with over half given to the actions of Antiochus IV. Daniel's description of his three-week fast (10:2) probably reflects the author's own action over the increasing persecutions suffered by the people near the end of Antiochus's rule. The coming of the archangel Gabriel, described variously as "a man clothed in linen" (10:5), "like the appearance of a human being" (10:16, 18), heightens the drama. Gabriel's message that he had been delayed in coming because he had been fighting against the angelic prince of the kingdom of Persia aided by the archangel Michael, and that he will soon return to fight against the angelic prince of Greece, is told to ensure the audience that God's compassion for the faithful has been there all through their history.

Dan 11:2–20 describes the events that took place after the "warrior king," Alexander, died, and his kingdom divided "to the four winds" (11:3–4). It deals with the constant fighting back and forth of the Ptolemies and Seleucids up to the time of the death of Antiochus III and succession of Seleucus IV. One intriguing verse (11:14) situated at the time of the defeat of Egypt's army at Paneas by Antiochus III, speaks of the "sons of violence of your people" as "lifting themselves up in order to fulfill the vision, but they shall stumble." The phrase would refer to those prophetic visionaries in Upper Galilee who believed that Antiochus III at the battle of Paneas (198 BCE) would fulfill the prophetic vision, but were wrong.[33] This would constitute a mild indictment by the author of his fellow visionaries to the north for being ready to take up arms to achieve the divine plan.

Dan 11:21–30 describes the rise of a "contemptible person" who obtains "the kingdom through intrigue," Antiochus Epiphanes. He is described as destroying armies and eliminating the high priest Onias III, "the leader of the covenant" (11:22), acting deceitfully, lavishing gifts on the rich to gain their favor, waging war against the south, making a false alliance to return to his land with great wealth (11:23–28). But it is only for a time, for soon will be the appointed time for his end (11:24, 27). His being enraged at Jason's revolt and invading Jerusalem, slaughtering many of its inhabitants and taking much gold from the temple is described tersely as "his heart shall be set against the holy covenant" (11:28). Then in grim detail the author documents Antiochus's growing antagonism and tyranny toward those who persist in remaining firm in their faith, but particularly his

---

33. See Collins, *Daniel*, 379.

resentment and persecution of their leaders—"those who have insight" (*Maskilim*) and teach the people to remain strong (11:29-35). He takes action against the holy covenant and sides with the Hellenizers who have forsaken that covenant (11:30). His forces occupy the fortress and the temple and profane it; he abolishes the daily sacrifices and sets up "the abomination that desolates" (11:31). Those who have acted wickedly against the covenant he reduces to apostasy with falsehood.

However, those loyal to their God stand firm, taught by the *Maskilim* how to be the true Servant of Yahweh (11:32; cf. Isa 53:11). This the *Maskilim* demonstrate even with their lives as they are subjected to sword and flame, captivity and confiscation of property for some days (11:33). That they receive "a little help" from the Maccabean revolt, whose use of force would not have been welcomed by the author of Daniel, particularly as he saw many joining the revolt with ulterior motives.[34] However, the suffering of the *Maskilim* like the Servant of Isa 53 will refine, purify, and make them white (an allusion to Isa 1:18 and 1 En 90:32) until the time of the end of the persecution and the judgment foretold in Dan 7:10-11. Their witness to the people is that judgment is in the hands of God who will bring it about at the appointed time (11:35). One does not bring about righteousness by retaliation and war but by demonstrating a faithful relationship with God and with one another is the message of the *Maskilim*. Nevertheless, the period of wrath is not yet complete. Antiochus continues to exalt himself above God and every god, and while he may experience success, the judgment awaits him. Those, too, will share his fate who have supported him for the gain of wealth, power, and confiscated land (11:36-40).

Up to this point the author of Daniel has described what he has seen and experienced. He now predicts that Egypt will come against Antiochus but will be defeated, and Antiochus will carry off all its riches. Tens of thousands will fall victim to Antiochus before he comes to his end between the sea and the holy mountain (11:40-45). For the place of the final judgment of the nations had traditionally been set in the vicinity of Jerusalem (Ezek 38:14-16; 39:2-4; Joel 3:1, 12-15; Zech 14:2-12). This prediction, however, did not eventuate. That final battle between Egypt and Antiochus did not happen, and Antiochus dies in Persia around 163 BCE, after this book of Daniel had been completed (cf. 1 Macc 6:1-17; 2 Macc 1:11-17; 9:1-29). Finally, the author can now elaborate on the judgment scene given in the first vision (Dan 7:9-14). The kingdom of God will be given to the Servant who has insight and has been ready to give his life in order to make many righteous. Michael the archangel and protector of Israel, who has been fighting the angelic powers behind the Seleucid throne, now comes in a judicial capacity to defend and vindicate the faithful.[35] Everyone who is found written in the book will be delivered (12:1). This is the book of the living, the record of the righteous (Ps 69:28; Isa 4:2-6; Mal 3:16; Exod 32:32-33), and not all who have died during this whole period of foreign domination will be found recorded there. For "many of those who sleep in the dust of the earth shall awake, some to everlasting life, and some to disgrace and everlasting abhorrence" (12:2). In Isa 53 the Servant was depicted as rising up from the death of the exile to prolong his days and fulfill his purpose by causing many

---

34. Cf. Hartman and Di Lella, *Book of Daniel*, 299.
35. So Nickelsburg, *Resurrection*, 11-14.

to become righteous. These ideas were later picked up in Isa 26:19 where the conviction was expressed that God would make the faithful dead to live, to awake and rise from the dust and sing for joy, while the wicked who had died would not live and their shades would not rise (Isa 26:14). Isaiah 24–27 had a strong influence of the apocalyptic writings. So also here in Dan 12:2 the influence of Isa 26:19 is evident, but it goes further in that it speaks of the resurrection of individuals—the righteous to everlasting life and the wicked who had rejected their faith and opposed the faithful to everlasting disgrace and abhorrence (cf. Isa 66:24). Now those who have insight, that is, those who exemplify the role of the Servant of Yahweh of Isa 52:13—53:12 and lead many to righteousness "will shine like the brightness of the firmament," "like the stars forever and ever," reflecting the brilliance of God's presence as in Isa 60:1–3, 19–20 (Dan 12:3; cf. 1 En 103:3–4; 104:2; 108:11–12).[36]

After these revelations, Daniel is told to keep the words secret and the book sealed until the time of the end. However, two angels appear and one addresses the inevitable question of those suffering under the Seleucid regime: "How long will it be until the end of these extraordinary events?" (12:6). Gabriel makes a solemn oath that it will be for "a time, two times and half a time," the same response given in 7:25, and described in 9:27 as "half a week," that is, of years. Of course, the point that it would be half of seven, a number symbolizing fullness, emphasized that it was for a limited time. To that oath, the archangel adds "and that when the purging[37] of the power of the holy people comes to an end, all these things would be accomplished" (12:7). This is the cleansing of the holy people of every influence of the Hellenizers. For Daniel, that is further explained in that "many shall be purified, made white, and refined, but the wicked shall continue to act wickedly" because they lack understanding. So they will be purged from the community of the *Maskilim* who understand the ways of God (12:10). Through the instruction and struggle many will become part of that community.

The book ends with two attempts to interpret literally the three and a half times, first as 1,290 days (3.6 years) and then 1,335 days (3.7 years). Evidently, the death of Antiochus IV had not yet been reported, nor had the temple been cleansed and rededicated at the time of writing. These suggested calculations were probably later additions to the book. Daniel is now told to go his way and await his reward at the end of days.

Conclusion

The undercurrent throughout the book of Daniel has been about the faithful exemplifying the role of the Servant of Yahweh. The author was evidently part of a community which sought to live up to that ideal by witnessing by word and action to the power

---

36. Cf. Nickelsburg, *Resurrection*, 17–26; Davies, *Daniel*, 109–11; Collins, *Daniel*, 390–96; Hartman and Di Lella, *Book of Daniel*, 306–10.

37. The NRSV and other translations have "the *shattering* of the power of the holy people," but that has been found problematic. Porteous, *Daniel*, 172, emends it to translate "when the power of the *oppressor* of the holy people" comes to an end. Similarly, Hartman and Di Lella, *Book of Daniel*, 312, have "the *desecrator* of the holy people." However, the word *nafats* is used in Isa 27:9 where it has the meaning of purging sacred poles and incense altars from Israel, and this seems to be the meaning here.

of the one true God. The leaders of this community, the *Maskilim*, those who have the insight of the Servant of Isa 52:13, sought to live up to this ideal and to teach others to be that Servant in whatever situation they found themselves. The author himself was evidently one of the *Maskilim* who used the stories of Daniel and his companions to illustrate how the faithful could live out that role under foreign rule. In this context it is obvious that the figure of "the one like a son of man" who is to succeed to the throne of God's earthly kingdom as his representative after the judgment is that Servant of Isa 40–66, a collective concept for the faithful, the holy people of God. Consequently, there is no hope expressed for a Davidic messiah, and dominion, glory and kingship are given to the Servant, the holy ones of the Most High (Dan 7:13–27). It is quite apparent from the stance of non-violence expressed in these chapters that the holy ones were not part of those "pious ones" who joined up with the Maccabees to fight.

Throughout Daniel's apocalypses the focus of the final judgment has been on Antiochus IV because of his cruelty and attacks on Yahweh and his people. The author has seen the pivotal point of those attacks being against the temple worship with the banning of the daily sacrifices and the erection of an altar to Zeus Olympius. This desecration of the temple had made it impossible to continue the worship of Yahweh there. Concern for this and his indictment of Antiochus for the murder of the last good high priest, Onias III, indicate that the author of Daniel was much closer to the Jerusalem scene and more sympathetic toward those priests who remained faithful to their religious convictions than those of the Enochic communities.

HISTORICAL INTERLUDE

By December 164 BCE Judas Maccabeus and his followers were able to gain control of Jerusalem and the temple. Choosing "blameless priests devoted to the law," Judas had the temple cleansed and rededicated, and Mount Zion fortified against attacks from the Hellenizers and the Syrian garrison (1 Macc 4:42–60). Not long after, Antiochus died (1 Macc 6:1–16). His son Antiochus V rescinded the decrees of his father (1 Macc 6:59–60), but was soon murdered. Civil war broke out and soon led to the death of Judas in battle (160 BCE; 1 Macc 9:18). His brother Jonathan then took over the leadership, and by 152 he had gained the upper hand, taking over the office of high priest. However, with the growing instability of the Syrian government, Jonathan was drawn into more fighting which led to his death in 142 BCE (1 Macc 12:46—13:24). He was succeeded by Simon, the last surviving son of Mattathias, who was soon ratified as high priest and ethnarch by the assembly of the priests and the people of Judea (1 Macc 14:41), but in 134 he was murdered together with two of his sons by his son-in-law Ptolemy. Simon's one remaining son, John Hyrcanus, was soon able to put down the rebellion and gain control of the leadership, and thus served as high priest and military leader until his death in 104 BCE.

By this time, the Hellenizers were no longer a force to contend with, and other movements were gaining strength. Primary among these was the party of the Pharisees, an offshoot of the Hasidim, concerned with the keeping of Mosaic law and ancestral traditions, and thus popular among the common people. Closely aligned with them were the scribes who had gained prominence through the need for copies of the Torah after the destruction of so many scrolls under Antiochus IV. Under the Hasmoneans, as the descendants of Mattathias became known, the Pharisees had been influential particularly under John Hyrcanus until one of their members questioned the legitimacy of Hyrcanus holding the office of high priest. John Hyrcanus then turned to the priestly party, the Sadducees ("sons of Zadok"), who were influential among the wealthy and more sympathetic to Hellenizing tendencies (cf. *War* II.8.14; *Ant.* XIII.10.6).

When John Hyrcanus died after thirty years of rule, his eldest son, Aristobulus, took over but died within a year. His widow, Salome Alexandra then released his brother Alexander Janneus whom Aristobulus had imprisoned, married him and declared him the new king and high priest. Under Alexander Janneus (103–76 BCE), the Hasmonean leadership moved to secular rule and to the way of the Hellenizers.[38] The opposition of the Pharisees to his lawlessness and cruelty during his reign eventually led to civil war, at the end of which 800 leading Pharisees were crucified. However, when Alexander Janneus died, his widow Salome Alexandra took over the rule of Judea (76–67 BCE), appointed her elder son, John Hyrcanus II, as high priest, and made reconciliation with the Pharisees, allowing them to have control in matters of religion and law, and to avenge those who had supported Alexander Janneus against them. Josephus claimed that while Salome Alexandra ruled others, the Pharisees ruled her (*War* I.5.2).

Salome Alexandra died in 67 BCE, and John Hyrcanus II now succeeded to the throne as well as retaining the high priesthood but was opposed by his brother, Judas Aristobulus II. This led to fighting between the two sides, leading eventually to both seeking Pompey in Damascus to settle the dispute. But when fighting broke out again Pompey came to Jerusalem with his army, laid siege to the temple, where Aristobulus's followers had taken refuge, for three months before the walls were breached. As a result, thousands of Jews lost their lives, and many were taken as slaves to Rome together with Aristobulus and his children to be paraded in Pompey's triumphal procession there in 62.

In this way the Jewish people once again lost their independence, and now had to pay tribute to Rome with the Roman governor of Syria ruling them and with Hyrcanus serving as high priest. However, the whole world soon seemed to be returning to chaos as fighting for power broke out in both Palestine and Rome. Through all of this Antipater, an Idumean, who had befriended Julius Caesar, was made procurator of Palestine in 47 BCE. Antipater then placed two of his sons as governors—Phasael in Jerusalem and Herod in Galilee. When Caesar was assassinated in 44 and Antipater was poisoned the following year, Phasael and Herod, always ready to switch sides, quickly sought Antony's favor who named them as tetrarchs in spite of the fact that delegations from Jerusalem brought all kinds of accusations against both of them. Earlier, as governor of Galilee, Herod had rounded up Hezekiah, a so-called brigand chief together with his men and summarily executed them. These were people who had lost their land either because of debt caused by heavy taxes and tribute or through confiscation by foreign rulers,[39] and had turned to robbing wealthy merchants bringing goods from Damascus to the coast. Charges had been brought against Herod and he was summoned to stand trial in

---

38. Tcherikover, *Hellenistic Civilization*, 253.
39. See Richardson, *Herod*, 110–11, 250–51.

Jerusalem, but he had been acquitted because of the intervention of the Syrian governor at that time.

The Parthians had been a continuing threat to the Roman hold on Syria, so Antigonus, Aristobulus's last remaining son, now gained their support in taking over control of Judea. The Parthians proclaimed Antigonus "king" in Jerusalem in 40 BCE. Herod escaped and made his way to Rome where he convinced the Roman senate to name him as king of Judea. Herod returned in 39 BCE and landed in Ptolemais, gathered an army, and together with Roman legions sought to take over the kingdom. Taking back control of Galilee, which he had governed since 47 proved more difficult than he had expected. Much of the local population joined with some of Antigonus's soldiers to fight against Herod, causing him constant harassment. So he had to proceed against the so-called brigands who were living in the cliff caves near the village of Arbela. Herod tried to wipe them out, but because of the difficulty of getting to the caves, many survived and returned to attack again. This time Herod was ready to go to great lengths to eliminate every cave inhabitant as well as those who had fled to hide in the Huleh marshes at the Jordan river (*War* 1:309–13; *Ant.* 14:420–33). Only then could he return to campaigning against Antigonus and the Parthians. Herod left his brother Joseph in charge of Galilee, but Joseph and his men were ambushed and killed near Jericho by the forces of Antigonus. This gave some of the common people in Galilee the opportunity to rise up against some of the mighty who had supported Herod. They dragged them to the Sea of Galilee where they drowned them.[40]

After two years of fighting, Herod with the assistance of Mark Antony's legate Sosius, laid siege against Antigonus in Jerusalem. After four months the soldiers of Herod and the Romans were able to scale the walls and take the city. Indiscriminately, they massacred the whole population, men, women and children. So by 37 BCE Herod was now finally proclaimed "King of Judea," and wasted no time in executing those who had supported Antigonus, confiscating their property and wealth. Just prior to the siege of Jerusalem Herod had married Mariamme, granddaughter of Hyrcanus II, hoping thus to link himself with the Hasmonean line, but he always feared for his throne. It was this fear and the popularity of the young high priest, Aristobulus III, Mariamme's brother, that led Herod to have him drowned. By 30 BCE he also had the elderly Hyrcanus II put to death. Herod ordered the death of Mariamme herself soon after, as well as her mother Alexandra. Growing paranoia soon led him to suspect that his two sons by Mariamme were plotting to take over his kingdom, so he had them executed. A few days before his own death at the age of 70 in 4 BCE, Herod had his eldest son, Antipater, executed believing he was conspiring against him. Herod had maintained control over his kingdom by the use of fear, but he himself became a victim of fear, even of his own family.

Psalms of Solomon

During these tumultuous and desperate times, a pious community expressed itself in a series of psalms, known as the *Psalms of Solomon*. These psalms are prayers for God's

40. Cf. ibid., 153–57.

mercy and protection, and for strength to remain faithful in times of persecution and distress. They are the psalms of a community of the righteous, the afflicted and dispossessed (Ps 5). The many allusions to the Isaianic literature in particular indicate the influence of the prophetic vision on this community. Psalms 2 and 8 speak of the events of 63 BCE with Pompey entering the city of Jerusalem and laying siege of the temple against the followers of Aristobulus II. Then, we are told, "he killed their leaders and everyone wise in counsel, he poured out the blood of the inhabitants of Jerusalem like dirty water. He led away their sons and daughters, those profanely spawned" (8:20–21).[41] While the psalmist rejoices over the death of Pompey (2:26–29), he acknowledges that the real causes of the trouble were the Hasmonean leaders and their priests, "the sons of Jerusalem" who had "defiled the sanctuary of the Lord" (2:3), defiling "Jerusalem and the things that have been consecrated to the name of God" (8:22). Psalm 4 speaks further of their hypocrisy. In spite of Pompey's cruelty, he was seen as God's agent in bringing judgment on them.

Psalm 17 appears to have been written after Herod had taken over control of the kingdom in 37 BCE.[42] Herod, an Idumean, is described as "a man alien to our race" (v. 7), as "the lawless one" who laid waste their land, and massacred young and old. He is "the enemy, a stranger" whose heart is alien to their God. With his coming, the pious had to flee and become refugees in the wilderness in order to save their lives from evil, leaving behind in Jerusalem a "Gentile rabble" and those Jews who adopted Gentile ways (vv. 11–18).

The Psalmist's answer to all of this (vv. 4–5) is to revive the hope for a Davidic messiah by recalling the everlasting covenant made with David in 2 Sam 7:14. Such a Davidic messiah would destroy the unrighteous rulers, purge Jerusalem from Gentiles and drive out those "sinners," the false priests, from their inheritance (vv. 22–23). Using the messianic language of Ps 2 and Isa 11:2–5, the writer depicts this son of David as destroying "unlawful nations with the word of his mouth" (v. 24), gathering a holy people whom he will lead in righteousness (v. 26), and then Gentile nations will serve "under his yoke" (v. 30). The nations will come to see the glory of this king, taught by God, and bring back those who had been driven out as gifts in fulfillment of Isa 66:18–21.[43] He will be the "anointed lord" under the kingship of God, and he will not rely on war and collecting armies but on his strong hope in God (vv. 32–34). Filled with God's holy spirit his rule will be "wise in the counsel of understanding, with strength and righteousness" (v. 37).[44]

These psalms thus appear to have been written somewhere between 63 and 30 BCE. It has often been assumed that the group responsible for these psalms was either the Pharisees or the Essenes.[45] However, the emphasis on the covenant with David coupled

---

41. Translation used is from Wright, "Psalms of Solomon," 2:639–70.

42. Cf. Atkinson, "Herod the Great," 313–22; Atkinson, "On the Herodian Origin," 435–60.

43. Davenport, "Anointed of the Lord," 67–91.

44. See further discussions in Wright, *OTP* 2:641–46; Pomykala, *Davidic Dynasty Tradition*, 159–70; Nickelsburg, *Jewish Literature*, 238–47.

45. For a list of those attributing authorship to the Pharisees, Essenes and others, see Atkinson, "On the Herodian Origin," 437.

with the prophetic influence may indicate Levite authorship. They had long condemned the arrogance of the Zadokite priesthood and disdained the Hasmoneans. Nevertheless, it was during the horrendous reign of Herod that many thought back to the time of David as king and longed for such a ruler.

THE PARABLES OF ENOCH (1 ENOCH 37–71)

The author of the Parables of Enoch was evidently living during these times and responded to the sufferings and persecution of the faithful both in Galilee and Judea with further assurances of God's impending judgment on their oppressors and the final vindication of God's chosen, righteous, and holy ones. He came to this task imbued with the prophetic vision, the Isaianic expression of their purpose as God's people, the vision of a new heaven and new earth, the heritage of the earlier Enochic literature, and the message of the book of Daniel.

That these parables had their origin during the time of Herod is evident from the reference to the Parthians and Medes in 1 En 56:5—57:3, since the threat of the Parthians to the Roman expansion in the east was the main reason why the Roman senate had been ready to give Herod the title "king" and helped him to be installed as such. The probable references in the Noachic interpolation to the thermal waters of Calirrhoe in which Herod had bathed hoping to find healing shortly before his death (1 En 67:4–12) is another indication that these parables saw the light of day soon after Herod's death in 4 BCE.[46] Another clue to the time of Herod is in the numerous references to the kings, the mighty and the exalted possessing the land. Many people in Galilee and elsewhere had lost their land through debt because of heavy taxation or through confiscation and had become the dispossessed, sometimes seeking to survive by robbing the people who had "robbed" them, living in caves and in swamp lands. The situation became far worse under Herod. Even after Herod had annihilated the cave dwellers (*Ant.* 14:20–30) and left Ptolemy as general over Galilee, "the men who had formerly disturbed Galilee" killed Ptolemy and "fled in a body to the marshes and other inaccessible places, harrying and plundering the entire country thereabout" (*Ant.* 14:431–33). Such was the resentment of the people of Galilee against those who had taken over their ancestral land.

Out of the pall of persecution, dispossession and the slaying of many Galileans by Herod and his henchmen came these Parables of Enoch. The three parables are described as "the vision of wisdom that Enoch saw, spoken in the presence of the Lord of Spirits according to his insight and according to the good pleasure of the Lord of Spirits" (1 En 37:1–5).

---

46. Most recent scholars are now in general agreement that these two historical allusions call for a dating of the parables around the turn of the era. See the various articles by different scholars in Boccaccini, *Enoch and the Messiah Son of Man*. Also Nickelsburg, *1 Enoch 2*, 62. Arguments to the contrary by Ehro, "Historical Allusional Dating," 493–511, remain unconvincing.

The First Parable (Chapters 38–44)

The first parable begins with a description of the time of the coming judgment when the righteous and chosen are gathered together with the Righteous One (Isa 53:11), and when the righteous, chosen and holy ones who dwell on the earth will be reflecting the brilliant presence of God (Isa 60:1–3), and the hidden things promised in Isa 42:9; 43:10; 48:3–8 will finally be revealed. It is the time when the sinners, the kings, the mighty and the exalted who possess the land will be driven out and will perish, with no one seeking mercy for them (38:1–6). A brief reference is made to the story of the fallen angels in the book of the Watchers (cf. 1 En 14:24—16:4) to remind readers of the origin of the evil and violence they have experienced (39:1–2).

Enoch is then taken up into heaven where he has another vision. This time he sees the holy and righteous ones who have died dwelling with the righteous angels, joining them, in interceding and praying for humanity. Before these chosen ones, who shine like fiery lights as they reflect the brilliance of the divine presence (Isa 60:1–3; Dan 12:3), he sees the Chosen One of righteousness and faith who dwells "beneath the wings of the Lord of Spirits," the poetic place of refuge for the righteous (Pss 17:8; 36:7; 57:1; 61:4; 63:7; 91:4; cf. Matt 23:37–39). There, in that perfect realm of righteousness and truth, all join in songs of blessing and praise for the Lord of Spirits (39:3–7; cf. Isa 42:10–12). Enoch, longing for that experience too, offers his songs of praise and blessing and is joined by the holy angels singing the song of the seraphs of Isa 6:2–3 (39:8–14). Among the myriads of angels, he hears the voices of the four archangels who are blessing the Lord of Spirits, his Chosen One and the chosen ones, petitioning and praying for those who dwell on earth (40:1–10). Enoch learns the secrets of heaven, how justice is carried out and how those who deny the Lord of Spirits will be driven away from the dwelling places of the chosen and holy ones (41:1, 2, 9). He observes the order and secrets of the cosmos (41:3–8; 43:1–4; 44:1) and notes that they are a parable for "the holy ones who dwell on the earth and believe in the name of the Lord of Spirits" (43:4).[47] The order and permanence of the heavenly bodies is an example for the faithful and an assurance to them of God's abiding care for them (cf. Isa 40:26–31).

The Second Parable (Chapters 45–57)

This parable concerns those "who deny the name of the dwelling of the holy ones and of the Lord of Spirits." There will be no place for them in the new heaven or the new earth, but they will be kept for the day of affliction and tribulation when God's Chosen One, sitting on the throne of glory, will test their works. At that time, the righteous and chosen ones will dwell in peace with the Chosen One in the divine presence in the transformed heaven and earth (45:1–6; cf. Isa 65:17; 66:22).

Enoch now sees the judgment scene taken from Dan 7 in which the Lord of Spirits is now called the "Head of Days" and the Chosen One is referred to as "that Son of Man who has righteousness," who will reveal "the hidden things" to the faithful and judge the kings and the mighty whose deeds are unrighteous, who trust in their wealth, worship

---

47. See Suter, "*Mašal* in the Similitudes," 193–212.

false gods, and persecute the faithful who trust in the Lord of Spirits (46:1–8). The kings and the mighty are categorized in the same terms as the arrogant king of Babylon in Isa 14:4–20. The significant addition to the scene of judgment in Dan 7 is that here the Chosen One / Son of Man is seated on the throne of glory, presumably that "other" throne mentioned in Dan 7:9, 14 (cf. Ps 110:1), and the judgment is handed over to him as God's representative (46:1–8; cf. Ps 2:7–9). For the prayers of the righteous and the blood of the Righteous One had been rising up from the earth, and the angels of heaven had been interceding on their behalf that judgment might be executed for them. Alternating between the blood of the Righteous One and that of the righteous ones picks up the integral nature of the relationship between the "one like a son of man" in Dan 7:13 and "the holy ones of the Most High" in Dan 7:21–22. In response to the prayers, as in Dan 7:9–10, the Head of Days had taken his seat on the throne of his glory to avenge the blood of the Righteous One and the righteous ones. However, this time the books that are opened are the books of the living, as in Dan 12:1, to emphasize the vindication of the righteous who had suffered (47:1–4).[48]

Following this, the commissioning and function of "that Son of Man" is described as having been part of God's plan from the beginning (48:2–3; cf. Isa 46:8–11). It is highly significant that this Son of Man of Dan 7:13–14 is described here in terms of the Servant of Yahweh. He is to be a staff for the righteous, the light of the nations, and a hope for those who grieve in their hearts (48:4–9; cf. Isa 42:1–6; 49:6, 8), and all on earth will prostrate themselves before him (48:5; cf. Isa 49:7; 52:15). Like the Servant he was chosen and hidden in God's presence from the beginning until he is revealed to the holy and righteous according to the wisdom of the Lord of Spirits (48:6–7; cf. Isa 49:1–3; 51:16). The kings and the mighty who possess the land will not be able to stand before him and will perish like stubble in the fire (48:8–9; cf. Isa 24:21–22; 47:14–15). For "they have denied the Lord of Spirits and his Anointed" (48:10). This allusion to Ps 2:2, calling the Son of Man, "Anointed One" (again in 52:4) is not a Davidic messiah as in *Pss. Sol.* 17. It picks up two ideas: one, in Isa 55:3–5 that everlasting covenant made with David has been transferred to the faithful as the Servant (Isa 61:1); and second, that kingship has been given to the Son of Man in Dan 7:14. As such, he is described with all the royal attributes of Isa 11:2–5 (49:1–3) and will bring forth justice as the Chosen One in whom God delights (49:4; cf. Isa 42:1–3). Then the light of God's presence will dwell upon the holy, chosen and righteous who will conquer and cause others to repent and be saved (50:1–5; cf. Isa 60). The dead will be raised, as in Dan 12:1–3, and the earth will rejoice, as in Isa 55:12, because the Chosen One has arisen to sit upon the throne and to choose the righteous and holy to dwell upon the land (51:1–5).

Metals used by the powerful to make instruments of war will all melt before the Chosen One like wax before the fire when the Chosen One appears before the Lord of Spirits (52:1–9). Next, Enoch sees a deep valley where instruments of punishment are being prepared for the kings and mighty and where they will perish. Then "the Righteous and Chosen One" can cause "the house of his congregation" to come into being. There the faithful can live unhindered, free from oppression (53:1–7). Turning to another area, Enoch sees another deep valley with burning fire where iron chains are being forged for

---

48. For influence of Dan 7 in the Parables of Enoch, see further VanderKam, "Daniel 7," 291–307.

Azazel and the rebel angels who became servants of Satan, leading many astray. The four archangels will throw them and their demonic offspring (cf. 1 En 12–16) into the burning furnace on the day of judgment (54:1–6). They will be judged by the Chosen One upon the throne of glory and witnessed by the kings and mighty who are soon to receive their own punishment. With the depiction of the final battle in which the forces of evil are destroyed and peoples come from east and west to fall down and worship the Lord of Spirits, the second parable ends (56:5—57:3; cf. Ezek 38-39; Zech 14).

The Third Parable (Chapters 58–69)

This final parable is about the future of the righteous and chosen ones dwelling in the light of everlasting life and in the presence of the Lord of Spirits. This light will endure because darkness will have passed away, and truth and righteousness will be forever (58:1–6; cf. Isa 60:1–3, 19–21; Zech 14:7; Dan 12:2–3). There they will be cared for, for Enoch learns the secrets of the lightning, luminaries and winds, how they all have function and orderly purpose by which God nourishes the earth and cares for those who dwell in the Garden of Righteousness (59:1–3; 60:11–23; cf. Isa 51:3; 58:11; 61:11; 1 En 32:3; 77:3). The flood of Noah's time was a sign of divine judgment but also of the mercy and longsuffering of the Lord of Spirits (60:1–10, 24–25). Enoch sees angels with measuring cords by which they gather all the righteous and chosen, including those who have died by various means, so that all may return for the day of the Chosen One (61:1–5). This day is the day of celebrating the seating of the Chosen One upon the throne of glory when he is given authority to judge even the angels in heaven as well as people on earth, according to the word of the Lord of Spirits. In response, all the heavenly host and the chosen who dwell in the garden of life join the Chosen One in singing songs of praise and blessing for the mercy and longsuffering of the Lord of Spirits (61:6–13).

The kings and the mighty and the exalted and those who possess the land are now commanded by the Lord of Spirits to face the Chosen One whom the Lord of Spirits has seated on his throne to judge (cf. Isa 11:4). They will see that Son of Man seated there and will be terrified; pain, like birth pangs, will seize them. They had not recognized him before because the Most High had preserved him in the presence of his power and revealed him only to the chosen and holy ones who will be planted and stand in his presence (cf. Isa 60:21). The petitions of the kings and the mighty will be of no avail, and they will be delivered to the angels for punishment, while the righteous and chosen will be vindicated (62:1–12). For they will now live and eat with the Son of Man, having put on the garment of glory, the garment of life (cf. Isa 60:10–11), garments which will never wear out and glory that will not fade (62:13–16).

The kings and the mighty, the exalted and those who possess the land (63:1–12) together with the fallen angels (64:1–2) will all vanish from the face of the earth, corruption will disappear, for the judgment has been given to the Son of Man whose word will prevail in the presence of the Lord of Spirits (69:26–29).

The Righteous, Chosen and Holy Ones

These terms have largely derived from Isa 40–66. In Deutero-Isaiah the singular was used in a corporate sense: Israel was referred to as "my servant, my chosen one" (41:8, 9; 42:1; 43:10, 20; 44:1, 2; 45:4; 49:7) or as "the righteous one, my servant (Isa 53:11). This changed in Trito-Isaiah to the plural and was used to indicate those who were the faithful (Isa 65:9, 15, 22). In Isa 62:2, 12 the faithful were given a new name, "the holy ones, the redeemed of Yahweh" which was to include all the righteous (Isa 60:21). Such designations became the favorites of the earlier Enochic literature (1 En 1:1, 3, 8; 5:6, 7, 8; 25:5; 93:2, 8, 10). Calling them "the holy ones" is found only in 93:6 and 100:5, 10 but gained popularity after Dan 7:18–27. They are the faithful who believe and trust in the power of God to deliver them and who will be vindicated and inherit the land once again. They are those who have suffered and died at the hands of the kings and mighty and have their resting place in heaven, having been raised from the dead. Yet together with the living they look forward to a new heaven and new earth where they will all dwell in peace and security and in righteousness and truth in the presence of God, reflecting his brilliance.

The Righteous, Chosen, Anointed, Son of Man

The journey through these Parables of Enoch has taken us through the ethereal mists of an imaginative drama in both the heavenly and earthly spheres, centering on the Day of Judgment for the oppressors and the vindication of the oppressed, always relating to the prophetic vision of the divine plan and its ultimate fulfillment. The hero of this drama, the Righteous, Chosen, Anointed Son of Man, has been drawn from the corporate personality of the Righteous Chosen One in Isa 40–55, and the Son of Man from Dan 7, all of which have come under the umbrella of the Servant of Yahweh. While this last title originally stood for Israel in Isa 40–55, it soon became restricted to the faithful. However, in these parables the titles take on an extended sense of one who is a leader and representative of the righteous, chosen, holy ones. He is seen as one who is a staff for the righteous, a light to the nations, hope for those who grieve in their hearts (48:2–4). Like the Servant in Isa 49:1–3, he had been hidden and now revealed to the holy and righteous and chosen (48:6–7; 62:7). While he acts as God's representative by sitting on his glorious throne and judging the kings and the mighty, he also represents the righteous and holy by leading them in their vindication. In the new age, the Righteous One will appear in the presence of the righteous and chosen (38:2), will dwell among them (45:4; 62:13–14) and will be joined by them in blessing the name of the Lord of Spirits (61:10–12). This Righteous, Chosen Son of Man is thus depicted as being in solidarity with the righteous, chosen, holy ones.

That solidarity is particularly significant in 47:1–4 where the blood of the Righteous One and the prayers of the righteous are said to have risen to the presence of the Lord of Spirits, while the holy ones in heaven have been interceding and praying "in behalf of the blood of the righteous ones that had been shed."[49] The Chosen One is seen as rising in

---

49. Cf. Black, "Messianism of the Parables of Enoch," 161, and VanderKam, "Righteous One," 170.

the resurrection scene in 51:1–5,[50] and in 39:6, 7 the Chosen One is seen by Enoch with all the righteous and chosen who had died, in heaven. There the archangel Raphael "who brings healing to every wound of the sons of men" is heard blessing the Chosen One and the chosen ones who depend on the Lord of Spirits (40:5, 9). The precedent for this is seen already in Isa 53:10–12 where the exile was described as a death from which the Righteous One would rise to fulfill his God-given purpose (cf. Isa 57:1–2; 1 En 92:3–5). In Dan 7 the "one like a son of man" represents those who have insight (Isa 52:13), who are raised in Dan 12:2–3 from the dust of the earth to shine like the brightness of the sky forever. The interpretation of Isa 52–53 in Wis Sol 2–5, probably written before the Parables of Enoch,[51] is closely parallel to the parables, particularly chs. 62–63.[52] There the Righteous One who "professes to have knowledge of God and calls himself the servant of the Lord" (Wisd 2:13; cf. Isa 53:11) is killed by the ungodly and taken into the presence of God where he becomes the accuser of the ungodly who oppressed him. The confession of the kings and the mighty in 1 En 63 is very similar to the confession of the unrighteous in Wis Sol 5.[53] So the Righteous, Chosen, Anointed Son of Man is the resurrected representative of the righteous, chosen and holy ones and will act in their behalf in judging and condemning their oppressors, thus inaugurating the new age.

The longing for a strong leader to come forth against the powerful oppressors of an earlier time gave rise to the renewal of hope for a descendant of David in *Pss. Sol.* 17, and the figure of the Righteous, Chosen, Son of Man is the Enoch community's response to this. Chapters 70–71, in which Enoch was identified as the Son of Man (71:14), is generally regarded as secondary.[54] In a later addition to the book of Enoch (1 En 108), it is said of all the righteous that God "will seat each one on the throne of his honor" (108:12). The tension between the corporate and the individual continues.

Brief Summary

This apocalyptic literature has transported us over three hundred years of exploitation, persecution and oppression under the Diadochoi, the Ptolemies, Seleucids, and worsening to a state of desperation under Herod. The hope for freedom to live as the people of God which arose under Alexander the Great expressed in Isa 24–27, quickly turned to an emphasis on the hope for an imminent Day of Judgment when their persecutors and oppressors would get their just deserts and the new age would come into being. The new age became more idyllic as time went on with a return to the garden of life, where only

---

50. The translation by Isaac of 51:4b is "the faces of all the angels in heaven shall glow with joy because on that day the Elect One has arisen," "1 Enoch," 37.

51. See Horbury, "Christian Use," 182–96.

52. Nickelsburg, *1 Enoch 2*, 258–59, makes this point (also earlier in *Resurrection*, 68–78) but argues that the exalted figure in the parables does not suffer but "is instead a transcendent figure," "the heavenly patron of the suffering chosen and righteous ones." Also, Collins, *Apocalyptic Imagination*, 147–50, who argues that "the Son of Man is not a personification of the righteous community, but is conceived, in mythological fashion, as its heavenly Doppelgänger."

53. For influence of Isa 52–53 on Wis Sol 2–5, see Suggs, "Wisdom of Solomon 2:10—5," 26–33.

54. Nickelsburg, *1 Enoch 2*, 322–23; Collins, *Apocalyptic Imagination*, 151–53.

righteousness and truth would be known and darkness banished forever as the righteous live in the brilliant presence of God. Meanwhile the sinners and oppressors, together with the rebel angels, receive more descriptive punishment in the fiery abyss. While the apocalypses were written to give comfort and assurance of God's almighty plan for the righteous under persecution and stress, the emphasis on the Day of Judgment has been central throughout, and thus the prophetic vision had become narrowed.

Chapter IX

Jesus and the Kingdom of God in Matthew's Gospel

MATTHEW'S GOSPEL

It is now generally acknowledged that the Gospel of Matthew was written by a Jewish Christian primarily for Jewish Christians to reassure, comfort, and encourage them in spite of harassment or rejection by some of their Jewish contemporaries.[1] The Gospel emphasizes the fulfillment of the Hebrew Scriptures, deals with concerns regarding Jewish understanding of the law, the acts of righteousness, Sabbaths, temple tax, sacrificial ritual, Pharisaic traditions and scribal interpretations, and accentuates the controversies with the Jewish leaders. There is a strong concern to counteract Pharisaic rejection of Jesus by emphasizing Jesus' Jewish roots as "son of Abraham," and his royal heritage as "son of David." The Gospel contains many Semitisms, words and phrases in Hebrew idiom, unexplained Jewish customs which indicate that Jewish readers are foremost in mind. It emphasizes that Jesus' mission was first to gather "the lost sheep of the house of Israel" into the kingdom of God to be a light to the nations. More so, the author assumes that his hearers/readers know a lot about the prophetic heritage and that they are familiar with the Hebrew Scriptures, particularly the prophetic writings.

A more prominent feature of the Gospel is the frequent use of quotations and allusions to the Hebrew Scriptures, many of which are found only in Matthew. It becomes clear that the ten so-called formula citations (1:22–23; 2:15; 2:17–18; 2:23; 4:14–16; 8:17; 12:17–21; 13:35; 21:4–5; 27:9–10) are not just superimposed on the narrative but are an integral part of the context to which they give meaning and significance. These follow in similar pattern to quotations spoken by Jesus in Matthew's Gospel (e.g., 11:10; 13:14–15; 15:7–9; 21:16; 21:42). The author shows that he is thoroughly familiar with the context of the prophetic quotations and expects the same of his readers. He often combines words

---

1. See, e.g., Overman, *Matthew's Gospel*; Saldarini, *Matthew's Christian-Jewish Community*; Sim, *Gospel of Matthew*; Hagner, "Matthew: Apostate, Reformer, Revolutionary," 193–209. See further the discussion in Carter, "Matthew's Gospel," 155–79.

The Prophetic Vision and the Real Jesus

from two different texts in one quotation in order to alert the reader to the context of both (e.g., 2:6 [Mic 5:1–2 2 Sam 5:2]; 2:23 [Isa 11:1 60:21]; 11:10 [Exod 23:20 Mal 3:1]; 21:5 [Isa 62:11 Zech 9:9]; 27:9 [Jer 18:1–13; 19:1–12 Zech 11:12–13]). The author's thorough knowledge of the Old Testament Scriptures, and that of his community, is also indicated sometimes in subliminal messages. For example, in 3:4 he uses words to describe the Baptist's clothing which are almost identical with 2 Kgs 1:8, a description of the garments worn by Elijah, in order to alert the reader to recognize John as fulfilling the role of the returning Elijah (cf. 11:14; 17:13). Similarly, in 27:41–43 he characterizes the chief priests, scribes, and elders in Jerusalem with the very words used to describe the "wicked" in Ps 22:8 and Wis 2:10–20, in order to make the point that these leaders are actually the evil ones who persecute Jesus as the one who exemplifies the righteous Servant of Ps 22 and Isa 53.

Fulfillment is the all-pervading basic concept in Matthew (cf. 26:54, 56). All Israel's history, hopes, and purpose are seen as coming to fulfillment through Jesus. However, it is not the legal, catechetical or rabbinic tradition which provides the main focus, but the prophetic. The author of Matthew's Gospel understands that the most profound influence on the message and mission of Jesus comes from Deutero-Isaiah, and to varying degrees from those prophets who followed in that prophetic tradition from Trito-Isaiah to the Parables of Enoch (1 En 37–71).[2]

One can readily understand why the early church universally claimed that the Gospel of Matthew had originally been written in Hebrew which had to be translated into Greek for the Diaspora Jews and the growing number of Gentiles who became part of the early church. In spite of its Jewish orientation, this Gospel was always regarded as the primary Gospel for understanding the teaching and mission of Jesus by the church fathers. Jerome (347–420 CE) tells us that he found a Hebrew copy of the Gospel in the library at Caesarea, and that he translated into Greek and Latin a copy used by the Nazoreans (*de viris illustribus* 2, 3). Eusebius of Caesarea (260–340 CE) in his *Ecclesiastical History* (V.10.1–3) tells of Pantaenus, head of the catechetical school in Alexandria, going to India around 180 CE and finding that people there were already using a Hebrew version of the Gospel of Matthew.

In spite of popular opinion, the Gospel must have been written prior to the destruction of the temple in Jerusalem in 70 CE since the temple's existence is always assumed (cf. 5:23–24; 23:16–22; 17:24–27). There is no evidence of the war with Rome having already taken place, nor allusions to any of the Pauline letters.[3] Because the Gospel is directed primarily to Jewish Christians, the place of origin was most likely in Palestine, probably in Galilee or the surrounding area.[4] While the early church universally held

---

2. See further Leske, "Isaiah and Matthew," 152–56.

3. Cf. France, *Matthew: Evangelist and Teacher*, 82–91. David Sim argues that there are two valid arguments for dating Matthew's Gospel after 70 CE: "Matthew's use of Mark and his explicit allusion in 22:7 to the destruction of Jerusalem" in his *Gospel of Matthew and Christian Judaism*, 33–40. However, the destruction of the faithless and the burning of the city in 22:7 is simply a repeat of the prophetic warning of judgment found in Isa 5:24–25; Jer 25:8–9; Mal 4:1; etc. So the only argument left is based on the Two-source Hypothesis, which, of course, is a circular argument.

4. So also Overman, *Matthew's Gospel*, 159; Segal, "Matthew's Jewish Voice," 26–29 and White, "Crisis Management," 299; Stanton, "Revisiting Matthew's Communities," 17.

that the author of this Gospel was Matthew, the apostle and former tax collector referred to in 9:9, most scholars today hold that he was probably an anonymous disciple of Jesus. At this point I do not wish to presume who the author is or the date of the writing of this Gospel. They can best be arrived at on the basis of the results of our study of its historical and cultural background. However, it should be readily acknowledged that the Gospel with the most Jewish content is likely to have been the first. It is unfortunate that so much of Matthean scholarship has worked from the premise that Matthew redacted Mark's Gospel instead of seeing his work in its Jewish context. For the sake of brevity, I shall simply refer to the author as "Matthew."

Given the thorough familiarity of Matthew with the prophetic vision, it is entirely appropriate to consider this Gospel as the primary source for understanding the message and mission of Jesus against the background of his Jewish environment and to see how Jesus responded to the prophetic vision. Matthew's basic purpose in writing his Gospel was obviously to set down for posterity and for the Diaspora Jews an abiding record of Jesus' teaching and mission, which he had been teaching to his community, so that it would be the foundation for their faith and mission. Moreover, he wanted to warn his readers to beware of the teachings of the scribes and Pharisees lest they be led astray from fulfilling their mission. Matthew also needed to respond to a number of wrong assumptions made popular by the scribes and Pharisees, such as: that the Messiah had to be the "son of David"; that the judgment on the forces of wickedness (e.g., Gentiles, tax collectors, sinners) had to take place before the kingdom of God could be established; that this kingdom would be a political, national kingdom as in the days of David and Solomon, ruled by the law as the Pharisees taught it; also that hostility to Gentiles had to be maintained lest one's purity as the people of God be jeopardized.

THE INFLUENCE OF THE PHARISEES

The Pharisees as a movement appear to have originated among the "pious ones" (*chasidim*) who had taken a stand against Hellenism and had joined forces with Judas in the Maccabean revolt. As a non-priestly group they developed their own set of beliefs based on the Mosaic law and the traditions of the elders. Under the Hasmoneans they were able to flourish and became particularly influential among the masses, and as such became powerful politically. Josephus tells us that John Hyrcanus (135–104 BCE) was a disciple of the Pharisees and "greatly loved by them" (*Ant.* XIII.289). Understandably so, because Hyrcanus had extended the borders of his control, conquering Shechem and Samaria and destroying the rival temple on Mount Gerizim. This gave the Pharisees the opportunity to exert their influence and religious authority further north. That Hyrcanus was motivated by religious fervor as well as by political power is evident also in his conquering the Idumeans to the south and forcing them to become Jews and live according to the Mosaic Law (*Ant.* XIII.257). The Pharisees later had a falling out with Hyrcanus over the validity of his high priesthood (*Ant.* XIII.290–96), which made Hyrcanus move to the Sadducees, abrogate the Pharisaic regulations and punish any who continued to observe them. Nevertheless, the Pharisees retained their popularity with the people and were immediately believed when they spoke against king or high priest

(*Ant.* XIII.288). Later, opposition of the Pharisees to the rule of Alexander Jannaeus (103–76 BCE) even led to civil war which resulted in 800 of the leading Pharisees being crucified by Alexander (*Ant.* XIII.372–83).[5]

However, the power of the Pharisees was such that before Alexander died, he counseled his wife and successor, Alexandra Salome (76–67 BCE), to win back the masses by yielding some power to the Pharisees (*Ant.* XIII.400–402). This she did, allowing the Pharisees to reinstate the regulations abrogated by John Hyrcanus, and gave them free rein in carrying out executions of those who had urged Alexander to crucify the 800 (*Ant.* XIII.408–12; cf. *J.W.* I.111–13). However, the growing power of the Pharisees soon led Aristobulus II to begin a revolt against his dying mother, Alexandra, which led to civil war with his brother, finally resulting in Pompey taking over power for Rome in 63 BCE.[6]

During the reign of King Herod, the Pharisees maintained their influence and popularity with the masses, and this often protected them from some of the severe reprisals of Herod, even though the Pharisees often opposed him. This was evident when the Pharisees refused to take the oath of allegiance to him. While others were punished "by every means possible," the Pharisees, some 6,000 of them, were only made to pay a fine (*Ant.* XV.366–70; XVII.41–42), although some who were found to be conspiring against Herod with the wife of Pheroras, Herod's brother, were put to death (*Ant.* XVII.44).[7] During the Roman rule, the Pharisees continued to wield their political influence in more subtle ways, but it was particularly their religious stance that helped them to retain a hold over the common people.

According to Josephus, the Pharisees were thought to be more pious than others, and to interpret the laws more accurately and were regarded as the leading sect (*J. W.* I.110; II.162). In their interpretations, they had passed on to the people regulations which had been handed down from former generations and which were not recorded in the Mosaic Law, but were regarded by them as equally valid (*Ant.* XIII.297, 408; XVII.41). This use of oral tradition was the central and most distinctive element of Pharisaic teaching (*Ant.* XVIII.12).[8] They also taught that the thoughts and actions of human beings were governed by a complex blend of fate and God on the one hand, and human free will on the other. The soul, being imperishable, of a good person would then be free to live again, while the soul of the wicked would suffer eternal punishment (*J.W.* II.162–63; *Ant.* XIII.172; XVIII.14). It is on account of these views, says Josephus, that the Pharisees happened to be the most persuasive to the people so that their prayers and sacred rites and all their faith and worship were conducted according to Pharisaic interpretation, even their manner of life and discourse were governed by Pharisaic views (*Ant.* XVIII.15).

---

5. This was referred to also in the *Nahum Pesher* (4Q169) where Alexander Jannaeus is referred to as the "Angry Lion" and the Pharisees as the "seekers of smooth things" (cf. Isa 30:10; Dan 11:32). Cf. Schiffman, "Pharisees and Their Legal Traditions," 264–65.

6. See Mason, *Flavius Josephus on the Pharisees*, 255–59.

7. Ibid., 260–74.

8. Ibid., 293.

However, the reason for the popularity of the Pharisees may be more in what Josephus does not say. Writing principally for Roman readers, he did not want to say anything about the aspirations of the Pharisees to be free from Roman or any foreign control and to be able to have an ideal kingdom governed by the laws of God as they understood them for their own people. In their fight against the Hellenizing priesthood and the decrees of Antiochus Epiphanes, the Pharisees had taught the people that their salvation was dependent upon their keeping the Law and following the traditions of the fathers with devotion and thoroughness. Only by doing so would the nation be living up to the covenant and become righteous in the eyes of God. Only as such would God deliver them from the tyranny of foreign rulers and bring judgment on their persecutors and those who collaborated with their oppressors. Only then could they live in freedom and justice in the kingdom of God. God's agent in destroying the oppressor and establishing his kingdom would be a descendant of David whom God would raise up at the right time to carry out the judgment and to restore on earth an ideal kingdom for the righteous. This "son of David" would be God's Anointed One, the Messiah. The righteous ones who had died would be raised up to live again in this earthly kingdom.

To hasten the coming of this kingdom, the Pharisees believed that both the written and the oral law should be kept in every detail. Even those purity laws meant only for the priesthood and the temple were developed to cover every aspect of people's lives. In their interpretations of the Law, the Pharisees developed meticulous detail about dietary practices, ritual purity for meals and for households, table fellowship, agricultural tithing, and keeping the Sabbath. Such devotion to the interpretation of law to achieve righteousness soon led to the formation of exclusive fellowships of the "righteous" and the "pure." This kind of perfectionism or "holiness" inevitably led to arrogance and self-righteousness and a judgmental attitude towards those who did not or could not meet all their requirements. Such people were referred to as "sinners" or the "people of the land," the unclean who would be excluded from the future kingdom.[9] The common people had turned to the Pharisees because they believed they were the ones who could preserve their covenant with God and uphold the traditions of their faith, but it eventually became a new tyranny of the law in which they could never be sure whether their righteousness had reached the standard required for being God's covenant people and ultimately being part of his future kingdom.

THE PRIMARY LOCATION OF JESUS' MINISTRY

According to Matt 2:23, Jesus grew up in the Galilean village called Nazara/Nazareth[10] which was about an hour's walk south of Sepphoris, the city where Herod Antipas had his seat of government and which he was rebuilding to make it, as Josephus called it, "the ornament of all Galilee" (*Ant.* XVIII.27). After the Assyrian conquest of Galilee in 732 BCE, most of the population of the tribal areas of Zebulon and Naphtali had been

---

9. Cf. Dunn, "Pharisees, Sinners, and Jesus," 264–89; Regev, "Pure Individualism," 176–202; Neusner, *From Politics to Piety*, 82–90.

10. Both terms are found in Matthew and Luke. *Nazara* would be the normal name (like Magdala), while *Nazareth* is really the Hebrew construct form used with Galilee (e.g., *nazaret galil*).

deported, leaving that area sparsely populated. Settlements increased in the area and in the Golan during the Hellenistic period.[11] As we have seen in 1 En 13 and learn from the Aramaic Levi Document 4, these settlements would have been communities of the prophetic visionaries, Levites, and others who had joined them. Jewish population of Galilee increased considerably during the Hasmonean rule.[12] So by the time of Jesus, Galilee was mostly Jewish with the Pharisees exercising considerable influence among the population,[13] having become a powerful influence there already during the time of John Hyrcanus (135–104 BCE).

In Matt 2:23 we are told that Joseph took Mary and the child Jesus to Galilee "and he went and dwelt in a town called *Nazaret*, so that what was spoken by the prophets might be fulfilled, 'He will be called a *Nazôraios*.'" The town of Nazareth, which archeological evidence suggests was only settled in the second century BCE as a thoroughly Jewish agricultural village,[14] seemed to have derived its name from the Hebrew *netser*, "shoot," from Isa 60:21 where the community of the righteous was referred to as the "shoot" of God's planting. So the village was very likely settled originally by a group who were prophetic visionaries since, as we have seen, the "planting of the Lord" had become a way by which the prophetic visionaries in this area often referred to themselves (cf. 1 En 10:26; 84:6; 93:2, 5, 8, 10; 62:7, 8; Jub 1:16; 16:26; 21:24; 36:6; 1QH XIV.15–16; XV.18–19; XVI.6–11; cf. also Matt 15:13).[15] Matthew's reference to the "prophets" (2:23) may be covering all these references. The term, *Nazôraioi*, then, is the equivalent of the Hebrew *Notsrim*, the "shoots" of God's planting.

Over the years the *Notsrim* / Nazoreans of Nazareth would have witnessed much political activity in neighboring Sepphoris. They may have been caught up in the turmoil of Herod the Great's tempestuous rule there, and of the rebellion after his death led by Judas the son of Ezekias, as well as the consequent sacking and burning of the city by the Roman Legate, Varus, and the enslaving of its inhabitants. While living under the shadow of this important city had its negative effects, it would also have given them the opportunity to sell their produce there. These circumstances would have necessitated the Nazareth community taking a neutral position, which resulted in it becoming isolated from the majority of the prophetic communities in Upper Galilee, thus meriting the later remark by Nathanael: "Can anything good come out of Nazareth?" (John 1:46). Nevertheless, Jesus would have been well educated in the prophetic tradition there, particularly in the book of Isaiah.

JESUS AND HIS RELATIONSHIP TO JOHN THE BAPTIST

It would have been familiarity with the book of Isaiah that led Jesus to go to the Jordan where John the Baptist was carrying out his ministry, calling people to repentance

---

11. See Reed, "Galileans, 'Israelite Village Communities,'" 95–97.
12. Freyne, "Geography of Restoration," 299.
13. Chancey, *Myth of a Gentile Galilee*; Lee, *Galilean Jewishness of Jesus*.
14. Meyers and Strange, *Archeology*, 56–57; Reed, *Archaeology and the Galilean Jesus*, 131–32.
15. See further, Leske, "Jesus as a *Nazôraios*," 69–81.

because of the nearness of the kingdom of God. That John was seen as fulfilling the words of Isa 40:3 was attracting many from Jerusalem, Judea and the region around the Jordan (Matt 3:5) to undergo his baptism of repentance. So Jesus, with others from Galilee, went to be baptized by John. It appears that John became impressed with Jesus' knowledge and understanding of the prophetic vision and saw in him the spirit of the prophet Elijah. So he hesitated to baptize Jesus, suggesting that their roles be reversed (Matt 3:13, 14). Jesus' answer to this, according to Matthew, was "Let it be so now, for thus it is fitting for us to fulfill all righteousness" (3:15). It is evident from this that Jesus saw John's and his own mission as inseparable in initiating God's plan and purpose for Israel, expressed so often in the book of Isaiah (14:2, 6; 25:1; 55:10, 11). They would share the role of preparing the way of God and announcing the kingdom not only to the cities of Judah but elsewhere as well (Isa 40:6–11). They were to fulfill all righteousness, the bringing together of both divine and human righteousness as often expressed in the prophetic vision, exemplified particularly in Isa 45:8: "Shower, O heaven from above and let the skies rain down righteousness (*tsedeq*), let the earth open, that salvation may spring up and let it cause righteousness (*tsedaqah*) to sprout up also" (cf. Hos 10:12–13). God, being faithful to the covenant, would bring about his righteousness by delivering his people (cf. Isa 45:21–24; 46:12–13; 59:16–17) and reigning as King (Isa 40:9; 41:21; 43:15; 44:6; 52:7). Israel would then respond with righteousness and by witnessing to others (Isa 43:10, 12; 44:8; 55:3–5). Thus through them God would cause righteousness to shoot forth before all nations (Isa 61:11). In this way, Israel as the Righteous One, Yahweh's Servant, would cause many to be righteous (Isa 53:11).[16] Righteousness, as understood in the prophetic literature, is essentially the whole realm of faithfulness in the covenant relationship between God and people.[17] After Jesus had been baptized, it appears that he stayed in the wilderness with John during which time he wrestled with the implications of his divine calling (Matt 4:1–11).

The close working relationship between John the Baptist and Jesus is indicated in Matt 4:17 where Jesus, after hearing that John had been arrested by Herod Antipas, and having returned to Galilee and taken up residence in Capernaum, began to carry on with the same basic message John had preached: "Repent, for the kingdom of heaven is at hand." Later, he commanded his disciples to do the same (10:7). The Baptist's epithet for the Pharisees and Sadducees, "brood of vipers," was also used by Jesus against the Pharisees in 12:34 when they accused him of healing a demoniac by the power of Beelzebul, the prince of demons. He employed the epithet again in his woes against the scribes and Pharisees (23:33) because of their rejection of the prophetic vision. Jesus also repeated the "tree" motif used earlier by John (3:10) in 7:19–20; 12:33 and 15:13. Both John and Jesus had employed these phrases or motifs, as did the Teacher of Righteousness at Qumran, because they had obviously become common terms used by those seeking to fulfill the prophetic vision. The term, "brood of vipers," had originated in Isa 59:2–8 to

---

16. Leske, "Matthew," 1266.

17. This is true of all seven uses of *dikaiosynê* in Matthew's Gospel (3:15; 5:6, 10, 20; 6:1, 33; 21:32). To limit the meaning to human conduct or obligation is to ignore the whole concept of the divine-human relationship emphasized in the prophetic vision and in the teaching of Jesus. So e.g., Przybylski, *Righteousness in Matthew*, 75–76; Luz, *Matthew 1–7*, 177; Strecker, *Der Weg der Gerechtigkeit*, 153–58.

describe those who, motivated by greed or power, sought to lead people away from God. The tree motif, the "planting of the Lord" (Isa 60:21) had long been a common term for the prophetic visionaries.

That John the Baptist, like Jesus, had been proclaiming more of Isa 40 than just 40:3 is indicated by the popular belief of the close association of Jesus with the message of the Baptist. When the fame of Jesus became known to Herod Antipas (14:1-2), he was concerned that this was John the Baptist who had been raised from the dead, whom he had recently executed. That close relationship between John and Jesus, is illustrated further by the fact that after John's disciples had taken his body and buried it, they came and told Jesus (14:12). When Jesus heard it, he withdrew to a lonely place apart (14:13), only to be followed by a large crowd, which probably included disciples of the Baptist (14:13-21). Only Matthew's Gospel mentions this.[18] Matthew also mentions that Herod Antipas had earlier wanted to put John to death because he had criticized his marriage to his brother's wife Herodias, but he had feared the people because they regarded John as a prophet (14:5; cf. 21:26). The same was said about Jesus when the chief priests and elders wanted to arrest him (21:45-46; cf. 23:29-31).[19]

That Jesus understood John to have the same divine authority as he had is evident from his question put to the chief priests and elders in the temple: "The baptism of John, whence was it? From heaven or from men?" (21:25). When they refused to answer, Jesus chided them, saying that "John came to you *in the way of righteousness* (cf. 3:15) and you did not believe him" (21:32). So Jesus here saw John as bearing the same divine authority and having the same divine commission as himself.

Jesus told them the parable of the wicked tenants of the vineyard (21:33-40). The basis of this parable is the Song of the Vineyard in Isa 5:1-7, where the owner is God and the vineyard is Israel (cf. Isa 27:2-6). Jesus tells this to illustrate the rejection of the prophets sent by God by the leaders in Jerusalem. The chief priests and elders are the tenants of the vineyard who take the servants who are sent and "beat one, kill another, and stone another" (21:35, 36; cf. 23:29-33). So the vineyard owner sends his son whom they cast out of the vineyard and kill him so that they might retain the vineyard for themselves. The reference to the "son" has almost always been interpreted as Jesus referring to himself and his destiny at the hands of the chief priests. Yet the context is talking about chief priests and elders having rejected John the Baptist who had come in the "way of righteousness," and who had been put to death by Herod, something which would have pleased those who saw John's ministry as a threat to them. Nevertheless, the argument is given that "son" has to be a self-designation by Jesus because only Jesus is referred to as God's son (Matt 3:17; 11:27; 16:16; 17:5).[20] However, for the prophetic visionaries, acknowledging God as Father meant that they saw themselves as Servant/son (cf. Isa 63:16; 64:7; also Wis. 2:13, 16-18), and Jesus taught that peacemakers, the bringers of God's *shalom*, would be called "sons of God" (5:9) and throughout the Sermon on the Mount (chs. 5-7) encouraged kingdom members to think of themselves as sons and daughters of their heavenly Father (5:45). Earlier, Jesus had spoken of John as "more

---

18. Cf. Nepper-Christensen, "Die Taufe im Matthäusevangelium," 192.
19. Cf. Meier, "John the Baptist in Matthew's Gospel," 399-400.
20. So Kingsbury, "Parable of the Wicked Husbandmen," 643-55.

than a prophet" and that there was "no one greater than John the Baptist" (11:9–11), so why not as a "son" of God.[21]

Instead of giving an explanation of the parable, Jesus asks the chief priests and elders whether they have ever read Ps 118:22–23, which was regularly used in the Passover procession. It is important to see the prophetic significance behind this quotation. At the time of the Assyrian threat Isaiah of Jerusalem had told the leaders in Jerusalem who preferred to make foreign alliances rather than put their trust in God, that they had lies as their refuge and had taken shelter in falsehood, but that Yahweh was "laying in Zion a foundation stone, a tested stone, a precious cornerstone, a sure foundation: one who trusts will not panic" (Isa 28:14–16). Psalm 118 refers to this (v. 22), and was a song of thanksgiving to God for having saved them from their enemies. The "builders" who had rejected the stone were the faithless leaders, just as the present leaders in Jerusalem had rejected John,[22] so the kingdom of God will be taken away from them and given to those who will produce its fruits (21:43). Jesus' indictment continues in 21:44, "And he who falls on this stone will be broken to pieces, but when it falls on anyone, it will crush him." This verse is usually relegated to a footnote because it does not seem to fit, but it is actually an important part of the whole stone motif. For in Zech 10:4 the faithful of Judah are called that "cornerstone" (an allusion to Isa 28:16) who shall save Jerusalem, and in Zech 12:1–3 which begins with a quotation of Isa 42:5 in which God says, "I will make Jerusalem a heavy stone for all the peoples; all who lift it shall grievously hurt themselves." The "heavy stone" referred to the faithful of Judah. Jesus gave this as a further warning to those who would persist in working against the kingdom which he and John had been sent to proclaim.

However, differences did develop in the way Jesus and John approached their commissions. This became evident already when disciples of John came to Jesus asking why his disciples did not fast while they and the Pharisees did (9:14). Fasting was carried out as a sign of repentance, mourning, or the fear of coming judgment. So John's disciples were still focusing on the impending Day of Judgment, and John was expecting Jesus to be doing the same in the role of Elijah *redivivus*. Malachi 4:5–6 had described the returning Elijah as being sent before the Day of Judgment to warn the people to be reconciled to one another lest God strike the land with destruction. Ben Sira had spoken of Elijah as a prophet like fire, his word burning like a torch, who was destined to calm the wrath of God before it broke out in fury (Sir 48:1–10). Yet Jesus and his disciples were already celebrating the kingdom with tax collectors and sinners who had turned in repentance and faith in God's forgiveness (9:10–13). Jesus' response to John's disciples was: "Can the wedding guests mourn as long as the bridegroom is with them?" (9:15). Jesus was using the metaphoric language of Isa 61:10–11; 62:5 which spoke of the Servant who brings good news as one who is clothed in the garments of salvation, covered with a robe of righteousness as a bridegroom decks himself with a garland (cf. also Jer 33:11; 1 En 62:14–15). Jesus told John's disciples this was not a time to try to patch up an old

---

21. Suggested by Parker, "Jesus, John the Baptist," 10; argued also by Stern, "Jesus' Parables," 57–65.

22. There appears to be a play on words in Hebrew in this psalm between "builders" (*bonim*), "stone" (*eben*), and "son" (*ben*) in the parable, as in 3:9. See the discussion in Snodgrass, "Recent Research," 202–5.

worn-out garment (9:16) when the prophetic promise was that the old would pass away and God would cause new things to spring forth (Isa 42:9–10; 43:18–19; 48:6). Similarly, one could not put new wine into old wineskins, which symbolized the old ways (9:17). The new wine was the symbol of joy and gladness at the annual harvest thanksgiving, and so it was the symbol of the new age now being inaugurated (cf. Gen 49:10; Zech 9:16–17; Isa 55:1–2) through the proclamation of the good news (Isa 40:9–10).

The difference between Jesus and John in regard to the perception of their missions came up again later when John in prison was hearing reports of Jesus' works which did not sound like the works of Elijah. John wanted to know whether he should look for someone else to carry out that role (11:2–3). John's understanding of his mission according to Isa 40 was to prepare the way for the coming of God to restore his kingdom, but before that kingdom could be proclaimed as being present there were a series of events that would have to happen first—Elijah had to come to warn the people, then that great and terrible Day of Yahweh would follow in which the wicked would be judged and the tyrants destroyed, and then, and only then could the kingdom of God be established. Like most people, John was convinced that the judgment had to come first, and he was expecting Jesus to carry out that role of Elijah. Jesus' answer to John demonstrated that Jesus saw his mission according to Isa 40 in a different light. It was to go further and proclaim the good news of the kingdom of God *now*, God coming *now* to feed his flock like a shepherd (Isa 40:9–11). For Jesus, Isa 40 was just the introduction to the whole proclamation and mission expressed in Isa 40–66. Judgment would come later when people had had an opportunity to respond to the kingdom. So Jesus answered by referring back to his "works" of proclaiming the good news and acts of healing as signs of the kingdom promised in Isa 26:19; 29:18; 35:5–6; 52:1–7; 57:18–19; 61:1–3, works which Matthew had already recorded in chs. 5–9.

After the disciples of John had left, Jesus then addressed the crowds about the role of John in God's plan (11:7–15). Of course, the people had known John as a prophet, but Jesus tells them that he was more than a prophet, he actually fulfilled the role of the Coming One himself. He was Elijah *redivivus*. The quotation from Mal 3:1 is combined with Exod 23:20 in Matt 11:10 because the messenger who went before Moses was to lead the people of Israel into the promised land, just as John in the role of Elijah prepared the way for the promised kingdom. The idea of a second exodus and entry into the promised land was implicit in Isa 40:3 which was the verse to which Mal 3:1 alluded. Evidently, the crowds who had accepted John as a prophet from God had not made the connection to Elijah, the one "more than a prophet" (Matt 11:9). So Jesus further elaborated: "For all the prophets and the law prophesied until John, and if you are willing to accept it, he is Elijah who is to come" (11:13–14).[23] In other words, John as Elijah was more than the earlier prophets and was rather the culmination of their prophecies. As such, among humanity in general there was no one greater than him. Yet even the least one who enters

---

23. From the point of view of the prophetic vision, "prophets and the law" is the proper order since "law" was understood as the "teaching" of God by the prophets, rather than as a set of laws and statutes as emphasized by the Pharisees. In the light of this saying, it is unlikely that John ever saw himself as Elijah. In 3:3 Matthew was already alerting his readers to what Jesus is saying here by pointing out the similarity of John's apparel to that of Elijah in 2 Kgs 1:8. Contra Öhler, "Expectation of Elijah," 470–73.

the kingdom and experiences the good news of the Heavenly Father's restoring love and healing was greater than John. The "least one" is simply the diminutive form of "little one," a term used in 10:42; 18:6, 10, 14 for new members in the kingdom. Jesus explains why: "From the days of John the Baptist until now, the kingdom of heaven is treated violently and violent men are trying to grab it for themselves" (11:12). John's preaching of repentance and coming judgment had raised the hopes of freedom from oppression and foreign rule, leading some with nationalist ideals to seek to force the issue. This only created tension and fear of an uprising which led to John's imprisonment. This approach was the opposite of what Jesus had been teaching in 5:38–48.[24]

Jesus acknowledged the difference between his and John's approach to their roles once more in 11:16–19 in his condemnation of "this generation," that is, those leaders who found fault with and rejected both their messages, claiming a higher wisdom. Jesus' answer to them was simply: "Wisdom is declared righteous (only) by her works!" Jesus implies that in spite of their different approaches, both he and John were carrying out God's plan in action, whereas the wisdom of the "wise and understanding" (Matt 11:25; cf. Isa 29:14b) was nothing but vanity.

One final mention of John the Baptist comes after the Transfiguration when Moses and Elijah were seen in a vision with Jesus (17:1–13). As they came down from the mountain, Jesus told the disciples to say nothing about the vision until the Son of Man was raised from the dead (17:9; cf. 16:21). At this point the disciples asked: Then why do the scribes say that first Elijah must come?" They were referring to the scribal contention that Elijah had to come to restore relations between fathers and children and herald the judgment in line with Mal 4:5–6 before the resurrection could take place. Jesus acknowledged that the scribes were right to expect Elijah but they did not recognize him when he came in the person of John the Baptist, "but did to him whatever they pleased. So also the Son of Man will suffer at their hands."[25] Once again the destinies of Jesus and John are in parallel.

The relationship between Jesus and John the Baptist was as coworkers in seeking to fulfill God's plan as expressed in the book of Isaiah. Jesus came to be baptized by John, not as his disciple[26] but to work together with him to bring about the fulfillment of the Isaianic vision. The fundamental difference that developed between them was in their understanding of when the kingdom would come. For John, and for so many others, it could only come after the Great Judgment, which had been foremost in the minds of those who had long suffered under tyrants since the time of the death of Alexander the Great. Jesus understood the message of Isa 40–66 differently, and his interpretation was to meet with opposition, in spite of the hope and healing it brought to so many, even among some within the prophetic and Levite communities.

---

24. Leske, "Matthew," 1291.

25. See the discussion about Elijah coming first raised by Faierstein, "Why Do Scribes," 75–86; Allison, "Elijah Must Come First," 256–58; Fitzmyer, "More about Elijah Coming First," 295–96.

26. Cf. Frankemölle, "Johannes der Täufer und Jesus," 196–218.

The Prophetic Vision and the Real Jesus

THE SETTING FOR THE PROCLAMATION OF THE GOOD NEWS (THE SERMON ON THE MOUNT)

The reason why Jesus made his home in Capernaum after the arrest of John the Baptist was partly because it was on the north-west corner of the Sea of Galilee, a busy city, on one of the trade routes between Damascus and the Mediterranean, and so was a center from which he could access the region roundabout. But first and foremost, it was because Capernaum was the gateway to Upper Galilee and the surrounding area where many of the prophetic and Levite communities had settled. Jesus would announce the good news of the reign of God to them first. To accentuate this point, Matthew quotes Isa 9:1–2 as being fulfilled by this move (Matt 4:14–16), giving only the geographical locations and the promise of the future light of God's presence. In that quotation, Isaiah of Jerusalem had expressed the hope that the two northern tribes, Zebulun and Naphtali, which had been deported by the Assyrians in 733 BCE, would soon be brought out of the gloom of the exile into the light. For God would not forsake his people. The areas of these two tribes were the hill country of Galilee (Zebulun) and Upper Galilee (Naphtali). The area had been called "Galilee of the nations" because Assyria had populated the area with people from various parts of their empire (2 Kgs 15:29; 17:24–27), but by the time of Jesus the population was mostly Jewish.[27] By giving this quotation Matthew was saying that in Jesus' proclamation of the good news to people in these areas, the promise of light was finally being fulfilled. Matthew made a slight change to Isaiah's proclamation to "the people who *sit* in darkness" to bring it into line with Isa 42:7 in order to connect it to Jesus' mission, identified at his baptism with Isa 42:1 (3:17). The quotation was to focus on the *light* that comes to people with the proclamation of the kingdom of God soon to be announced rather than confrontation with the Roman power.[28]

The first four disciples Jesus called to follow him would have been members of the prophetic communities, and when they heard Jesus' message they were ready to follow immediately (4:18–22). Simon and Andrew were originally from Bethsaida, a town a few kilometers east of Capernaum (John 1:44). Andrew had already been a follower of John the Baptist (John 1:35–40). James and John, the sons of Zebedee, were from a family that remained committed to Jesus' mission (20:20; 27:56). All four fishermen were ready to become "fishers of men" (Jer 16:15–16; cf. 1QH XIII.9–15) for the kingdom.

In the next verse (4:23), Matthew has summarized Jesus mission in Isaianic terms: "*teaching* in their synagogues" (cf. Isa 42:4, 21; cf. 51:4, 7), "*proclaiming* the good news of the kingdom" (Isa 40:9–11; 41:27; 52:7), "*healing* every disease and every sickness among the people" (Isa 53:3, 4; 57:18, 19). This verse (4:23) is an *inclusio* verse repeated in 9:35 to indicate that all in between is an elaboration of that verse. It is significant that Jesus' fame is mentioned as spreading first "throughout all Syria" which would indicate the whole area to the north and east where the prophetic and Levite communities had spread. This then led to many crowds coming to Jesus "from Galilee and the Decapolis, and Jerusalem and Judea, and from beyond the Jordan" (4:24–25).

---

27. Nazareth was in Zebulun and Capernaum was in the area of Naphtali.

28. Contra Carter, "Evoking Isaiah," 513–18. The Matthean context shows no interest here in the phrase "Galilee of the nations." Cf. Menken, "Textual Form," 532–33.

More importantly, Matthew has introduced the essential teaching and proclamation of Jesus about the kingdom of God with the words: "Seeing the crowds, he went up on the mountain . . . and he opened his mouth and taught them."[29] This is not a new Moses on the mountain to proclaim a new law;[30] this is Jesus responding to the call in Isa 40:9 and 52:7 to get up to a high mountain and with a loud voice as the herald of good news to proclaim that "Your God reigns!" Much has been written regarding the source, structure and setting of the Sermon on the Mount with little consensus. In its context in Matthew, the Sermon is Jesus' proclamation of the kingdom of God to those who have been longing for its coming. It is the good news that the kingdom *has* come, and giving instructions on how to live in this kingdom—quite different from the teaching of the scribes and Pharisees.

The Beatitudes, Matt 5:3–12

The announcement of the good news is expressed in a series of blessings drawing together epithets of the faithful and corresponding promises to them taken from Isa 40–66. The Greek word for blessing, *makarios* has generally been seen as translating the Hebrew *ashre* which is found predominantly in wisdom literature, such as wisdom psalms, proverbs, Sir 14:1–2, 20–25; 4Q525.[31] However, this would imply a wisdom context for the beatitudes and consequently an ethical interpretation of them. Yet these beatitudes are decidedly prophetic and are based on covenant promises. They respond to the promise of Isa 44:3: "I will pour out my spirit upon your offspring and my *blessing* (*birakti*) on your descendants." This is repeated in Isa 61:8, 9: "Their descendants will be known among the nations and their offspring in the midst of the peoples, all who see them shall acknowledge them, that they are the people whom Yahweh *has blessed*" (*berak*). This is mentioned again in Isa 65:13–16 with the promise that they will finally inherit the land and prosper in it, "for they shall be the offspring of the *blessed of Yahweh*" (*beruke Yahweh*) and their descendants with them" (Isa 65:23; cf. Ps 37:22). These are the covenant blessings mentioned in Deut 28:2–8. The beatitudes of Matt 5:3–12 are the proclamation of the fulfillment of all these promises, the *baruk* blessings of the everlasting covenant spelled out in detail![32]

Presented in good rhetorical style, these beatitudes form the foundation of the whole message and mission of Jesus. There are nine blessings with the ninth one made more personal: "Blessed are *you*." The first and eighth both finish with the declaration,

---

29. Jesus going up on "the mountain" is mentioned several times in Matthew's Gospel (14:23; 15:29). In 16:13 he is in the district of Caesarea Philippi at the foot of Mt. Hermon and six days later he takes Peter, James and John "up a high mountain alone" where they experience the vision of Jesus with Moses and Elijah. In 28:16, after the resurrection, the disciples are told to meet Jesus on the mountain in Galilee. Cf. 1 En 13:7–9; Aramaic Levi Document 4; Jubilees 32; Test. Levi 2:3–5.

30. So often stated, e.g., Bacon, "Jesus and the Law," 207–8; Davies and Allison, "Reflections on the Sermon on the Mount," 297; Evans, *Matthew*, 97.

31. See Puech, "4Q525 et les Péricopes des Béatitudes," 80–106.

32. See further, Leske, "Beatitudes," 823–25.

"For theirs is the kingdom of heaven," thus forming an *inclusio* indicating all the blessings are essentially giving the same message: "The kingdom is yours!"

5:3: *hoi ptôchoi tô pneumati*, "the poor in spirit" is a Semitic phrase, *anave ruakh*, found in 1QH XIV.3 and 1QM XIV.7, meaningless in Greek, and is really a summary of a number of phrases used in Isa 40–66. In Isa 61:1 it is the *afflicted* (*anavim*), paralleled with *the broken-hearted* who have the good news brought to them. Another such parallel is found in Isa 66:2: "This is the person to whom I will look, to the *afflicted* (*ani*) and to the *smitten in spirit* (*nekah ruakh*) who tremble at my word." This latter refers to the Servant of Isa 53:4 ("smitten of God and afflicted"). Similarly, Isa 57:15 speaks of the "crushed and lowly in spirit." All these phrases commonly expressed the dependent relationship of the faithful on God as they waited for his deliverance, and are here summarized in Jesus' "afflicted in spirit." They are the ones waiting for the fulfillment of Isa 40:9–11. To them Jesus announces the good news that the kingdom of God has come, and it is theirs![33]

5:4: "Those who mourn . . . shall be comforted" is the response to Isa 40:1: "*Comfort, comfort* my people, says your God." In Isa 61:2–3, the role of the Servant is "to *comfort* all who *mourn*; to grant to those who *mourn* in Zion, to give them a garland instead of ashes, the oil of gladness instead of *mourning*" (cf. also Isa 49:13; 51:3, 12; 52:9; 60:20; 66:7–11, 13). Again, these refer to those who are afflicted and waiting for the restoration of the reign of God. So this is just another way of saying, Rejoice! The kingdom of God is here and it's yours!

5:5: "those who are meek (*hoi praeis*) . . . shall inherit the land." Once again, the Greek gives a misleading translation of the original Hebrew. The beatitude is practically a quotation of Ps 37:11, where *praeis* translates *anavim*, "afflicted ones." The psalm expresses many of the same sentiments as Isa 40–66, where possession of the land after the return from exile was certainly an issue (cf. Isa 49:8; 57:13–14; 60:21; 61:7; 63:16—64:2; 65:8–9, 13–16, 17–25). Over generations of continued domination by foreign powers, Ps 37 which mentioned the possession of land six times (Ps 37:3, 9, 11, 18, 29, 34), would have been in the minds of many who had lost their inheritance because of heavy taxes and confiscation. Like Isa 40–66, the Psalm bears many allusions to the hopes of the faithful and emphasizes that God will always uphold the righteous.[34] As such it forms an integral part of the blessings as proclamation of the kingdom (Ps 37:22).

5:6: "Those who hunger and thirst for righteousness . . . shall be satisfied." In Isa 40–66 hunger and thirst became a metaphor for longing for God's deliverance and restoration. For example, Isa 44:3: "I will pour water on the thirsty land, and streams on the dry ground. I will pour my spirit upon your descendants and my *blessing* on your offspring" (cf. also Isa 41:17–20). In Isa 49:10 the restoration is described as: "They shall not hunger or thirst . . . for he who has compassion on them will lead them, and by

---

33. *Ptôchos* generally means "beggar, poor man," but the LXX used it to translate a number of Hebrew words that came out of the covenant context referring to the afflicted and dispossessed (*ani* 38x, *anav* 4x, *ebyon* 11x, *dal* 20x) which bear nuances of meaning that created difficulties for the LXX translators. Cf. Leske, "Beatitudes," 825–26. Powell, "Matthew's Beatitudes," 465, prefers to translate *autôv estin hê basileia tôn ouranôn* as "heaven rules them," but *basileia* is more than that. It is living in the whole realm of God's love, compassion, and righteousness as the following blessings elaborate.

34. Cf. Leske, "Beatitudes," 829.

springs of water will guide them." This leads up to the celebration of the kingdom in 55:1: "Ho, everyone who thirsts, come to the waters; and he who has no money, come, buy and eat!" In this celebration the "everlasting covenant" made with David (2 Sam 7:14; Ps 89) is transferred to the faithful (55:3–5). The righteousness for which the blessed hunger and thirst is God's righteousness. It is that righteousness which comes in the form of an outpouring of his spirit and brings redemption and salvation. Those who seek Yahweh's righteousness (Isa 51:1) are assured that it comes speedily (51:5), and it will be forever (51:6). Those who experience it will have his instruction in their hearts (51:7) and will be able to carry out their God-given purpose to be a people-covenant, a light to the nations (42:6; 49:6, 8) because he who causes them to be righteous is always near (50:8). There is always this interplay between divine and human righteousness. Righteousness is a relational term, often coupled together with "faithfulness," "steadfast love," "compassion," "justice," and "salvation,"[35] as will be demonstrated further in the rest of the Sermon. So it is clear that those "who hunger and thirst for *the* righteousness" are seeking the fulfillment of God's covenant faithfulness, the restoration of the kingdom of God, and now "they will be satisfied!"

5:7: "The merciful" (*eleêmenos*). The clue to the Hebrew behind *eleêmenos* can be found in the use of *eleos* in Matt 9:13 and 12:7 which quote Hos 6:6. There *eleos* translates *khesed*, "steadfast love." Hosea had exhorted the people to sow righteousness and reap the result of steadfast love, so that Yahweh might rain down righteousness upon them (10:12). During and after the exile the message in Isa 40–66 emphasized Yahweh's saving, redeeming steadfast love and compassion, and it became a constant expression of the hope for deliverance (49:10, 13, 15; 54:7, 8, 10; 55:3, 7; 60:10; 63:7). Their hope was sure, for as Isa 54:10 put it: "The mountains may depart and the hills be removed, but my steadfast love shall not depart from you." In this beatitude both the human and divine elements of *khesed* are brought together in a proper relationship. The faithful who seek Yahweh's steadfast love in the kingdom are those who practice it (cf. Isa 57:1; Ps 37:28). This relational concept is central to Jesus' teaching about living in the kingdom in Matthew's Gospel (cf. 9:13; 12:7; 23:23; 18:21–35; 25:31–46). However, the emphasis here is on the proclamation that the faithful "shall obtain mercy." They shall experience God's steadfast love.

5:8: "The pure in heart . . . shall see God" draws on Ps 24:4–5 where it says that "he who has clean hands and a *pure heart* . . . will receive *blessing* from Yahweh, and righteousness from the God of his salvation." This expression brings together and summarizes those references to the faithful in Isaiah as the "fearful of heart" (35:4), "the people in whose heart is my teaching" (51:7), the "crushed in heart" whom God revives and with whom he dwells, and who shall "sing for gladness of heart" (65:14). "They shall see God" (cf. Isa 30:20) is the promise of being in God's presence (cf. Isa 35:2; 40:9; 52:8; 60:1–2). To be ushered into the kingdom is to "see" God and be in a trusting relationship with him. When Israel refused to live faithfully, it was commonly said that God's face was "hidden" from them (cf. Isa 54:8; 57:17; 59:2; 64:6), but with steadfast love and compassion God comes to those who seek him. Once again, the beatitude is a summary

---

35. Leske, "Righteousness as Relationship," 125–37.

The Prophetic Vision and the Real Jesus

of the promise to those who are waiting for the kingdom, it is the proclamation that it is now theirs.

5:9: "Peacemakers . . . shall be called sons of God." The one who announces the coming of the kingdom is the one who proclaims peace and salvation (Isa 52:7). For God's covenant of peace and his steadfast love are forever (54:10). The people will be taught by Yahweh and they will be established in peace and righteousness (54:13, 14) which are to govern their lives (57:10). What this means is further elaborated in the Sermon (Matt 5:38–48). Those who thus reflect the peace and steadfast love of God in their lives are "peacemakers" and shall be called "sons of God." Israel had been called by that title before (Exod 4:22, 27; Deut 14:1; Hos 2:1 [1:10]; 11:1) and it had been used of Israel's monarch (2 Sam 7:14; Ps 2:7; 89:26, 27). But here it is used of those who reflect God's love and will and acknowledge God as Father (Isa 63:16; 64:8).

5:10: "Persecuted . . . for the sake of righteousness." After the return from exile, Trito-Isaiah lamented that "the righteous one perishes and no one takes it to heart, people of steadfast love are taken away, while no one understands" (57:1). Yet Yahweh promised those who are "crushed and afflicted in spirit" (57:16; 66:2) that they would see those put to shame who are "your brethren who hate you and cast your name out for my name's sake" (66:5). A prime example of this is given in Wis 2:6–20 where the righteous poor man (*dikaios penês*) is persecuted by the godless simply because of his living righteously as a child of God. The "persecuted" are the same as the "afflicted in spirit" in the first beatitude, and both finish with the same apodosis, "theirs is the kingdom of heaven." This *inclusio* brings all the blessings together as one. The only difference is that the last four beatitudes illustrate more the active stance of the faithful, while the first four show more their dependent relationship on God. However, in each case, the emphasis is on the apodosis because that is where the good news lies. Far from being a set of requirements or "a series of uncompromising demands,"[36] they are the proclamation of the good news of God's gracious steadfast love. The people to whom Jesus addresses these blessings were well familiar with affliction and persecution suffered during the period of the Ptolemies, Seleucids, and Herods, and were waiting for this consoling message.

5:11–12: In this final beatitude Jesus expands on the previous one using the words of assurance given to the righteous in Isa 51:7, addressing his hearers directly in the second person, and relating it to his own teaching. The prophets before them had always experienced persecution because of their message. So rather than being humiliated or discouraged by the reviling, they can "rejoice and be glad" (v. 12). Those being reviled in Isa 51:7 were told that they will "obtain joy and gladness, and sorrow and sighing shall flee away" (51:11). This was a constant refrain in Isaiah when referring to the restoration of the kingdom of God (Isa 25:9; 29:19; 35:1, 2, 10; 55:12; 61:3, 7, 10; 62:5; 65:13, 18, 19; 66:5, 10). "For your reward is great in heaven" draws the theme of "reward and recompense" referred to in Isa 40:10 to describe God's gracious rule and his caring for his people like a good shepherd. It is used in Isa 62:11, 12 to describe receiving God's salvation and redemption. The "reward" is the culmination of the blessings of the kingdom announced in all the beatitudes—the reign of God breaking into their lives here and now.

---

36. So Luz, *Matthew 1–7*, 243.

The impact of all these blessings can only be appreciated fully when one comes from an understanding of the prophetic heritage, of the struggles and hopes expressed by the prophets. Each blessing is a joyous proclamation to all those who have been waiting for the kingdom that it is theirs now! It is God's gift! Each one couched in Isaianic phrases is a call to all the prophetic visionaries to recognize that God's promises are sure and to discover anew their place in God's plan. There is no need to wait for the Judgment. They are called to live as God's kingdom members now!

Kingdom Members: Salt of the Earth, Light of the World: 5:13–16

It is in the context of such an astonishing proclamation that these sayings about salt and light must be seen. Deutero-Isaiah had made the point that up to the time of the exile, Israel had not known what its real purpose was (49:1–4). That purpose was announced in Isa 42:6: "I have called you in righteousness . . . I have given you as a people-covenant, a light to the nations." It was not enough for Yahweh to use the exiles simply for restoring the nation of Israel, but that his salvation might "reach to the ends of the earth" (Isa 49:6). Having addressed them as "the people in whose heart is my teaching" (Isa 51:7), it is as such that they are called to be a living covenant, a people who through demonstration of their covenant faithfulness would draw all people into a bonded relationship with their only God and Father (Isa 45:20–22). The priestly law had required that after the exile all sacrifices were to be offered with salt (Ezek 43:24; Lev 2:13; Num 18:19). Because salt acted as a preservative, the "covenant of salt" came to be the term used to emphasize the everlasting nature of their covenant with God. The Chronicler used the same term in arguing for the permanent nature of the Davidic covenant (2 Chr 13:5).[37] So when kingdom members are told: "You are the salt of the earth," they would know that they were to be that permanent living covenant which would draw others into that living relationship with God and with one another. Salt by its very *nature* does not lose its saltiness.

"You are the light of the world" (v. 14) clearly covers the other purpose stated in Isa 42:6; 49:6 and which draws on the common Isaian theme of bringing light to those who dwell in darkness, beginning with Isa 8:23—9:1 (quoted in Matt 4:14–16) and continuing in 42:6, 7, 16; 48:8, 10; 49:6; 51:4; 59:9. It reached its climax in 60:1–3 where Yahweh's *kabod*, his brilliant presence, is reflected in his people so that nations come to their light and kings to the brightness of their rising (cf. also 60:19, 20; 62:2). The purpose of that witness is to give glory to the heavenly Father (v. 16). Restored Israel was called to be the witness of God's power and glory before the nations (Isa 43:10, 12; 44:8; 55:4–5; cf. 44:23) and thus it is through them that God is glorified (Isa 49:3; 60:21; 61:3). In this way the nations will come to experience God's presence, and from them others shall go forth and declare the presence of God to the far ends of the earth (66:18–23). This is what is being referred to in Matt 5:16. Light by its very *nature* dispels the darkness. This is what kingdom people are like.

---

37. Cf. also Dumbrell, "Logic of the Role of the Law," 12.

The Prophetic Vision and the Real Jesus

The True Understanding of Law in the Kingdom: 5:17–48

For kingdom members, 5:17–20 points out, it is vitally important to have the true understanding of the law of God, and it is *not* as has been popularly taught by the scribes and Pharisees. The proper understanding of law and righteousness is fundamental for the kingdom and is expressed in greater detail in the rest of the Sermon as well as in Jesus' teaching throughout the Gospel. Jesus' discussion of the law is both polemical and defensive: "Think not that I have come to abolish the law or the prophets; I have not come to abolish but to fulfill" (v. 17). By saying "law *or* the prophets" he may have been responding to criticisms coming not only from those who had been taught by the scribes and Pharisees but also from those who followed the prophetic tradition. Both groups would have been astonished at Jesus proclaiming that the kingdom is here now, since both, in their different ways, expected the Judgment to come first before there could be any kingdom, to say nothing of their assumption of what that kingdom would be. Moreover, the scribes and Pharisees regarded "law" as a series of statutes and demands. The rabbis later listed these as 613 commandments which, together with doing the "acts of righteousness," were requirements for entering the kingdom of God.

Jesus' pronouncement that "until heaven and earth pass away, not an iota, not a hook[38] will pass from the law until all is accomplished" (v. 18) directly relates to what Jesus had just said about kingdom members being the salt of the earth and light of the world. The saying about heaven and earth passing away alludes to Isa 51:4–6, a passage that Jesus had just previously alluded to in v. 11. In that passage the emphasis was on promises of God that a *law* would go forth and his justice for a *light* to the peoples, and even though heaven and earth may pass away, his salvation and his righteousness would be forever. Israel, as God's Servant, was to establish justice in the earth and bring God's law to the nations (Isa 42:4, 21) in fulfillment of the hope long expressed that all the nations would eventually flow to the house of Yahweh acknowledging that "out of Zion goes forth the law and the word of Yahweh from Jerusalem" (Isa 2:3; Mic 4:2).[39] This was part of Jesus' mission. In the prophetic literature "law" (*torah*) was understood primarily as the "teaching" of God transmitted through the Mosaic Decalogue and through his servants the prophets. Only God is referred to as "Teacher" in the prophetic literature (Isa 30:20) and it is as such that he teaches his Servant (Isa 50:4–5). "Law" and "word" of God were often used in synonymous parallelism (Isa 1:10; 2:3; 5:24), and are related primarily to the covenant relationship. For faithfulness to the covenant relationship—to Yahweh and to one another—was always the concern of the prophets.

This understanding of "law" often brought the prophets into conflict with the priesthood and their priestly law (e.g., Hos 8:1–13; Amos 5:21–25; Isa 1:10–15; Mic 6:6–8; Zeph 3:4; Mal 2:6–8). A similar conflict is seen in Jesus' dispute with the Pharisees over their laws of purity (Matt 9:12) and Sabbath (Matt 12:7) where Jesus answered them with a quote from Hos 6:6: "I desire steadfast love and not sacrifice." This quotation gets to the heart of the matter in fulfilling every aspect of the law for Jesus. This is brought

---

38. In Hebrew this would have referred to a *yodh* and a *waw*, which when used as vowel-letters, were sometimes dropped.

39. Cf. Dumbrell, "Role of the Law," 14.

out very clearly again in Jesus' response to the lawyer who came to him asking, which was the great commandment in the law. Jesus readily responded with the word from the *Shema* (Deut 6:5) and added Lev 19:18 as a second one like the first. Together these two made up the "great" commandment to love. On these, Jesus explained, "hang" all the law and the prophets (22:34–40). While "hang" may be a technical term used by the later rabbis for the dependence of one law upon another,[40] the two love commandments essentially are summary of the two tables of the covenant law in the Decalogue which defined one's relationship with God and one's neighbor.

Consistent with this is the answer given to the rich young man in Matt 19:16–22 who asked what good deed he must do to have eternal life. Jesus first points out that the young man is entirely dependent on the goodness of God rather than on his own. It is only in that light that one can keep the commandments in the second table of the covenant stipulations. These Jesus cites together with the defining summary from Lev 19:18: "You shall love your neighbor as yourself." When the young man claims that he has kept all these, Jesus gives him a test, asking him to demonstrate his claim by giving up his wealth to the needy and finding "treasures in heaven" (cf. 6:19–23). This he was not ready to do, for his riches were more important to him than helping those in need. This is not an indication that Jesus was setting up new requirements for the kingdom, but that he is pointing out how love for God and neighbor takes precedence over everything else in the kingdom, and as fulfilling the law and the prophets (cf. 7:12).[41] In the account of the final judgment in Matt 25:31–46, the defining point for the judgment is whether one has practiced love.[42]

The saying about being least or great in the kingdom in 5:19 must be seen in the light of the above. It is a matter of levels of commitment to the love commandments which are being discussed here. It parallels the saying about the seed that falls on good soil that brings forth various yields of grain in the Parable of the Sower and the Seed (Matt 13:3–9). So the relaxing of one of the least of these commandments would refer to not carrying out fully some aspect of the love commandment. The term "commandment," is always used in Matthew in regard to the basic covenant stipulations (15:3; 19:17; 22:36, 38, 40), to love God and neighbor.

There is no conflict between v. 10 and v. 20 when the latter states that "unless your righteousness greatly surpasses that of the scribes and Pharisees you will never enter the kingdom of heaven." Although they were generally regarded by the people as the interpreters of the law, their righteousness, Jesus is saying, does not even put them in the "least in the kingdom" list, because their interpretations often deny the very intention of the law. This is clarified in the rest of the Sermon, but it is particularly evident in their confrontations with Jesus throughout the Gospel. For example, in 9:10–13 their rigid interpretation of the laws of purity, which they had taken over from the priestly law, precluded them from associating with those they regarded as impure, and thus excluded them from loving their neighbor as themselves. The same was true with their multiplication of oral laws regarding the Sabbath (12:1–14) and with their regarding

---

40. See Donaldson, "Law That 'Hangs,'" 14–33.

41. Contra Banks, *Jesus and the Law*, 219.

42. See further, Snodgrass, "Matthew and the Law," 99–127; Hagner, "Law, Righteousness," 364–71.

The Prophetic Vision and the Real Jesus

Jesus' compassionate acts of healing as demonic (12:22–32). The Pharisees' insistence that everyone was required to keep not only the written law but also their own oral tradition, which they even distorted for their own purposes (15:1–20), only laid heavy burdens on the people (23:4). The accusations against the scribes and Pharisees were finally set down in a series of woes, similar to the prophetic woes in Isa 5:8–23. These woes in 23:13–36 essentially function as covenant curses in contrast to the covenant blessings given in 5:3–12 (cf. Deut 27–28). A major indictment against the scribes and Pharisees was that they required people to tithe even the herbs of their garden, but yet they neglected the weightier matters of the law: justice, steadfast love, and faithfulness (23:23), the sum of God's requirements according to Mic 6:6–8. Righteousness, then, is not to be understood simply as fulfilling the obligations of a set of laws, rather, it is to respond to the steadfast love of the Father in loving faithfulness to him and to one's fellow human beings. Righteousness is a relational term which means living in that faithful relationship with God and neighbor in accordance with God's covenant teaching.[43]

The antitheses which follow (5:21–48) give examples of what true righteousness is over against common practice and beliefs. These are not a set of new laws but an expression of what it means to follow fully the love commandment. Members of the kingdom will begin to look at law in a different way. Transgressions of the law are not just those that are identifiable and which can lead to a judgment in court, but every thought, word, or action which goes against the intention of the covenant relationship. So the fifth commandment (5:21) is not just about the action of killing someone, it also deals with the intention in one's thoughts and expression in harsh words which indicates a loveless attitude towards others (5:22). The two tables of the law, love for God and love for neighbor, are inseparable. Therefore it is necessary to seek reconciliation with one's neighbor before one can expect to be reconciled with God (5:23–25). Throughout the prophetic literature God is always depicted as seeking reconciliation with his erring people, always ready to forgive. So these are two actions, central to the love commandment, which the people of God will reflect in their lives towards others (cf. 6:12; 18:21–35). In this understanding, a loveless attitude towards others is essentially a rejection of God's love and his kingdom, and leads to final judgment (5:25, 26).

Similarly, the commandment, you shall not commit adultery, also condemns the desire or intention to do it (5:27–30). In this case, this commandment is closely related to the commandment not to covet one's neighbor's wife (*gynê*). The legal traditions of the rabbis tended to identify women as property, and in the case of adultery the law usually put the blame on women (cf. Gen 38:12–26; Num 5). Jesus directed the statement here particularly to men, and must have been referring to an attitude in the School of Hillel, later expressed by his disciple, R. Akiba (m. Gittin 9:10), that if a man found a woman fairer than his wife, that was reason enough to divorce his wife on the basis of Deut 24:1. Such an attitude called for some drastic spiritual surgery (5:29–30)!

Closely related to the law on adultery is the matter of divorce (5:31–32) which in Jesus' day was consistently abused. The law of Deut 24:1–4 was interpreted by the rabbis who developed a vast oral tradition which gave men many opportunities to practice divorce and defile the marriage covenant (cf. Mishnah: Yebamoth, Ketuboth, Gittin

---

43. Cf. Frankemölle, *Jahwebund und Kirche Christi*, 281–83.

passim; also Matt 19:1–9). Such abuse only led to all parties becoming guilty of adultery. For marriage was the essential form of a covenant relationship, an image of the intimate relationship between God and his people (cf. Jer 3:1–14; Isa 50:1; 54:4–8; Hos 2:14–20; Mal 2:10–16), and as such is a divine institution (Matt 19:6). The only reason for a man to divorce his wife on the basis of the love commandment was *porneia*, which must be understood as "persistent unfaithfulness," such as prostitution, because it destroys the covenant relationship irreparably.[44]

Again, the casuistry regarding the taking of oaths (5:33–37) was rampant among the scribes and Pharisees who debated among themselves as to what constituted a valid or invalid oath. Such casuistry allowed them to make an invalid oath to a person ignorant of their traditions and in that way they could be excused for not carrying out the oath (cf. 23:16–22; also Mishnah: Shebu 4:3 and *passim*; Ned 1:3; 3:4; Sanh 3:2). Jesus' answer to this was simply to speak with sincerity and honesty so that taking an oath was unnecessary. Jesus himself refused to speak under oath except when ordered to later by the high priest (26:63–64). False oath-taking had long been a problem (cf. Deut 29:19–21; Zech 5:1–4; 8:17; Sir 23:7–11; 27:14), so there is no reason to argue for Matthean authorship of these verses.[45]

The law of retaliation, found in all three law codes (Exod 21:22–25; Lev 24:17–22; Deut 19:21), is clearly abrogated by Jesus because it ignores the love commandment and only increases violence (5:38–42). Even the full statement about loving one's neighbor in Lev 19:17–18 does not go far enough when it limits the love response to "sons of your own people" (Lev 19:18a). By referring to the hated Roman practice of *angareia*, the rule by which Roman soldiers were permitted to force anyone to carry their equipment for one mile (v. 41),[46] Jesus was implying that one's neighbor also includes Gentiles, even anyone regarded as the enemy. This is made explicit in the final antithesis (5:43–48) which describes what it really means to live as a member of the kingdom of God. Part of Jesus' mission was calling the people to be the Servant of Yahweh, and turning the other cheek is an allusion to Isa 50:4–9 where the Servant puts his trust in God for his vindication. It is to see oneself as a son or daughter of the heavenly Father, to be ready to be molded in his image (cf. Isa 63:16; 64:8) to reflect his steadfast love to even one's persecutors, and thus bring about transformation instead of violence, to be the Righteous One to cause many to be righteous (Isa 53:11). This is what it means to be "perfect (*teleios*) as the heavenly Father is perfect" (v. 48; cf. 19:21). This is what it means to be a member of the kingdom—it is to see oneself as a child of the heavenly Father and to live as such in this world.

---

44. The close connection between *pornê* ("prostitute") and *porneia* rules out it being translated as adultery during betrothal or marriage, which is still *moicheia*. Contra Janzen, "Meaning of *Porneia*," 66–80.

45. As do many. Cf. Luz, *Matthew 1–7*, 318. Cf. also Duling, "[Do not swear . . .] by Jerusalem," 291–309, who argues for a pre-Matthean community as author.

46. Cf. Wink, "Neither Passivity Nor Violence," 215–19.

The Prophetic Vision and the Real Jesus

Doing the Acts of Righteousness (6:1–21)

The people had been taught by the scribes and Pharisees that keeping the 613 commandments and doing the acts of righteousness, almsgiving, prayer and fasting, constituted total righteousness (cf. Tob 12:8-9; m. Abot 1:2), which for them often in practice became ritualized and a display for one's own "glory." The verb used here (6:2) is *doxazein* which elsewhere in Matthew is only used for God (5:15; 9:8; 15:31), implying that people who gave alms for show were seeking the glory that belongs to God. Just as Jesus had expressed in regard to the law, so here he places these acts of righteousness in the proper perspective. In each case the acts are motivated by spontaneous acts of love for God and neighbor. So almsgiving done purely out of compassion for others receives God's blessing (v. 4; cf. Isa 58:7-10). Similarly prayer is personal communication with God, which cannot be ritualized or put on display. It is entering into a quiet place to converse with one's heavenly Father in sincere trust that God is listening (vv. 5-8; cf. Isa 65:24). Fasting also, which originally had been a sign of mourning and sorrow, had become ritualized and exhibited rather than sincere sorrow shared with the family of God and as motivation for relieving the suffering of others (vv. 16-18; cf. Isa 58:1-11).

These acts of righteousness were often called "treasures" which were better than gold (Tob 4:9; 12:8-9; Sir 29:11-12). By saying, "where your treasure is, there is your heart also" (6:21), Jesus was alluding to Isa 51:7 where the righteous are described as "the people in whose heart is my teaching," who will not fear the reproach of men "for the moth will eat them up like a garment, and the worm will eat them like wool" (51:8). The same will happen to acts that are motivated by self-righteousness.

The model prayer which Jesus gives his disciples (6:9–15) is formulated against the background of the prayer of the faithful in Isa 63:13—64:12 with the divine response in Isa 65:1-25. It is the prayer for kingdom members. The address, "Our Father who is in heaven," expresses the intimate relationship which kingdom members have with God (Isa 63:16; 64:8), a relationship which Jesus emphasizes throughout this Sermon (17 times) and in his teaching generally (another 28 times). "Hallowed be your name" expresses the hope that with the restoration of God's people they would glorify his name before the nations (Isa 29:22-23; 44:23; 49:3; 55:5; 60:21; 61:3, 9–11). "May your kingdom come": Jesus has already proclaimed that the kingdom has come to the faithful (5:3–12), so the petitioner is expressing the desire that through the witness of its members, the kingdom will come to all peoples and nations (Isa 43:10-12; 44:8; 55:4-5) and reach its final consummation. "May your will be done, as in heaven, so on earth" expresses further the desire that God's purpose for all people might be fulfilled and all live under him in his kingdom through his people being a living covenant and a light to the nations (Isa 42:1-4, 21; 53:10-11). In this context, the petition: "Give us this day our daily bread" (v. 11) likely has a meaning relating explicitly to the kingdom and the prayer's Isaianic background. The word *epiousios*, which has traditionally been translated as "daily" is not found elsewhere in the New Testament or in classical Greek literature. So it probably refers to the coming celebration of the kingdom mentioned in Isa 55:1-2 where "bread" symbolizes the spiritual blessings of being in the kingdom. The promised restoration had been spoken of in terms of satisfying hunger and thirst (Isa 49:10; 65:13-14). So the petition is a request for the spiritual blessings of the kingdom, made with joy and confidence, knowing that their hunger and thirst for righteousness is being satisfied (5:6; cf. 6:25–33).

The petition, "Forgive us our debts, as we also have forgiven our debtors" (v. 12) points to the central expression of the love commandment, emphasized by the further explanation in vv. 14 and 15, to remind the hearers that readiness to forgive others is the basis on which they can receive the forgiveness of God and be restored into full relationship with the heavenly Father, confident that the Father has swept away their failures and remembers them no more (Isa 40:2; 43:25; 44:22; cf. Matt 5:23–26). The final petition, dealing with temptation and deliverance from evil (v. 13), is the confident plea that in the trials and vicissitudes of life one will not be tested beyond one's strength, knowing that such testing in the "furnace of affliction" leads to refinement of one's faith "like silver" (Isa 1:25; 48:10; Zech 13:9; Mal 3:3). Such is the prayer of a child of God to the heavenly Father for living in the kingdom.

The Lamp of the Body Is the Eye (6:22–24)

For an understanding of this saying, interpreters have usually turned to Greek and Roman philosophy or Jewish wisdom sayings, and have assumed that it is an isolated saying here.[47] However, the only other time *lychnos* ("lamp") is used in Matthew is in this Sermon (5:15), where it is used in the context of kingdom members being "the light of the world." Moreover, Jesus had just been speaking of the duplicity of fasting simply to make a display of one's piety, a so-called treasure on earth. This must have recalled Isa 58:1–12 where the fast that God chooses is to take care of the hungry, the homeless, the naked, and the afflicted (58:6, 7, 10), and then their "light" would "break forth like the dawn," their righteousness would go before them, and the brilliant presence (*kabod*) of Yahweh would be their rearguard (58:8, 10b). In Isa 6:10, because of the people's duplicity, the prophet had been told to "make their ears heavy, and shut their eyes, lest they see with their eyes and hear with their ears," but later Isaiah had expressed the hope that in the future out of the gloom and darkness the eyes of the blind would see (29:18; 30:20; 32:3). Part of Servant Israel's role as a people-covenant and as a light to the nations was "to open the eyes of the blind" (Isa 42:6, 7) and God would turn their darkness before them into light (42:16). The parallel between eyes seeing and the mind understanding (cf. Isa 44:18) has relevance for this saying that if the eye is sound the whole body will be full of light (Matt 6:22). The word *haplous* has the meaning here of being "single-minded," "sincere"[48] and the word *phôteinos* is only found elsewhere in Matthew in 17:5 where it refers to the brilliant cloud, the *kabod*. Thus, Jesus is saying over against those who do acts of righteousness for self-aggrandizement, that it is the single-minded who will be enlightened by God's presence in their lives, whereas those whose eye is duplicitous will be full of darkness (v. 23).

---

47. See discussions in Betz, *Essays on the Sermon on the Mount*, 71–87; Elliott, "Evil Eye," 51–84; Zöckler, "Light within the Human Person," 487–99; Hauck, "Like a Gleaming Flash," 557–73; Moss, "Blind Vision and Ethical Confusion," 757–76.

48. See Zöckler, "Light Within," 489–90.

Verse 24, dealing with serving God and "mammon," serves as a transition verse to the section dealing with anxiety (6:25–34). "Mammon" is a Hebrew term, generally meaning "property, wealth, possessions" (cf. m. Aboth 2:12; 1QS VI 2; CD XIV 20). The verse affirms the previous saying by calling for single-minded devotion to God and his kingdom, while it serves as a caution to those who make material needs their prime concern instead of putting their full trust in their heavenly Father.

About Earthly Concerns (6:25–34)

One can understand that for many people living in Galilee at the time of Jesus, life would not have been easy. The requirement to pay taxes and tribute for the Roman government and for Herod Antipas, as well as tithing for the temple priesthood, would have put a heavy strain on families, so it would have been easy to allow concerns for the basic needs of daily living to dominate their lives. The scribes and Pharisees would have been ready to remind them of the curses of the covenant if their written and oral traditions were not kept. Deut 28:48 contains a summary statement of those covenant curses which warned the people that if they did not serve God with joy and gladness of heart, they would serve their enemies "in hunger and thirst, in nakedness and in want of all things." Many would have thought that this was happening to them. However, in this section Jesus reminds his audience that they are God's children, members of his kingdom, and as such they are not under the covenant curses, but live now under the covenant blessings, the good news he had proclaimed earlier. They should just observe how God takes care of his creation, even the birds of the air and flowers of the field, so surely God would take care of his children as their heavenly Father. So their prime concern should be for his kingdom and living in his righteousness in faith and trust, and the rest will be theirs as well.[49]

On Being Judgmental and the Gift of the Kingdom (7:1–12)

This Sermon has been about what it means to be members of the kingdom of God. As a consequence much of it has been contrasting what that means over against the practice and teaching of the scribes and Pharisees since 5:20. So in these verses Jesus appears to be addressing them directly, berating them for their self-righteous judgmental attitude that would exclude others from the kingdom. Using a carpenter's hyperbole of a speck of sawdust (*karphos*) and a beam (*dokos*) he accuses them of judging others when their faults and attitudes are far worse. With such an attitude they could only expect to be judged by their own measure.

In this context, v. 6 must be taken as an example of their prevailing judgmental attitude and of the consequences of that attitude.[50] Dogs and pigs were regarded as unclean animals. The Mishnah stated: "None may rear swine anywhere. A man may not rear a dog unless it is kept bound by a chain" (Baba Kamma 7:7). So these terms easily became derogatory epithets for enemies, Gentiles, fools, or male prostitutes (cf. Ps 22:16–20;

---

49. See further Leske, "Matthew 6:25–34," 15–27; Pregeant, *Knowing Truth*, 139–41.
50. Cf. Bennett, "Matthew 7:6," 371–86.

59:6, 14; Prov 26:11; Deut 23:18). To associate with them would render one unclean. Such an attitude towards others was to prevent any outsider from ever being part of the kingdom. The "holy thing" and the "pearls" symbolize the good news of the kingdom (cf. 13:45). The story of the Canaanite woman (also a derogatory term for a Greek) and the healing of her daughter (15:21–28) is an example of Jesus sharing the blessings of the kingdom with a Gentile, while testing her faith by using the diminutive form of the derogatory "dog" (*kynarion*, "puppy"). The positive response made to the Canaanite woman who *asked* is also an illustration of what Jesus now tells his audience is the proper way (7:7–12).

The prophetic message had always been: "Seek Yahweh while he may be found, call upon him while he is near" (Isa 55:6; cf. Jer 29:12–14; Isa 65:1–2) with the promise that the wicked who turn from their ways God would abundantly pardon (55:7). That included foreigners and eunuchs who held fast to the covenant, for God's house is a house of prayer for all peoples (Isa 56:3–8). So God freely offers the gift of the kingdom to all those who ask, seek, knock and wish to enter the kingdom.[51] Those who are addressed as "you who are evil" (v. 11) would refer to those who judged others and would exclude them from the kingdom. Instead, they should heed the saying: "Whatever you wish that people should do to you, do so to them." This saying was known to the Pharisees in its negative form as uttered by Hillel the Elder (b. Shabbat 31a), and in Tobit 4:15. By putting it into a positive form Jesus had transformed a wisdom saying into an action of love instead of self-protection. Thus it becomes the love commandment on which hangs "all the law and the prophets" (v. 12. Cf. 5:17; 22:34–40). In this way, the whole of 7:1–12 forms a unity as another expression of rejecting false teaching and fulfilling the law and the prophets.[52]

Final Warnings about Entering the Kingdom (7:13–27)

The exhortation to enter through the narrow gate (7:13–14), then, follows on from 7:1–12, warning the audience against simply following the crowd and giving in to social pressure and the pervading influence of the Pharisees. Rather, they should choose life, even though it may sometimes mean the way of affliction (cf. Matt 5:10–12; 10:17–25; 13:21; 24:9–31). For through it they will hear the voice of their Teacher: "This is the way; walk in it" (Isa 30:19–21).[53]

This is followed by warnings against being misled by false prophets who claim to be speaking on God's behalf about obeying his law yet show no change for good in their own lives and only seek to gain for themselves influence, power, reputation or wealth (7:15–20). John the Baptist had warned the Pharisees and Sadducees that they needed to bear the fruits of repentance (3:10) and Jesus later repeated that warning to the Pharisees in 12:33. So he is probably referring to the Pharisees and their scribes here as false

---

51. This saying is not to be understood as just talking about prayer generally but about seeking the kingdom. Luke's placing this saying in the context of prayer is misleading (11:9–13) and secondary. Contra Murphy-O'Connor, "Prayer of Petition," 359–416.

52. See McEleny, "Unity and Theme," 490–500.

53. Cf. Mattill, "Way of Tribulation," 531–46.

prophets. The prophets of God in the past repeatedly had to warn the people to beware of those who gave "lying visions, worthless divination, and the deceit of their own minds" (Jer 14:14; cf. 27:14–15). Jesus is here doing the same as a true prophet of God. However, the people are also warned to beware of those who claim to be the followers of Jesus and to have done many works in his name, yet were not doing the will of the heavenly Father and thus were leading people astray (7:21–23; cf. Isa 29:13). For this reason they will be condemned as "workers of iniquity" (Ps 6:8),[54] and come under judgment "on that day" (v. 22) with the coming of the Son of Man (24:29–44).

The Sermon on the Kingdom concludes with an exhortation to "hear and do" the message proclaimed. This echoes the frequent exhortations to hear and do the covenant message found in Deuteronomy (e.g., 4:6; 5:1; 7:12; 8:1, 15) which results in Yahweh's steadfast love. By using these words Jesus is encouraging his hearers to have this covenant written in their hearts (cf. Jer 31:31–34; Isa 51:7) which is the basis of their relationship with God and with one another, and to see themselves as part of God's family in the kingdom. For when they build their lives on the Rock, which is God (cf. Deut 32:4, 15, 18; Isa 17:10; 26:4; 30:29; 44:8; Ps 18:2, 31; 19:14; 62:6), they are on a firm foundation against which no force can prevail (7:24–25; cf. 16:18). This is the "precious cornerstone of a sure foundation" of Isa 28:16 which stands firm while "hail will sweep away the refuge of lies and water will overwhelm the shelter" of falsehood (28:15–17). Thus their lives in the kingdom are to be based on a living relationship with their God.

The response of the crowds to the message of the kingdom is one of astonishment because it was so radically and refreshingly different. They were used to their scribes and the Pharisees hedging the kingdom around with all kinds of regulations and requirements and making it into some quasi-political institution governed by the traditions of the elders in some future time after the Great Judgment. They could be part of the kingdom of God now, living in covenant relationship with their heavenly Father and with one another, a kingdom which reaches beyond boundaries of all kinds, whether they be geographical, national, or boundaries of social status and gender. Moreover, Jesus' manner of teaching was radically different from that of their scribes, for he spoke directly, like the prophets of old, as having authority which came from relationship with the heavenly Father.

RESTORATION AND THE GROWTH OF THE KINGDOM (8:1—9:34)

In these two chapters, following directly after the proclamation of the kingdom, Matthew has brought together ten miracles arranged in sets of three interspersed with incidents dealing with discipleship. By weaving together stories of healing and discipleship, Matthew thus demonstrates signs of the restoration of Israel and of the growth of the kingdom. All this shows the kingdom of God in action. The prophets had often spoken of the restoration of God's people as the healing of their wounds (Hos 6:1–3; 14:4; Jer 3:22; 8:11, 22; 17:14; 30:17; 33:6; Isa 30:26; 57:18, 19). In Isaiah the promised restoration

---

54. The Greek in this verse uses *anomia*, "lawlessness," the usual LXX translation of the Hebrew *aven*, "iniquity." There is no evidence here at all to indicate that Matthew is accusing Paul of antinomianism. Contra Sim, "Matthew 7:21–23," 325–43.

was always depicted as healing the deaf, the blind, the afflicted, the weak, the lame and the dumb, as well as those broken-hearted or in prison (29:18-19; 35:3-7; 42:7, 16-22; 49:9-13; 61:1-3). Servant Israel, the one despised and rejected by men (Isa 53:3), would be restored to health in order that the purpose of God could be brought to fulfillment through his Servant, causing many to become righteous (53:11). The promise of God, given in Isa 55:11, was that his dynamic word would not return empty but would accomplish that which he purposed, and would prosper in the thing for which he sent it. In these chapters, it is demonstrated how that word, the good news of the kingdom proclaimed in the Sermon on the Mount bears fruit in healings, in discipleship, in faith, and in recognition of the authority of that word over against the teaching of the scribes and Pharisees.[55]

The years of persecution, oppression, and land confiscation under Herod and his minions had left a heavy toll on the people, particularly in Galilee, leaving many in poverty, experiencing traumatic stress, malnutrition, depression and despair. The aftermath of Herod's reign of terror was not much better. Much of the land which people would have inherited was still in the hands of big land owners, and the little the poor had was still heavily taxed. With subsistence living and malnutrition came disease, sickness, mental illness and psychosomatic disorders.[56] It did not help when the scribes and Pharisees pointed out that all these were the curses of the covenant for not keeping all their laws. To many who were experiencing depression, disconnectedness and resentment, the proclamation of the kingdom gave them new hope and meaning and a feeling of belonging, knowing that they could be part of God's family in spite of their circumstances.

Because Matthew's purpose is to illustrate the growth of the kingdom, he just emphasizes the main points of each miracle, assuming that the reader is already well familiar with the details. The verb that Matthew prefers to use for healing is *therapeuô* (16 times), which has the meaning of "care for, treat, heal" and always implies both physical and spiritual healing. In the case of the centurion and the Canaanite woman, the verb *iaomai* is used, meaning to "heal" physically (8:8, 13; 15:28).

Three Healing Stories

Significantly, the first healing is that of a leper (8:1-4), since the rabbis sometimes thought that the description of the Servant in Isa 53:4 as "Stricken, smitten by God and afflicted" was that of a leper, because similar terms were used in Lev 13 to describe such a person (cf. b. Sanh. 98b). Obviously familiar with Jesus' message of the kingdom, the leper approaches Jesus in faith and Jesus heals him, a prime example of the restoration to wholeness for Servant Israel. With certification from the priest that he is clean of the

---

55. Cf. Kingsbury, "Observations," 559-73, who argues that Matthew arranged these miracles to treat Christology (8:1-17), discipleship (8:18-34), questions pertaining to the separation of Jesus and his followers from Israel (9:1-17), and faith (9:18-34), with the prime emphasis on Jesus as Messiah, Son of God (572). I shall deal with Christology in the next chapter.

56. Cf. Hollenbach, "Jesus, Demoniacs, and Public Authorities," 567-88; Carter, "Jesus' Healing Stories," 488-96.

disease he becomes a "witness" to the crowds of the presence of the kingdom and of God's power (Isa 43:10, 12; 44:8).

The second healing is that of the centurion's *pais* (8:5–13). The word *pais* can be translated as "child" or "servant," but here it is most likely the centurion's son (cf. Matt 2:16; 17:5, 18; 21:15).[57] Significant in this miracle is the fact that the centurion is a Gentile who expresses total faith that Jesus can heal his son with an authoritative word without entering his home and thus be open to criticism from the Pharisees. His sensitivity to Jewish tradition, recognition of Jesus' God-given authority, and deep faith become an illustration how Gentiles will enter the kingdom before unbelieving "sons of the kingdom."

After that, Matthew reports on the healing of Peter's mother-in-law of a fever, as well as those who were brought to him who were demon-possessed and those who were "suffering badly" (8:14–16). This first triad of healings is concluded with a quotation from Isa 53:4 to indicate that Servant Israel is thus being healed to carry out its God-given purpose. Jesus is thus depicted as God's authoritative instrument to bring about the fulfillment of that purpose in the kingdom of God.

Two Discipleship Stories

The two discipleship stories follow to point out that discipleship means total commitment to the cause of spreading the good news of the kingdom. A certain scribe addresses Jesus as "teacher" and says that he will follow him wherever he goes (8:20). Jesus tells him that "the Son of Man has nowhere to lay his head." By this Jesus was implying that the scribe saw him as having a role similar to that of the rabbis of his day, who would settle into a secure position as a great teacher surrounded by pupils who would one day aspire to become teachers themselves. Jesus was indicating to the scribe, as he later told his disciples: "The Son of Man came not to be served but to serve and to give his life as a ransom for many" (20:28); in other words, he came to live out the role of Servant Israel. The same would be the role of his disciples (20:26, 27). The term "Son of Man," used here for the first time in this Gospel, always carries a tension between the collective and the individual meaning as an expression of the Servant, the Chosen One of Isa 40–66, especially as expressed in Isa 53 and pictured in Dan 7–12. Jesus was pointing out to the potential disciple that discipleship meant servant-hood, a total commitment to the mission of the kingdom.[58] The second disciple (8:21–22) wanted to delay his following until he had completed his responsibility of transferring the bones of his father's corpse into an ossuary, sometimes called the "second burial," which would be carried out a year after the corpse had been placed in a tomb.[59] Jesus' response, "Follow me, and let the dead bury their own dead," was again to emphasize the commitment to the kingdom and to his *heavenly* Father, which must become the prime concern of a disciple.

57. So Luz, *Matthew 8–20*, 10.

58. Keeping in mind that this saying comes in the context of restoring Servant Israel for its God-given task, Jesus cannot be understood here as rejecting the scribe as an "outsider" but urging him to take up this task. Contra Kingsbury, "On Following Jesus," 52.

59. See McCane, "Let the Dead," 31–43.

Three More Miracle Stories

The second triad of miracles begins, strangely enough, describing Jesus calming the storm as they head across the water to the other side of the Sea of Galilee (8:23–27). How does this fit in with the general theme of healing Servant Israel and the growth of the kingdom? It has been argued that Matthew placed this story here to continue the theme of discipleship and to warn his community that discipleship meant going through the storms with him, that it was not all glory as the willing scribe may have thought. Others have contended that Christology, Jesus' divine power and authority, is the main emphasis.[60] While these elements may certainly be part of it, there seems to be more to this story. The storm is described as a "great earthquake" in the sea, which is later contrasted with a "great calm." Two motifs are brought together here. The one is that the earthquake was seen as a symbol of God breaking into his ordered universe to bring about judgment on evildoers and justice for the righteous (Isa 29:6; Zech 14:5; cf. Matt 27:51–54; 28:2). Sometimes, this was also spoken of in terms of storm and tempest (Isa 28:2; 30:30; 40:24; 41:16). The other motif was to see storm and sea as symbols from which God provides shelter and refuge for the faithful (Ps 46:1–3; Isa 25:4; Pss 77:16–20; 107:23–32; 106:7–12; 18:16–19). Perhaps even more significant is the mention of famine and earthquakes as signs of the ushering in of the new age, the consummation of the kingdom in Matt 24:7, as the beginning of the birthpangs of the new age (cf. 1 En 62:4). Added to this are the overtones of the story of Jonah (Jesus is asleep, the disciples cry, "Save us, we are perishing!" Cf. Jonah 1:5–6, 14) who was turned back to carry out his God-given purpose, and so the waters became calm. Thus, at a time like this, when God is breaking into his universe to establish his kingdom and bring salvation to all people, this was no time for the disciples to be timid or to be of "littleness of faith." It was a time for complete trust in God's protection to carry out their God-given calling of witnessing for the kingdom. Curiously, Matthew then refers to the disciples as *hoi anthrôpoi*, "the men" who marvel that even the winds and waves obey Jesus (v. 27).[61] This may be to point out that they are the "men" with the "Son of Man" (*ho huios tou anthrôpou*) with all that that implies (cf. 9:6 and 8). In sum, the stilling of the storm is an indication of the presence of God and renewal of all his creation. Second, as part of that transformation, disciples are called to grow in faith in order to be participants in the work of the kingdom, as children of the heavenly Father. Third, as the Son of Man, Jesus exemplifies what that really means—acting in fullness of faith, filled with the Spirit of God, speaking and acting with the authority given from the Father.

This authority is further demonstrated in the healing of the Gadarene demoniacs (8:28–34). Jesus and his disciples had crossed the Sea of Galilee in order to bring the good news of the kingdom to those Jews, particularly those of the prophetic tradition,

---

60. Bornkamm, "Stilling of the Storm," 52–7; Held, "Matthew as Interpreter," 200–204. Cf. Luz, *Matthew 8–20*, 20–22 who describes the purpose as Christological with a "soteriological-ecclesiastical dimension" added.

61. Bornkamm, "Stilling of the Storm," 56, argues that *anthrôpoi* represents men who later hear this story in preaching, which is a bit incongruous. Luz, *Matthew 8–20*, 20, follows suit. Hagner, *Matthew 1–13*, 222, suggests that it simply reminds us that the disciples had not yet been constituted as "the twelve."

who were scattered in the predominantly Gentile region of Gadara. As they enter that region they are met by two fierce demoniacs coming out of the tombs. They confront Jesus with the cry: "What have you to do with us, Son of God? Have you come here to torment us before the time?" (v. 29). The demons know how to address Jesus and know his authority because of the failure of their leader, the devil (also known as Satan or Mastema, Jub 10:1-6) to tempt Jesus (4:1-11). The "time" they refer to is the day of the consummation of the Great Judgment (1 En 15:8—16:3), the day when they will finally be destroyed with all the forces of evil. These demons, the evil spirits of the giants that once devastated the earth, were popularly believed to be the cause of corruption, violence, blindness, infant deaths, and all manner of illnesses in people. To show that he had authority as the herald of the kingdom even over these demonic forces, Jesus cast them out, where they went into a herd of pigs (unclean and prohibited to Jews). These fled down the steep hill into the sea and were drowned in the water over which Jesus had already exercised his authority. Because of this the Gentile community of Gadara barred Jesus and his disciples from entering their city, and so they returned across the Sea to Capernaum. No further mention is made of the men who were healed (cf. Mark 5:1-20). Matthew was concerned simply to identify Jesus' authority in eliminating demonic forces as a sign of kingdom growth.

The healing of the paralytic (9:1-8), highlights yet another aspect of the kingdom of God, and Jesus' representative authority. Seeing the faith of the people who brought the paralytic to him, Jesus addressed the paralytic and told him, "Your sins are forgiven." This was part of the good news of the kingdom, for God who reigns had said: "I, I am he who blots out your transgressions for your own sake, I will not remember your sins" (Isa 43:25; cf. 44:22). Thus forgiveness was to take the central position in the growth of the kingdom (cf. 5:21-25; 6:12, 14-15), for forgiveness has always been part of the healing process. The Servant's function was to bind up the broken-hearted, free from prison those who were bound, open the eyes of the blind (Isa 42:7; 61:1) and thus to restore (Isa 49:6). To the scribes this was blasphemy because in their belief only God can forgive, and that only on the Day of Atonement. But then they had not read the prophets. So Jesus' response to them, "that you may know that the Son of Man has authority on earth to forgive sins" (v. 6), demonstrates that he was obediently carrying out the role of Servant Israel. Then, when at Jesus' bidding, the paralytic rose up, took his bed and went home, the crowds feared and glorified God that God had given such authority to the people (*tois anthrôpois*, v. 8). Once again we see an alignment between "the Son of Man" and "men," indicating the representative nature of the term "Son of Man."

The Call of Matthew and Discipleship

The call of Matthew the tax collector and Levite (he is called Levi in parallel accounts in Luke 5:27 and Mark 2:14) to discipleship (9:9), and to be one of the Twelve (10:1-4), was a significant act for the growth of the kingdom. As a Levite who had responded to the good news, he would be well suited to witness to the Levite communities in Upper Galilee. However, tax collectors were regarded as collaborators with the forces of oppression and were always under suspicion of using their office to enrich themselves.

The rabbis classified them with murderers and robbers, and approved of lying to them in order to escape taxation (m. Nedarim 3:4). Moreover, a tax collector entering one's home was said to render it unclean (m. Tohoroth 7:6). Jesus and his disciples dining with Matthew and his fellow tax collectors and "sinners" later was thus bound to give cause to the Pharisees to question his actions (vv. 10, 11). Jesus' response to them (vv. 12, 13) was threefold: (1) Those who are sick are the ones who need a physician, not those who regard themselves as healthy. Jesus had come to bring healing to Servant Israel, the man of sickness and acquainted with pain (Isa 53:3). (2) In quoting Hos 6:6: "I desire steadfast love and not sacrifice," Jesus was pointing out that having compassion on one's neighbor was acting according to God's will, whereas their priestly purity laws were not. (3) Jesus came to call sinners into the kingdom, not those who considered themselves "righteous" in their arrogance (cf. 5:20). The indictment of the Pharisees in all this is obvious. This story illustrates how integrally connected are forgiveness, healing and discipleship in the kingdom. The same message was true for the disciples of John the Baptist as well (9:14–17). Both groups could do well to hear the divine word: "From this time forth I make you hear new things, hidden things which you have not known" (Isa 48:6).

Three More Healing Stories

The next two healing stories, the raising of the ruler's daughter and the woman with a hemorrhage (9:18–26) are woven together because they both deal with forms of death and restoring to life. The woman who had suffered from a hemorrhage for twelve years had lived in a constant state of uncleanness during that time, making it difficult to do anything without rendering unclean whatever she touched (Lev 15:19–30; m. Zabim 5:1, 6). So she approached Jesus from behind and touched only the tassel of his garment, which symbolized the covenant with God (cf. Num 15:38, 39; Deut 22:12; Zech 8:23). This way she hoped to be "saved" (*sôthêsomai*, v. 21) from her situation. Jesus turned and assured her that her faith had saved her. Similar cases were reported later (14:36). In the case of the ruler's daughter, the professional mourners were already in the house when Jesus arrived. These Jesus asked to leave because, he told them, the little girl was not "dead but sleeping" (v. 24). They laughed at this, but Jesus took the girl by the hand and raised her up. Both of these cases were signs of new life being given as the ushering in of the kingdom.

The healing of Servant Israel had always been described in Isaiah as the blind receiving their sight, the ears of the deaf unstopped, and the tongues of the dumb singing for joy (Isa 29:18; 35:5, 6; 42:7, 16, 18, 19; 43:8). These signs of the kingdom are now illustrated in the final two healing stories, drawn from different occasions (9:27–31 from 20:29–33; 9:32–34 from 12:22–24). In the first, the two blind men, regarded as under a covenant curse because of their blindness (cf. Deut 28:28–29; John 9:1–34), address Jesus as "son of David." Evidently, the hope for a Davidic messiah, expressed in Psalm of Solomon 17, had become popular among the people with the belief that he would be the one to usher in the kingdom of God. Jesus healed them both because of the faith they had expressed, but then instructed them to tell no one. This strange demand was because they had addressed him as "son of David," a title often associated with political and nationalist hopes, which was not the way of Jesus. The second case was of a deaf and dumb demoniac (9:32–34) whom Jesus exorcised. To be deaf and dumb was attributed to demonic forces, and the word *kôphos* was used for both disorders (cf. 11:5). Matthew mentioned this healing here, taken from 12:22–24, to bring to completion all the signs of the kingdom as mentioned in Isa 29:18 and 35:6 before Jesus reports to John the Baptist the list of his works in 11:2–5.

Matthew now finishes up this section on the restoration of Israel and the growth of the kingdom by repeating the *inclusio* verse from 4:23 (9:35), emphasizing once again the restoration of the one despised and rejected, acquainted with pains and sickness (Isa 53:3, 4). Jesus then expresses compassion for the crowds which had followed him, seeing them "like sheep without a shepherd," "harassed and helpless" (cf. Zech 10:2, 6–10). For they are the ones for whom "the Lord God comes with might and . . . will feed his flock like a shepherd, he will gather the lambs in his arms and carry them in his bosom, and gently lead the mother sheep" (Isa 40:10–11). That is the message Jesus had come to proclaim in word and deed. It was now time to send out the Twelve he had chosen, symbolically representing the twelve tribes of Israel, to go and proclaim the same good news in word and deed throughout all Galilee, but only "to the lost sheep of the house of Israel" (10:6; cf. 15:24; 18:10–14). In one sense this was a training run for the Twelve, reaching out particularly to those communities familiar with the prophetic vision. At this stage they are not instructed to teach, only to proclaim the good news that the kingdom is here and to heal giving indications of its presence, and then move on.

DESCRIBING THE KINGDOM IN PARABLES (MATTHEW 13)

That Jesus' primary concern was to reach out first to those prophetic communities, who were already familiar with the hopes and promises of Isaiah, is clear from Matt 10:40–42, his final words to the Twelve as he sent them out. There he reminded them that those who received them into their homes were receiving the good news of the kingdom and were accepting the ministry of Jesus himself. Those who received them as prophets of God would receive the rewards and recompense proclaimed by the prophets in Isa 40:10; 49:4; 61:8; 62:11, 12. Putting it another way, those who received them as representatives of the "Righteous One, my Servant" (Isa 53:11) would be accounted righteous before God and come under his protection (cf. also Isa 57:1; 1 En 38:2; 53:6–7). Prophets and the righteous were often mentioned synonymously in the prophetic literature, so also in Matthew (e.g., 13:17; 23:29). Even the smallest acts of hospitality (a cup of cold water) towards Jesus' disciples ("these little ones," v. 42; cf. 18:1–10; 11:25; Isa 40:10; 60:22; Zech 13:7; 1 En 62:11) would be rewarded.

However, not all would accept Jesus' proclamation of the good news of a spiritual kingdom. Many were still holding on to a more concrete concept of the future kingdom where the righteous would physically inherit the land from the large landowners who had taken it from their families by political or usurious means, a utopian theocratic state of the righteous, no longer under alien rule, after all the oppressors of their people were no more. For many, as long as the powerful landowners in collaboration with their foreign or Herodian oppressors had control of their ancestral land, there could be no kingdom. Many who saw themselves as the "shoot," the planting of the Lord, expected that during the "week of righteousness," the righteous would execute judgment on the wicked. Then, and then only, would they "acquire possessions in righteousness" and God would reign in his temple forever, and all people would become righteous (1 En 91:12–17).

So in spite of the initial euphoria and the many healings Jesus had performed as signs of the restoration of the kingdom, there was a lack of understanding and growing opposition to Jesus' message. Even John the Baptist had become impatient with Jesus, whom he had regarded as his protégé, and questioned his whole understanding of the coming kingdom (11:2–6). Yet, as Jesus reminded the crowds (11:7), John had a God-given role to play, but there were those of "this generation" who rejected both John and Jesus because their messages did not resonate with their own "wisdom." But true wisdom, Jesus pointed out, shows itself in action (11:19; cf. 11:2). Even those cities where prophetic influence was strong (Chorazin, Bethsaida, and Capernaum) where Jesus had healed many, were looking for a different kingdom than the one Jesus proclaimed (11:20–24). These were like the "wise and understanding" of Isaiah's day whose "wisdom" would soon perish and their "understanding" vanish (Isa 29:13–14), while true wisdom was being revealed "to babes" (11:25; cf. Isa 28:9). The main representatives of "this generation" were, of course, the Pharisees and their followers who saw their influence being eroded, and so opposed Jesus (12:1–14, 22–45) in spite of the good works Jesus did in fulfillment of Isa 42:1–4 (Matt 12:15–21). With the growing publicity of Jesus' mission, even Jesus' own family feared for him and did not understand his message or mission at this time (12:46–50).

It was because of this growing opposition and lack of understanding that led Jesus to change his strategy and begin to describe the kingdom in parables. Jesus recognized that the crowds who came to him to hear his preaching contained not only those who were moved by his message of the kingdom and believed with the ears of faith (13:9), but also those who were there to criticize and debate. These Jesus saw as not only lacking understanding but also obstinate in their unbelief, much like the people of Isaiah's time (13:14–15, quoting Isa 6:9–10). But those who sought the word of God in faith would be given the "secrets" (*ta mysteria*) of the kingdom (13:11; cf. 11:25), a common theme in the prophetic literature (see Isa 42:9; 48:6–8; 52:15; 53:1; 1 En 38:3; 51:3; 58:5; 61:13). In spite of the opposition, Jesus assured the disciples that they were witnessing the gathering of the faithful into God's kingdom to be a light to the nations, something that had been longed for by prophets and the righteous since the time of the exile (13:16–17).

In the light of this, the parable of the sowing of the seed (13:3–9, 18–23) describes how the "word of the kingdom" works to accomplish its purpose and causes the kingdom of God to grow. While that word may fall on the ears of the spiritually deaf and have no effect, or be initially received with joy only to be denied in the face of any opposition, or be accepted for a time only soon to be forgotten in the concern for material things, it nevertheless will bear the fruits of righteousness at various levels in the lives of the faithful and thus demonstrate the growth of the kingdom. Behind this parable are some Isaianic expressions: (1) Isa 40:6–8, 24 had spoken of people being like grass which withers and fades, but the word of God stands forever; (2) in Isa 55:1–11 the invitation to the celebration of God's reign and the installation of the faithful as God's witnesses to the nations is followed by the promise that God's word will not return to him empty but will accomplish that which he purposes—like rain and snow which waters the earth, making it bring forth and sprout.[62]

The parable of the weeds among the wheat (13:24–30, 36–43) carries on and extends the metaphor of the seed falling on good soil. It illustrates that the kingdom is already present in the germination of the seed in the faithful responding to the word and proclaiming the good news. All are given the opportunity to grow, even while evil is still present, and the judgment on those who bear no fruit only comes at the close of the age. This follows the role of Servant Israel who will not break a bruised reed or quench a dimly burning wick until he has established justice in the earth (Isa 42:1–4; cf. Matt 12:18–21). To judge prematurely would negate God's plan for his Servant to be a light to the nations. The Servant's task is to dissipate the darkness, and those who ultimately resist that light will be destroyed at the close of the age, while the righteous "will shine like the sun in the kingdom of their Father" (v. 43; cf. Mal 3:20 [E 4:2]; Dan 12:3; 1 En 59:36). That time is depicted in 1 En 58:1–6 as the time when the righteous and chosen enter into eternal life, which appears to be implied here. They will then be in the presence of the heavenly Father reflecting fully his brightness (cf. Isa 60:19–21). The point being made is that the kingdom has its beginning in this world with the righteous witnessing to the good news of the kingdom before there can be any final judgment of the wicked and ultimate blessing of the righteous. That is why the disciples needed an explanation of this parable.[63]

The parables of the mustard seed and the leaven (13:31–33) are told to illustrate that the kingdom does not come about by means of a great battle in which the wicked are destroyed and the righteous are victorious. Rather, it comes about by quiet growth of faith and understanding as more and more people are touched by the good news and relate to their heavenly Father. Like the tiny mustard seed which quickly grows into a large bush some three meters high, so the reign of God in the hearts and lives of people may have small beginnings but it grows and spreads into the hearts and lives of others, and without force or violence becomes a powerful influence in the world. That "it becomes a tree" echoes Isa 60:21—61:3 where the shoots of God's planting grow into "oaks of righteousness" (cf. also 1QH XIV, 15–16; XV.18–19; XVI.6–11). "Birds nesting in its branches" (v. 32) symbolizes the openness of the kingdom to all, offering security and protection (cf. Ps 104:10–12, 16–17).[64] The parable of the leaven (v. 33) similarly describes how the kingdom becomes great from small and inconspicuous beginnings but emphasizes the quiet and unassuming nature of its growth.

The telling of these parables, addressed to the crowds, Matthew (13:34–35) sees as fulfillment of Ps 78:2 and Isa 40:29; 42:9; 48:6–8 (cf. particularly 1 En 51:3; 52:1–5). Thus Matthew once again emphasizes the revelation of new things, hidden things, to the faithful in parables, as in 13:11 (cf. 11:27). After this Jesus began to concentrate more on explaining the kingdom to his disciples.

62. Cf. Evans, "On the Isaianic Background of the Sower Parable," 464–68.
63. Cf. a different approach to the parable by McIver, "Parable of the Weeds," 643–59.
64. Cf. Bailey, "Parable of the Mustard Seed," 449–59.

In the privacy of his house in Capernaum Jesus then told three more parables to his disciples to bring home to them the great value and urgency of the kingdom of God for anyone. It is like hidden treasure which, when discovered, a person is ready to give up everything else in order to have it because he/she acknowledges that being part of God's kingdom must take precedence over everything else (13:44); or the kingdom is like a merchant who has been searching for the very finest pearl, and when he finds it, sells everything he has to purchase it. So also a person searching for the ultimate answers to life is ready to give up every other approach in order to embrace the kingdom and live in that relationship with the heavenly Father (13:45–46). The urgency for them to share this good news of the kingdom with others is then implied in the parable of the dragnet (13:47–50). Using a metaphor thoroughly familiar to his disciples of fishermen using a dragnet to gather in all kinds of fish, sorting the good into containers and throwing away the bad, Jesus reminded them of the final judgment before which the gathering in had to be done. As scribes of the kingdom of God, therefore, they will share the "new things" which have now been declared (Isa 42:9; 48:6–8), as well as the old (13:51–52).

Throughout this chapter we have seen how Jesus sought to draw his hearers into a true understanding of the kingdom of God as expressed in the prophetic vision found in its truest form in Isa 40–66. Instead of some future kingdom after the great Day of Judgment, a geo-political kingdom brought about by the destruction of their oppressors, Jesus described this kingdom as the gracious reign of God in the hearts and lives of his faithful people. It would be manifest as the people live in a faithful relationship with their heavenly Father as his sons and daughters here and now. That kingdom would grow by their witness to the love of God through their love for all humankind. Much more could be said about Jesus' understanding of the kingdom, but it is important to move now to a discussion of how Jesus perceived his mission in the light of the prophetic vision as presented in Matthew's Gospel.

Chapter X

The Prophetic Vision and the Mission of Jesus

THE OPENING VERSE OF Matthew's Gospel states: "The book of the origin of Jesus Anointed, son of David, son of Abraham."

THE PROPHETIC UNDERSTANDING OF DAVIDIC KINGSHIP

Considering the prophetic orientation of Matthew's Gospel, it seems strange that the Gospel should begin with an emphasis on Jesus as "son of David." As we have seen, from the time of Deutero-Isaiah the idea of a future Davidic king was dismissed because of the failure of the kings to represent God's justice and righteousness. In the plan for the future, God alone would be king (Isa 40:9–11; 41:21; 43:5; 44:16; 52:7–10), and the everlasting covenant made with David would be transferred to the faithful (Isa 55:3–5). The people were to be God's representatives through their covenant faithfulness and witness to God's reign over all. As such, they would be a living "people-covenant" and a "light to the nations" (Isa 42:1–6; 49:1–8). Designations which had been used of David such as "servant" and "chosen one" now constantly referred to the faithful as a corporate group, sometimes been referred to as "collective messianism."

That concept, we have seen, was carried on within the prophetic community after the exile. Trito-Isaiah, speaking in the role of Servant Israel, announced that Yahweh had *anointed* him as David had been (1 Sam 16:13; 2 Sam 23:5; Ps 89:39, 52) to bring the good news of God's reign to the afflicted (Isa 61:1), so that they might all become the recipients of the "oil of gladness" (61:3, like the king in Ps 45:8). In Isa 60:21, the righteous are even called the "shoot" of God's planting, that rare term used formerly by Isaiah of Jerusalem of a future Davidic king (11:1). Even Jeremiah's famous prophecy in Jer 23:5: "I will cause a righteous *shoot* to shoot forth for David" was democratized in Isa 61:11, which said of the faithful that "the Lord Yahweh will cause righteousness and praise to "*shoot forth* in front of the nations." This same democratization of the kingship followed in Zech 9:9 where the faithful of Judah were seen as representing God's kingship, in Dan 7–12 where "one like a son of man" is a corporate figure signifying "the holy ones of the Most High," and in Wis 2:10—6:11 where the corporate figure (based on the Servant of Isa 53) is referred to as the "righteous poor one" (2:10). We have seen that, as well, throughout the Enoch literature—especially in 1 En 37–71 where much of the corporate terminology ("that Son of Man," "the Righteous One," "the Chosen One," "the Anointed One") are merged together. Such a one there is placed on the throne of glory to represent God's kingship as a non-Davidic, non-royal messianic figure (1 En 61:3; 62:5). It is clear that this was the prophetic vision from the time of the exile on, one which Jesus is portrayed in Matthew's Gospel as bringing to fulfillment.

Jesus as "Son of David"?

So why this strong emphasis at the beginning of the Gospel on Jesus as "Son of David"? While the hope for a future Davidide had diminished with the disaster of the exile, it was kept alive to a limited degree by the Zadokite priesthood as a secular adjunct to the high priest, by Davidic descendants, and by the Levite hope for the validation of their priesthood (cf. Jer 33:14–26; the Chronicler, Jubilees). However, with the devastation brought on by Pompey's aggression in 63 BCE, the hope for a descendant of David to rise up and establish rule to free Israel from this continuous oppression was expressed in *Pss. Sol.* 17:23 (21), and this became the popular hope. The Messiah (Anointed One) had to be a "son of David," a notion supported by the scribes and Pharisees on the basis of 2 Sam 7:12–16, and became the prevailing messianic hope among the people, spreading even among the Jewish Diaspora. That this hope continued even after the destruction of the temple in 70 CE is evident in Shemoneh Esreh 14 and in the tradition about Rabbi Akiva (d. 135 CE) who held that the plural "thrones" in Dan 7:9 were for God and the Davidic Messiah (b. Hag 14a; b. Sanh 38b).

It was this popular messianic hope which led "all the populace," amazed at Jesus' healing powers, to raise the question: "Can this be the Son of David?" (12:22–23). That Jesus came to be popularly viewed as that Son of David, in spite of his rejection by the Pharisees (12:24; cf. 9:32–34), is clear from the cry of the two blind men (9:27; 20:30–31), and the pilgrims proclaiming Jesus' entry into Jerusalem with the cry: "Hosanna to the Son of David," followed by their children singing the same in the temple (21:9, 15). That this popular belief had spread widely was recognized even by an outsider, the Canaanite (Greek) woman who appealed to Jesus to save her daughter with the same cry: "Have mercy on me, O Master, Son of David" (15:22). This Gentile woman, as well as the blind men, appeal to Jesus as Son of David, not because they saw David or his son Solomon as having therapeutic power[1], but because of the tradition that David's Son would reestablish God's rule of justice and righteousness (2 Sam 8:15; Ps 72:1–4, 12–14) from which the blind and the lame (on the basis of 2 Sam 5:6–8; Deut 28:23, 29; cf. John 9:1–41), as well as Gentiles, had been excluded.[2]

---

1. In spite of the emphasis on this aspect in Duling, "Solomon, Exorcism," 235–52; Duling, "Therapeutic Son of David," 392–410; Duling, "Matthew's Plurisignificant 'Son of David,'" 99–116; Poffenroth, "Jesus as Anointed," 547–54. Moreover, it is unlikely that Matthew is suggesting a connection with Ezek 34 since in that passage it is God who does the healing, not David, and second, Matthew never quotes or alludes to Ezekiel because of that work's Zadokite priestly orientation. Contra Baxter, "Healing," 36–50.

2. See Leske, "Matthew," 1287, 1301–2.

Disciples of Jesus never refer to Jesus as Son of David, nor does Jesus ever claim to be such in Matthew's Gospel. Apart from the above few references by others the only other reference to "Son of David" outside of the infancy narrative is in Matt 22:41–46. There Jesus puts the question to the Pharisees: "What do you think of the Anointed One? Whose son is he?" and receives the expected answer: "The Son of David." Jesus then questions their interpretation of Ps 110:1 upon which they had based their answer: "If David thus calls him lord, how (*pôs*) is he his son?" (22:41–45). *Pôs* in this context does not mean "in what sense"[3], but in its general meaning in Matthew as "how can it be possible" (cf. 12:26, 29, 34; 16:11; 23:33).[4] For in the prophetic understanding, it is faithful Servant Israel who will be exalted and lifted up (Isa 52:13), and now bears the title, "Anointed" (Isa 61:1). This interpretation of Ps 110:1 is confirmed in Matt 26:63–64 where the high priest accuses Jesus of claiming to be the "Anointed One, Son of God," implying Davidic sonship. Jesus response is: "*You* have said so" and then continues with an allusion combining both Ps 110:1 and Dan 7:13 with 1 En 62:1–6: "From now on you will see the *Son of Man* seated at the right hand of Power, and coming on the clouds of heaven." Clearly, the implication here is that the designation "Son of David" is rejected for the title "Son of Man."[5] For it is reminiscent of the sayings in 1 En 51:3; 55:4; 61:8; 62:5 where it is the Son of Man / Chosen One who is enthroned and revealed to the "holy and chosen ones" who are the "planting of the Lord" (cf. Isa 60:21; 61:3).[6]

This is further borne out in the rest of the New Testament. In his Pentecost speech in Acts 2:14–36 Peter defends the position that it is Jesus who has been exalted and sits at the right hand of God according to Ps 110:1, not an earthly David or his son (vv. 33–36). According to Acts 13:32–37, Paul's speech in the synagogue of Pisidian Antioch makes the same claim, combining Pss 2:7; 110:1 and 16:10 as being fulfilled by the risen Jesus in relation to Isa 55:3–5, rather than a Davidide. In Paul's Letter to the Romans in which he defends his position before Jews in Rome who expected the messiah to be the Son of David, he felt constrained to refer to Jesus as being a descendant of David "according to the flesh," but affirms he has been "designated Son of God in power according to the spirit of holiness by his resurrection from the dead" (Rom 1:3). In the rest of the letter, while he does refer to the Psalms of David, he nowhere mentions Jesus' Davidic descent again.

What we therefore find in Matt 22:41–46 is the time when Jesus has finally shed the cloak of David in order to give way to a fuller disclosure of his role and mission as Servant Israel. However, throughout his ministry that mantle with its political implications, as held by the chief priests, elders and Pharisees, continued to follow Jesus, leading finally to his crucifixion as "King of the Jews" (27:37). Matthew's narrative thus ultimately "overturns the textuality of Davidic messianism" after having gone along with it in order

---

3. So Duling, "Therapeutic Son of David," 405–6; Poffenroth, "Jesus as Anointed," 553.

4. Luke 20:41 also includes the double *pos*, and Mark 12:35–37 makes the negative even more explicit with *pos . . . pothen*.

5. Contra, e.g., Davies and Allison, *Gospel according to Saint Matthew*, 2:254.

6. Cf. Hengel, *Studies in Early Christology*, 181–88.

to draw his audience to a new messianic understanding,[7] rather than emphasizing and developing the importance of Jesus' kingship.[8]

So it must be that Matthew has begun his Gospel with this deliberate stylized genealogy for "Jesus Anointed One, son of David, Son of Abraham" to respond to the accusation that Jesus could not be the Anointed because he was not a descendant of David, and to assert that in representing the faithful, he has inherited the everlasting covenant made with David. Matthew has deliberately formed this genealogy into three sections of fourteen generations covering the whole history of Israel up to the time of Jesus (1:17). Since the number fourteen in Hebrew is made up of the letters *d-v-d* which make up the name "David," Matthew may be subtly reminding his readers that all Israel, which Jesus represents, is called to take over the role of David to witness to the nations. Even after this elaborate genealogy, the connection of Jesus to the Davidic line is tenuous at best: it is only through Joseph, "son of David" (1:20), who is not his biological father!

By following "son of David" with the title "son of Abraham" Matthew not only identifies Jesus as a true Israelite but reminds the reader that as such the covenant made with Abraham to become a blessing to all nations (Gen 12:3; 18:18; 22:18) would finally reach its fulfillment in Jesus' mission, as Deutero-Isaiah had proclaimed about the role of Servant Israel (Isa 42:6–7; 49:6–8). For in Isa 41:8 Servant Israel is addressed as "offspring of Abraham" when called to be God's witness to the nations.

CONCEPTION FROM THE HOLY SPIRIT (1:18, 20)

A second unique aspect of Matthew's stylized genealogy is the mention of four women: Tamar, Rahab, Ruth, and Bathsheba. In each case there was something highly irregular in their giving birth to Israel's ancestors, yet all were seen as having been led by the Spirit of God to act in accordance with the divine purpose. Tamar was the widowed daughter-in-law of Judah and acted as a prostitute in order to have progeny by Judah (Gen 38). Rahab was a Canaanite prostitute who was spared from the destruction of Jericho because she hid the Israelite spies (Josh 2) and was seen as thus helping to fulfill God's purpose for Israel. Ruth was a Moabite woman who became an ancestor of David by seducing Boaz into marriage (Ruth 3). Matthew refers to Bathsheba pointedly as "the wife of Uriah" the Hittite with whom David committed adultery (2 Sam 12:9–10). In spite of this Bathsheba was held in high esteem as one who was destined by God to continue the Davidic line.[9] Matthew's purpose in including these women in Israel's history in the genealogy was to give the setting of Mary's irregular conception of Jesus—both to answer criticism that Jesus was illegitimate and thus could not be the promised Messiah, but also to demonstrate that God had destined Jesus to fulfill his divine purpose.

This is the basic message of 1:18–25. In his particular way, Matthew is setting down in summary fashion how Jesus is to fulfill the role of Servant Israel in proclaiming the good news of God's compassionate reign. Being "conceived from the Holy Spirit" in this

---

7. So Jones, "Subverting the Textuality," 256–72. Cf. also Dunn, "Messianic Ideas," 370–76.
8. Contra Bauer, "Kingship of Jesus," 306–23; Verseput, "Role and Meaning," 532–56.
9. See further, e.g., Schaberg, *Illegitimacy of Jesus*, 20–34; Weren, "Five Women," 288–305.

The Prophetic Vision and the Real Jesus

context carries on from the many references in Deutero-Isaiah to Yahweh putting his Spirit upon his Servant, his Chosen One (42:1; 44:3; cf. 61:1), of having formed Israel "from the womb" and having carried Israel from birth (43:1; 44:2, 24; 46:3). In Isa 49:1, 5, Servant Israel acknowledges: "Yahweh has called me from the womb, from the body of my mother he named my name . . . who formed me from the womb to be his Servant." In none of these instances does it indicate a virgin birth. In fact, Yahweh had exonerated Israel (43:22–25) in order for Israel to be his Servant. The same may be said for Matt 1:18, 20. There, in 1:21, Joseph is instructed to take Mary as his wife and to legitimize her son's birth by naming him with the name God has designated, "Yeshua" (cf. Isa 43:1; 49:1), for "he will save his people from their sins." This, in a nutshell, is Jesus' mission. It is the announcement of the good news of God's compassionate reign over Israel as well as over the nations. For Servant Israel was commissioned by God "to be a light to the nations that his "salvation (*yeshuah*) may reach to the ends of the earth" (Isa 49:6; 52:7, 10).

In Deutero-Isaiah's time the exile was commonly held to be the punishment for Israel's sin of breaking covenant with God (cf. Isa 50:1; 59:2, 12–14), and "saving from sin" expressed God's deliverance from exile and restoration of the covenant relationship in God's kingdom (cf. 35:4; 43:11–12; 45:20–22). With the legalistic teaching of the Pharisees, the common people were led to believe that all the oppression and suffering they experienced were the covenant curses. The same message at the end of the exile that the people had paid the penalty and God would sweep away their sins like mist (40:2; 43:25; 44:22) was to be the message Jesus was to proclaim. For the role of Servant Israel was to "bear the sin of many, and make intercession for the transgressors (Isa 53:5–12). By this authority Jesus was to announce the forgiveness of sins (Matt 9:2–6; 12:31; 26:28) and thus restore the relationship with God, to assure the sufferers that God was with them. This is the reason why Matthew quotes Isa 7:14 in 1:23 with its parallel of a young woman having conceived and giving birth to a son as a sign that God is with his people. The Hebrew word used in that quotation was *almah*, meaning simply "a young woman." That is the term that would have been used in Matthew's original Hebrew version. Our Greek version, however, has *parthenos*, usually translated as "virgin," and taken over from the LXX translation of Isa 7:14, although this word does not always have that meaning.[10] Later Greek versions of Isaiah such as those of Theodotion, Aquila, and Symmachus used the more general word *neanis*, "young woman."[11] Matthew's use of Isa 7:14 was simply to emphasize that through this birth Israel would be able to experience God's presence among them once again, joyfully announced in the name "Emmanuel . . . God is with us" (cf. Isa 41:10; 43:5).

THE BIRTH OF JESUS AS SERVANT ISRAEL

In his second chapter of the infancy narrative Matthew continues to reveal the child Jesus as having come to fulfill the role of Servant Israel. Tradition has it that magi,

---

10. Cf. Schaberg, *Illegitimacy*, 62–77. See particularly Lincoln, "Contested Paternity," 215n10.

11. The early church fathers using the LXX condemned as heretics the Jewish Christians known as the "Ebionites" who used only the Hebrew Gospel of Matthew and thus did not accept the virgin birth. Cf. Ireneus, *adv. Haer.* III.11.7; 21.1; V.1.3; Origen, *Contra Celsum* V.61.

renowned as astrologists, had foretold the birth of Cyrus who eventually established the Persian Empire.[12] This same Cyrus Deutero-Isaiah heralded as God's coming "Anointed One" and "shepherd" to restore the exiles to their homeland (Isa 44:28; 45:1). Now the restoration of God's reign is foretold by the magi coming to Jerusalem from the east to announce Jesus' birth as "Anointed One" (Matt 2:4) and "shepherd" (2:6) of Israel. Matthew has modified the quotation from Mic 5:2 by changing "clans" and "ruler" to "leaders" and "one who leads" and adds a quotation from 2 Sam 5:2 to make it conform more with the Servant role. The magi bringing gifts of gold, frankincense and myrrh recalls Servant Israel being acknowledged as God's representative by the nations in Isa 45:14; 55:5 and 60:6. These gifts were to indicate that Servant Israel would become God's crown of beauty, his royal diadem (Isa 62:3; cf. 28:5).

In the next verses (2:13–23), the young child's mission as representing true Israel is more explicit, reliving Israel's history in microcosm, leading up to Israel's mission. Warned of Herod's intention to destroy the child, Joseph takes the child and his mother to Egypt in order to fulfill Hos 11:1: "Out of Egypt have I called my son" (2:15), where "son" is Israel. Deutero-Isaiah had often implied that the return from exile was like a new exodus, and Israel was often referred to as God's "son" and "servant" (cf. Exod 4:22–23). Just as Pharaoh had ordered that all male children be put to death (Exod 1:15, 22), so Herod orders that all male children two years and under in Bethlehem be killed (Matt 2:16). Matthew sees this as fulfilling Jer 31:15, which expresses the people's bitterness over the exile, but given in a context of hope and reconciliation with God through a new living covenant (Jer 31:31–34). In that same chapter Jeremiah had spoken of God as "a father to Israel" (v. 9) and of Israel as God's "dear son" (v. 20). The return from Egypt after the death of Herod (Matt 2:19–21) parallels the departure of the Israelites from Egypt to eventually enter the land which became Israel. In Matt 4:1–11, this exodus motif is extended further in that Jesus is tested in the wilderness for forty days and nights, just as Israel was tested in the wilderness for forty years. All this is not to imply that Jesus was to be a new Moses,[13] but that he was to live out the role of Servant Israel. That the child Jesus should grow up and begin his mission from Nazareth completes the divine plan—that he should be one of those who maintained the prophetic vision and were known as the *Notsrim/Nazoreans* (from the term *netser*, the *shoot* of God's planting, Isa 11:1; 60:21; 1 En 10:16; 84:6; 93:2, 8, 10; 62:7, 8; 1QH XIV:15–16; XV:18–19; XVI:6–8; CD 1:7–8).[14]

THE COMMISSIONING OF JESUS

One can expect that the first time Jesus is depicted as speaking in Matthew's Gospel his words would be an important indication of his mission. Those words were spoken to John the Baptist when John questioned Jesus' request to undergo baptism. Jesus' reply

---

12. Herodotus I.107–28, 204. See Aus, "Magi at the Birth," 99–114.

13. So Davies, "Jewish Sources," 503–11; Allison, *New Moses*, 140–65. While Moses may be lurking in the background, the typology in this narrative is of Israel. The same must be said of Jesus being tested in the wilderness, contra Allison, *New Moses*, 165–72. We have already seen that the Sermon on the Mount is a response to Isa 40:9–11 rather than to Moses receiving the Law on Mount Sinai (chapter 9).

14. See further Leske, "Jesus as a *Nazoraios*," 69–81.

("Let it be so now, for thus it is fitting for us to fulfill all righteousness," 3:15) was referring to the significance of their combined missions in bringing God's righteousness to the people that they might then respond in righteousness to God and to one another. Deutero-Isaiah had expressed this as: "Shower, O heavens, from above, and let the skies rain down righteousness, let the earth open up that salvation may spring up also, and let it cause righteousness to sprout up also" (Isa 45:8). John's approach was to call people to act in righteousness and thus invoke God's righteous response, but Jesus saw his mission as first proclaiming the good news of God's deliverance so that the people might respond in covenant faithfulness and become God's witnesses before all the nations (Isa 61:11). By this Israel, as Yahweh's Servant, as the Righteous One, was to cause many to be accounted righteous (Isa 53:11).

The baptism then becomes the commissioning of Jesus as Yahweh's Servant, the Righteous One. The cry of the faithful for God's righteousness to come to them in Isa 64:1("O that you would rend the heavens and come down") is echoed in "behold the heaven were opened" (Matt 3:16) and Jesus seeing "the Spirit of God coming down like a dove and alighting upon him" is the fulfillment of Isa 42:1 ("I will put my Spirit upon him), further expressed in 44:3; 48:16; 57:16; 59:21; 61:1. In this context, "the voice from heaven" is God's response to the faithful, who have addressed him as "Father" (Isa 63:16; 64:8), in recognition that they are God's Servant and son. The words of the heavenly Father to Jesus, "This is my son, the beloved, in whom I am well pleased," follow quite naturally and indicate that Jesus is that Servant. The statement thus combines many of the descriptions of Israel as Servant of Yahweh using Isa 42:1 as the basic quotation. The insertion of "the beloved" instead of "my chosen" of Isa 42:1 adds a theme often expressed in Deutero-Isaiah regarding the Servant (cf. 43:4; 44:2 ["Jeshurun" was a term of endearment which the LXX translated as "the beloved"]), as a true son of Abraham who had been called God's "beloved" in Isa 41:8. "Son" and "servant" were interchangeable designations in a covenant relationship (cf. 2 Sam 7; 2 Kgs 16:7; also Wis Sol 2:12–18). So by naming Jesus "my son," God was identifying him as Servant Israel, as the ideal representative of God's faithful people (called "sons of God" in Matt 5:9).

That Isa 42:1–4 thus played such an important role in describing Jesus' mission, the reader is reminded once more in Matt 12:18–21 where Matthew quotes the passage at length with slight changes to emphasize that Jesus as Servant will bring justice to victory and that in his role the nations have hope. The disciples Peter, James and John are again reminded of Jesus commissioning according to Isa 42 when they see Jesus transfigured before them in a vision on the high mountain, and the voice from the bright cloud announcing: "This is my beloved son in whom I am well pleased; listen to him" (Matt 17:1–8). As this is said to have taken place six days after their visit to Caesarea Philippi where Simon Peter made his bold confession, the mountain was likely Mount Hermon where Enoch and Levi had been commissioned and received visions according to 1 En 12–16 and Aramaic Levi Document 3–4. It was at Mount Hermon where Enoch in a vision was called up by the clouds into heaven where he saw the "Great Glory" sitting on a throne with his garments "shining more brightly than the sun, whiter than any snow" (1 En 14:20), and who addressed him as "scribe of righteousness" and commanded him to "listen to my voice" (1 En 15:1). Enoch was then charged to pass judgment on the fallen watchers and their offspring and promise deliverance to the faithful.[15] Similarly, in the vision on the high mountain, Peter, James and John see Jesus transfigured before them—"his face shone like the sun, and his garments became white as light" from reflecting the "Great Glory" of 1 En 14:20. The voice from the cloud commanding them to "listen to him" is the reaffirmation of the commissioning of Jesus as Servant Israel. The transfiguration is essentially a vision of the foretaste of the new age when "the righteous will shine like the sun in the kingdom of their Father (Matt 13:43; cf. Dan 12:1–3; 1 En 58:3).

The testing of Jesus in the wilderness as God's son, which follows his baptism (Matt 4:1–11), shows that Jesus is capable of fulfilling the role of Servant Israel. Where Israel had failed in the wilderness, Jesus passes every test as God's son, rejecting every temptation by quoting relevant passages from the account of Israel's wandering in the wilderness in Deut 8:3; 6:16 and 6:13. Thus Jesus had met the test of covenant faithfulness and was worthy to function as Servant Israel.

JESUS AS SON OF GOD / ANOINTED ONE

By now it should be clear that "Son of God" does not necessarily have connotations of divinity but signifies one who acts on God's behalf as his Servant, as his witness, being in harmony with God's will, plan and purpose. This has been evident in the infancy narrative, both in the quotation from Isa 7:14 in 1:23 and from Hos 11:1 in 2:15, as well as in the baptismal quotation from Isa 42:1 (3:17) and the account of the testing in the wilderness (4:1–11).[16] In the past, the term "Son of God" was a designation for Israel (Exod 4:22–23; Hos 1:10 [Heb 2:1]; 11:1; Jer 3:14, 19, 22; 31:20; Isa 63:8) or kings (2 Sam 7:14) who were to be God's servants and witnesses before the nations. It was this understanding that led to the messianic "son of David" to be referred to as "son of God," as one who was to bring about God's justice and righteousness.

The case of the disciples in a boat caught in a storm in which they see Jesus coming to them and calming the sea is different. When they cry out in amazement and gratitude: "Truly, you are God's Son" (14:33), they were acknowledging with traditional prophetic understanding that Jesus was God's Spirit-filled Servant. It is this way also that the centurion and those with him who experienced the earthquake at the time of Jesus' death must be understood when they uttered similar words: "Truly, this was God's Son" (27:52). In neither of these cases does it imply divinity any more than Jesus was implying divinity for the peacemakers when he called them "sons of God" (5:9). In each case it is the recognition and acknowledgment that Jesus has been representing the will and purpose of God.[17] All this is brought to greater clarity in Peter's confession at Caesarea Philippi, where he responds to the question of who Jesus is as Son of Man with: "You are the Anointed One, the Son of the Living God" (16:16). The term, "Son of the Liv-

---

15. In the Aramaic Levi Document, Levi is seen praying and being commissioned as "worthy of the priesthood" at the mountain. Cf. Stone, "Enoch, Aramaic Levi," 159–70; Kugler, *From Patriarch to Priest*. In Test. Levi 2:7, which draws on 1 En 12–16, Levi receives his commission on the "high mountain," Mt. Hermon. See Nickelsberg, "Enoch, Levi and Peter," 575–800.

16. Contra Luz, *Theology*, 30–37, who regards all of these as presenting divine sonship.

17. Contra, e.g., Verseput, "Role and Meaning of the 'Son of God' Title," 532–56.

ing God" recalls the title given to Israel as God's people restored to faithfulness in Hos 1:10. Peter was thus emphasizing the representative nature of Jesus' mission as Son of Man / Servant.

However, it must be recognized that the two aspects of Peter's confession, "the Anointed One" and "Son of the Living God" stand together. This is the first time a disciple of Jesus refers to him as the "Anointed One." As we have seen, those who followed the prophetic vision would understand that term quite differently than those who connected that title to a royal son of David. Here Peter, on behalf of the disciples, is claiming that Jesus is that "Anointed One" as Servant Israel in terms of Isa 61:1. That is unquestionably made clear by the use of that term in Matt 11:2 where John the Baptist inquires about Jesus' role, having heard of "the works of the Anointed One." The list of works in Jesus' reply (11:4–6) clearly recalls Isa 61:1–3 which draws on signs of the restoration of God's people spoken of earlier in Isa 25:8; 26:19; 29:18; 35:5, 6; 42:7, 16–21.

After Peter had made that declaration and received Jesus' acknowledgment for having understood Jesus' mission, Jesus charges the disciples to tell no one that he is the "Anointed One" (16:20). The reason for this is obvious, because in the popular thinking that title would have been understood politically as referring to a royal figure, a son of David. That is how the high priest used it in seeking to condemn Jesus of rebellion against Rome (26:63), as also by some members of his Sanhedrin (26:68). This was the basis of their condemnation of Jesus before Pontius Pilate as one claiming to be "king of the Jews" (27:11–14). Pilate may already have been made aware of Jesus' ministry as a peacemaker and healer rather than some militant messiah. We are told that Pilate saw no fault in Jesus but knew that it was out of jealousy that the chief priests and elders were condemning him. As well, his wife had pleaded with him that Jesus was "that righteous man" (27:19). So Pilate offered as one for release either Barabbas, a known criminal, or "Jesus who is called Anointed One." When the chief priests and elders asked for the release of Barabbas, Pilate seemed taken aback and asked: "Then what shall I do with Jesus who is *called* Anointed One?" Pilate may have been apprised of the ambiguity of that title for he saw Jesus as innocent and refused to take on the responsibility of Jesus' crucifixion (27:23–25).

GATHERING DISCIPLES FOR THE MISSION

Acknowledged now as one who is to exemplify Servant Israel, Jesus sets about gathering twelve close disciples to represent the twelve tribes to train and teach them to be Servant Israel and to carry on the mission after him. After John the Baptist was arrested by Herod Antipas, Jesus returned to Galilee and, leaving his hometown of Nazareth, set up the center for his mission in Capernaum because this was the gateway to the whole area of Upper Galilee and the surrounding districts, previously known as Zebulon and Naphtali. Quoting from Isa 9:1–2, Matthew changed "walking in darkness" to "*sat* in darkness" to bring it into line with Isa 42:7 to refer to those who were to become a *light* to the nations. In gathering Israel together to be the corporate Servant of Yahweh, Jesus first had to go to those who had always maintained the prophetic vision.

The Prophetic Vision and the Mission of Jesus

After Jesus had become known there as proclaiming a message similar to that of John the Baptist (4:17), he began to gather his first disciples to join him in the mission. The first four, Simon who was later named Peter, his brother Andrew, and two other brothers, James and John, the sons of Zebedee (4:18–22), would have been members of the prophetic communities in that area. So when they heard Jesus' call they were ready to follow immediately. Simon and Andrew were originally from Bethsaida, a few kilometers east of Capernaum (John 1:44) and Andrew had already been a follower of John the Baptist (John 1:35–40). James and John were evidently from a family that held to the prophetic tradition and who remained committed to Jesus' mission (Matt 20:20; 27:56). All four fishermen were ready to become "fishers of men" to gather the people of Israel "out of the land of the north" (Jer 16:14–16) to carry out God's plan. For, they were all familiar with the preaching of the Baptist, and the intense hope that had built up among the people for the coming of the kingdom of God. Jesus' message of the good news of God's reign further inspired them, and they were ready to participate in the inauguration of the kingdom.

The only other disciple mentioned specifically as being called to be one of the Twelve is Matthew whom Jesus saw sitting in his tax office in Capernaum and said to him, "Follow me." To this, like the others, Matthew immediately complied (9:9), evidently also one who was familiar with the prophetic vision. In parallel verses in Luke 5:27 and Mark 2:14, he is known as "Levi" which would indicate that Matthew was of Levite background. In fact, "Matthew" is the Greek equivalent of the Hebrew "Maththiah" (cf. 1 Chr 9:31; Neh 8:4), or "Mattaniah" (cf. 2 Kgs 24:17; Neh 11:17, 22), both meaning "Gift of Yahweh" and both common Levite names. Levite tradition had always emphasized education, which would have stood Matthew in good stead as a customs official responsible for collecting duty on goods being brought into or leaving the territory of Herod Antipas.

The long and notorious history of tax collectors, particularly during the Ptolemaic and Seleucid periods, had left tax collectors with a reputation for using their offices to enrich themselves, and regarded as collaborators with the forces of oppression. Such persons were regarded as shut out of the messianic kingdom and were commonly associated with "sinners" and "Gentiles." By inviting Matthew to become one of the chosen Twelve, Jesus was acknowledging that he would certainly be a member of God's kingdom, and by further inviting him to dine at his house (9:10) was indicating that the "unclean" label was false, much to the chagrin of the Pharisees (9:11). Even though Jesus is depicted in this Gospel as using the common Pharisaic saying of rejection which labels tax collectors together with Gentiles and sinners (5:46–47; 18:17; cf. 9:11), it is the only Gospel that also records that Jesus told the chief priests and elders that the tax collectors and the harlots would enter the kingdom of God before them (21:32).

Matthew evidently was not only moved by Jesus' open proclamation of God's forgiveness and invitation to become part of the kingdom of God, but had already been a member of the prophetic community with all its hopes for the faithful, and so eagerly responded to Jesus' call. However, there may well have been another reason for Jesus choosing Matthew to be one of the Twelve. This first Gospel is the only one that mentions certain scribes in a good light while others related to Pharisees and chief priests are condemned as hypocrites or working against the kingdom. In 8:19–22, a certain *scribe* wants to be a disciple and to follow Jesus wherever he goes. At the end of his explanation to the disciples of the parables, Jesus concludes: "Therefore every *scribe* who has been trained for the kingdom of heaven is like a householder who brings out of his treasure what is new and what is old" (13:52). Then in the list of covenant curses condemning "scribes, Pharisees, hypocrites" given in Jerusalem (23:13–33) Jesus finishes by saying: "Therefore I send you prophets and wise men and *scribes*, some of whom you will kill and crucify and some you will scourge in your synagogues and persecute from town to town" (23:34). The scribes referred to in these verses would be those who copy and disseminate the prophetic writings. Matthew himself may well have served as such a scribe, and as such would have been well versed to understand and record Jesus' prophetic mission. One cannot escape the possible conclusion that the author of this Gospel with all its prophetic quotations and allusions may very well be that Apostle Matthew writing a decade or so after the resurrection event as the first Gospel.[18]

JESUS AS SON OF MAN

So much has been written on the origin and meaning of the ambiguous title, "Son of Man," and why only Jesus uses this term in the Gospels; whether Jesus uses it as a self-designation or whether he is sometimes speaking of some future individual. However, when one sees the development of this designation in the prophetic vision, it becomes clear why Jesus uses it. It is the development of the Servant concept as understood from the time of the persecution under Antiochus Epiphanes down through the reign of Herod. The book of Daniel had used that term to describe those who remained faithful during persecution and who would be finally vindicated, calling them "the holy ones of the Most High." We have seen how the author of the Parables of Enoch combined all the Servant descriptions—the Righteous One, the Chosen One, Anointed One—under the general title, "that Son of Man," as one who would exemplify, represent, and lead the righteous, chosen people of God to carry out God's plan as his Servant. However, like the Servant designation, it retains the tension between the individual and the faithful community. As the individual or as the corporate body of the faithful, the Servant / Son of Man has the role of speaking with authority in representing the divine purpose, and bringing about the restoration of God's reign in the hearts and lives of people in every nation. Whether as individual or corporate body the ultimate goal of the Servant / Son of Man is to bring God's almighty plan to victory (cf. Matt 12:20—Isa 42:4). It is this goal which Jesus calls the people of Israel to fulfill.[19]

18. Once again we are reminded of those words of Papias, bishop of Hierapolis (ca. 100–110) who stated: "Matthew put together the sayings [of Jesus] in the Hebrew language and each one interpreted them as he was able" (quoted by Eusebius, *His. Eccl.* 3.39.16).

19. Without a thorough acquaintance of this prophetic development, one is left in a sea of different hypotheses, muddied by questions of whether this figure is heavenly or human, or of some foreign origin. However, there have been a number of scholars who have recognized the tension between the individual or corporate concepts in the sayings of Jesus, e.g., Moule, *Origin of Christology*, 11–22; Black, "Aramaic Barnasha," 200–206; Hooker, *Son of Man in Mark*. Hooker, however, denies any connection of the term with the Servant motif.

Jesus obviously used this concept to describe his ministry and that of his disciples because it incorporates all those prophetic descriptions of the faithful as combined in the Parables of Enoch under the designation "that Son of Man" who is the leader and exemplifier of the righteous and chosen ones in an intimate union with them in both suffering and vindication. Jesus both uses this term of himself while at the same time retaining the corporate nature of the term as portrayed in Dan 7–12.

One has to assume that since Jesus uses this title without explanation that he takes it for granted that most of his hearers have some idea of the significance and meaning of this designation. Jesus had, after all, begun his ministry in Capernaum in order to reach out to those who had espoused the prophetic vision. The first two references to "Son of Man" are uttered in Capernaum, and it is probably from there that Jesus sends out the Twelve to proclaim the good news of the kingdom to those who were waiting for it. The first time Jesus is said to use this term is in response to that scribe in Capernaum who exclaimed: "Teacher, I will follow you wherever you go." Jesus reminded him that "foxes have holes and the birds of the air have nests but the Son of Man has nowhere to lay his head" (8:19, 20). Jesus was warning him that commitment to the kingdom does not promise political or economic security, and there would be suffering before vindication. This scribe was likely familiar with the prophetic writings and its message and would have known how "Son of Man" was used in Dan 7 and in the Parables of Enoch. He would have understood that Jesus was speaking about the mission of the Servant and its hazards under Jesus' leadership.

This corporate understanding is also evident in the story of the healing of the paralytic (9:1–8). In Deutero-Isaiah the proclamation of the good news always involved the message of God's forgiveness (40:2; 43:25; 44:22), so it was quite natural for Jesus to announce that to the paralytic as part of the process of his healing. When this was challenged Jesus' response was to show that "the Son of Man has authority on earth to forgive sins." Seeing this, the crowds glorified God that he had give such authority to *human beings*. The crowds here understood "Son of Man" as representing God's faithful people of which Jesus was the exemplar.[20] Practicing forgiveness for one another as God forgives is a part of being the children of God (6:12, 14–15). Jesus later reminds his disciples of *their* authority both to forgive sins and pronounce judgment (16:19; 18:18).

THE MISSION OF JESUS AND THE TWELVE, AND THE SON OF MAN

After Jesus had chosen twelve close disciples to represent the twelve tribes of Israel, he sent them out among the people of Galilee with the same good news he had been proclaiming, and to carry out healings as he had done as signs of the restoration of God's people. He strictly commanded them to go "only to the lost sheep of the house of Israel" and not to the Gentiles or Samaritans. The Twelve would have recognized that Jesus was directing them at this stage to go house to house only to those who were looking for the fulfillment of the prophetic vision but lacked anyone to lead them. The "lost sheep of the house of Israel" were those who had just been described as "harassed and helpless, like

---

20. Cf. Hooker, *Son of Man in Mark*, 90–92.

The Prophetic Vision and the Real Jesus

sheep without a shepherd" (9:36). In the past, the phrase described the faithful who had been either led astray or abandoned by leaders who were self-serving and corrupt (cf. Jer 50:6–7; Ezek 34:1–16; Zech 10:2–3). It was not any different in Jesus' time with the Jerusalem priesthood seen as corrupt and with the Pharisees requiring strict adherence to their traditions without practicing them themselves (cf. 15:1–14; 23:13–36). The people needed to be gathered together first of all to live as members of God's kingdom as a true covenant people. Only then could they be a light to the nations and be the Servant / Son of Man. It was this gathering of Israel into the kingdom, that Jesus saw as his mission first and foremost, as he told the Canaanite woman (15:21–28).

This initial mission into Upper Galilee and the surrounding area had all the elements of being a brief foray into all the towns and villages where the prophetic communities were dominant in order to call them to join in bringing about the transformation of Israel. The Twelve are dependent on the goodwill of the people they call on. They take no supplies for a long stay, nor do they remain to dispute with those who reject their message, for their task is simply to proclaim and demonstrate that the kingdom of God has come, calling all to be part of it. For with the coming of the kingdom, there also comes judgment on those who reject it. It is because of this that there is a sense of urgency about it.

That sense of urgency was later carried over to Matthew's own community who continued to carry on the mission to the "lost sheep of the house of Israel" after Jesus had handed over his ministry to the apostles.[21] They are also reminded that they are sent out as "sheep in the midst of wolves," recognizing that they are constantly facing the influence of the Pharisees in Galilee with their false interpretation of the Law (10:16; cf. 7:15–20). They are to be wise in the ways of the Pharisees ("serpents," cf. 23:33) but keep themselves pure, motivated only by the Spirit of God ("doves," cf. 3:16; 10:19–20). Like Jesus, their master and teacher, they could expect to suffer at the hands of those in power and dragged before governors and kings for a *witness* to them, for they *are* God's witnesses (Isa 43:10–12; 44:8; 55:4–5), a light to the nations (Isa 42:6–7). The message of the good news of the reign of God, which brings joy and gladness to those who respond, also brings a message of judgment on those who reject it, bringing conflict even within families when some resist the call to faithfulness, as in the days of Micah (Mic 7:5–6). All this is a sign of the coming end of the present age (10:21; cf. 1 En 100:1–9).

There is much in this exhortation to mission that draws on the apocalyptic language of 1 Enoch. "I have not come to bring peace, but a sword" (10:34) picks up the idea expressed in the Apocalypse of Weeks (1 En 91:11–17) wherein in the eighth week, the period of righteousness, a sword is given to all the righteous to carry out righteous judgment against the wicked (4Q212.IV.14–16). In the Animal Apocalypse (1 En 90:20–27) it is the Lord of the sheep who carries out judgment on all the forces of evil and oppression, as well as on the blind sheep. All are bound and cast into the fiery abyss in the Valley of Hinnom (cf. also 1 En 26:1—27:5). The statement in Matt 10:28, "rather fear him who can destroy both soul and body in Gehenna," draws on this graphic picture of judgment, as do all the other references in this Gospel to *geenna* (5:22, 29, 30; 18:9; 23:15, 33). After the judgment, the sword that has been given to the sheep can be laid down and sealed

---

21. Cf. Brown, "Mission to Israel," 73–90.

before the Lord (1 En 90:34). However, in the later Parables of Enoch, it speaks of the "Son of Man who has righteousness" as the one who will unseat the kings and the mighty and the exalted and judge them (1 En 46:1–8; 38:1–2). The Chosen One will be seated on God's throne (1 En 51:1–5) and "will slay the sinners with the word of his mouth" (1 En 62:12; cf. Isa 11:4). Thus, when Matthew's community is told that they "will not have finished going through all the towns of Israel before the Son of Man comes" (10:23), this coming of the Son of Man should be understood simply as a way of referring to the Day of Judgment when the faithful will finally be exonerated. "All the towns of Israel" would include all towns, cities and villages throughout Galilee, Judea, and the Diaspora where people of Israel resided. The corporate nature of the Son of Man coming as judge is further illustrated by Jesus' remark to Peter that in the restoration "when the Son of Man shall sit on his glorious throne" those who have followed him "will also sit on twelve thrones judging the twelve tribes of Israel" (19:28).

Because of centuries of living under oppressive rule, both foreign and native, and with the growing expectation among the population that the time of judgment on their oppressors was near, the specter of that Day and the end of that age of suffering lurks behind everything in Jesus' teaching. The urgency of gathering Israel together to witness as God's covenant people, therefore, has to be the foremost mission of Jesus and his disciples, but the ultimate goal of being a light to the nations in never forgotten. For the end of the age will only come after the good news of the kingdom of God has been proclaimed throughout the whole world, as a witness to all nations (24:14). This point is already hinted at in 10:18: "for a witness to them and to the nations." It is only when the training of his disciples is completed and after Jesus has been vindicated in the resurrection that Jesus can then send out his disciples, as Servant Israel, to be that light to the nations (28:18–20).[22] Meanwhile, the mission to Israel to join them as witnesses to the nations will continue until the close of the age and the "coming of the Son of Man" (10:23).

GROWING RESISTANCE TO AND REJECTION OF THE MISSION

It is evident from the theme of persecution that the initial mission did not result in complete success. While crowds of those harassed and helpless continued to seek the message of renewal, there were many, even among those who held to the prophetic tradition, who resisted Jesus' and the disciples' call to become Servant Israel. Even John the Baptist had not understood Jesus' mission (11:2–6), and Jesus expressed frustration with "this generation" (11:16) for their inability to see beyond their preconceived notion of how the kingdom of God would come about. They had rejected the strict preparations for the coming kingdom by the Baptist and his followers, and criticized Jesus and his disciples for celebrating the coming kingdom with tax collectors and sinners (11:17–19). The use of the term "Son of Man" here (11:19) would cover both Jesus and his disciples, for Jesus condemns some of the towns where he and the disciples had proclaimed the good news in their mission to the "lost sheep of the house of Israel," but where they were met with

---

22. Cf. Jeremias, *Jesus' Promise to the Nations*, 38–39.

diffidence and rejection. Even Capernaum, where Jesus lived, came under a judgment to be worse than that of the land of Sodom (11:20–24; cf. 10:12).

Jesus' response to this growing lack of understanding and commitment was a prayer of thanksgiving to God for those whose hearts have been open to his message, a prayer which reveals much about how Jesus saw his mission in terms of the prophetic vision (11:25–30). The unique address, "Father, Lord of heaven and earth," recalls the urging of Deutero-Isaiah for Israel in exile to know that *their* God is the Lord, the creator of heaven and earth, who redeems them (Isa 40:12–31; 42:5), and who calls them forth to be his witnesses before the nations (43:8–13). "Father" is the intimate title by which Jesus had taught his followers to address God, based on the cry of the faithful in Isa 63:16; 64:8 (cf. 29:16!). That God has "hidden these things from the wise and understanding" recalls the words of Isa 29:13–14 which refers to false leaders who regard themselves as such and honor God with their lips but not their heart, a passage which Jesus later quoted against the Pharisees and scribes from Jerusalem (15:8). That God has "revealed these things to babes" alludes to Isa 28:9 in the same general context ("To whom will he teach *knowledge*, and to whom will he explain the message? Those weaned from the milk? Those taken from the breast?"). The *babes* are, of course, the disciples who have accepted the "knowledge" which Jesus has taught. That "knowledge" (v. 27) is to be understood in the Semitic sense of "being in relationship with" God. "Well-pleasing" in v. 26 has its origin in Isa 42:1, quoted in Matt 12:18 and used in the divine pronouncement at Jesus' baptism (3:17) and transfiguration (17:5). In these pronouncements the Father acknowledged his relationship with Jesus as Son/Servant.

The crucial word in v. 27, and really for this whole prayer, is "know" which emphasizes that intimate relationship between Father and Son. Servant Israel was called to "know" God (Isa 42:21–23, 28; 43:10), for "by his knowledge" the righteous Servant "shall make many to be accounted righteous" (53:11). In this context the statement that "no one knows the Son except the Father" alludes to the cry of the faithful in Isa 63:16 ("For you are our Father, though Abraham does not know us and Israel does not acknowledge us"). The statement "no one knows the Father except the Son and anyone to whom he chooses to reveal him" alludes to Isa 45:14 where the nations are depicted as finally coming to Israel seeking to become part of the covenant people, acknowledging that "God is with you only, and there is no other, no god beside him." In any case, the two sayings together make up a classic statement of covenant relationship (cf. Hos 2:20), and it is the role of Servant Israel to gather all the scattered of Israel to be a people-covenant and a light to the nations so that God's salvation may reach to the ends of the earth (Isa 49:108; 42:6). It is through his Servant/Son that God reveals the hidden things according to Isa 48:6–8; 52:15; 53:1, 11. According to the Parables of Enoch, it is this Righteous One of Isa 53:11 who reveals the hidden things to the righteous and chosen ones and judges the wicked (1 En 8:3; 51:3; 61:13; 62:7; 69:26), just as Jesus reveals the "secrets of the kingdom of heaven" to the disciples (Matt 13:11).

The open invitation which now follows (v. 28) to all those who labor and are burdened is the call of Isa 40:28–30 to the faint and weary to find renewal and strength in the good news that God reigns. It is an invitation to the kingdom, to become as "babes." Recalling once again the failure of those religious leaders in Isa 28:12 to heed God's call to find rest and repose for the weary, Jesus promises the weary: "I will give you rest." It has the meaning of experiencing peace and security without fear of oppression or hostility (cf. Deut 12:9, 10; Isa 32:18). With the invitation, "Take my yoke upon you and learn from me, for I am afflicted[23] and lowly in heart . . . for my yoke is easy and my burden is light" (11:29–30), Jesus was expressing solidarity with the faithful, with those "afflicted and broken-hearted" (Isa 61:1), the "crushed and lowly in spirit" (Isa 57:15; 66:2; cf. Ps 34:18–19), with the suffering Servant (Isa 53:4, 7). It expresses the same solidarity and relatedness as the term "Son of Man" with humankind, and the "Righteous and Chosen One" in the Parables of Enoch with the "righteous and chosen ones." His yoke of commitment which brings freedom is contrasted with the yoke of the Pharisees which binds the people with heavy burdens of uncertainty with their legalism. There appears to be a deliberate allusion here to the invitation of wisdom in Sir 24:19–34; 51:23–30 to show that the words of the "wise and understanding" is not enough—true wisdom must be demonstrated by action (11:19).

THE GROWING OPPOSITION OF THE PHARISEES TO JESUS' MISSION

In spite of Jesus' emphasis on his mission being to gather the "lost sheep of the house of Israel" together, to bring them into the kingdom of God in a meaningful relationship with their heavenly Father, Jesus always had as his ultimate goal their thus becoming a living people-covenant, a light to the nations. That was evident when Jesus lauded the great faith of the centurion who had requested that Jesus heal his servant. The faith of this Gentile led Jesus to exclaim: "I tell you that many will come from east and west and sit at table with Abraham, Isaac, and Jacob in the kingdom of heaven, while the sons of the kingdom will be thrown into outer darkness; there men will weep and gnash their teeth" (8:11–12). This was evident also in the healing of the Canaanite woman's daughter because of her mother's great faith (15:21–28). On the basis of this, it has been argued that part of the reason for opposition to Jesus' mission was that he spoke of Gentiles becoming part of the kingdom of God without mentioning punishment or revenge for centuries of oppression by Gentile nations. Jesus had always taught that kingdom members would overcome evil with love rather than hate, with forgiveness rather than revenge. Yet those who had experienced oppression and injustice, even among those who followed the prophetic tradition, could point to those passages in the prophets which spoke of the day of vengeance (e.g., Isa 35:4; 61:2), or which spoke of the nations serving Israel (e.g., Dan 7:14; Isa 61:5). Yet Jesus would tell his disciples that the Son of Man came not to be served but to serve (20:28) as the righteous Servant of Isa 53.[24] Jesus did, of course, speak about judgment, but it was always for those who rejected God's compassionate rule.

---

23. Cf. Matt 5:3, 5.

24. Jeremias, *Jesus' Promise to the Nations*, 40–54.

The Prophetic Vision and the Real Jesus

Pharisaic Opposition to the Mission

However, the greatest opposition to Jesus and his mission came from the Pharisees and scribes who had had such influence among the people in Galilee since the time of John Hyrcanus. Certainly, they bore no love for the Gentile nations, but their main bone of contention was over Jesus' teaching of the kingdom and the basis on which people could enter it. Jesus' message of an easy yoke and light burden were drawing the common people away from the hold scribes and Pharisees had maintained on them with their heavy legalistic "yoke of the Torah" (cf. *m. Abot* 3:5; *m. Berakot* 2:2). Their confrontation with Jesus was thus always over matters of law and the tradition of the elders.

The first confrontation over law which Matthew highlights is regarding the Sabbath. The Pharisees had taken the law of the Sabbath and hedged it around with thirty-nine prohibitions of activities on that day (*m. Sabb* 7:2). One of those activities was "reaping," and when the Pharisees saw Jesus' disciples plucking a few heads of grain to eat (permissible by law, Lev 19:9–10; Deut 23:25) on the Sabbath they regarded that as reaping (12:1–8). The Sabbath had been originally established in the Sinai covenant as a day for rest and reflection on their covenant relationship with God in thankfulness for having been delivered from slavery, where they were never given rest. The Pharisees had turned a compassionate law into a heavy burden. Once again Jesus had to remind them of the divine word in Hos 6:6: "I desire steadfast love and not sacrifice," which if they had heeded, they would have recognized that "the Son of Man is lord of the Sabbath" (12:7–8). "Son of Man" here is used in the corporate sense of those who remain in covenant faithfulness with their God and thus can understand God's intention in the law (cf. Matt 23:8–10). The Pharisees even categorized Jesus' healing on the Sabbath as work, rather than compassion, and thus of breaking the law of Exod 31:14, an action deserving of death. Jesus counters with their own interpretation of that law allowing a man to rescue his sheep from a pit on the Sabbath. Left without rejoinder, the Pharisees planned how they might destroy Jesus (12:9–14).

Matthew then interrupts these episodes of Pharisaic confrontations with the full quotation of Isa 42:1–4 to remind the reader that Jesus is fulfilling the role of Servant Israel, and as such will not stay and argue which would only lead to further polarization. Instead, Jesus continues to gather the faithful to be that Servant and thus bring God's justice to the nations (12:18–21).

The confrontation continues (12:22–37) when Jesus heals a blind and dumb demoniac. The Pharisees would have interpreted this man's condition as a result of a covenant curse for some sin committed (Deut 28:28–29; cf. John 9:1–34) and so they ridicule Jesus' healing as the work of Satan. But it is by the Spirit of God (Isa 42:1) that Jesus casts out demons, and so the kingdom of God has come upon them (12:28). By alluding to Isa 49:22–25, Jesus was saying that by healing and casting out demons he was gathering people into the kingdom and thus *binding* Satan. Anyone, therefore, who did not *gather* with him was *scattering* and thus preventing the people from being gathered into God's kingdom. So Jesus warns the Pharisees that speaking against the Son of Man, the faithful Servant, can be forgiven, but to speak against the Spirit of God is unforgivable (12:31–32).

The Prophetic Vision and the Mission of Jesus

When the scribes and Pharisees ask Jesus for a sign from God regarding his prophetic authority, the only sign Jesus will give is the sign of Jonah (12:38–42). Just as Jonah, as Israel, had to undergo a death and resurrection experience in order to do God's will and preach to Gentile Nineveh, so would the scribes and Pharisees need such a drastic experience to finally see and fulfill Israel's mission to the nations. Just so, the Son of Man as true Israel would be three days and three nights in the "heart of the earth" as Jonah was in the "heart of the seas" (Jonah 2:2) in order to be fully directed to the ultimate goal of making disciples of all nations. It was the same pattern laid down in Hos 5:14—6:2 and identified of Servant Israel in Isa 53. While this is usually understood as Jesus referring to his own later death and resurrection,[25] Matthew does not say that. Moreover, it would not have been understood that way by the disciples prior to Matt 16:21, or by the Pharisees. Israel needed to undergo this transformation in order carry out its God-given task. Nevertheless, this is a sign Jesus himself would exemplify, for the kingdom of God being at hand urgently called for Israel to fulfill its purpose (12:41–42).[26]

It was this opposition and lack of understanding that prompted Jesus to address the crowds by speaking in parables. Those who had the ears of faith would understand but those who sought to criticize his teaching would find it difficult. This was the "Son" revealing the Father to those whom he chooses (11:27), the Son of Man revealing the "hidden things" to the righteous ones (1 En 62:5). Thus Jesus' response to the disciples who asked why he spoke in parables was: "To you it has been given to know the "secrets" of the kingdom of heaven, but to them it has not been given" (13:11), those who still suffered from the spiritual deafness and blindness described long ago in Isa 6:9–10. These are the weeds among the wheat which cannot be dealt with by violent confrontation (cf. Matt 12:15–21; Isa 42:1–4) but would come under judgment at the close of the age when the Son of Man sends his messengers to gather out of the kingdom all cause of sin and all evildoers (13:37–43). The imagery behind this parable is drawn from the Parables of Enoch where Enoch sees "all the secrets of heaven, how the kingdom is divided, and how the deeds of humanity are weighed in the balance" (1 En 41:1–2), and where evildoers are delivered by the Son of Man to the angels of punishment so that the righteous can rejoice in the presence of the Lord of Spirits (1 En 62:9–12; cf. Matt 13:49; 16:27; 24:31; 25:31).

Matthew alternates stories of opposition with stories of the crowds of the "harassed and helpless" seeking out Jesus. This is to point out that while those influential leaders oppose him, the common people are still responding to Jesus in great numbers. So while even people of his hometown of Nazareth reject him (13:53–58), when Jesus goes to a lonely place to pray and reflect on the beheading of John the Baptist by Herod Antipas (14:1–12), crowds follow him there on foot, and Jesus heals their sick and feeds them (14:13–21). Again, when he and his disciples land at Gennesaret the word gets around and many come bringing those who were sick. Others simply touch the tassels on Jesus' shawl as a sign of their seeking renewal of their covenant relationship with their forgiving God in order to "be saved through it" (14:34–36; cf. 9:20–21).

---

25. E.g., Luz, *Matthew 8–20*, 217–18.
26. See further Leske, "Matthew," 1293–96; cf. also Black, "Aramaic Barnasha," 200–206.

A further confrontation with Pharisees and scribes coming from Jerusalem follows (15:1–9). This time it is to accuse Jesus' disciples of not washing their hands before they eat—a trivial matter, but it was seen as acting against the strict purity laws of the elders. Jesus countered by condemning them for not honoring their parents, one of the basic covenant stipulations, by using their legal tradition of *qorban* to evade any financial obligations to parents.[27] In the list of covenant curses against the scribes and Pharisees as hypocrites (23:13–33), Jesus condemns them for being so concerned about trivial matters and neglecting the weightier matters of the law such as justice, steadfast love, and faithfulness. They had become "blind guides, straining at a gnat and swallowing a camel!" (23:23–24). Such legalism indicated that they were obviously not part of the planting of the Lord (Isa 60:21) and so would be uprooted (Matt 15:13).

The story of the faith of the Canaanite woman follows as a contrast to that of the scribes and Pharisees (15:21–28). Then ensues the story of the "great crowds" coming to Jesus to be healed and glorifying God, the occasion of Jesus and his disciples feeding the five thousand (15:29–38) as a second kind of celebration of the reign of God according to Isa 55:1–2. However, before long it is back to the Pharisees who have joined up with members of the priestly party of the Sadducees to try to test Jesus by asking him for a sign from heaven (16:1–6). Once again Jesus tells them that the only sign he will give is the sign of Jonah.

These confrontations illustrate the great gulf that existed between Jesus and the scribes and Pharisees in their perceptions of God, his kingdom, and Israel's mission. For the Pharisees, God was a God of stern justice who required keeping all his laws as they interpreted them. For Jesus, God was the loving, compassionate and forgiving God of Isa 40–66, who brings recompense and reward to his people, feeding his flock like a shepherd, gathering the lambs in his arms and carrying them in his bosom, gently leading those with young (Isa 40:10–11). He is a God who calls Israel to turn to him and be gathered into his kingdom with the promise: "My steadfast love will not depart from you, and my covenant of peace shall not be removed, says Yahweh, who has compassion on you" (Isa 54:10). Such a compassionate God calls Israel to show the same compassion to the nations and bring them into the kingdom. Law, for Jesus, was always to be interpreted according to the double commandment to love God and one's neighbor (Matt 22:40).

The words Jesus later addressed to the crowds and to his disciples to practice and observe whatever the scribes and Pharisees say, but not what they do (23:2–3) has been widely misunderstood.[28] The situation in Galilee at the time of Jesus was such that for

---

27. Leske, "Matthew," 1301.

28. E.g., Sanders, *Jesus and Judaism*, 292, through a series of anomalous arguments which deny the authenticity of the above confrontations comes to the conclusion that "we *know* of no substantial dispute about the law, nor any substantial conflict with the Pharisees." Mason, "Pharisaic Dominance," 363–81, expresses the common assumption: "The saying explicitly affirms Pharisaic primacy in legal interpretation" (372) and concludes that Jesus endorses the Pharisaic system and yet accuses the Pharisees in general of hypocrisy (380). Others, such as Viviano, "Social World," 3–21, and Saldarini, "Delegitimation of Leaders," 659–80, regard the whole chapter as deriving from the Matthean community in their struggle with formative Pharisaism after 70 CE. This is taken to the bizarre conclusion by Runesson, "Rethinking Early Jewish-Christian Relations," 95–132, that the Mattheans were a group of Pharisees after 70 CE

many people the only access to the law and the prophets to which Jesus often referred (5:17; 7:12; 11:13; 22:40) was hearing the readings in the synagogues which the Pharisees had established for that purpose. By attending the synagogues on the Sabbath, the crowds would hear the spoken covenant law as well as the prophetic writings. Jesus was certainly not condoning the ways in which the scribes and Pharisees interpreted the laws in their oral tradition. "Do and observe . . . but do not do according to their works" would involve not following their interpretations of the law.[29] It was these interpretations and their failure to live up to them that led Jesus to warn the people not be taken in by the scribes and Pharisees who aggrandized themselves as such interpreters by making their phylacteries wide and their tassels long (both symbols to emphasize the law), claiming places of honor at festivals and in their synagogues, and being called rabbi (23:4–7). For, Jesus reminds his disciples (23:8–12), as members of the kingdom of God, God is their only Teacher (cf. Isa 30:20–21; 50:4–9; 54:13–17)[30] and Father (Isa 63:16; 64:8), and with God's teaching in their hearts (Isa 51:7; Jer 31:31–34) they were all equal. Neither are they to be called "guides, ones who lead the way," for there is only one guide, "the Anointed One" (the Servant who is anointed, Isa 61:1) of whom Jesus is the exemplar (Matt 11:27).

What follows is a series of prophetic woes (Isa 5:8, 11, 18, 20–22; 10:1, 5), the equivalent of covenant curses (Deut 28:15–46) on the scribes and Pharisees as hypocrites, expressed near the end of Jesus' ministry (23:13–36) in stark contrast to the covenant blessings given at the beginning of Jesus' proclamation of the kingdom in Matt 5:3–12. Specifically emphasized in relation to their synagogue reading of the law and the prophets is that the scribes and Pharisees give only lip service to the prophets but do not follow and even negate them by persecuting the prophets sent to them (23:29–37).

REASSESSMENT AND INTENSIFICATION OF THE MISSION

With this growing opposition of the religious leaders and the lack of understanding of his mission even by some who were followers of the prophetic vision, Jesus felt the need to go to the holy place of the prophetic communities at the foot of Mount Hermon, the place of revelation, to reassess his mission strategy. Most of all, he needed a renewed commitment from his disciples that they understood the mission they were deeply involved in and were aware of the ramifications of that commitment. The old stereotypes of the kingdom of God and how it would come about which had been developed over years of struggle and oppression had been hard for the disciples to erase. It would take them until after Jesus' resurrection to gain a full understanding of what it meant to be a kingdom member and live as such, and thus to carry on the mission. This is why Jesus led his disciples up to Caesarea Philippi (16:13), into the heart of the prophetic and apocalyptic communities where Enochic and Levite literature had originated.

---

who had become convinced that Jesus was Israel's Messiah and wished to remain a movement within Pharisaism, yet were in conflict with those Pharisees who did not accept Jesus (125–28).

29. Cf. Powell, "Do and Keep What Moses Says," 419–35.
30. Cf. Derrett, "Mt 23, 8–10 a Midrash," 372–86.

The Prophetic Vision and the Real Jesus

There Jesus asked his disciples, who did people understand "the Son of Man" to be. The disciples, well acquainted with the prophetic literature, would have been familiar with this term from its use in Dan 7 and its subsequent use in the Parables of Enoch (1 En 37–71). In Matthew's Gospel up to this point Jesus had used the term "Son of Man" some eight times in which that tension between the corporate and individual meaning was always evident as we have already seen.[31]

When the Pharisees and Sadducees came asking for a sign from heaven, Jesus had to point out to them that they needed to die to their old ways of self-righteousness and arrogance and be raised up to see and fulfill their covenant relationship with God and carry out God's plan. He did this by once again referring to the sign of Jonah (16:1–4), and then warns the disciples against the teachings of the Pharisees and Sadducees (16:5–12) just prior to putting this question to them about the Son of Man. For the sign of Jonah was important for them to understand too, particularly in terms of the Son of Man (cf. 12:39–41).

Simon Peter's Declaration

By asking this question Jesus was not trying to find out people's opinion about himself[32] but how the people in the prophetic communities understood the term "Son of Man" in their apocalyptic literature. That they had no clear understanding is evident from the answer of the disciples, who report that some of the people surmised that it referred to John the Baptist, others to Elijah, still others to Jeremiah or one of the prophets (16:14). Jesus then turns to asking the disciples how they perceive *him* in relation to the term "Son of Man." To this question Simon Peter responds with a spontaneous exclamation: "You are the Anointed One, the son of the Living God!" (16:16). It is important to see this answer in the context of the prophetic vision, particularly in Isa 61:1 where Trito-Isaiah, speaking on behalf of the faithful, proclaimed: "Yahweh has *anointed* me to bring good news to the afflicted." In some early Qumran manuscripts influenced by the prophetic vision, the plural "anointed ones" was used of the faithful (4Q521 and 11QMelch). Even more significant, in the Parables of Enoch "that Son of Man" is not only referred to as "the Righteous and Chosen One" but also as "his [God's] Anointed One" (48:10; 52:4). Simon Peter's response must be understood in this context.

The representative and corporate nature of Jesus' function as "the Son of Man," "the Anointed One" is further emphasized in the phrase, "son of the Living God." That phrase comes from Hos 1:10 where it referred to Israel being restored as God's people. That was picked up again in Jub 1:23–25 where the author has God assuring Moses that there will come a time when the people will return to him and he will purify them and be a father to them, and they will all be called "sons of the Living God." Similarly, in Dan 6:21 Daniel is called "servant of the living God." Simon thus sees Jesus as the harbinger

---

31. Cf. also Moule, *Origin of Christology*, 20–21.

32. So Luz, *Matthew 8–20*, 361, and others, following the post-Easter understanding found in Mark 8:27–30 and Luke 9:18–21.

and representative of that restoration.³³ It is vitally important to note here that both these titles that Simon has used of Jesus are, from the prophetic point of view, collective or corporate terms.

In response, Jesus blesses Simon for having been inspired by God to recognize his role as the representative of restored Israel, calling him "son of Jonah" for having understood the "sign" (16:4). Because of this, Jesus names him "Peter" meaning "rock," a term commonly used to indicate a sure foundation. Thus God was often depicted as Israel's rock of salvation (cf. Deut 32:15, 18, 30, 31; Isa 8:14; 26:4; 30:29; 44:8; 1QH VII.28; XIX.18; cf. Matt 7:24-27). Abraham was a rock of faithfulness to whom people should look (Isa 51:1-2). In Isa 28:16 those who have faith in God are described as "a stone, a tested stone, a precious cornerstone of a sure foundation." Those faithful to the covenant, God would establish as the foundation of his kingdom (cf. Zech 1:2:3; Dan 2:34, 35, 45). Referring to this, the Teacher of Righteousness could thank God for rescuing him from the "gates of death" and laying his foundation upon rock, making all the tested stones into a strong building that could not be shaken (1QH XII.4; XIV.27-31; XV.11-12). The Qumran Community regarded itself as this rock which is to be an everlasting plantation, a holy house for Israel (1QS VIII.4-9; IX.6; XI.2-9). It was this same expression of faith and understanding of Jesus' mission by Simon that led Jesus to name him "Peter" and on this rock (*petra*) he would build his community,³⁴ and the gates of death would not be able to prevail against it (16:18; cf. Isa 28:15-18; 38:40).

On the basis of Simon Peter's understanding of Jesus' role, Jesus promises him the keys of the kingdom of heaven. The imagery behind this promise is the account in Isa 22:15-22 where the steward Shebna is dismissed for abuse of his office, and the faithful servant Eliakim is installed in his place. Eliakim is entrusted with the keys of the house of David and is told that what he opens none shall shut, and what he shuts none shall open (v. 22). It is an image of complete trust in delegating authority, knowing that the person so entrusted will exercise that authority as the master himself would wish. Peter is thus entrusted with the authority to "bind or loose on earth" on God's behalf (16:19). This has most often been understood along the lines of later rabbinic usage to describe authority given to the rabbis to decide what was prohibited and what was permitted according to the law,³⁵ or the power to exorcise evil spirits.³⁶ However, while it may entail forgiving and retaining sins and casting out demons the concepts of binding and loosing are a development deriving from the prophetic literature.

The statement in Isa 24:22 that the hosts of heaven and the kings of the earth who were guilty of oppression and injustice would be "gathered together as prisoners in a pit . . . shut up in prison, and after many days they will be punished" became the basis of the frequent stories in the Enochic literature of the fallen angels and their human collaborators, the kings and the mighty, being *bound* hand and foot and cast into

---

33. See Leske, "Influence of Isaiah," 259; cf. also Goodwin, "Hosea," 265-83.

34. The idea of "building" the community of God's people derives from Isa 58:12 and 61:4. Cf. Betz, "Felsenmann und Felsengemeinde," 49-77.

35. So e.g., Cullmann, *Peter, Disciple, Apostle, Martyr*, 204-5; Derrett, "Binding and Loosing," 112-17; Marcus, "Gates of Hades," 443-55; Powell, "Binding and Loosing," 438-45.

36. Hiers, "'Binding' and 'Loosing,'" 233-50.

darkness until the fire of the great judgment (1 En 10:4–6, 11–14; 14:5; 18:15; 21:1–10; 88:3; 90:23–26; cf. Jub 5:10; 10:9). The righteous would then be freed ("loosed") from oppression and injustice. Jesus used the same language of the guest without a garment in the parable of the kingdom being like a marriage feast (Matt 22:1–14; cf. Isa 61:10). "Loosing" is the proclamation of the good news of the kingdom. It is to proclaim *liberty* to the captives, the *opening* of the prison to those who are bound, *loosing* the bonds of wickedness (Isa 61:1; 42:7; 49:9; 52:2; 58:6; Zech 9:11–12), to *give light* to those who sit in darkness.[37]

Essentially, being given the keys of the kingdom meant to be able to participate fully in the mission of Jesus as the Anointed One of Isa 61:1, and as the Son of Man of Dan 7. This mission was vastly different from the one expected by those who were still looking for a powerful Davidic king to eradicate oppressors and establish a national kingdom as the Anointed One. So Jesus charged his disciples to tell no one that he was the Anointed One (16:20).

That Simon Peter did not fully understand the implications of his confession nor the responsibility he had been given became clear when Jesus elaborated on his mission by announcing that he must go to Jerusalem, suffer death, and be raised on the third day (16:21). The opposition to the good news of the kingdom that Jesus had experienced, not only from the Pharisees and Sadducees but also from some of those of the prophetic tradition, led Jesus to the conviction that decisive action was needed. As the representative of true Israel he would undergo that necessary death and resurrection experience himself on Israel's behalf. For Jesus saw confrontation with the priesthood and their associates for their corruption of the temple as a necessary part of the prophetic mission. Peter is shocked and tries to deny it, but Jesus instructs him and the disciples that in order to fulfill God's plan they must deny themselves and follow him. For soon the Son of Man will come with his angels in the presence of his Father (16:22–28). This alludes particularly to 1 En 45:1–6 where it states that after the day of affliction and tribulation for those who deny the name of the Lord of Spirits, the Chosen One will sit on the throne of glory surrounded by the chosen ones dwelling in the presence of God.[38] (Cf. also Dan 7:13, 14, 27; 1 En 55:4; 61:8; 62:5; 69:29; Matt 19:28.) Greatness in the kingdom would only come through humble service and putting the kingdom first. The role of the disciples is intimately involved in the concept of the Son of Man and the role of Jesus.

It is six days later that Jesus then takes Peter, James and John up Mount Hermon by themselves where they experience the vision of Jesus being transfigured before them with Moses and Elijah (17:1–8). This is essentially a vision of future vindication. While Peter is moved to recognize Jesus as being equal to Moses and Elijah, the voice from heaven commands that it is Jesus as the Servant who is to be followed first and foremost.

---

37. Leske, "Influence of Isaiah," 259.
38. Tödt, *Son of Man in the Synoptic Tradition*, 223. Contra Hare, *Son of Man Tradition*, 156–58.

Greatness in the Kingdom Is in Serving

While Peter had been given the keys of the kingdom, Jesus had addressed all of the disciples, for they all received those keys as Matt 18:15–18 illustrates. However, this did not give them superior status. For when they asked Jesus who was the greatest in the kingdom, Jesus put a child in their midst to illustrate that whoever humbles himself is greatest in the kingdom (18:1–4), for everyone is equally precious in God's sight (18:10–14), even one's erring brother (18:15–18). However, the very image of the coming vindication of the Son of Man soon to be sitting on his glorious throne together with all twelve disciples on their thrones (19:28) sparked that desire for future greatness once again. This led the sons of Zebedee, James and John, through their mother, requesting to sit on the thrones next to Jesus in his kingdom (20:20–21). Jesus' response to them was to ask them if they were able to drink the "cup" that he is to drink, the cup of suffering mentioned later in 26:39. During the time of the suffering of the exile the prophets had referred to it as the "cup of God's wrath because of Israel's idolatry (Jer 25:15–31; Ezek 23:31–33), but with the announcement of the coming end of the exile came the promise that God would now take that cup from them and put it in the hands of their tormentors (Isa 51:17–20). However, with the opposition to the good news of the kingdom and the failure of Israel to fulfill its purpose as a light to the nations, Jesus saw that he would have to go through that suffering, death, and resurrection experience as Servant Israel in order to make many to be accounted righteous (Isa 53:11),[39] and the disciples would be participants in this. For the kingdom of God is not about power and control but about serving others, helping many to find their purpose and to be raised to newness of life. So the Son of Man is "to give his life as a ransom for many" (20:28).[40]

When they had returned from Caesarea Philippi, and the Galileans were meeting together to arrange for their mass pilgrimage to Jerusalem for the Passover, Jesus once again reminded his disciples of the importance of this trip to Jerusalem, for "the Son of Man is to be betrayed into the hands of men (cf. 9:6–8; 16:13) and they will kill him, and on the third day he will be raised" (17:22–23). The emphasis again is on the resurrection as the vindication of the Servant / Son of Man (Isa 52:13; 53:10; Dan 12:2–3). The representative nature of the term "Son of Man" is not lost in this statement, and the distress of the disciples may be because of their uncertainty about their own involvement in this death and resurrection experience. Jesus had warned them that following him meant taking up the cross of suffering in order to find their life (16:24–26).

Entry into Jerusalem and Action in the Temple

For centuries the prophets had been critical of the priesthood in Jerusalem and the temple rituals which were often seen as contaminated by idolatrous practices. Such prophetic criticism prior to the exile reached its intensity under Jeremiah, and the destruction of Jerusalem and its temple, as well as the subsequent exile, were seen as judgment on the corruption and idolatry of temple worship. When, after the return from exile, a

---

39. Contra Luz, *Matthew 8–20*, 456.
40. See further, Leske, "Isaiah and Matthew," 167–69.

new temple was eventually built with the Zadokite priesthood in control in the province of Yehud as representatives of foreign powers, the prophetic criticism of temple and priesthood resumed. The "house of Yahweh" was seen as polluted and corrupt from its beginning (1 En 89–90). To some degree the temple had become irrelevant because in the future the word of God would be written in the hearts of the righteous. The office of the high priesthood had become a political and financial function open to the highest bidder by the Hellenists, and a military power during the time of the Hasmoneans. The Zadokite high-priesthood was frequently associated with wealth, corruption, and greed, and rejected by the prophetic community, Levites, the Qumran community, and even some of the low-ranking priests. With the urgency of establishing the kingdom of God and fulfilling the promises to the chosen and righteous, the temple and priesthood had to be confronted and the corruption condemned.

Whether the temple was to be destroyed or cleansed, a strong statement needed to be made since the crowds who had followed Jesus needed to be assured that the establishment of the reign of God would bring about transformation of the house of God. Conscious of this, Jesus deliberately chose to act out the imagery of Zech 9:9 by sending two of his disciples to Bethphage to fetch a donkey and its colt tied up there—likely arranged beforehand with a local follower (21:1–3). The purpose of this was two-fold—to proclaim the inauguration of God's reign on the one hand and to rebuke the priesthood for polluting the house of God on the other. In its original setting, Zech 9:9 drew on Gen 49:10–12; Isa 62:10–12; Zeph 3:11–15 to create an image of the people of Judah minus their shepherds (Zech 10:3) coming as God's holy and redeemed people (Isa 62:12), a people afflicted and lowly, the faithful remnant (Zeph 3:12–13) to represent God's presence as King among his people. All these hopes expressed in the prophetic vision are summarized in Zech 9:9, based on Isa 55:3–5.[41] Matthew only summarizes the verse to explain why Jesus chose to ride into Jerusalem on the colt of a donkey (21:5), and would have expected his initial audience/readers to have understood the implications of this quotation.

So Jesus rode into Jerusalem as the representative of faithful Israel, as the Servant of Yahweh, and as such to represent God's kingship. The time had come to proclaim the restoration of the reign of God in Jerusalem, the elimination of the corruption of his house and the reinstatement of justice for his people. The crowds who followed appeared to have understood some of the symbolism of that entry and seemed to connect it with the triumphal entry into Jerusalem by Judas Maccabeus in 164 BCE, who cleansed the temple and celebrated the Feast of Booths although it was well after the harvest season (2 Macc 10:6–8). For many cut down branches as required for that Feast (cf. Lev 23:39–43; Neh 8:13–18) and spread them on the road as they sang the last of the Hallel psalms (Ps 118:25–26). In their excitement the pilgrims connected this procession to the popular hope for the son of David, as had the blind men earlier (20:29–34). These crowds coming from Galilee were hoping for change which Jesus exemplified, although Jesus had never claimed to be king. However, when the people of Jerusalem, disturbed by the noise of

---

41. See the discussion of Zech 9:9 and the whole message of Zech 9–14 in chapter 7.

the Galilean crowds, asked who this was, their answer was quite reserved: "This is the prophet Jesus from Nazareth of Galilee" (21:11).[42]

This deliberate entry into Jerusalem as the Servant representing God's kingship carried with it certain expectations. In Zech 9–14, it is the Jerusalem leadership, particularly the priesthood, who were seen as corrupt (10:3), collaborating with and enriching themselves through collecting the tribute for foreign overlords (11:4–17), for there would come a time when the Lord would suddenly come to his temple (Mal 3:1) and oust the false leaders. Coming into the Court of the Gentiles, Jesus and the Galilean pilgrims would have been confronted by the sheer commercialism that had developed around the temple and its rituals. The priests, as the certifiers of the purity of the lambs (Exod 12:5) and as the ones who would have to carry out the ritual slaughter for the people had the monopoly on the whole business, and prices for their work were often inflated (cf. *m. Ker.* 1:7). Because Roman currency with its images of the emperor could not be used in the temple, it meant that people would have to exchange their money for Tyrian coinage to pay for their Passover lambs. The whole process had become big business for the priesthood and destroyed the whole concept of celebrating God's deliverance of his people from slavery. Jesus' action of disrupting these dealings (21:12) was a rejection, like that of the prophets of old (Amos 5:21–25; Hos 6:6; Isa 1:10–17; Jer 6:20), of what the whole sacrificial system and its priesthood had become. Driving out the traders from the temple (as in Zech 14:21), Jesus responded to the abuse of the temple by combining quotations from Isa 56:7 and Jer 7:11—the temple was supposed to be a place of prayer but it had become a den of robbers. As Jeremiah had once warned of the destruction of the temple because of its misuse (Jer 7:11–15), so Jesus' actions and words were implying the same.[43] The whole action was essentially symbolic as a foretaste of the coming of the Son of Man in judgment which Jesus will soon explain to his close disciples (Matt 24–25). The next morning Jesus illustrated that coming destruction together with judgment on the priesthood with his action parable of cursing the fig tree which bore no fruit (21:18–22).

With the backing of the Galilean pilgrims who had accompanied Jesus, some seeking healing and others singing his praises, the chief priests, scribes and elders of Jerusalem were unable to retaliate immediately. For they knew that the crowds revered Jesus as a prophet, as they had also John the Baptist, another one whom the priests had rejected (21:14–17, 23–32). For the time being all the priests could do was question his authority and encourage further confrontations by their local adherents, the Sadducees, as well as by the Pharisees and Herodians (21:45—22:45). Although the chief priests and elders maintained authority in Jerusalem, the Pharisees still had a presence and some influence there and were ready to join with the others in their opposition to Jesus, as they had done with John the Baptist. Nevertheless, the final lament and judgment over

---

42. Sanders, *Jesus and Judaism*, 306, regards this passage as "being one of the most puzzling in the Gospels" because he interprets it as Jesus claiming to be king on the basis on Zech 9:9. This is a common assumption, but is a misunderstanding of the meaning. See, e.g., Verseput, "Jesus' Pilgrimage to Jerusalem," 115; also Davies and Allison, *Gospel according to Saint Matthew*, 3:112, 128.

43. Evans, "Jesus' Action in the Temple," 237–70, has good reason to criticize much of Sanders' statements (in *Jesus and Judaism*) about this event. Nevertheless, the action of cleansing the temple was a portent of its coming destruction as well. Cf. also Sanders, "Jerusalem and Its Temple," 189–96.

Jerusalem for its unbelief and opposition meant that even the temple must come under judgment, for it is the house of the chief priests and elders, no longer the house of God. It would be a desolation (23:37-39) like that visited on the faithless King of Judah in Jer 22:5-9. Herod's magnificent building (still being completed) would not stand, and "not one stone will be left here upon another" (24:1-2).

THE END OF THE AGE AND THE PRESENCE OF THE SON OF MAN

As Jesus and his close disciples sat on the Mount of Olives overlooking Jerusalem, the disciples asked him when this destruction of Jerusalem and temple would happen, and what would be the sign of his "presence" (*parousia*) and the "end of the age" (24:3). First of all, it must be understood that the essential meaning of *parousia* is "presence" as opposed to "absence" (*hapousia*; cf. Phil 2:12; 1 Cor 16:7; 2 Cor 10:10, 11) rather than "coming," and so does not speak of a "return" or "second coming."[44] Second, behind the questions, and certainly in the answers given, the understanding is that Jesus as the exemplar of the Servant / Son of Man is the forerunner of all those who follow and thus make up the corporate Servant / Son of Man. Third, the background of the phrase, "end of the age" is primarily the Apocalypse of Weeks (1 En 93:1-10; 91:11-17) where the "weeks" are the different ages. Jesus and his disciples are near the end of the seventh age as those chosen as part of "the eternal plant of righteousness" to uproot the foundations of violence and deceit of this "perverse generation" (cf. Matt 12:30-39; 15:13).

It is rather significant that Jesus does not specifically respond to the question: "What will be the sign of *your* presence?" but later refers more objectively to the "sign of the Son of Man in heaven" (24:30). While Jesus may represent the Son of Man now, in the future it is going to be up to his followers to carry on the role of the Son of Man. In a sense, all these "Son of Man" sayings contain a challenge to his disciples, as M. D. Hooker has put it, "to be included and to make a corporate interpretation a reality instead of a possibility."[45] For this reason Jesus begins by warning the disciples not to be led astray from their task by false leaders claiming to be the Anointed One who will cause others to join them in fighting against the oppressing forces, thus bringing about nation rising against nation and kingdom against kingdom (24:5, 23-24). This will only lead to chaos and natural disasters, and these are "but the beginning of the birth pangs" (24:8). This was a common metaphor for the suffering that would suddenly come upon evil peoples or nations (Isa 13:8; Mic 4:9-10; Jer 13:21) and particularly in the time leading up to the presence of the Son of Man being revealed to the kings, the mighty, and the exalted who possess the land" (1 En 62:3-5). The disciples themselves can expect to be caught up in this and become the focus of confrontation and conflict as Jesus himself has been, but by remaining faithful to their task they would be saved. For the good news of the kingdom

---

44. The word *parousia* in the Gospels is only found in Matt 24:3, 27, 37, 39. In the parallel in Luke 17:26, 30, the author speaks of "in the days of the Son of Man" and "on the day when the Son of Man is revealed." Other uses of the term are found in 1 Cor 15:23; 2 Cor 7:6, 7; Phil 1:26; 1 Thess 2:19; 3:13; 4:15; 5:23; 2 Thess 2:1, 8, 9; James 5:7, 8; 2 Pet 1:16; 3:4, 12; 1 John 2:28. Cf. Harris, "Comings and Goings," 51-70, particularly 59-63.

45. Hooker, "Is the Son of Man Problem Really Insoluble?," 155-68.

of God had to be proclaimed throughout the whole world as a witness to all the nations (Isa 42:6; 43:10, 12; 44:8) before the end of the age can come (24:9–14).

As for Jerusalem and the temple, they too will be part of the great tribulation, the destruction of violence and deceit spoken of in 1 En 93:9–10; 91:11. Such will be a foretaste of the presence of the Son of Man in judgment. For "where the body is, there the vultures will be gathered together" to devour (24:15–28). Jesus is using some of the graphic imagery here of Jeremiah's prediction of judgment on Judah and Jerusalem and its temple for the abominations set up in the house of God (Jer 7:30–34; 15:1–6).[46] It would be similar to the situation referred to in Dan 9:27; 11:31; 12:11. So when the disciples see the same abominations happening in the temple, they know it is time to get out, for the judgment is coming (24:15–20).

"Immediately after the affliction of those days" (24:29) leads into the "eighth week" (1 En 91:12), the time when the righteous will execute judgment on the wicked as God's agents, as the Son of Man coming on the clouds of heaven with power and great glory, as in Dan 7:13–14. That Jesus was expecting this transformation to begin to take place during the lifetime of the disciples is evident from his statement that all these things would happen before the present generation passes away (24:34), but he was quick to point out that only the heavenly Father knows when this will take place (24:36). Then, while the chosen will be gathered "from the four winds" (24:31), there will be many left behind because they had not remained watchful and had fallen back into godlessness (24:37–51). So Jesus exhorted the disciples to be always in a state of readiness for the coming judgment and be always faithfully going about the work for which they had been called—gathering Israel to be a light to the nations before the Day of Judgment comes. Such warnings to watchfulness and faithfulness to their task are told in a series of parables in 24:45—25:30.

Such exhortations to endurance under affliction and being faithful to their calling are given against the background of Jesus' own impending affliction, death, and resurrection as the suffering Servant / Son of Man. With the Pharisees, chief priests and elders of Jerusalem all plotting Jesus' death, the disciples cannot expect anything different for them, for it is only through suffering and endurance can transformation come about. What happens to Jesus as Servant / Son of Man is a microcosm of what will happen to the corporate Servant / Son of Man in the ongoing struggle for righteousness leading into the new age.

The Coming Day of Judgment

The Day of Judgment was always on the minds of those who felt oppressed by foreign nations and their clients. It had become part of the fabric of the culture of Israel after continued domination by other nations. The Pharisees particularly had played into this by popularizing the idea of a coming Davidic messiah who would destroy oppression and establish a national kingdom, inevitably through war, bloodshed, and violence. Over

---

46. While *aetos* may mean "eagle," the imagery here is of vultures feeding on dead bodies, "food for the birds of the air" (Jer 7:33) and the emphasis is on the corruption of the temple rather than on destruction by Rome. Contra Carter, "Are There Imperial Texts in the Class?," 467–87.

the years there had been those who tried to begin a rebellion but were brutally put down, only to cause more rage, resentment and continuing hostility. Even within the prophetic movement there were those who looked with longing to the great Day of Judgment and called for the destruction of kings and the mighty and the exalted who possessed the land (cf. 1 En 62:11).

In the parable concerning the final judgment in Matt 25:31–46, Jesus uses apocalyptic language to describe the judgment to come. As in Daniel and the Parables of Enoch, the Son of Man is seen sitting on the throne of his glory (25:31; cf. Dan 7:13–14; 1 En 45:3; 55:4; 61:8; 62:5; 69:29), placed there by God to carry out the judgment on God's behalf. The corporate Son of Man made up of the chosen righteous, as in Matt 19:28, is here even called "king" (v. 34) because God has designated the Son of Man to act on behalf of his kingship (cf. Zech 9:9). This kingdom of God had not come about by war and violence, for Jesus had taught that the kingdom comes about only when God rules over the hearts and minds of the faithful, no matter what their outward circumstances may be. With their hearts ruled by the love of God, their lives would be moved to an attitude of love and forgiveness towards others which would ultimately bring about transformation within society. The acts of compassion highlighted in 25:35–36, identified already in Isa 58:6–11 as true worship, are depicted as the natural response to the Father's love, and as spontaneous actions without ulterior motive. Those who act in these ways are Jesus' brothers and sisters, just as Jesus identifies those in need as his kin, in total solidarity with them (25:40, 45). These acts are the ultimate examples of covenant faithfulness and show no discrimination of race, nation, culture or creed. For it is only by acts of caring and compassion that one gives witness to the kingdom and the love of the heavenly Father. Those who reject all this, and are motivated by greed and self-centeredness, whether Jew or Gentile, are cast out, in typical apocalyptic language, "into the eternal fire prepared for the devil and his angels" (25:41). They go into eternal punishment, but the righteous into eternal life" (25:46).

Meanwhile, the judgment imposed on Jesus by the chief priests and elders of Jerusalem and the Pharisees overshadows the days of the Passover event. The Galilean crowds which had accompanied Jesus and his disciples into Jerusalem, who had cheered him on with their hosannas will observe the events soon to unfold. But not fully understanding, they will remain silent as the Jerusalem crowds, coached by their elders, cry against Jesus. Afraid of being implicated and attacked, like the disciples, they will slink away and reflect on all that has taken place. Matthew, writing perhaps decades later, plays down the impact of these crowds who had followed Jesus, but many of them would have formed the nucleus of the Jesus movement and the later church after the resurrection. Their presence during Jesus' mission must have had an effect on Jesus' expectation of their future influence in bringing about change as the "holy ones of the Most High," the corporate Son of Man (cf. 10:23; 16:28; 19:28).

THE ULTIMATE MISSION

Throughout his ministry Jesus had been living out the role of Servant Israel as an example of what Israel was to become, but the hesitancy of many to understand that role

The Prophetic Vision and the Mission of Jesus

and to accept that they were to become a light to the nations had led Jesus to the conviction that it would only be when he himself underwent that death and resurrection experience, vindicated by God. As the Servant he would be cut off from the land of the living (Isa 53:7-9), pour out his soul to death (Isa 53:12), but be raised to prolong his days, to make many to be accounted righteous. Thus he would bear their iniquities (Isa 53:10-11). For those witnessing his resurrection might finally believe in God's plan for them and be transformed to a new understanding of their role as witnesses of God to the nations. They would finally understand the meaning of the sign of Jonah. The passion story (26:1—28:10) is thus a remarkable account of Jesus' determination to fulfill Israel's history and thus draw all into the resurrection experience, into a new beginning as the people of God.

So Jesus reminds his disciples that he has come to the major task set before him: as the Son of Man to be "handed over to be crucified" (26:2). Matthew then records three significant events that lead up to that. First, the chief priests and elders meet with the high priest, Caiaphas, to plot how to get rid of Jesus (26:3-5). Second, while Jesus is dining with one of his followers, Simon the leper (cf. 8:4) in his home in Bethany, a woman enters and anoints his *head* with very expensive perfumed oil. Obviously, she did this out of enthusiastic devotion as a way of declaring him her king.[47] While the disciples condemned this as waste, Jesus declared it to be a beautiful act of anointing his *body* for burial (26:6-13). Third, Judas Iscariot, one of the Twelve, offers to betray Jesus for thirty pieces of silver (26:14-16), the actual price of a slave (Exod 21:32; cf. Zech 11:12).

Having previously arranged with a Jerusalem disciple to use his house for the Passover meal, Jesus celebrates it with his twelve disciples on 14th Nisan following the solar calendar of 364 days as had always been used by the prophetic movement, the Levites and the Qumran community.[48] At the meal Jesus first warns that one of them, sharing in this bond of fellowship, will betray him, for "while the Son of Man goes as it is written of him" (Isa 53; Jonah 1:17—2:10), it would be better that the one who betrays him had never been born (26:20-25; cf. 1 En 38:2). During the meal, which commemorated God delivering Israel from slavery in Egypt, Jesus takes the unleavened bread, blesses God, breaks the bread and gives it to his disciples—actions which recall the feeding miracles in Matt 14:19 and 15:36 with their allusions to the messianic banquet (Isa 25:6-9; 55:1-3).[49] As he does this, Jesus tells them: "Take and eat, this is my body." Then taking the cup of wine, he gives thanks and gives it to them, saying: "Drink from it all of you, for this is my blood of the covenant which is poured out concerning many for the forgiveness of sins" (26:26-28). These sayings are loaded with meaning and significance. The disciples are to incorporate Jesus, the Servant / Son of Man, into themselves in a sense that they are now to take on that role themselves. The language of v. 28 draws heavily on

---

47. In a Jewish setting this can hardly have had any sexual connotations as it may have had in Greek society. Such has been suggested by Corley, "Anointing of Jesus," 61-72.

48. This would have been earlier than the official Passover, following the lunar calendar. See Jaubert, *La date de la cène*; English translation: *The Date of the Last Supper*; Saulnier, *Calendrical Variations in Second Temple Judaism*.

49. This may be the *afikoman*, a portion of unleavened bread that was shared later in the meal as a symbol of hope for the coming of the messiah. Cf. Carmichael, "David Daube on the Eucharist," 45-67.

Isa 53:12, for Jesus is that Servant who will pour out his soul to death and bear the sins of many. "This is my blood of the covenant" recalls the words of Moses as he sprinkled the blood over the people as a symbol of sealing their covenant relationship with God (Exod 24:8; cf. Zech 9:11). The disciples were now to be the Servant which Jesus has exemplified for them. "For the forgiveness of sins" has always been the good news, the basis for restoring people into the kingdom of God. In other words, in this dramatic action Jesus was passing on to the disciples the role he had exemplified—they are soon to be that Servant / Son of Man and that light to the nations (28:18–20). The fourth cup of the Seder which celebrates the kingdom of God[50] Jesus puts off by saying: "From now on I shall not drink from the fruit of the vine until that day when I drink it with you new in the kingdom of my Father" (26:29). The reference here is the consummation of the new age when the righteous and chosen are saved, no longer to see the faces of the unrighteous, when "the Lord of Spirits will abide over them, and with that Son of Man they will eat, and they will recline and rise up forever" wearing the garments of glory (1 En 62:1016; cf. Matt 22:11–14; Isa 61:10).

On leaving, Jesus warns the disciples that they will be scattered because of what is about to happen, but after he has been raised up he will go before them to Galilee (26:31–35). Soon after, action takes place in the Garden of Gethsemane at the foot of the Mount of Olives where pilgrims often slept during the week of the Passover. There Jesus struggles over the cup of suffering he must take on for Israel (26:36–46; cf. Jer 25:15–31; Ezek 23:31–33; Isa 51:17–20) before Judas appears with a crowd sent by the chief priests and elders to arrest Jesus. Jesus offers no resistance because the writing of the prophets must be fulfilled (26:47–56; cf. Hos 6:1–6; Isa 53; Jonah 1:17—3:3).

Taken before Caiaphas, the chief priests and elders at an informal meeting of the Sanhedrin during the night, false witnesses are brought forward to accuse Jesus but he remains silent until Caiaphas puts him under oath to answer whether he is the Anointed One, the Son of God, both titles popularly understood as referring to the hoped for Davidic messiah. Caiaphas was hoping for an affirmative answer so that Jesus could be put to death by the Romans for treason. But Jesus turns the question back onto the questioner with his: "You have said so" and then adds: "From now on you will see the Son of Man seated at the right hand of Power and coming on the clouds of heaven" (26:64). The significance of this statement which combines Ps 110:1; 1 En 62:5–7 and Dan 7:13, is that it puts the high priest and his chief priests and elders into the category of the mighty and the exalted who will come under judgment before the Son of Man (1 En 62:3–5). Whatever Caiaphas may have understood by the reference to the Son of Man it gave him the opportunity to claim that Jesus had uttered blasphemy, which according to priestly law (Lev 24:10–23) carried the death penalty. So this was the decision which was ratified when the Sanhedrin was able to meet legally in the morning (27:1–2).

However, the charge they would take to Pontius Pilate was one of treason, that Jesus claimed to be king of the Jews and was inciting an insurrection (27:11–14). It is likely that Pilate was already familiar with who Jesus was and what he had been teaching and saw him as a righteous man of peace (27:19), but the chief priests and elders were able to incite the Jerusalem crowd to call for Jesus' crucifixion with such vehemence that he

---

50. See Carmichael, "David Daube on the Eucharist," 65n2.

let them have their way lest they start a riot (27:15–26). So after suffering scourging, ridicule and humiliation Jesus was led away to be crucified. Nailed to a cross, Jesus is further reviled by the Jerusalem crowd. Matthew appropriately describes the mocking of the chief priests, scribes and elders in words of the wicked who seek to condemn the righteous poor one to death in Wis 2:10–20, a passage based on Isa 53 (27:27–44).

Matthew focuses very little on the suffering of Jesus on the cross but rather concentrates on the significant events that happen at the time of the crucifixion. From noon until three in the afternoon darkness came over the land (27:45). The prophets often spoke of the coming Day of Yahweh as being a day of darkness and gloom, when the sun would turn to darkness and the moon to blood (Isa 13:10–13; Joel 2:1–2; 3:4; Zeph 1:15). Amos had said that the sun would set at midday and cover the earth with darkness to turn their feasts into mourning (8:9–10). Earlier Jesus had told his disciples that this would be a sign of the presence of the Son of Man (24:29). Jesus then cries out with a loud voice the opening words of Ps 22, the cry of agony of the righteous one who later receives divine vindication and finishes praising God (Ps 22:22–31). So in this cry Jesus was acknowledging the role of the suffering Servant who will triumph in his death and bring about new life for others. Soon after this, Jesus yields up his spirit (27:50) which appears to set off a series of apocalyptic events.

There is an earthquake and the veil of the sanctuary was torn in two from top to bottom (27:51). Since this veil was seen as a symbol of the firmament of heaven, it may have indicated that God was answering the prayer of the faithful who had cried out to God: "O that you would rend the heavens and come down, that the mountains might quake at your presence, to make your name known to your adversaries" (Isa 64:1).[51] However, the combination of the curtain in the temple being split in two, the earth shaken by an earthquake, rocks being split and the holy ones who had died being raised, appears to follow the pattern of Zech 14:4–5. This describes God coming upon Jerusalem with power with "all the holy ones" just prior to establishing divine rule, when the Mount of Olives is split in two, and the people flee as from an earthquake. This is the only time Matthew has used the term "holy ones" for the faithful, a term originating in Isa 62:12 and used in Dan 7:18–27 and 1 En 51:2–5. Both allusions would be emphasizing God coming in power to establish his reign through his Servant. The phrase, "the bodies of many holy ones who had fallen asleep were raised" (27:52), alludes to Dan 12:2: "Many of those who sleep in the dust of the earth shall awake." This was part of the message that was to be sealed until the end-time (Dan 12:4). The image of these bodies coming forth from their tombs after Jesus' resurrection and entering the holy city (27:52–53) has all the markings of an apocalyptic vision, since Jerusalem at this time could hardly be called "holy."[52] With the darkness and the earthquake happening simultaneously with Jesus expiring, the Roman centurion and his soldiers are led to utter, "Truly, this was God's son," in stark contrast to the chief priests and elders who had acted like the devil in Matt 4:1–11 with their taunts: "If you are God's son . . ." (27:54; cf. 27:40).[53]

---

51. So Gurtner, *Torn Veil*, 172.
52. For a different approach see Waters, "Matthew 27:52–53," 489–515.
53. See Troxel, "Matt 27:51–4 Reconsidered," 31.

THE PROPHETIC VISION AND THE REAL JESUS

With the eleven disciples scattered, many women disciples who had followed Jesus from Galilee had kept watch on the events, and when a wealthy disciple, Joseph of Arimathea, requested to take the body of Jesus and lay it in his new tomb (27:57–60), two of the women, Mary Magdalene and Mary the mother of James and Joseph (27:56, 61), who is also the mother of Jesus (cf. 13:55), followed and kept watch over the tomb. They had not come to anoint the body of Jesus, but to witness the resurrection. The sealing of the tomb and the placing of guards there by the chief priests and Pharisees would not change that (27:62–66).

THE RESURRECTION OF JESUS

The empty tomb and the resurrection of Jesus come as the climax of Jesus' ultimate mission. It has not only been the growing opposition of the Pharisees and the antagonism of the chief priests and elders of Jerusalem that had led Jesus to this ultimate mission of demonstrating the power of God to raise his Servant up to fulfill Israel's purpose, it was also the diffidence and lack of understanding of many of those who had accepted and espoused the prophetic vision. The promises of a resurrection had been there in the prophetic writings for a long time, well before the exile. As early as the prophet Hosea there had been the promise that, "after two days he will revive us, and on the third day he will raise us up that we may live before him" (6:2). During the exile God's plan for Israel had been made so clear that they as his Servant were to be a people-covenant and a light to the nations, and that even though cut off from the land of the living, the Servant would see his offspring and prolong his days so that the will of Yahweh might prosper in his hand (Isa 53:10). This promise continued to be echoed down through history in the ongoing, developing prophetic vision, as the people suffered death and deprivation under numerous oppressors. It was portrayed in Jonah, in Isa 26:19; 1 En 103:1–4; 104:1–6; Dan 12:2–3; 1 En 51:1–5; 62:15. Jesus' absolute conviction that God would raise him up as his Servant had led him to Jerusalem, and now in his resurrection his mission had been accomplished, he had been vindicated, and God's righteousness would be fulfilled (cf. 3:15).

It was the two Marys who believed and were the first to witness his resurrection when they returned to the tomb on the third day. They experienced a further earthquake tremor during which the messenger of God rolled back the stone from the opening of the tomb. Arriving there, the messenger verified the resurrection and reminded them that they would see Jesus in Galilee. They were shown the empty tomb and were eager to hurry and tell the disciples the good news, but further proof of the resurrection came in the form of Jesus himself appearing to them and encouraging them to tell the brethren to go to Galilee to meet him there (28:1–10).

Before coming to the very climax of Jesus' whole mission and the point of his Gospel, Matthew briefly refers to the recalcitrance of the chief priests and their deceit in bribing the guards who had to explain to them what had happened. The guards were to say that the disciples had come during the night and stolen the body, and so this was circulated among the Judeans[54] "to this day" (28:11–15).

THE COMMISSIONING OF THE DISCIPLES

Jesus had been persistent that after he was raised up, he would go before the disciples to Galilee (26:32). The messenger of the Lord had told the two Marys that the risen Jesus was going before them to Galilee (28:7), and when they met Jesus soon after, he repeated: "Go and tell my brethren to go to Galilee, and there they will see me" (28:10). So the eleven disciples went to the mountain in Galilee to which Jesus had directed them (28:16). There can be little doubt that this is Mount Hermon where Jesus had taken them once before (16:13—17:13), a mountain sacred to the prophetic and Levite communities living in that area. Commissioning his disciples in the midst of these communities who held to the prophetic vision to go now to the nations was important. For those within these communities who had been diffident to Jesus' call to be a light to the nations and had not accepted his authority as Servant / Son of Man, nor understood the sign of Jonah, would now have to reconsider. Now after witnessing that God had raised Jesus from the dead, surely they would be moved to change their thinking, reexamine the whole prophetic vision and become disciples and a light to the nations.

The mountain had always been a place of revelation, and the prophetic vision had originally spoken of the nations coming to Mount Zion in Jerusalem to worship the one true God (e.g., Isa 2:2–4; 25:6; 56:7; Zech 8:20–23; 14:16–19),[55] but Jerusalem and its temple were now under judgment. The nations were now to be invited into the fellowship of God's people in the kingdom of God which is not governed by time or space. When Jesus had told the Pharisees that "something greater than the temple is here" (12:6) or greater than Jonah or Solomon (12:41, 42), he was not referring to himself, but talking about the kingdom of God. For, it was the good news of the kingdom that was to be preached throughout the world as a witness to the nations, before the end of the age would be accomplished (24:14).

When the disciples saw Jesus they prostrated themselves before him (28:17) although some hesitated because they were meeting someone raised from the dead. So Jesus came to them and reminded them that "all authority has been given to me in heaven and on earth" (v. 18). That authority had been given to him as the Son of Man by God (Dan 7:13–14) and had already been recognized in his teaching (7:29), healing (8:9), acts of forgiveness (9:6, 8), and expulsion of unclean spirits (10:1), and now verified by his resurrection.

Previously, Jesus' mission had been to *gather* "the lost sheep of the house of Israel" to carry out what Israel had been chosen by God to do. Now he could send them out to do that and to draw all in Israel and in all nations into that covenant relationship with God. This had been Jesus' goal from the beginning and would now be carried out through his disciples. "Baptism" would be the sign of entering into the renewed life as

---

54. For Matthew, *Ioudaios* always referred to the people of Judea as opposed to Galilee.
55. Cf. the point of view and discussion by Donaldson, *Jesus on the Mountain*, 176–85.

a child of God, in intimate relationship with the heavenly Father, revealed through the Son, and filled with the Holy Spirit (cf. 11:25–27; 12:28–32). They were to teach the nations to observe everything that Jesus had taught them, the good news of the kingdom of God, a kingdom motivated by God's love for them and their love for God and for one another. "And remember I am with you to the end of the age" (v. 20), a commitment given to them before (18:20) and now affirmed as an answer to the question the disciples had asked Jesus earlier: "What will be the sign of your presence and the end of the age?" (24:3). Jesus was now telling them that as they take on the role of Servant / Son of Man he is still with them as part of the corporate function until God's plan is accomplished and God's benign reign is over all. Now across the centuries that assurance comes to all who follow in the footsteps of Jesus as the Servant / Son of Man.

Chapter XI

Conclusion

FOLLOWING THE DEVELOPMENT OF the prophetic vision, as it has travelled through history, responding and reacting to the many changes in the social and political climate of the people of Israel, has allowed us to see the continuity and progress of that vision, and the struggle of those who held fast to those prophetic ideals. We have been able to witness the highs and lows of that vision, carried forward by one prophet after another, as it moved through times of foreign domination, injustice, despair, and also recovery. Sometimes the vision under the pressure of oppression and exploitation became narrowed to a focus on descriptions of the coming Day of Judgment, and at other times it expanded into visions of hope and the active presence of God among his people encouraging them to live as his children in love and forgiveness. In that spirit the people were to reach out even to those nations which had exploited them, in the recognition that all peoples and nations come under the beneficent rule of the one and only God, the Creator of all.

One of the significant contributions of this study has been to demonstrate the aspect of intertextuality, the way that later prophets have absorbed the words and messages of the prophets who have preceded them, often wholeheartedly taking into their thinking and preaching the concepts and expressions used by others. Sometimes, they have consciously expressed differences because of changing circumstances and attitudes of the people, but nevertheless, testifying to their knowledge and understanding of the earlier oracles. Highly significant in this process has been discovering how dominant and continuously influential in the postexilic era have been the oracles of hope expressed by Deutero-Isaiah with his conviction that the everlasting covenant made with David had now been transferred to the faithful. This has been so evident in the later prophets and in the apocalyptic writings, and taken up again by Jesus who made it the foundation of his proclamation and his mission as the mission of Israel.

We have observed how the prophets saw their function as calling the nation back to the ancient covenant ideal of relationship with God, an agreement to live as the people of Yahweh fulfilling the divine purpose for all his creation. That covenant concept had been so deeply ingrained in the prophetic vision from the very beginning that in some cases the word "covenant" hardly needed to be mentioned. That covenant called for a deep trust in faithfulness to that partnership, expressed in terms of their righteousness responding to God's righteousness. In that light, the making of covenants or alliances with other nations and acknowledging their gods would be seen as a rejection of their covenant with Yahweh and could only lead to suffering on their part.

Important in this study has been the clarification of the relationship of the prophetic visionaries to other movements such as the Levites and the Zadokite priesthood. Through the prophets' call for a return to the covenant relationship, the Levites could understand that they had much in common with them. Moreover, both had become minority groups in opposition to the Zadokites who often sought to wield power and control over the people through their collaboration with foreign overlords. Yet there were differences. The Levites could agree with many of the concerns of the visionaries, and some like Jeremiah, Malachi, and Joel readily took up the role of prophet calling for justice and faithfulness to the covenant. Nevertheless, many of them still held firmly to the hope of one day being able to serve honorably as faithful priests under the rule of one like David. During periods of transition we have also seen Zadokite priests such as Ezekiel and Zechariah (Zech 1–8), taking up the prophetic role as visionaries, but with a different vision. In that vision the Zadokite priesthood would be exonerated of any corruption to continue the sacrificial rituals, maintaining their power and leadership together with a secular Davidic ruler. Distinguishing these different movements has been important in clarifying and understanding these often contrary visions and their effect on later times.

Prominent also in the development of the prophetic vision has been the rise of the apocalyptic literature to express the hopes and fears of the prophetic and Levite communities in cryptic language for the faithful. Arising out of the strong disappointment and despair when the short but benign reign of Alexander the Great turned into the harsh and predatory domination of the Ptolemies and Seleucids, descriptions of the Day of Judgment and the destruction of the wicked were given greater emphasis. Eventually, however, through the continuing influence of Deutero-Isaiah it evolved into the final exaltation of the Servant of Yahweh as the Son of Man, a corporate concept for the faithful which became personified in the Parables of Enoch as the representative and leader of the faithful. This was the concept which Jesus was soon to take up to describe his whole mission.

All this has led the way to a clearer comprehension of the cultural context and prophetic influence culminating in the coming of John the Baptist and Jesus the Nazorean. We have noted how each, coming from different places and environments, have seen their missions based on Deutero-Isaiah, and also why they eventually differed in their understanding of their missions. While John's vision was colored by the imminence of the Day of Judgment and the need for repentance in preparation of the kingdom of God, Jesus felt constrained to go further and proclaim the presence of the kingdom here and now in the light of the full message of Deutero-Isaiah. The Day of Judgment would come later for those who had rejected the kingdom. Jesus' message proved to be inspired by the joyous and positive message in Isa 40–66, leading him to personify the role of Israel as the Servant of Yahweh / Son of Man in order to lead all to live out that role as the children of God, fulfilling the divine purpose for their own vindication and the salvation of all peoples. The images of a loving and forgiving God and Father, particularly emphasized in Hosea and Isa 40–66 and their call to all to respond in love and forgiveness to all peoples, finds its home in the fundamental message of Jesus in the Sermon on the Mount.

The study of the development of the prophetic vision has also shed much light on Christology. It has often been argued that the Gospel of Matthew has a high Christology, higher than that of the Gospel of Mark and consequently later than that Gospel. However, that has proved not to be the case. The Christology developed in the prophetic vision in the terms, Son of God, Son of Man, Anointed One, Servant, is both human and corporate. Throughout Jesus' ministry these terms have always borne a tension between their description of Jesus as an individual personifying faithful Israel, and what the faithful were to be as a corporate body. Not recognizing the tension between individual and corporate in the central christological terms, Servant / Son of Man has led to a diminution of the mission of the church as the corporate Son of Man, a point picked up, however, by the Apostle Paul in calling the church the "body of Christ." Matthean Christology is thus a far cry from that of the Council of Nicaea in 325 CE. However, one can readily understand how early Christians could find God in Jesus, as the one who represented God's love and almighty plan for them.

It is also noteworthy, and brings light on the ministry of Jesus, that because of the suppression and exploitation of the Ptolemies and Seleucids, that the prophetic visionaries and the Levites found refuge in the less accessible reaches of Upper Galilee and the surrounding areas. This has been evident from the literature deriving from the area around Mount Hermon. This explains why Jesus as a Nazorean concentrated his mission in Galilee to reach out to those who had inherited the prophetic vision and to inspire them to carry out that mission as members of the kingdom of God to all peoples. Understandably, because of their conviction that the Day of Judgment had to come first, there were some who were not open initially to Jesus' message that the kingdom was already here.

This study has not only revealed the *real* historical Jesus, but has also given us a greater appreciation of the Jewish nature of the Gospel of Matthew. Besides the many indications of its Jewishness and its familiarity with the prophetic literature, we can now see its depth of understanding of the prophetic vision, and the impact of that vision on the ministry of Jesus. Considering that the whole mission and ministry of Jesus was carried out in a totally Jewish environment, it stands to reason that the Gospel that best depicts this situation is the most fundamental and earliest account on which the others have built. Matthew's Gospel contains no indication of or allusion to the destruction of the temple in 70 CE. Jesus spoke of its future destruction as the common expectation of the prophetic visionaries because they all saw it hopelessly polluted. A new temple of the kingdom would later be built to which all nations would come in the new age (cf. 1 En 89:73; 93:9, 10; 91:11). Nor does the Gospel contain any hint of the murders of James the brother of the Lord in 62 CE and of James, the son of Zebedee in 41 CE, nor of events recorded in the Acts of the Apostles. So the Gospel of Matthew must have been written early. The claim of Eusebius in his *Chronicon* that the Gospel was written in the third year of Caligula's reign (i.e., ca. 40 CE) may be somewhere near the mark after all.

The Jewish nature and the informed use of quotations and allusions to the prophets in the Gospel of Matthew reveal that the author was himself very likely a member of the Notsrim (Nazoreans), in the prophetic and Levite communities. The references to a good scribe in Matt 8:19 and 13:52 would point to the author himself being that scribe, but a scribe of the prophetic writings. This scribe has to be that Matthew, the tax collector, mentioned in Matt 9:9 who was ready to leave his lucrative position in his tax office in Capernaum to follow Jesus in spite of Jesus' warning in Matt 8:20. This, of course, was the view held unanimously by the early church, but long denied by most New Testament scholars. Nevertheless, his Levite background, indicated in his name and in the fact that he is called "Levi" in Mark and Luke would point to Matthew being well educated, and a reason why Jesus would have called him to follow. He was thus an ideal candidate to understand Jesus as the fulfillment of the prophetic vision and well suited to record the story of Jesus' message and ministry. Moreover, as a Levite, he could more readily reach out to the Levite community. The fact that he began his Gospel with an initial emphasis on Jesus as "son of David," as well as his references to Jeremiah, may have been Matthew's way of bringing fellow Levites to accept and follow Jesus.

Matthew's assumption that his readers understood the significance of his biblical quotations and allusions, and his brief summaries and significance of Jesus' miracles would confirm what the early church had always said, that Matthew wrote his Gospel in Hebrew for fellow Hebrews, and these were likely members of the prophetic and Levite communities in Galilee. After the great commission given on the mountain in Galilee, it appears that Matthew continued to proclaim the good news to these communities for a decade or so before feeling that he had accomplished that task which Jesus had started. Then he wrote up in Hebrew what he had been teaching them before departing to join other apostles in proclaiming the good news to the nations. This confirms what Eusebius had said in his *Ecclesiastical History* III.24.5 that "Matthew had begun by preaching to the Hebrews, and when he made up his mind to go to others too, he committed his own gospel to writing in his native tongue, so that those with whom he was no longer present, the gap left by his departure was filled by what he wrote."

It follows from all of this that the two-source hypothesis of the formation of the Synoptic Gospels which was conceived in the climate of the *Kulturkampf* in Bismarck's Germany cannot stand up to its claims, and any quest for the real historical Jesus will have to begin in the Gospel of Matthew as the culmination of the prophetic vision.

In the light of this it can readily be seen why Luke felt constrained to write his Gospel when Matthew's Gospel was already in circulation. He needed to restate the gospel in terms more meaningful to a Gentile audience. Some of the aspects of Matthew's Gospel would have been difficult to understand for Gentiles without a thorough knowledge of its prophetic background, and the fact that Jesus had said that he was sent only to the lost sheep of the house of Israel (Matt 10:5; 15:24) could have led to misunderstanding. For this reason the universality of the gospel is strongly emphasized by Luke. However, the differences between these two Gospels and the way they were perceived among diaspora Jews in Rome may have been the cause of the situation that developed there during the reign of Emperor Claudius (41–54 CE) who, we are told, "expelled from Rome the Jews who were constantly rioting under the leadership of Chrestus" (Suetonius, *Claudius*

XXV.3; cf. Acts 18:2). Mark's Gospel, then, may well have been written as a bridge between the two after the deaths of Peter and Paul in 64 CE.

Finally, and most important of all, is the continuing call of Jesus to his present-day followers to be the corporate Servant / Son of Man, to be an abiding witness to all the nations, to transform our world into the Eden of long ago with peace, love, and caring as the nations come to understand how to live together as the children of God.

Bibliography

Achtemeier, Elizabeth. *The Community and Message of Isaiah 56-66*. Minneapolis: Augsburg, 1982.
Ahlstrom, G. W. *Joel and the Temple Cult of Jerusalem*. VTSup 21. Leiden: Brill, 1971.
Albertz, Rainer. *A History of Israelite Religion in the Old Testament Period*. 2 vols. Translated by John Bowden. Louisville: Westminster John Knox, 1994.
Allison, Dale C., Jr. "Elijah Must Come First." *JBL* 103 (1984) 256-58.
———. *The New Moses: A Matthean Typology*. Minneapolis: Fortress, 1993.
Anderson, Bernhard W. "Exodus and Covenant in Second Isaiah and the Prophetic Tradition." In *Magnalia Dei, The Mighty Acts of God: Essays on the Bible and Archeology in Memory of G. Ernest Wright*, edited by F. M. Cross et al., 339-60. Garden City: Doubleday, 1976.
Anderson, Francis I., and David Noel Freedman. *Hosea: A New Translation and Commentary*. AB 24. New York: Doubleday, 1980.
Anderson, T. David. "Renaming and Wedding Imagery in Isaiah 62." *Bib* 67 (1986) 75-80.
Andinach, Pablo R. "The Locusts in the Message of Joel." *VT* 42 (1992) 433-41.
Atkinson, Kenneth. "Herod the Great, Sosius, and the Siege of Jerusalem (37 BCE) in Psalm of Solomon 17." *NovT* 38 (1996) 313-22.
———. "On the Herodian Origin of Militant Davidic Messianism at Qumran: New Light from *Psalm of Solomon 17*." *JBL* 118 (1999) 435-60.
Aus, Roger. "The Magi at the Birth of Cyrus, and the Magi at Jesus' Birth in Matt 2:1-12." In *New Perspectives on Ancient Judaism, II: Religion, Literature, and Society in Ancient Israel, Formative Christianity & Judaism*, edited by Jacob Neusner et al., 99-114. New York: University Press of America, 1987.
Bacon, Benjamin W. "Jesus and the Law: A Study of the First 'Book' of Matthew (Mt 3-7)." *JBL* 47 (1928) 203-31.
Bailey, Mark L. "The Parable of the Mustard Seed." *BSac* 155 (1988) 449-59.
Balentine, Samuel C. "The Politics of Religion in the Persian Period." In *After the Exile: Essays in Honour of Rex Mason*, edited by John Barton and David J. Reimer, 129-46. Macon, GA: Mercer University Press, 1996.
Baltzer, Klaus. *Deutero-Isaiah: A Commentary on Isaiah 40-55*. Translated by Margaret Kohl. Hermeneia. Minneapolis: Fortress, 2001.
Banks, Robert. *Jesus and the Law in the Synoptic Tradition*. SNTSMS 28. Cambridge: Cambridge University Press, 1975.
Basser, Herbert. "Derrett's 'Binding' Reopened." *JBL* 104 (1985) 297-300.
Bauer, David R. "The Kingship of Jesus in the Matthean Infancy Narrative: A Literary Analysis." *CBQ* 57 (1995) 306-23.
Baxter, Wayne. "Healing and the 'Son of David': Matthew's Warrant." *NovT* 48 (2006) 36-50.
Becker, Michael. "4Q521 und die Gesalbten." *RevQ* 18 (1997) 73-96.
Bedford, Peter Ross. "Discerning the Time: Haggai, Zechariah, and the 'Delay' in the Rebuilding of the Jerusalem Temple." In *The Pitcher Is Broken: Memorial Essays for Gösta W. Ahlström*, edited by Steven W. Hollaway and Lowell K. Handy, 71-94. JSOTSup 190. Sheffield: Sheffield Academic, 1995.

Bennett, Thomas J. "Matthew 7:6: A New Interpretation." *WTJ* 49 (1987) 371–86.
Berges, Ulrich. "Die Armen im Buch Jesaja: Ein Beitrag zur Literaturgeschichte des A. T." *Bib* 80 (1999) 153–77.
Berquist, Jon L. *Judaism in Persia's Shadow: A Social and Historical Approach*. Minneapolis: Fortress, 1995.
Betz, Hans Dieter. *Essays on the Sermon on the Mount*. Translated by L. L. Wilborn. Philadelphia: Fortress, 1985.
Betz, Otto. "Felsenmann und Felsengemeinde: Eine Parallele zu Mt 16:17–19 in den Qumranpsalmen." *ZNW* 48 (1957) 49–77.
Beuken, W. A. M. "Isa 29:15–24: Perversion Revisited." In *The Scripture and the Scribes: Studies in Honour of A. S. Van der Woude*, edited by F. Garcia Martinez et al., 43–64. Leiden: Brill, 1992.
———. "The Main Theme of Trito-Isaiah: 'The Servants of Yahweh.'" *JSOT* 47 (1990) 67–87.
———. "Servant and Herald of Good Tidings: Isaiah 61 as an Interpretation of Isaiah 40–55." In *Book of Isaiah / Le Livre d'Isaïe: Les Oracles et Leurs Relectures Unité et Complexité de L'Ouvrage*, edited by Jacques Vermeylen et al., 415–24. Leuven: Leuven University Press, 1989.
Beuken, Wim. "Does Trito-Isaiah Reject the Temple? An Intertextual Inquiry into Isaiah 66:1–6." In *Intertextuality in Biblical Writings: Essays in Honour of Bas van Iersel*, edited by Sipke Draisma, 53–66. KIampen: Kok, 1989.
Biddle, Mark E. "Lady Zion's Alter Ego: Isaiah 47:1–15 and 57:6–13 as Structural Counterparts." In *New Visions of Isaiah*, edited by Roy F. Melugin & Marvin Sweeney, 124–39. JSOTSup 214. Sheffield: Sheffield Academic, 1996.
Black, Matthew. "Aramaic Barnasha and the 'Son of Man.'" *ExpTim* 95 (1983–84) 200–206.
———. "The Messianism of the Parables of Enoch: Their Date and Contribution to Christian Origins." In *The Messiah: Development in Earliest Judaism and Christianity*, edited by James H. Charlesworth, 145–68. Minneapolis: Fortress, 1992.
Blenkinsopp, Joseph. *Isaiah 56–66: A New Translation with Introduction and Commentary*. AB 19B. New York: Doubleday, 2003.
———. *Opening the Sealed Book: Interpretations of the Book of Isaiah in Late Antiquity*. Grand Rapids: Eerdmans, 2006.
Block, Daniel I. *The Book of Ezekiel*. 2 vols. NICOT. Grand Rapids: Eerdmans, 1997–98.
Boadt, Lawrence. "Rhetorical Strategies in Ezekiel's Oracles of Judgment." In *Ezekiel and His Book: Textual and Literary Criticism and Their Interrelation*, edited by J. Lust, 182–200. BETL 74. Leuven: Leuven University Press, 1986.
Boccaccini, Gabriel, ed. *Enoch and the Messiah Son of Man: Revisiting the Book of Parables*. Grand Rapids: Eerdmans, 2007.
Bornkamm, Günther. "The Stilling of the Storm in Matthew." In *Tradition and Interpretation in Matthew*, edited by Günther Bornkamm et al., 52–57. Philadelphia: Westminster, 1963.
Briant, Pierre. *From Cyrus to Alexander: A History of the Persian Empire*. Translated by Peter T. Daniels. Winona Lake, IN: Eisenbrauns, 2002.
Brown, Schuyler. "The Mission to Israel in Matthew's Central Section (Mt 9:35—11:1)." *ZNW* 69 (1978) 73–90.
Bruehler, Bart B. "Seeing through the *eynim* of Zechariah: Understanding Zechariah 4." *CBQ* 63 (2001) 430–43.
Carmichael, Deborah Bleicher. "David Daube on the Eucharist and the Passover Seder." *JSNT* 42 (1991) 45–67.
Carter, Warren. "Are There Imperial Texts in the Class? Intertextual Eagles and Matthean Eschatology as 'Lights Out' Time for Imperial Rome (Matthew 24:27–31)." *JBL* 122 (2003) 467–87.
———. "Evoking Isaiah: Matthean Soteriology and an Intertextual Reading of Isaiah 7–9 and Matthew 1:23 and 4:15–16." *JBL* 119 (2000) 503–20.
———. "Jesus' Healing Stories: Imperial Critique and Eschatological Anticipations in Matthew's Gospel." *CurTM* 37 (2010) 488–96.
———. "Matthew's Gospel: Jewish Christianity, Christian Judaism, or Neither." In *Jewish Christianity Reconsidered: Rethinking Ancient Groups and Texts*, edited by Matt Jackson-McCabe, 155–79. Minneapolis: Fortress, 2007.
Cazelles, Henri. "Jeremiah and Deuteronomy." In *A Prophet to the Nations: Essays in Jeremiah Studies*, edited by Leo G. Purdue and Brian W. Kovacs, 89–111. Winona Lake, IN: Eisenbrauns, 1984.

Childs, Brevard. *Isaiah*. Louisville: Westminster John Knox, 1993.
Clements, R. E. "Beyond Tradition History: Deutero-Isaianic Development of First Isaiah's Themes." *JSOT* 31 (1985) 95–113.
———. "Isaiah 53 and the Restoration of Israel." In *Jesus and the Suffering Servant: Isaiah 53 and Christian Origins*, edited by William H. Bellinger Jr. and William R. Farmer, 39–54. Harrisburg, PA: Trinity, 1998.
———. *Prophecy and Covenant*. SBT 43. London: SCM Press, 1965.
———. "The Unity of the Book of Isaiah." *Int* 26 (1982) 117–29.
Clines, David J. A. *He, We and They: A Literary Approach to Isaiah 53*. JSOTSup 1. Sheffield: JSOT Press, 1976.
Collins, John J. *The Apocalyptic Imagination: An Introduction to the Jewish Matrix of Christianity*. New York: Crossroad, 1987.
———. *A Commentary on the Book of Daniel*. Hermeneia. Minneapolis: Fortress, 1993.
———. "The Son of Man and the Saints of the Most High in the Book of Daniel." *JBL* 93 (1974) 50–66.
Cook, Stephen L. "Innerbiblical Interpretation in Ezekiel 44 and the History of the Priesthood." *JBL* 114 (1995) 193–208.
Corley, Kathleen E. "The Anointing of Jesus in the Synoptic Tradition: An Argument for Authenticity." *JSHJ* 1 (2003) 61–72.
Crenshaw, James L. *Joel: A New Translation with Introduction and Commentary*. AB 24C. New York: Doubleday, 1995.
Cullmann, Oscar. *Peter, Disciple, Apostle, Martyr*. Translated by Floyd V. Filson. New York: Living Age, 1958.
Darr, Katheryn Pfisterer. "Isaiah's Vision and the Rhetoric of Rebellion." In *SBL 1994 Seminar Papers*, edited by Eugene H. Lovering, 847–82. Atlanta: Scholars, 1994.
Davenport, Gene L. "The 'Anointed of the Lord' in Psalm of Solomon 17." In *Ideal Figures in Ancient Judaism: Profiles and Paradigms*, edited by John J. Collins and George W. E. Nickelsburg, 67–91. SBLSCS 12. Chico, CA: Scholars, 1980.
Davies, Graham. "The Destiny of the Nations in the Book of Isaiah." In *The Book of Isaiah / Le Livre d'Isaïe: Les Oracles et Leurs Relectures Unité et Complexité de L'Ouvrage*, edited by Jacques Vermeylen et al., 93–120. Leuven: Leuven University Press, 1989.
Davies, Philip R. *Daniel*. Old Testament Guides. Sheffield: JSOT Press, 1985.
Davies, W. D. "The Jewish Sources of Matthew's Messianism." In *The Messiah: Developments in Earliest Judaism and Christianity*, edited by James H. Charlesworth, 503–11. Minneapolis: Fortress, 1992.
Davies, W. D., and Dale Allison Jr. *The Gospel according to Saint Matthew*. ICC. 3 vols. Edinburgh: T. & T. Clark, 1988–97.
———. "Reflections on the Sermon on the Mount." *SJT* 44 (1991) 283–309.
Dell, Katherine J. "Reinventing the Wheel: The Shaping of the Book of Jonah." In *After the Exile: Essays in Honour of Rex Mason*, edited by John Barton & David J. Reimer, 85–101. Macon, GA: Mercer University Press, 1996.
DeRoche, Michael. "The Reversal of Creation in Hosea." *VT* 31 (1981) 400–409.
———. "Zephaniah I 2–3: The 'Sweeping of Creation.'" *VT* 30 (1980) 104–9.
Derrett, J. Duncan M. "Binding and Loosing (Matt 16:19; 18:18; John 20:23)." *JBL* 102 (1983) 112–17.
———. "Mt 23, 8–10 a Midrash on Is 54, 13 and Jer 31, 31–34." *Bib* 62 (1981) 372–86.
Donaldson, Terence L. *Jesus on the Mountain: A Study in Matthean Theology*. Sheffield: JSOT Press, 1985.
———. "The Law That 'Hangs' (Mt 22:40): Rabbinic Formulation and Matthean Social World." In *SBL 1990 Seminar Papers*, edited by David J. Lull, 14–33. Atlanta: Scholars, 1990.
Dozeman, Thomas B. "Inner-Biblical Interpretation of Yahweh's Gracious and Compassionate Character." *JBL* 108 (1989) 207–23.
Duling, D. C. "'[Do Not Swear . . .] by Jerusalem because It Is the City of the Great King' (Matt 5:35)." *JBL* 110 (1991) 291–309.
———. "Matthew's Plurisignificant 'Son of David' in Social Science Perspective: Kinship, Kingship, Magic, and Miracle." *BTB* 22 (1992) 99–116.
———. "Solomon, Exorcism, and Son of David." *HTR* 68 (1975) 235–52.
———. "The Therapeutic Son of David: An Element of Matthew's Christological Apologetic." *NTS* 24 (1978) 392–410.

Dumbrell, W. J. "The Logic of the Role of Law in Matthew V 1–20." *NovT* 23 (1981) 1–21.
Dunn, James D. G. "Messianic Ideas and Their Influence on the Jesus of History." In *The Messiah: Developments in Earliest Judaism and Christianity*, edited by James H. Charlesworth, 370–76. Minneapolis: Fortress, 1992.
———. "Pharisees, Sinners, and Jesus." In *The Social World of Formative Christianity and Judaism*, edited by Jacob Neusner et al., 264–89. Philadelphia: Fortress, 1988.
Ehro, Ted M. "Historical Allusional Dating and the Similitudes of Enoch." *JBL* 130 (2011) 493–511.
Eichrodt, Walther. "Prophet and Covenant: Observations on the Exegesis of Isaiah." In *Proclamation and Presence: Old Testament Essays in Honour of Gwynne Henton Davies*, edited by John I. Durham and J. R. Porter, 167–88. New corrected edition. Macon, GA: Mercer University Press, 1983.
Eissfeldt, Otto. "The Promises of Grace in Isaiah 55:1–5." In *Israel's Prophetic Heritage: Essays in Honor of James Muilenburg*, edited by Bernhard W. Anderson and Walter Harrelson, 196–207. New York: Harper, 1962.
Elliott, John H. "The Evil Eye and the Sermon on the Mount: Contours of a Pervasive Belief in Social Scientific Perspective." *BibInt* 2 (1994) 51–84.
Evans, Craig A. "Jesus' Action in the Temple: Cleansing or Portent of Destruction?" *CBQ* 51 (1989) 237–70.
———. *Matthew*. Cambridge: Cambridge University Press, 2012.
———. "On the Isaianic Background of the Sower Parable." *CBQ* 47 (1985) 464–68.
Faierstein, Morris M. "Why Do Scribes Say That Elijah Must Come First?" *JBL* 100 (1981) 75–86.
Farmer, William R. "State *Interesse* and Markan Primacy: 1870–1914." In *Biblical Studies and the Shifting of Paradigms: 1850–1914*, edited by Henning Graf Reventlow and William Farmer, 15–49. JSOTSup 192. Sheffield: Sheffield Academic, 1995.
Fitzmyer. Joseph A. "More about Elijah Coming First." *JBL* 104 (1985) 295–96.
France, R. T. *Matthew: Evangelist and Teacher*. Exeter: Paternoster, 1989.
Frankel, Rafael. "Prehellenistic Galilee." *ABD* 2:879–95.
Frankemölle, Hubert. *Jahweh Bund und Kirche Christi: Studien zur Form-und Traditionsgeschichte des "Evangeliums" nach Matthäus*. Münster: Aschendorf, 1974.
———. "Johannes der Täufer und Jesus im Matthäusevangelium: Jesus als Nachfolger des Täufers." *NTS* 42 (1996) 196–218.
Freyne, Sean. "The Geography of Restoration: Galilee-Jerusalem Relations in Early Jewish and Christian Experience." *NTS* 47 (2001) 289–311.
Fretheim, Terence E. *The Message of Jonah: A Theological Commentary*. Minneapolis: Augsburg, 1977.
Fried, Lisbeth S. "Cyrus the Messiah? The Historical Background to Isaiah 45:1." *HTR* 95 (2002) 373–93.
———. *The Priest and the Great King: Temple-Palace Relations in the Persian Empire*. Winona Lake, IN: Eisenbrauns, 2004.
Galambush, Julie. *Jerusalem in the Book of Ezekiel: The City as Yahweh's Wife*. SBLDS 130. Atlanta: Scholars, 1992.
Gammie, John G. "On the Intention and Sources of Daniel I–VI." *VT* 31 (1981) 282–92.
Glazier-McDonald, Beth. "Intermarriage, Divorce, and the *Bat 'El Nekar*: Insights into Mal 2:10–16." *JBL* 106 (1987) 603–11.
———. *Malachi: The Divine Messenger*. SBLDS 98. Atlanta: Scholars, 1987.
———. "Malachi 2:12: *'er we'oneh*—Another Look." *JBL* 105 (1986) 295–98.
Goodwin, Mark J. "Hosea and the 'Son of the Living God' in Matthew 16:16b." *CBQ* 67 (2005) 265–83.
Gosse, Bernard. "Isaïe 52, 13—53, 12 et Isaïe 6." *RB* 98 (1991) 537–43.
Grabbe, Lester L. *Yehud: A History of the Persian Province of Judah*. Vol. 1 in *A History of the Jews and Judaism in the Second Temple Period*. London: T. & T. Clark, 2004.
Graffy, Adrian. *A Prophet Confronts His People: The Disputation Speech in the Prophets*. AnBib 104. Rome: Biblical Institute Press, 1984.
Greenberg, Moshe. "The Design and Themes of Ezekiel's Program of Restoration." *Int* 38 (1984) 181–208.
———. *Ezekiel 1–20: A New Translation with Introduction and Commentary*. AB 22. Garden City: Doubleday, 1983.
Greenfield, J. C., et al. *The Aramaic Levi Document: Edition, Translation, Commentary*. SVTP 19. Leiden: Brill, 2004.

Gregory, Bradley C. "The Postexilic Exile in Third Isaiah: Isaiah 61:1–3 in Light of Second Temple Hermeneutics." *JBL* 126 (2007) 483–88.
Gurtner, Daniel M. *The Torn Veil: Matthew's Exposition of the Death of Jesus.* SNTSMS 139. New York: Cambridge University Press, 2007.
Hagner, Donald. "Law, Righteousness, and Discipleship in Matthew." *Word and World* 18 (1998) 364–71.
———. *Matthew 1–13.* Word Biblical Commentary 33A. Dallas: Word, 1993.
———. "Matthew: Apostate, Reformer, Revolutionary." *NTS* 49 (2003) 193–209.
Hahn, Scott Walker, and John Sietze Bergsma. "What Laws Were 'Not Good'? A Canonical Approach to the Theological Problem of Ezekiel 20:25–26." *JBL* 123 (2004) 201–18.
Halpern, Baruch. "The New Names of Isaiah 62:4: Jeremiah's Reception in the Restoration and the Politics of 'Third Isaiah.'" *JBL* 117 (1998) 623–43.
Hanson, Paul D. *The Dawn of the Apocalyptic.* Philadelphia: Fortress, 1975.
Hare, Douglas R. A. *The Son of Man Tradition.* Minneapolis: Fortress, 1990.
Harris, Mark. "The Comings and Goings of the Son of Man: Is Matthew's Jesus 'Present' or 'Absent'? A Narrative-Critical Response." *BibInt* 22 (2014) 51–70.
Hartman, Louis F., and Alexander A. Di Lella. *The Book of Daniel: A New Translation with Notes and Commentary.* AB 23. Garden City: Doubleday, 1978.
Hauck, Robert J. "Like a Gleaming Flash: Matthew 6:22–23, Luke 11:34–36, and the Divine Sense in Origen." *Australasian Theological Review* 88 (2006) 557–73.
Held, Heinz Joachim. "Matthew as Interpreter of Miracle Stories." In *Tradition and Interpretation in Matthew*, edited by Günther Bornkamm et al., 165–300. Philadelphia: Westminster, 1963.
Hengel, Martin. *Studies in Early Christology.* Edinburgh: T. & T. Clark, 1995.
Hermann, Siegfried. *A History of Israel in Old Testament Times.* Rev. ed. Translated by John Bowden. Philadelphia: Fortress, 1981.
Hiers, Richard H. "'Binding' and 'Loosing': The Matthean Authorizations." *JBL* 104 (1985) 233–50.
Hillers, Delbert R. "*Berit 'am:* 'Emancipation of the People.'" *JBL* 97 (1978) 175–82.
———. *Covenant: The History of a Biblical Idea.* Baltimore: John Hopkins University Press, 1969.
———. *Micah: A Commentary on the Book of Micah.* Hermeneia. Philadelphia: Fortress, 1984.
Holladay, William L. *Jeremiah I: A Commentary on the Book of Jeremiah, Chapters 1–25.* Hermeneia. Philadelphia: Fortress, 1986.
———. *Jeremiah II: A Commentary on the Book of Jeremiah, Chapters 26–52.* Hermeneia. Philadelphia: Fortress, 1989.
———. "Plausible Circumstances for the Prophecy of Habakkuk." *JBL* 120 (2001) 123–42.
Hollenbach, Paul W. "Jesus, Demoniacs, and Public Authorities: A Socio-Historical Study." *JAAR* 49 (1981) 567–88.
Hooker, Morna D. "Is the Son of Man Problem Really Insoluble?" In *Text and Interpretation: Studies in the New Testament Presented to Matthew Black*, edited by Errnest Best and R. Mch. Wilson, 155–68. Cambridge: Cambridge University Press, 1979.
———. *The Son of Man in Mark: A Study of the Background of the Term "Son of Man" and Its Use in Saint Mark's Gospel.* Montreal: McGill University Press, 1967.
Horbury, William. "The Christian Use and the Jewish Origins of the Wisdom of Solomon." In *Wisdom in Ancient Israel: Essays in Honour of J. A. Emerton*, edited by John Day et al., 182–96. Cambridge: Cambridge University Press, 1995.
Horsley, Richard A. "Jesus and Galilee: The Contingencies of a Renewal Movement." In *Galilee through the Centuries: Confluence of Cultures*, edited by Eric R. Meyers, 57–74. Winona Lake, IN: Eisenbrauns, 1999.
———. *Jesus and the Spiral of Violence: Popular Jewish Resistance in Roman Palestine.* Minneapolis: Fortress, 1993.
———. *The Prophet Jesus and the Renewal of Israel: Moving Beyond a Diversionary Debate.* Grand Rapids: Eerdmans, 2012.
———. *Scribes, Visionaries, and the Politics of Second Temple Judea.* Louisville: Westminster John Knox, 2007.
Huffmon, Herbert B. "The Covenant Lawsuit in the Prophets." *JBL* 78 (1959) 285–95.
Hurowitz, Victor A. "Restoring the Temple—Why and When?" *JQR* 93 (2003) 581–91.

BIBLIOGRAPHY

Isaac, E. "1 (Ethiopic Apocalypse of) Enoch: A New Translation and Introduction." In *The Old Testament Pseudepigrapha*, vol 1., edited by James H. Charlesworth, 5–100. Garden City: Doubleday, 1982.

Janzen, David. "The Meaning of *Porneia* in Matthew 5.32 and 19.9: An Approach from the Study of Near Eastern Culture." *JSNT* 80 (2000) 66–80.

———. "The Mission of Ezra and the Persian-Period Temple Community." *JBL* 119 (2000) 919–43.

———. "Scholars, Witches, Ideologies, and What the Text Said: Ezra 9–10 and Its Interpretation." In *Approaching Yehud: New Approaches to the Study of the Persian Period*, edited by Jon Berquist, 49–69. Atlanta: SBL, 2007.

Japhet, Sara. *The Ideology of the Book of Chronicles and Its Place in Biblical Thought*. Rev. ed. Frankfort am Main: Lang, 1997.

Jaubert, Annie. *La Date de la Cène: Calendrier Biblique et Liturgie Chrétienne*. EBib. Paris: Gabalda, 1957.

Jenkins, Allan K. "The Development of the Isaiah Tradition in Isaiah 13–23." In *The Book of Isaiah / Le Livre d'Isaïe: Les Oracles et Leurs Relectures Unité et Complexité de L'Ouvrage*, edited by Jacques Vermeylen et al., 237–51. Leuven: Leuven University Press, 1989.

Jenkins, Philip. *Hidden Gospels: How the Search for Jesus Lost Its Way*. New York: Oxford University Press, 2001.

Jeremias, Joachim. *Jesus' Promise to the Nations*. Translated by S. H. Hooke. Philadelphia: Fortress, 1958.

Johnson, Luke Timothy. *The Real Jesus: The Misguided Quest for the Historical Jesus and the Truth of the Traditional Gospels*. San Francisco: HarperCollins, 1996.

Jones, Douglas Rawlinson. *Jeremiah*. New Century Bible Commentary. Grand Rapids: Eerdmans, 1992.

Jones, John Mark. "Subverting the Textuality of Davidic Messianism: Matthew's Presentation of the Genealogy and the Davidic Title." *CBQ* 56 (1994) 256–72.

Jonker, Louis. "The Chronicler and the Prophets: Who Were His Authoritative Sources?" *SJOT* 22 (2008) 275–95.

Joyce, Paul M. "King and Messiah in Ezekiel." In *King and Messiah in Israel and the Ancient Near East: Proceedings of the Oxford Old Testament Seminar*, edited by John Day, 323–37. JSOTSup 270. Sheffield: Sheffield Academic, 1998.

Kaiser, Walter C. Jr. "The Unfailing Kindnesses Promised to David: Isaiah 55:3." *JSOT* 45 (1989) 91–98.

Keiser, Thomas A. "The Song of Moses a Basis for Isaiah's Prophecy." *VT* 55 (2005) 486–500.

Kessler, John. "Building the Second Temple: Questions of Time, Text, and History in Haggai 1:1–15." *JSOT* 27 (2002) 243–56.

Kim, Hyun Chul Paul. "Jonah Read Intertextually." *JBL* 126 (2007) 512–16.

Kingsbury, Jack Dean. "Observations on the 'Miracles Chapters' of Matthew 8–9." *CBQ* 40 (1978) 559–73.

———. "On Following Jesus: The 'Eager' Scribe and the 'Reluctant' Disciple." *NTS* 34 (1988) 45–59.

———. "The Parable of the Wicked Husbandmen and the Secret of Jesus' Divine Sonship" *JBL* 105 (1986) 643–55.

Klein, Ralph W. *I Chronicles: A Commentary*. Hermeneia. Minneapolis: Fortress, 2006.

———. *Ezekiel: The Prophet and His Message*. Columbia: University of South Carolina Press, 1988.

Knibb, M. "Isaianic Traditions in the Book of Enoch." In *After the Exile: Essays in Honour of Rex Mason*, edited by John Barton and David J. Reimer, 217–29. Macon, GA: Mercer University Press, 1996.

Knight, George A. F. *Servant Theology: A Commentary on the Book of Isaiah 40–55*. Grand Rapids: Eerdmans, 1984.

Knoppers, Gary N. *1 Chronicles 1–9: A New Translation with Introduction and Commentary*. AB 12. New York: Doubleday, 2003.

———. *1 Chronicles 10–29: A New Translation with Introduction and Commentary*. AB 12A. New York: Doubleday, 2004.

———. "Hierodules, Priests, or Janitors? The Levites in Chronicles and the History of the Israelite Priesthood." *JBL* 118 (1999) 49–72.

———. "Intermarriage, Social Complexity, and Ethnic Diversity in the Genealogy of Judah." *JBL* 120 (2001) 15–30.

Koch, Klaus. "Der 'Menschensohn' in Daniel." *ZAW* 119 (2007) 369–87.

Kohn, Risa Levitt. "A Prophet Like Moses? Rethinking Ezekiel's Relationship to the Torah." *ZAW* 114 (2002) 236–54.

Kugler, Robert. *From Patriarch to Priest: The Levi-Priestly Tradition from Aramaic Levi to Testament of Levi*. Atlanta: Scholars, 1996.

Larkin, Katrina J. A. *The Eschatology of Second Zechariah: A Study of the Formation of a Mantological Wisdom Anthology*. Kampen: Kok Pharos, 1994.
Lee, Bernhard J. *The Galilean Jewishness of Jesus: Retrieving the Jewish Origins of Christianity*. Mahwah, NJ: Paulist, 1988.
Leske, Adrian M. "The Beatitudes, Salt, and Light in Matthew and Luke." In *SBL 1991 Seminar Papers*, edited by Eugene Lovering Jr., 816–39. Atlanta: Scholars, 1991.
———. "Context and Meaning of Zechariah 9:9." *CBQ* 62 (2000) 663–78.
———. "The Influence of Isaiah on Christology in Matthew and Luke." In *Crisis in Christology: Essays in Quest of Resolution*, edited by William R. Farmer, 241–69. Livonia, MI: Dove, 1995.
———. "Isaiah and Matthew: The Prophetic Influence in the First Gospel." In *Jesus and the Suffering Servant: Isaiah 53 and Christian Origins*, edited by William H. Bellinger and William R. Farmer, 152–69. Harrisburg, PA: Trinity, 1998.
———. "Jesus as a *Nazoraios*." In *Resourcing New Testament Studies: Literary, Historical, and Theological Essays in Honor of David L. Dungan*, edited by Allan J. McNicol et al., 69–81. New York: T. & T. Clark, 2009.
———. "Matthew." In *The International Bible Commentary: A Catholic and Ecumenical Commentary for the Twenty-First Century*, edited by William R. Farmer, 1253–330. Collegeville: Liturgical, 1998.
———. "Matthew 6:25–34: Human Anxiety and the Natural World." In *The Earth Story in the New Testament*, edited by Norman C. Habel & Vicky Balabanski, 15–27. London: Sheffield Academic, 2002.
———. "Righteousness as Relationship." In *Festschrift: A Tribute to Dr William Hordern*, edited by Walter Freitag, 125–37. Saskatoon: University of Saskatchewan Press, 1985.
Leuchter, Mark. "'The Prophets' and 'the Levites' in Josiah's Covenant Ceremony." *ZAW* 121 (2009) 31–47.
Levin, Yigal. "Who Was the Chronicler's Audience? A Hint from His Genealogies." *JBL* 122 (2003) 229–45.
Levinson, Jon Douglas. *Theology of the Program of Restoration of Ezekiel 40–48*. HSM 10. Missoula, MT: Scholars, 1976.
Lincoln, Andrew T. "Contested Paternity and Contested Readings: Jesus' Conception in Matthew 1:18–25." *JSNT* 34 (2012) 211–31.
Lindblom, J. *Prophecy in Ancient Israel*. Philadelphia: Fortress, 1962.
Luz, Ulrich. *Matthew 1–7: A Commentary*. Translated by W. C. Linss. Minneapolis: Augsburg/Fortress, 1989.
———. *Matthew 8–20: A Commentary*. Translated by James E. Crouch. Hermeneia. Minneapolis: Fortress, 2001.
———. *The Theology of the Gospel of Matthew*. Translated by J. Bradford Robinson. Cambridge: Cambridge University Press, 1995.
Marcus, Joel. "The Gates of Hades and the Keys of the Kingdom (Matt 16:18–19)." *CBQ* 50 (1988) 443–55.
Mason, Rex. *The Books of Haggai, Zechariah and Malachi*. Cambridge: Cambridge University Press, 1977.
———. "The Use of Earlier Biblical Material in Zechariah 9–14: A Study in Inner Biblical Exegesis." In *Bringing out the Treasure: Inner Biblical Allusion in Zechariah 9–14*, edited by Mark J. Boda and Michael H. Floyd, 1–208. JSOTSup 370. London: Sheffield Academic, 2003.
Mason, Steve. *Flavius Josephus on the Pharisees: A Composition-Critical Study*. Leiden: Brill, 1991.
———. "Pharisaic Dominance Before 70 CE and the Gospels' Hypocrisy Charge (Matt 23:2–3)." *HTR* 83 (1990) 363–81.
Mattill, A. J. "The Way of Tribulation." *JBL* 98 (1979) 531–46.
May, Herbert G. "The King in the Garden of Eden: A Study of Ezekiel 28:12–19." In *Israel's Prophetic Heritage: Essays in Honor of James Muilenburg*, edited by Bernhard W. Anderson and Walter Harrelson, 166–76. New York: Harper, 1962.
McCane, Byron R. "'Let the Dead Bury Their Own Dead': Secondary Burial and Matt 21–22." *HTR* 83 (1990) 31–43.
McEleny, Neil J. "The Unity and Theme of Matthew 7:1–12." *CBQ* 56 (1994) 490–500.
McEvenue, Sean. "Who Was Second Isaiah?" In *Studies in the Book of Isaiah: Festschrift Willem A. M. Beuken*, edited by J. Van Ruiten and M. Vervenne, 213–22. BETL 132. Leuven: Leuven University Press, 1997.

McIver, Robert K. "The Parable of the Weeds among the Wheat (Matt 13:24–30, 36–42), and the Relationship between the Kingdom and the Church as Portrayed in the Gospel of Matthew." *JBL* 114 (1995) 643–59.

McKeating, H. "Ezekiel the 'Prophet Like Moses'?" *JSNT* 61 (1994) 97–109.

McKenzie, John L. *Second Isaiah: Introduction, Translation, and Notes*. AB 20. Garden City: Doubleday, 1968.

Meier, John P. "John the Baptist in Matthew's Gospel." *JBL* 99 (1980) 383–405.

Menken, Maarten J. J. "The Textual Form of the Quotation from Isaiah 8:23—9:1 in Matthew 4:14–15." *RB* 105 (1998) 526–45.

Meyers, Carol L., and Eric M. Meyers. *Haggai, Zechariah 1–8: A New Translation with Introduction and Commentary*. AB 25B. New York: Doubleday, 1987.

———. *Zechariah 9–14: A New Translation with Introduction and Commentary*. AB 25C. New York: Doubleday, 1993.

Meyers, Eric M. "Messianism in First and Second Zechariah, and the 'End' of Biblical Prophecy." In *"Go to the Land I will Show You": Studies in Honor of Dwight W. Young*, edited by Joseph E. Coleson and Victor H. Matthews, 127–42. Winona Lake, IN: Eisenbrauns, 1996.

———. "The Persian Period and the Judean Restoration: From Zerubbabel to Nehemiah." In *Ancient Israelite Religion: Essays in Honor of Frank Moore Cross*, edited by Patrick D. Miller et al., 509–21. Philadelphia: Fortress, 1987.

Meyers, Eric M., and James F. Strange. *Archeology, the Rabbis, and Early Christianity*. Nashville: Abingdon, 1981.

Mettinger, Tryggve M. D. *A Farewell to the Servant Songs: A Critical Examination of an Exegetical Axiom*. Scripta Minora. Lund: Gleerup, 1983.

———. *Solomonic State Officials: A Study of the Civil Government Officials of the Israelite Monarchy*. ConBot 5. Lund: Gleerup, 1971.

Millar, William R. *Isaiah 24–27 and the Origin of Apocalyptic*. Missoula, MT: Scholars, 1976.

Mitchell, Hinckley G. *A Criticial and Exegetical Commentary on Haggai, Zechariah, Malachi and Jonah*. With John Merlin Powis Smith and Julius A. Bewer. ICC. Edinburgh: T. & T. Clark, 1912.

Moore, Daniel F. "Jesus: An Emerging Jewish Mosaic." In *Jesus Research: New Methodologies and Perceptions; The Second Princeton-Prague Symposium of Jesus Research, Princeton, 2007*, edited by James H. Charlesworth with Brian Rhea, 58–81. Grand Rapids: Eerdmans, 2014.

Moran, W. L. "The Ancient Near Eastern Background of the Love of God in Deuteronomy." *CBQ* 25 (1963) 77–87.

Moss, Candida R. "Blind Vision and Ethical Confusion: The Rhetorical Function of Matthew 6:22–23." *CBQ* 73 (2011) 757–76.

Moule, C. F. D. *The Origin of Christology*. Cambridge: Cambridge University Press, 1977.

Murphy-O'Conner, Jerome. "The Prayer of Petition (Matthew 7:7–11 and Par.)." *RB* 110 (2003) 359–416.

Nepper-Christensen, Poul. "Die Taufe im Matthäusevangelium im Lichte der Traditionen über Johannes den Täufer." *NTS* 31 (1985) 189–207.

Neusner, Jacob. *From Politics to Piety: The Emergence of Pharisaic Judaism*. Englewood Cliffs, NJ: Prentice-Hall, 1973.

Nickelsburg, George W. E. "Enoch, Levi, and Peter: Recipients of Revelation in Upper Galilee." *JBL* 100 (1981) 575–600.

———. *1 Enoch 1: A Commentary on the Book of Enoch; Chapter 1–36, 81–108*. Hermeneia. Mineapolis: Fortress, 2001.

———. *Jewish Literature between the Bible and the Mishnah*. 2nd ed. Minneapolis: Fortress, 2005.

———. *Resurrection, Immortality, and Eternal Life in Intertestamental Judaism*. HTS 26. Cambridge: Harvard University Press, 1972.

Nickelsburg, George W. E., and James C. VanderKam. *1 Enoch: A New Translation Based on the Hermeneia Commentary*. Minneapolis: Fortress, 2004.

———. *1 Enoch 2: A Commentary on the Book of Enoch, Chapters 37–82*. Hermeneia. Minneapolis: Fortress, 2012.

Niskanen, Paul. "Yhwh as Father, Redeemer, and Potter in Isaiah 63:7—64:11." *CBQ* 68 (2006) 397–407.

Öhler, Markus. "The Expectation of Elijah and the Presence of the Kingdom of God." *JBL* 118 (1999) 461–76.

Olmstead, A. T. *History of the Persian Empire*. Chicago: University of Chicago Press, 1948.
Otzen, Benedict. "Traditions and Structures of Isaiah XXIV–XXVII." *VT* 24 (1974) 196–206.
Overman, J. Andrew. *Matthew's Gospel and Formative Judaism: The Social World of the Matthean Community*. Minneapolis: Fortress, 1990.
Parker, Pierson. "Jesus, John the Baptist, and the Herods." *PRSt* 8 (1981) 4–11.
Petersen, David L. *Haggai and Zechariah 1–8: A Commentary*. OTL. Philadelphia: Westminster, 1984.
———. *Late Israelite Prophecy: Studies in Deutero-Prophetic Literature and in Chronicles*. SBLMS 23. Missoula, MT: Scholars, 1977.
———. *Zechariah 9–14 and Malachi: A Commentary*. Louisville: John Knox, 1995.
Peuch, Émile. "4Q525 et les Péricopes des Béatitudes en Ben Sira et Matthieu." *RB* 98 (1991) 80–106.
———. "Messianism, Resurrection, and Eschatology at Qumran and in the New Testament." In *The Community of the Renewed Covenant: The Notre Dame Symposium on the Dead Sea Scrolls*, edited by Eugene Ulrich and James VanderKam, 235–56. Notre Dame: University of Notre Dame Press, 1994.
Poffenroth, Kim. "Jesus as Anointed and Healing Son of David in the Gospel of Matthew." *Bib* 80 (1999) 547–54.
Pomykala, Kenneth E. *The Davidic Dynasty Tradition in Early Judaism: Its History and Significance for Messianism*. SBLEJL 7. Atlanta: Scholars, 1995.
Pons, Jacques. "Le Vocabulaire D'ezekiel 20: Le Prophète s'oppose à la vision deutéronomiste de l'histoire." In *Ezekiel and His Book: Textual and Literary Criticism and their Interrelation*, edited by J. Lust, 214–33. BETL 74. Leuven: Leuven University Press, 1986.
Porteus, Norman W. *Daniel: A Commentary*. OTL. Philadelphia: Westminster, 1965.
Powell, Mark Allan. "Binding and Loosing: A Paradigm for Ethical Discernment from the Gospel of Matthew." *CurTM* 30 (2003) 438–45.
———. "Do and Keep What Moses Says (Matthew 23:2–7)." *JBL* 114 (1995) 419–35.
———. "Matthew's Beatitudes: Reversals and Rewards of the Kingdom." *CBQ* 58 (1996) 460–79.
Pregeant, Russell. *Knowing Truth, Doing Good: Engaging New Testament Ethics*. Minneapolis: Fortress, 2008.
Przybylski, Benno. *Righteousness in Matthew and His World of Thought*. SNTSMS 41. Cambridge: Cambridge University Press, 1980.
Redditt, Paul. "Nehemiah's First Mission and the Date of Zechariah 9–14." *CBQ* 56 (1994) 664–78.
Reed, Jonathan L. *Archeology and the Galilean Jesus: A Re-examination of the Evidence*. Harrisburg, PA: Trinity, 2000.
———. "Galileans, 'Israelite Village Communities' and the Sayings Gospel Q." In *Galilee through the Centuries: Confluence of Cultures*, edited by Eric M. Meyers, 87–108. Winona Lake, IN: Eisenbrauns, 1999.
Regev, Eyal. "Pure Individualism: The Idea of Non-Priestly Purity in Ancient Judaism." *JSJ* 31 (2000) 176–202.
Rendtorff, Rolf. "Zur Komposition des Buches Jesaja." *VT* 34 (1984) 295–320.
Richardson, Peter. *Herod: King of the Jews and Friend of the Romans*. Minneapolis: Fortress, 1999.
Riley, William. *King and Cultus in Chronicles: Worship and Reinterpretation of History*. Sheffield: JSOT Press, 1993.
Roberts, J. J. M. *Nahum, Habakkuk, and Zephaniah: A Commentary*. OTL. Louisville: Westminster John Knox, 1991.
———. "The Old Testament Contribution to Messianic Expectations." In *The Messiah: Developments in Early Judaism and Christianity*, edited by James H. Charlesworth, 47–49. Minneapolis: Fortress, 1992.
Rofé, Alexander. "Isaiah 66:1–4: Judean Sects in the Persian Period as Viewed by Trito-Isaiah." In *Biblical and Related Studies Presented to Samuel Iwry*, edited by Ann Kort and Scott Morschauer, 205–17. Winona Lake, IN: Eisenbrauns, 1985.
Rowley, H. H. "The Unity of the Book of Daniel." In *The Servant of the Lord and Other Essays on the Old Testament*. 2nd ed. Oxford: Blackwell, 1965.
Rudolph, Wilhelm. *Haggai—Sacharja 1–8—Sacharja 9–14—Malachi*. KAT 13.4. Gütersloh: Gütersloher Verlagshaus Mohn, 1976.
Runesson, Anders. "Rethinking Early Jewish-Christian Relations: Matthean Community History as Pharisaic Intragroup Conflict." *JBL* 127 (2008) 95–132.

Saldarini, Anthony J. "Delegitimation of Leaders in Matthew 23." *CBQ* 54 (1992) 659–80.

———. *Matthew's Christian-Jewish Community*. Chicago: University of Chicago Press, 1994.

Sanders, E. P. "Jerusalem and Its Temple in the Beginnings of the Christian Movement." *Judaism* 46 (1997) 189–96.

———. *Jesus and Judaism*. Philadelphia: Fortress, 1985.

Saulnier, Stéphane. *Calendrical Variations in Second Temple Judaism: New Perspectives on the "Date of the Last Supper" Debate*. Leiden: Brill, 2012.

Schaberg, Jane. *The Illegitimacy of Jesus: A Feminist Theological Interpretation of the Infancy Narratives*. San Francisco: Harper & Row, 1987.

Schaefer, Konrad R. "Zechariah 14: A Study of Allusion." *CBQ* 57 (1995) 66–91.

Schaper, Joachim. "The Jerusalem Temple as an Instrument of the Achaeminid Fiscal Administration." *VT* 45 (1995) 528–39.

———. "The Temple Treasury Committee in the Times of Nehemiah and Ezra." *VT* 47 (1997) 200–206.

Schiffman, Lawrence H. "The Pharisees and Their Legal Tradition according to the Dead Sea Scrolls." *DSD* 8 (2001) 262–77.

Schmitz, Philip C. "The Grammar of Resurrection in Isaiah 26:19a–c." *JBL* 122 (2003) 145–49.

Schottroff, Willy. "The Prophet Amos." In *God of the Lowly: Socio-Historical Interpretations of the Bible*, edited by Willy Schottroff and Wolfgang Stegemann, 27–46. Translated by Matthew J. O'Connell. Maryknoll: Orbis, 1984.

Schramm, Brooks. *The Opponents of Trito-Isaiah: Reconstructing the Cultic History of the Restoration*. JSOTSup 193. Sheffield: Sheffield Academic, 1995.

Schwartz, Baruch J. "Ezekiel's Dim View of Israel's Restoration." In *The Book of Ezekiel: Theological and Anthropological Perspectives*, edited by Margaret S. Odell and John T. Strong, 43–67. Atlanta: SBL, 2000.

Scullion, John J. "An Approach to the Understanding of Isaiah 7:10–17." *JBL* 87 (1968) 288–300.

Segal, Alan F. "Matthew's Jewish Voice." In *Social History of the Matthean Community: Cross-Disciplinary Approaches*, edited by David L. Balch, 3–37. Minneapolis: Fortress, 1991.

Segal, Michael. "The Responsibilities and Rewards of Joshua the High Priest According to Zechariah 3:7." *JBL* 126 (2007) 720–26.

Seitz, Christopher R. "The Divine Council: Temporal Transition and New Prophecy in the Book of Isaiah." *JBL* 109 (1990) 229–47.

———. *Isaiah 1–39*. Interpretation. Louisville: John Knox, 1993.

———. *World Without End: The Old Testament as Abiding Theological Witness*. Grand Rapids: Eerdmans, 1998.

Sim, David C. *The Gospel of Matthew and Christian Judaism: The History and Social Setting of the Matthean Community*. Edinburgh: T. & T. Clark, 1998.

———. "Matthew 7:21–23: Further Evidence of Its Anti-Pauline Perspective." *NTS* 53 (2007) 325–43.

Smith, Mark. "*Berit 'am/Berit 'olam*: A New Proposal for the Crux of Isa 42:6." *JBL* 100 (1981) 241–43.

Smith, Morton. "Hellenization." In *Emerging Judaism: Studies of the Fourth and Third Centuries B.C.E.*, edited by Michael E. Stone and David Satran, 103–28. Minneapolis: Fortress, 1989.

Snodgrass, Klyne. "Matthew and the Law." In *Treasures New and Old: Recent Contributions to Matthean Studies*, edited by David R. Bauer and Mark Allan Powell, 99–127. Atlanta: Scholars, 1996.

———. "Recent Research on the Parable of the Wicked Tenants: An Assessment." *BBR* 8 (1998) 187–215.

Sommer, Benjamin D. "Allusions and Illusions: The Unity of the Book of Isaiah in Light of Deutero-Isaiah's Use of Prophetic Tradition." In *New Visions of Isaiah*, edited by Roy F. Melugin and Marvin A. Sweeney, 156–86. JSOTSup 214. Sheffield: Sheffield Academic, 1996.

———. *A Prophet Reads Scripture: Allusions in Isaiah 40–66*. Stanford: Stanford University Press, 1998.

Stanton, Graham N. "Revisiting Matthew's Communities." In *SBL 1994 Seminar Papers*, edited by Eugene H. Lovering Jr., 9–23. Atlanta: Scholars, 1994.

Steck, Odil Hannes. "Aspekte des Gottesknechts in Jes 52, 13—53, 12." *ZAW* 97 (1985) 36–58.

Stern, David. "Jesus' Parables from the Perspective of Rabbinic Literature: The Example of the Wicked Husbandmen." In *Parable and Story in Judaism and Christianity*, edited by Clements Thoma and Michael Wyschogrod, 57–65. New York: Paulist, 1989.

Stern, Philip. "The 'Blind Servant' Imagery of Deutero-Isaiah and Its Implications." *Bib* 75 (1994) 224–32.

Stordalen, T. *Echoes of Eden: Genesis 2–3 and Symbolism of the Eden Garden in Biblical Hebrew Literature.* CBET 25. Leuven: Peeters, 2000.

Stone, M. E. "Enoch, Aramaic Levi and Sectarian Origins." *JSJ* 19 (1988) 159–70.

Streeter, Burnett Hillman. *The Four Gospels: A Study of Origins, Treating of the Manuscript Tradition, Sources, Authorship, & Dates.* London: MacMillan, 1924.

Strecker, Georg. *Der Weg der Rechtigkeit: Untersuchung zur Theologie des Matthäus.* Göttingen: Vandenhoeck & Ruprecht, 1962.

Stuhlmueller, Carroll. "Deutero-Isaiah: Major Transitions in the Prophet's Theology and in Contemporary Scholarship." *CBQ* 42 (1980) 1–29.

———. *Rebuilding with Hope: A Commentary on the Books of Haggai and Zechariah.* Grand Rapids: Eerdmans, 1988.

Suggs, M. Jack. "Wisdom of Solomon 2:10—5: A Homily Based on the Fourth Servant Song." *JBL* 76 (1957) 26–33.

Suter, David. "Fallen Angel, Fallen Priest: The Problem of Family Purity in 1 Enoch 6–16." *HUCA* 50 (1979) 115–35.

———. "*Masal* in the Similitudes of Enoch." *JBL* 100 (1981) 193–212.

Sweeney, Marvin A. "The Book of Isaiah as Prophetic Torah." In *New Visions of Isaiah*, edited by Roy F. Melugin and Marvin A Sweeney, 50–67. JSOTSup 214. Sheffield: Sheffield Academic, 1996.

———. "The Reconceptualization of the Davidic Covenant." In *Studies in the Book of Isaiah: Festschrift Willem A. M. Beuken*, edited by J. Van Ruiten and M. Vervenne, 41–61. BETL 132. Leuven: Leuven University Press, 1997.

———. "Textual Citations in Isaiah 24–27: Toward an Understanding of the Redactional Function of Chapters 24–27 in the Book of Isaiah." *JBL* 107 (1988) 39–52.

Tcherikover, Victor. *Hellenistic Civilization and the Jews.* Translated by S. Applebaum. New York: Atheneum, 1977.

Tiemeyer, Lena-Sofia. "'The Haughtiness of the Priesthood' (Isa 65, 5)." *Bib* 85 (2004) 237–44.

Tiller, Patrick A. *A Commentary on the Animal Apocalypse of 1 Enoch.* Atlanta: Scholars, 1993.

Tödt, Heinz Eduard. *The Son of Man in the Synoptic Tradition.* Translated by D. M. Barton. Philadelphia: Westminster, 1965.

Trotter, James M. "Was the Second Temple Primarily a Persian Project?" *SJOT* 15 (2001) 276–94.

Troxel, Ronald L. "Matt 27:51–4 Reconsidered: Its Role in the Passion Narrative, Meaning and Origin." *NTS* 48 (2002) 30–47.

Tuell, Steven Shawn. *The Law of the Temple in Ezekiel 40–48.* HSM 49. Atlanta: Scholars, 1992.

VanderKam, James C. "Daniel 7 in the Similitudes (1 Enoch 37–71)." In *Biblical Traditions in Transmission: Essays in Honour of Michael A. Knibb*, edited by Charlotte Hempel and Judith Lieu, 291–307. JSJSup 111. Leiden: Brill, 2006.

———. *Enoch and the Growth of an Apocalyptic Tradition.* CBQMS 16. Washington, DC: Catholic Biblical Association, 1984.

———. "Joshua the High Priest and the Interpretation of Zechariah 3." *CBQ* 53 (1991) 533–70.

———. "Righteous One, Messiah, Chosen One, and Son of Man in 1 Enoch 37–71." In *The Messiah: Development in Earliest Judaism and Christianity*, edited by James H. Charlesworth, 169–91. Minneapolis: Fortress, 1992.

Vermeylen, Jacques. "L'Unité du Livre d'Isaïe." In *The Book of Isaiah / Le Livre d'Isaïe: Les Oracles et leurs Relectures Unité et Complexité de L'Ouvrage*, edited by Jacques Vermeylen et al., 13–53. Leuven: Leuven University Press, 1989.

Verseput, Donald J. "Jesus' Pilgrimage to Jerusalem and Encounter in the Temple: A Geographical Motif in Matthew's Gospel." *NovT* 46 (1994) 105–21.

———. "The Role and Meaning of the 'Son of God' Title in Matthew's Gospel." *NTS* 33 (1987) 532–56.

Viviano, Benedict. "Social World and Community Leadership: The Case of Matthew 23:1–12, 34." *JSNT* 39 (1990) 3–21.

De Vries, Simon J. "Moses and David as Cult Founders in Chronicles." *JBL* 107 (1988) 619–39.

Waters, Kenneth L., Sr. "Matthew 27:52–53 as Apocalyptic Apostrophe: Temporal-Spatial Collapse in the Gospel of Matthew." *JBL* 122 (2003) 489–515.

Webb, Robert L. *John the Baptist and Prophet: A Socio-Historical Study.* JSNTSup 62. Sheffield: Sheffield Academic, 1991.

Weren, Wim J. C. "The Five Women in Matthew's Genealogy." *CBQ* 50 (1997) 288–305.

Westermann, Klaus. *Isaiah 40–66*. OTL. Philadelphia: Westminster, 1969.

White, L. Michael. "Crisis Management and Boundary Maintenance: The Social Location of the Matthean Community." In *Social History of the Matthean Community: Cross-Disciplinary Approaches*, edited by David L. Balch, 211–47. Minneapolis: Fortress, 1991.

Whitelam, Keith W. *The Just King: Monarchical Judicial Authority in Ancient Israel*. JSOTSup 12. Sheffield: Sheffield University, 1979.

Whybray, R. N. *Isaiah 40–66*. London: Oliphants, 1975.

Wilcox, Peter, and David Paton-Williams. "The Servant Songs in Deutero-Isaiah." *JSOT* 44 (1988) 79–102.

Wildberger, Hans. *Isaiah 1–12: A Commentary*. Translated by Thomas H. Trapp. Minneapolis: Fortress, 1991.

———. *Isaiah 13–27: A Continental Commentary*. Translated by Thomas H. Trapp. Minneapolis: Fortress, 1997.

Willey, Patricia Tull. *Remember the Former Things: The Recollection of Previous Texts in Second Isaiah*. Atlanta: Scholars, 1997.

Williamson, H. G. M. "Isaiah 62:4 and the Problem of Inner Biblical Allusions." *JBL* 119 (2000) 734–39.

———. "Isaiah 63:7—64:11: Exilic Lament or Post-Exilic Protest?" *ZAW* 102 (1990) 45–58.

———. "The Messianic Texts in Isaiah 1–39." In *King and Messiah in Israel and the Ancient Near East: Proceedings of the Oxford Old Testament Seminar*, edited by John Day, 238–70. JSOTSup 270. Sheffield: Sheffield Academic, 1998.

———. *Variations on a Theme: King, Messiah, and Servant in the Book of Isaiah*. Carlisle, UK: Paternoster, 1998.

Wink, Walter. "Neither Passivity Nor Violence: Jesus' Third Way." In *SBL 1988 Seminar Papers*, edited by David J. Lull, 210–24. Atlanta: Scholars, 1988.

Wolff, Hans Walter. *Haggai: A Commentary*. Translated by Margaret Kohl. Minneapolis: Augsburg, 1988.

———. *Hosea: A Commentary on the Book of Isaiah*. Translated by Gary Stansell. Hermeneia. Philadelphia: Fortress, 1974.

———. *Joel and Amos: A Commentary on the Books of Joel and Amos*. Translated by Waldemar Janzen et al. Hermeneia. Philadelphia: Fortress, 1977.

———. *Micah the Prophet*. Translated by Ralph D. Gehrke. Philadelphia: Fortress, 1981.

———. *Obadiah and Jonah: A Commentary*. Translated by Margaret Kohl. Hermeneia. Minneapolis: Augsburg, 1986.

Wright, R. B. "Psalms of Solomon: A New Translation and Introduction." In *The Old Testament Pseudepigrapha*, vol. 2, edited by James H. Charlesworth, 639–70. Garden City: Doubleday, 1985.

Zimmerli, Walther. *Ezekiel 1: A Commentary on the Book of the Prophet Ezekiel, Chapters 1–24*. Translated by Ronald E. Clements. Hermeneia. Philadelphia: Fortress, 1979.

———. *The Law and the Prophets: A Study of the Meaning of the Old Testament*. Oxford: Blackwell, 1965.

Zöckler, Thomas. "Light within the Human Person: A Comparison of Matthew 6:22–23 and Gospel of Thomas 24." *JBL* 120 (2001) 487–99.

Modern Authors Index

Achtemeier, Elizabeth, 62, 65, 67, 68, 70
Ahlstrom, G. W., 109, 111
Albertz, Rainer, 17
Allison, Dale C. Jr, 159, 189
Anderson, Bernhard, 58
Anderson, T. David, 70
Andinach, Pablo R., 111
Atkinson, Kenneth, 141
Aus, Roger, 189

Bacon, Benjamin W., 161
Bailey, Mark L., 182
Balentine, Samuel C., 73
Baltzer, Klaus, 47, 51, 55
Banks, Robert, 167
Bauer, David R., 187
Baxter, Wayne, 185
Bedford, Peter Ross, 73
Bennett, Thomas J., 172
Berquist, Jon L., 81, 88
Betz, Hans Dieter, 171
Betz, Otto, 205
Beuken, W. A. M., 63, 65, 70, 71
Beuken, Wim, 66
Biddle, Mark E., 66
Black, Matthew, 146, 194, 201
Blenkinsopp, Joseph, 67
Block, Daniel I., 26, 29, 30
Boadt, Lawrence, 32
Bornkamm, Günther, 177
Briant, Pierre, 88, 98, 99
Brown, Schuyler, 196
Bruehler, Bart B., 78

Carmichael, Deborah B., 213, 214
Carter, Warren, 149, 160, 175, 211
Cazelles, Henri, 22

Chancey, Mark A., 154
Childs, Brevard, 115, 117
Clements, R. E., 40, 50
Clines, David J., 55
Collins, John J., 128, 132, 134, 135, 137, 147
Cook, Stephen L., 89
Corley, Kathleen E., 213
Crenshaw, James L., 109, 111
Cullmann, Oscar, 205

Darr, Katheryn Pfisterer, 49
Davenport, Gene L., 141
Davies, Graham, 14
Davies, Philip R., 128, 132, 137
Davies, W. D., 189
Davies, W. D., and Dale Allison Jr., 161, 186, 209
Dell, Katherine J., 113
DeRoche, Michael, 17
Derrett, J. Duncan M., 203, 205
Donaldson, Terence L., 167, 217
Dozemann, Thomas B., 113
Duling, D. C., 169, 185, 186
Dumbrell, W. J., 165, 166
Dunn, James D. G., 153, 187

Ehro, Ted M., 142
Eissfeldt, Otto, 57
Elliott, John H., 171
Evans, Craig A., 161, 182, 209

Faierstein, Morris M., 159
Farmer, William R., 3
Fitzmyer, Joseph A., 159
France, R. T., 150
Frankel, Rafael, 120
Frankemölle, Hubert, 159, 168

Modern Authors Index

Freyne, Sean, 154
Fretheim, Terence E., 114
Fried, Lisbeth S., 46, 73, 87

Galambush, Julie, 27
Gammie, John G., 128
Glazier-McDonald, Beth, 82, 83
Goodwin, Mark J., 205
Gosse, Bernard, 54
Grabbe, Lester L., 81, 82, 87
Graffy, Adrian, 26
Greenberg, Moshe, 25, 26, 35
Gregory, Bradley C., 72
Griesbach, J. J., 3
Gurtner, Daniel M., 215

Hagner, Donald, 149, 167, 177
Hahn, Scott Walker, and John Sietze Bergma, 30
Halpern, Baruch, 70
Hanson, Paul D., 62, 63, 64, 65, 68, 70, 102, 105
Hare, Douglas R. A., 206
Harris, Mark, 210
Hartmann, Louis F., and Alexander A Di Lella, 131, 132, 134, 136, 137
Hauck, Robert J., 171
Held, Heinz Joachim, 177
Hengel, Martin, 186
Hermann, Siegfried, 40
Hiers, Richard H., 205
Hillers, Delbert R., 16, 51
Holladay, William L., 19, 20, 68
Hollenbach, Paul W., 175
Holtzmann, H. J., 3
Hooker, Morna D., 194, 195, 210
Horbury, William, 147
Horsley, Richard A., 4, 124
Huffmon, Herbert B., 9
Hurowitz, Victor A., 73

Isaac, E., 147

Janzen, David, 86, 169
Japhet, Sara, 91, 92, 96
Jaubert, Annie, 213
Jenkins, Allan K., 14
Jenkins, Philip, 4
Jeremias, Joachim, 197, 199
Johnson, Luke Timothy, 4, 6
Jones, Douglas Rawlinson, 22
Jones, John Mark, 187
Jonker, Louis, 96, 97
Joyce, Paul M., 34

Kaiser, Walter C. Jr., 57
Keiser, Thomas J., 44
Kessler, John, 73
Kim, Hyun Chul Paul, 113
Kingsbury, Jack Dean, 156, 175, 176
Klein, Ralph W., 29, 35, 90, 91, 96
Knibb, M., 127
Knight, George A. F., 43
Knoppers, Gary N., 91, 94, 95
Koch, Klaus, 132
Kohn, Risa Levitt, 30
Kugler, Robert, 191

Larkin, Katrina J. A., 102
Lee, Bernhard J., 154
Leske, Adrian M., 8, 97, 99, 100, 104, 150, 154, 155, 159, 161, 162, 172, 185, 189, 201, 202, 205, 206, 207
Leuchter, Mark, 97
Levin, Yigal, 91
Levinson, Jon Douglas, 35
Lincoln, Andrew T., 188
Lindblom, J., 59
Luz, Ulrich, 155, 164, 169, 176, 177, 191, 201, 204, 207

Marcus, Joel, 205
Mason, Rex, 83, 100, 103, 105, 106, 110
Mason, Steve, 152, 202
Mattill, A. J., 173
May, Herbert G., 32
McCane, Byron R., 176
McEleny, Neil J., 173
McEvenue, Sean, 41
McIver, Robert K., 182
McKeating, H., 35
McKenzie, John L., 43, 53
Meier, John P., 156
Menken, Maarten J. J., 160
Meyers, Carol L., and Eric M. Meyers, 78, 105
Meyers, Eric M., 79, 86
Meyers, Eric M., and James F. Strange, 120, 154
Mettinger, Tryggve M. D., 50, 51, 53
Millar, William R., 115
Mitchell, Hinckley G. A., 106
Moore, Daniel F., 5
Moran, W. L., 82
Moss, Candida R., 171
Moule, C. F. D., 194, 204
Murphy-O'Conner, Jerome, 173

Nepper-Christensen, Poul, 156
Neusner, Jacob, 153

Modern Authors Index

Nickelsburg, George W. E., 120, 121, 122, 124, 125, 126, 136, 137, 141, 142, 147, 191
Niskanen, Paul, 65

Öhler, Markus, 158
Olmstead, A. T., 74
Otzen, Benedict, 115
Overman, J. Andrew, 149, 150
Owen, Henry, 3

Parker, Pierson. 157
Petersen, David L., 78, 79, 96, 100, 101, 105, 106
Peuch, Émile, 161
Poffenroth, Kim, 186
Pomykala, Kenneth E., 68, 90, 141
Pons, Jacques, 30, 31
Porteus, Norman, 134, 137
Powell, Mark Allan, 162, 203, 205
Pregeant, Russell, 172
Przybylski, Benno, 155

Redditt, Paul, 98
Reed, Jonathan L., 154
Regev, Eyal, 153
Rendtorff, Rolf, 40
Richardson, Peter, 139, 140
Riley, William, 90, 97
Roberts, J. J. M., 19, 68
Rofé, Alexander, 68
Rowley, H. H., 127
Rudolph, Wilhelm, 82
Runesson, Anders, 202

Saldarini, Anthony J., 149, 202
Sanders, E. P., 202, 209
Saulnier, Stéphane, 213
Schaberg, Jane, 187, 188
Schaefer, Konrad R., 106
Schaper, Joachim, 102
Schiffman, Lawrence H., 152
Schmitz, Philip C., 117
Schottroff, Willy, 8
Schramm, Brooks, 67
Schwartz, Baruch J., 33
Segal, Alan F., 150
Seitz, Christopher R., 41, 57, 115
Sim, David C., 149, 150, 174

Smith, Mark, 51
Smith, Morton, 100
Snodgrass, Klyne, 157, 167
Sommer, Benjamin D., 41, 51, 52, 53, 54, 70
Stanton, Graham N., 150
Steck, Odil Hannes, 55
Stern, David, 157
Stordalen, T., 32
Stone, M. E., 191
Streeter, Burnett Hillman, 3, 5, 6
Strecker, Georg, 155
Stuhlmueller, Carroll, 59
Suggs, M. Jack, 147
Suter, David, 143
Sweeney, Marvin A., 56, 58, 71, 116, 117

Tcherikover, Victor, 119, 121, 123, 139
Tiemeyer, Lena-Sofia, 68
Tiller, Patrick A., 126
Tödt, Heinz Eduard, 206
Trotter, James M., 73
Troxel, Ronald L., 215
Tuell, Steven Shawn, 35

VanderKam, James C., 77, 124, 126, 144, 146
Vermeylen, Jacques, 40
Verseput, Donald J., 187, 191, 209
Viviano, Benedict, 202
De Vries, Simon J., 94, 95

Waters, Kenneth L., Sr., 215
Weren, Wim J. C., 187
Westermann, Klaus, 63
White, L. Michael, 150
Whitelam, Keith W., 13
Whybray, R. N., 62, 72
Wilcox, Peter, and David Paton-Williams, 51
Wildberger, Hans, 12, 115, 116
Willey, Patricia Tull, 53
Williamson, H. G. M., 12, 64, 70
Wink, Walter, 169
Wolff, Hans Walter, 9, 10, 74, 109, 110, 111, 113, 114
Wright, R. B., 141

Zimmerli, Walther, 27, 59
Zöckler, Thomas, 171

Ancient Document Index

OLD TESTAMENT/HEBREW BIBLE

Genesis

5–7	121
12:1–3	51, 187
18:18	187
22:18	187
38	187
49:10–12	100, 158

Exodus

19:2–6	35
19:16–20	13
21:22–25	169
24–31	35
32:32–33	136
34:15–16	83

Leviticus

4:3–5	89
10:17	56
15:19–30	179
17–26	30
17:1–9	30
19:9–10	200
21:5	26
21:17–23	67
24:17–22	169
25:8–34	67
25:48–49	44
26:36–39	26

Numbers

6:23–27	82
15:38–40	80
16–18	89
17:10	93
28–36	35

Deuteronomy

4:16–19	29
4:28	31
4:29, 31	29, 30
7:1–6	83
7:6–13	30
12:1–7	30
12:6, 15–28	30
12:31	31
15:1–6	30
15:19–23	30
18:6–8	30
19:21	169
23:25	200
24:1–4	30, 168
27:15—28:15	22, 161
28:23, 29	185
29:1	30
32	44
33:8–11	81

Ancient Document Index

Joshua

2	187

Judges

2:14	45

Ruth

3	187

2 Samuel

5:6–8	185
6:1–15	14
7:12–16	7, 50, 185
8:15	185
12:9–10	187

1 Kings

22:19–23	13

2 Kings

9:1—10:11	7
11	36
16:7	11
16:10–18	12
18:14–16	12
21:4–16	17
21:18	36
23	18, 37
23:5	17
25:1–34	24, 39, 67

1 Chronicles

1–9	90–92
11:2–9	92
13:1–6	92
15:2–29	93, 94, 95
17:1–15	92

2 Chronicles

5:10	93
13:5	92–93, 97
23:1–32	94, 95
29:1–36	94
30:3–27	94–95
35:3–14	95
36:14	96
36:12–16	96, 97

Ezra

1:5–11	61
4:2–4	62, 67
6:3–9	61, 73
7:1–6	85, 90
7:7—8:20	86, 90
9:1–14	86
10:2–14	86
10:18–44	84

Nehemiah

5:1–13	88
6:1–19	87
8:1–18	86
10:29–32	67
13:1–31	88

Psalms

2:2, 7–9	144, 186
18:44	57
24:4–5	163
37:3–34	161, 162
44:11–18	24, 45
44:17	25
69:28	136
72:1–14	185
74	25
89	46, 50, 57
110:1	144, 186
118:22–23	157
137:1–3	24

Proverbs

25–29	13

Isaiah

1:2–4	10, 12
2:2–4	14, 16, 59
3:13–15	10
5	11
5:1–7	21
5:26–30	14
6:1–13	11, 22, 41, 48
6:5	14
7:1–14	11, 14, 188
7:17–20	14
8:1–8	14
8:14–15	11
8:16–17	12, 41
9:1–5	12, 160, 192
9:12–21	11
10	14
10:1–5	11
10:21–22	12
10:33–34	12
11:1–9	12, 13, 14, 23
12:1	41
13–23	14
13:4	13
14:26–27	14
14:28–32	14
14:30	13
17:10	11
18:7	14
22:1–14	206
22:15–22	205
23:1–14	116
24–27	115, 121, 127, 147
24	116, 205
25	117
26:1–19	117
26:4	11
26:12	12
27	118
28:1–16	11–13, 157
28:29	12
29:6–19	13, 41
30:1–5	13
30:8	41
30:27–28	13
30:29	11
31:1–3	13
33:5	14
35	42, 47, 50
37:1–7	12
40:1–11	41–42, 46, 161, 184
40:12–31	43
40:1	44
40:27	39
41:1–10	43, 50
41:21	42
42:1–12	51–52, 184, 188, 190
42:16–25	49
42:22	39
43	42, 45, 49, 51, 188
44:6	42
44	44–46
45	43, 46, 58, 155
45:23	42
46:1–7	43, 44
46:8–11	46
47	59
48	49
49:1–8	51–53, 184
49:7	39
49:10	162
49:24–25	47
50:1–2	45
50:4–9	50, 53
51:1–8	32, 51, 53, 58, 163
51:17–23	39, 48, 54
52:7	48, 161
52:11–12	46
52:13—53:12	54–56, 147
52:13–15	54, 127
53:4–5	48, 162, 176
54:4–17	45, 48, 56, 59
55:1–11	57, 60, 117, 184
55:11–13	42, 47, 60
56–57	63, 67
58–59	64, 67
59:2–8	155
60–62	68–73, 131
60:1–3	69, 165
60:21	70
61:1–3	70–72, 162, 184
63:1–15	64–65
64–65	65, 68
65:13–16	161
66	66, 162

Jeremiah

1:9	25
1:13–16	19
2:1—4:4	27
2:8, 26	21
2:20–21	21
3:19–20	21
4:1–4	22
4:5–8	19, 22

Jeremiah (continued)

4:9	21
4:13	21
4:14	22
5:10–17	19
5:21	22
6:1–5, 14	19, 22
6:7	22
6:13–15	22, 28
6:16–21	26
7:4	20
7:12–15	20
7:16–26	20
7:18	17
7:29	26
8:11, 12, 21	22
8:18	28
8:19	23
10:10	23
10:19	22
11:1–17	22
11:18–23	20, 55
12:6	20
13:12–14	22
14:12	22
15:2	22
15:6	25
15:16–18	21, 22
16:5–9	28
16:14–16	46, 193
17:14	21
18:1–18	20
19:1–15	20
19:5, 6	17
20:1–6	20
21:5	31
22:9	22
22:13–19	19, 20
23:1–8	33, 42, 184
23:5–6	23, 34
23:33–40	22
24:1–10	21, 29
25:11–12	133
25:15–31	22, 48
26:1–19	20
26:20–24	20
26:1–31	20
27:1–22	21
29:1–23	21, 29
29:10–14	23
29:15–32	28
30–33	23
30:12–17	22
31:13	41, 44
31:15	189
31:16–17	42
31:29–31	26
31:31–34	23, 58, 189
32:36–41	23
33:14–26	68, 81, 90
36:6–10	20, 21
38:1–13	21
39:1–10	24
39:11	21
40:1–7	21, 61
43:8–13	21
44:15–19	17, 18
52:4–27	24
52:5–17	21
52:31–34	39

Lamentations

1:1–21	41
4:9–10	24
5:1–18	61–62
5:25	24

Ezekiel

2:8–10	25
3:3	26
3:16–21	26
4:1—5:17	26, 27
7:25–27	28
8:1–18	29
8–11	28, 36, 38
9:1–11, 14	29
11:22–25	29
12:22–28	28
13:10–16	28
13:17–23	28
14:1–11	28, 29
16	27
17:22	35
18:2	26
20:3–44	30, 31, 46
21:6–7	29
22:16	28
22:28	28
23	27–28
24:2–21	28
24:17	29

25–32	31, 32
33:1–9, 12	26
33:21–22	33
33:22–29	38
33:30–32	29
34	33, 34, 35
35:1–15	31
36	33
36:5	31
36:35	32
37	34, 35, 55
38–39	34, 98, 112
39:21–25	31
40–48	35–38
44:6–14	37–38, 66, 67, 82, 89
44:15–19, 24	29, 95
44:20	26

Daniel

1–6	127–29
7–12	129–31, 184
7:1–14	131–32, 186
7:18–27	132
8:1–25	133
9:1–27	133–34
10:5–18	135
11:2–30	135
11:32–40	136
11:40–45	136
12:1–13	136–37

Hosea

1:10	9, 204
2:14–17	9, 46
2:19–20	9
3:5	9
4	9
4:1–3	10
4:1–4	9, 17
5:1	9
5:7	21
5:8	9
5:13–15	10
5:14—6:6	114, 201
6:1–3a	10, 48
6:6	9, 200
6:7	21
6:9–10	9
6:7	9
6:9–10	9
7:16	9
9:8	9
9:15	9
10:5	9
10:7	9
10:8	9
10:12	9
10:15	9
11:1–3	10, 21, 189
11:5–7	10
11:13	10
12:2	9
12:3–10	9
14:2, 5	10

Joel

1:4–6	111
1:9, 13	109–10
2:2–20	107–8, 111
2:3	32
2:18–29	108
3:1–17	108

Amos

1:9—2:8	17
2:6–7	8, 10
2:10–11	46
3:1–2	10
3:15	8
4:1	8
5:3–15	8
5:24	8, 9
5:26–27	8
6:4–6	8
6:12	8
7:14	8
8:4–6	8
9:8	8
9:15	8

Jonah

1:1–17	112–13
2:1–10	113
3:1–10	113
4:1–11	114

Micah

1:9–16	15
2:1–9	15
2:12–13	16
3:1–3	15
3:11–12	15, 16, 20
4	16
5:2–6	16, 189
6:4	16
6:6–8	16
7	16, 196

Nahum

1:3–7	18
1:15	18

Habakkuk

1:2–4	19
1:5–17	19
2:2–4	19
2:5–9	19
2:15–19	19, 22
3:2–19	19

Zephaniah

1:1–9	17
2:7, 9	18
2:14–15	17
3:1–4	17, 28
3:11–20	17

Haggai

1:1–12	74–75
2:7–14	75
2:20–23	75, 77

Zechariah

1:1–17	76
2:1–11	76
3:1–10	76–77
4:1–14	77–78
6:9–14	79
7:3–14	79
8:1–19	79
8:20–23	80
9–14	108–9
9:1–8	99
9:9–15	100–101, 184, 207–9
11:4–17	101–3
12:1–6	103
12:7–9	104
12:10—13:6	104–5
14:1–8	106–7
14:9–21	107

Malachi

1:8–13	82
2:1–16	83
3:1–3	84
4:1–6	84–85, 157

APOCRYPHA

Wisdom of Solomon

2–5	147
2:10—6:11	184

Sirach

13:19	124
48:1–10	157

1 Maccabees

1:20–35	133, 134
1:41–63	126, 132, 134
4:52–53	133, 138
6:1–17	136, 138
6:59–60	138
9:18	138
12:46—14:41	138

ANCIENT DOCUMENT INDEX

2 Maccabees

1:11–17	136
3:1—4:6	123
4:7–50	124
9:1–29	136

PSEUDEPIGRAPHA

1 Enoch

1–36	121–23
13:4–9	122
37:1–5	142
38:1–6	143
39:1–14	143
41–44	143
46:1–8	144
47:1–4	144, 146
48:2–10	144
51:1–5	144, 146
52–57	144–45
56:5—57:3	142
61:1–13	145, 185
62:1–16	145, 146, 185, 186
63–64	145
67:4–12	142
78–82	123
83–90	126
91:11—93:10	124–25
94–105	125

Psalms of Solomon

2–8	141
17:4–37	141

NEW TESTAMENT

Matthew

1:17, 20	187
1:18–25	187, 188
2:1–6	189
2:13–23	153–54, 189
3:5–15	155, 190
4:1–11	155, 189
4:14–16	160
4:18–22	160, 193
4:23–25	160
5:1–2	161
5:3–12	161–65
5:9	190
5:13–16	165
5:17–20	166–68
5:21–30	168
5:31–32	168–69
5:33–37	169
5:38–42	169
6:1–21	170
6:9–15	170–71
6:22–24	171–72
6:25–34	172
7:1–12	172–73
7:13–27	173–74
8:1–4	175–76
8:5–17	176, 199
8:18–22	176, 194, 195, 222
8:23–27	177
8:28–34	177–78
9:1–8	178, 195
9:9	178, 193, 222
9:10–15	157, 179, 193
9:18–26	179
9:27–34	179–80, 185
10	195–97
10:5	222
11:2–19	158–59, 181, 192, 197
11:25–30	198–99
12:1–14	200
12:18–22	194, 200
12:22–37	185, 200
12:34	155
12:38–42	201
12:46–50	181
13:1–9, 18–23	181
13:10–15	181
13:24–30, 36–43	182
13:31–33	182
13:34–35	182
13:43	191
13:44–52	183, 194, 222
13:53–58	201
14:1–21	156, 201
14:33	191
14:34–36	201

Matthew (continued)

15:1–9	202
15:21–28	185, 196, 202, 222
15:29–38	202
16:1–12	204
16:14–19	191, 195, 204–5
16:20	192, 206
16:21–28	206, 207
17:1–13	15, 190, 206
17:22–23	207
18:15–18	195, 207
19:16–22	167
19:28	197
20:20–28	207
20:30–31	185
21:1–11	207–9
21:9–15	185
21:25–40	156, 193
22:41–46	186
23:13–37	194, 202, 203
24	210–11
24:14	197
25:31–46	167, 212
26:1–29	213–14
26:31–35	214
26:39	207
26:63–64	186, 192, 214
27:11–26	192, 214–15
27:27–44	215
27:45–54	215
27:37	186
27:52	191
27:57–66	216
28:1–17	216–17
28:18–20	197, 218

Mark

2:14	193

Luke

5:27	193

John

1:35–44	193
9:1–41	185

Acts

2:14–36	186
13:32–37	186